WHISPERS FROM A CONTINENT

WHISPERS FROM

THE LITERATURE
OF CONTEMPORARY
BLACK AFRICA

WILFRED

CARTEY

VINTAGE BOOKS
A DIVISION OF RANDOM HOUSE
NEW YORK

A CONTINENT

So many have helped me in my preparation of *Whispers from a Continent*. To them all I offer a smile, a handshake, an embrace.

To Anna Winand, who traveled to Africa with me and saw and helped in the total fashioning of this book, my deepest thanks. To Sandra Nagel, whose help over the many years I deeply treasure, my thanks. To my friend Ime Ikiddeh, for his open hospitality and for his great bull sessions into the late night and early morning, I offer a calabash of palm wine. My thanks to Eileen Fox for her warm participation in all this jazz, and to my colleague and fellow traveler Ellen Kennedy for adding her talents as translator of the French texts in Chapter Five.

To Margery Duncan, Carol Bell, Susan Williams, Peter Jankc, Susan Hall, Dee Dee Vallenga, Anne Morrison, and Dorset Edmunds, my sincerest gratitude for their friendly and generous help, often in the face of my restlessness and impatience.

Thanks also to Naomi Rosenfeld, Bryna Mandel, Shannon Miller, Peggy Winkler, Penny Roach, Cecelia Gbeho, Carmen Hughes, Emily Card, Norma Foster, Louis Adams, Dr. Leeman and all the others who pitched in so willingly.

My thanks to Recording for the Blind, The Lighthouse, and The American Society of African Culture for opening up their services to me.

I am particularly grateful for the kind understanding of my editor at Random House, Alice Mayhew, and Cordelia Jason, of the editorial staff.

To you all and to all the others, if you look well in the *Whispers* you will see or hear in a word or in a line, your voices. So many breaths came into these whispers.

Walking in the hills of Legon, I heard the murmurs of the wind. Sitting by the Winneba Sea, I listened to the back-and-forth movements of the water. Standing on the African soil at that hour when the heart strums the guitar of dreams in voices of the children Araba and Adwoa, Alice and Ekua, Abena and Amawi, Qwasi and Ayeki, I received the whispers from a continent. To Mother, and to all those who listen to children's voices, I give back these whispers.

CONTENTS

THE MOVEMENT AWAY

ONE

AUTOBIOGRAPHY . . .
MOTHER AND CHILD

"Samba Diallo, the milk that has nourished you, from the breast of the country of the Diallobe, is very sweet and very noble. Be indignant whenever anyone contests that and correct the cretin who would doubt you because you are a Negro. But know also that the more tender the mother is, the sooner comes the moment for thrusting her aside."[1]

The nourishing milk comes not only from the natural mother but also from the earth of Africa; mother and earth cross-fertilize and link together to form a single symbol. This symbol recurs as a dominant motif throughout the literary autobiographical expressions that have become a strong element in recent African literature. Many writers of the autobiographical statement turn to childhood to recall the bliss and easy circumstances of life, as in Camara Laye's *L'Enfant Noir* (published in England as *The Dark Child*) and Robert W. Cole's *Kossoh Town Boy;* or, even if conditions were troubled and chaotic, writers reinvoke those quiet moments that were cushioned by mother. For instance, Samba Diallo, in Cheikh Hamidou Kane's *Ambiguous Adventure,* from the confusion of Paris, directs his yearning to the certainties of his childhood, to that time before he was propelled into ambiguity. He wishes to return to his African past—a past already undergoing dramatic changes, a past that may have already become mythical. Writers in their middle years treat their youth with nostalgia and find in the mother image an emblem of strength and support. The mother figure, though varying from novel to novel, always evinces qualities of affection, shrewd practicality, and possessiveness where the son is concerned. Movement away from the mother— "thrusting her aside"—is movement away from Africa.

The autobiographical presentations to be discussed reflect the young heroes' movement away from the Mother Africa to growth in awareness, with a resultant falling away. Some, such as the Dark Child of *L'Enfant Noir* and Robert Cole in *Kossoh Town Boy*, move only by a quiet process of growth, with little tension. Others, such as Njoroge in *Weep Not, Child*, Mphahlele in *Down Second Avenue*, and Lee in *Tell Freedom*, see the light closing over their lands; their childhood dreams and desires for education are obscured, at times obliterated, by social and political ferment. Some protagonists successively move out of the cocoon of childhood into a harsh outer reality, whose pressures force them to leave the land—the Mother—completely. Yet, each author would have his hero know and feel the intensity of the land before he can leave it. Whether the wheels inevitably take the Dark Child further away, or the eclipsed light darkens the lives of Njoroge and characters in other novels, the Mother, the earth, demands recognition before she allows them their ultimate freedom. Each hero is inevitably wrenched away from the world of beauty within the raindrop that Lee, in *Tell Freedom*, watches slip down the window. Each hero, in a sense, watches the world from a warm, cozy home, and is inevitably thrust from it, forced to grapple with the larger, hostile forces outside. Yet, often, nostalgia for the first world remains.

"O my mother, I am thinking of you . . ."[2] writes novelist Camara Laye, "For it is to a mother to whom you turn, of whom you speak when nostalgia grips you, when distress clouds the vision of the moment. . . . When there is sorrow and bitterness a man finds refuge in his motherland. The mother is there to protect you. She is buried there. And that is why we say that mother is supreme."[3]

Dâman of the great family of blacksmiths and goldsmiths,

mother to Camara Laye, the Dark Child, is also supreme. Her totem is the powerful crocodile. She alone could draw water from the Niger when its waters deepened, hiding the danger of the triangular green heads. She was "sayon," the child born after twin boys, endowed with special magical powers. She was black woman, the symbol, but *one* woman, though her son is the son of the continent.

"You who were the first to open my eyes to the wonders of the earth, how I should love to be beside you once again." Laye sets the tone for *L'Enfant Noir* in this dedication, a hearkening back to an African childhood, regret for the fields, rivers, and banks of pale sand. "Black woman . . . thank you for all you have done for me, your son . . . I am thinking of you."[4] His thoughts flow backwards in time and space to her who represents the land and rivers of Africa; she is the "Africanness" he has lost in fact but has retained in memory. Written in nostalgia, *L'Enfant Noir* recaptures through a rigid process of romantic selection the warm and secure parts of the past. This contrasts with other writers, such as Ngugi, Mphahlele, and Abrahams, who, focusing their attention on the political surroundings and using a different selective process, present the stresses of growth and the harsh encounters with colonial administration.

Laye was born into the Guinea caste of coppersmiths, one of the ancient craft aristocracies of West Africa. His huge household of innumerable kin, apprentices and ever-welcomed guests spread out from the workshop in a ring of separate huts formed into a compound around a single orange tree. Laye's special childhood domain was the veranda of his father's hut, a hut like all their dwellings, "of mud that had been pounded and moulded into bricks with water . . . round and proudly helmeted with thatch";[5] its interior was overhung with prayer rugs, chaplets of cowrie shells, and pots of mysterious magic liquids.

All business of the concession was governed by the craftsmaster father, but it was closely surveyed by Laye's mother: "My mother was very kind, very correct. She also had great authority and kept her eye on everything we did so that her kindness was not altogether untempered by severity . . . my mother was not a very patient woman."[6]

A duality is developed throughout the work by the play of her kindness and her severity, her love for the son and her tender strictness, her tender weakness and fierce strength. Dâman is a volatile, emotional woman, ready to command all her woman's wiles to keep her son with her, as her child. She hugs him tightly upon his return from the circumcision school, "as if she was wanting secretly to proclaim that I was still her son, that my second ritual birth had done nothing to alter the fact that I was still her son."[7] She was extremely protective: ". . . I could not help thinking that her affection for me might have been a little less exclusive and less tyrannical. And it was obvious that [others] enjoyed more freedom than I was allowed."[8] Even after he had his own hut, she would get up at midnight to make sure he was alone.

> If I still happened to be awake, I would pretend to be asleep; then, as if the lighted match had disturbed me, I would pretend to wake with a start.
> 'What's the matter?' I would cry.
> 'Are you asleep?' my mother would ask.
> 'Yes, I *was* asleep. Why did you wake me up?'
> 'Good, go to sleep again.'
> And I used to complain . . . to my most intimate friends. Am I not old enough to look after myself?[9]

When he wishes to depart for France and the university, she argues, feigns rejection, weeps, and rages to tie him to her, to the Africa of which she is the eternal symbol:

> 'Your place is here. What *are* they thinking about, at the school? Do they imagine I'm going to live my whole life apart from my son? Die with him far away? Have they no mothers, those people? But they can't have mothers, of course. They would not have gone so far away from home if they'd had mothers.'
> And she lifted up her eyes to the sky, and addressed the heavens:
> 'He's been away from me so many years already!' she said. 'And now they want to take him away to their own land! . . .'
> Then she lowered her gaze and looked at my father again . . . 'This child will fall sick; that's what will happen. And . . . what will become of me? Oh, I once had a son, but now I have a son no more!'
> I went up to her and pressed her to me.

'Get away from me,' she shouted. 'You're no son of mine.'

But she did not push me away; she was weeping and she held me closely to her.

'You won't leave me alone, will you? Tell me you won't leave me alone.'[10]

In spite of Dâman's pleas, the Dark Child, caught in the centrifugal patterns of his African experience, inevitably moves away from her and his homeland.

Dâman's protective instincts extended to her husband as well. She worried that the treasured work of melting gold into trinkets would ruin his health, that his lungs would be worn out by puffing the blowpipe, his eyes damaged by the smith's hot forge. She worried, too, that his generosity to the constant visitors would imperceptibly drain his goods and powers, for he was "an open-handed, and, in fact, a lavish giver"[11] who always put the community before himself.

The father is wise and, as a renowned coppersmith of district prestige, has understanding far above that of his wife. Within the household, she acts as the indirect head; she has her set of rules, but the father is the final rule; his authority is clear and extends to all blacksmiths in five cantons. He is a master among them, almost divinely guided. As he forges, his lips move in prayer and incantations—he seems to be in communication with the spirit of creation.

His is an ecstasy unknown to quiet farmers, such as Uncle Lansana, who seems to hold the spirit of the fields in the silence of his eyes. The father's God-given visionary creativity is heralded by the praise-singers, for his totem strength is in the black snake; the spirit and continuity of the race flow through him.

Peacefulness and innocence are secure within the structure of the Dark Child's African family. His life has a distinct pattern, guided by traditional goals of excellence. His ritual course of growth is clear. There is a sense of inevitability in his growth, like the recitation of an old psalm. He is fatalistically resigned to an unknown future that is somehow assured to be benevolent.

"Are you afraid?" Laye's father asks on the night of the boy's Konden Diara, when the drummer comes to take the young men to the initiation to manhood. "I, too, went through this test . . . there is nothing you cannot overcome by your will-power. Remember: you have only to control your fear, you have to control yourself. Konden Diara will not take you away: he will roar; but he won't do more than roar. . . . Even if you are frightened, do not show it."[12]

Although its themes play upon those of tradition, progress is as inevitable as that ritual and spiritualism in which *L'Enfant Noir* is steeped. The mother cannot accept Laye's movement out into the other world that the French university will open to him, but the father, perceiving the dynamics of generational processes, understands that his son is not growing up in the same way as he, nor in the same social circumstances. "You see," he said, "it's something I've often thought about . . . I knew quite well that one day you would leave us. I knew it the very first day you set foot in school . . . Yes, since that day I knew it would be; and gradually I resigned myself to it."[13]

Laye cannot make his entry into the wider world without a painful spiritual desertion of his native culture. Through long rhythmical periods of soft rhetorical questions, of affirmations stating the spirituality and beliefs which Laye himself cannot explain rationally but passively accepts, the Dark Child slowly but irrevocably moves away from his first certainties. He is caught in a centrifugal force moving him away from the center of belief. He can no longer feel the singing of his peoples as they go out to labor in the fields. He can no longer feel the power of the black totem snake as can his father, and he bemoans his own loss of faith. He is caught in

> the workings of the inner wheels which, from the school in Kouroussa lead to Conakry and finally to France; . . . the wheels going round and round: first this wheel, then that one, and then this third and greater wheel, then still more wheels, many more wheels perhaps that no one else could see. And how could their workings be stopped?[14]

Education in the European style has its own dynamics to which the Dark Child must sacrifice old ways. But any education, any growth of awareness demands its proper sacrifice. Such is its nature: to create a contrast so startling that the past must be abandoned in favor of the future it promises or the reality it so starkly reveals.

The contrast between the past, present, and uncertain future is presented in *Ambiguous Adventure,* the sensitive autobiogra-phical novel of Kane. Samba Diallo is the center of a con-flict between the spiritualism of his early Islamic training and the materialism of the conquering West. This conflict is presented in a series of stark dialectical dialogues and philo-sophical oppositions. As a young boy, his world revolves entirely around the Master and the learning and perfected recitation of the Islamic Word, the Koran. This is a period of certainty when all is structured. Everything derives its value by relation to the ultimate totality, God.

Samba Diallo is the heir apparent to the noble Diallobe line, and the chief's sister, the Most Royal Lady, insists that his main responsibility lies in insuring the perpetuation of the tribe. She disapproves of the Master's emphasis on death and the absolute, and she warns that Samba and his generation will have to cope with a world of the living in which death is bereft of value. She desires, therefore, that Samba Diallo be taken away from the Glowing Hearth of the Master and into the new school established by the French in Senegal so that he might learn the art of conquering "without being in the right."[15]

As the Master's hope and the first son of the Diallobe chief, Samba Diallo is chosen as guardian of both spiritual and tem-poral leadership and becomes the focus of a controversy be-tween these two designs. There is contradiction between alle-giance to God, the Master, and the Word, and the necessity for flexibility, metamorphosis, and mutation in order to make pos-sible the physical perpetuation of the tribe. From the French school in Senegal, the next step is inevitably to move to Paris to study. In France, his feeling of separateness and ambiguity be-comes more acute. Torn from the tenderness and certainty that he had experienced during his youth with the Master, he now experiences a deepening loss-of-self: "Master, what is left for me? The shadows are closing in on me. I no longer burn at the heart of people and things."[16]

The Master dies, Samba Diallo is recalled—still perplexed, still suffering a profound sense of alienation from both East and West. Unable to slip back into the soft shadows, to be the continuum of his lofty lineage, he finally chooses death as an end to torment. Only then can he be reunited with the Ulti-mate.

In *Weep Not, Child,* the hero, Njoroge, is saved by his

mother from committing suicide. There is no such person for
Samba Diallo. Mother for him is metaphysical. Childhood has
been not proximity to mother but to traditional beliefs and to
God. He has never cut the cord that holds him to the womb of
Nature and Earth, and to all those noble Diallobe who have
preceded him. Thus it is into this eternal flow of the river of life
that he must finally return in order to be absorbed, to shed the
weight that is crushing him.

From the beginning, the Master sees in Samba Diallo a
purity that he feels can rise to the most exalted heights of
human grandeur—the possibility of complete devotion to the
spirit. This can only come through total dedication to the
Koranic Word—a task that demands excruciating suffering
even as it imparts an unspeakably beautiful mystery and sense
of the whole.

Samba Diallo is harshly chastised for the slightest failure to
reproduce the Word in its purest form: he is burnt with faggots
from the fire, his ears are twisted until they bleed. "The child's
ear already white with scarcely healed scars, was bleeding anew
. . . This sentence which he did not understand, for which he
was suffering martyrdom—he loved for its mystery and its
somber beauty . . . It was a miracle, it was as God Himself had
uttered it."[17]

The Word lends totality and continuity to life. Samba Diallo
feels that he is a part of all things and that through God all
things are part of him. The Word is all-embracing and encom-
passes mother, matter, love, and spirit. At one point, Jean, his
young French friend, fears that Samba Diallo is close to death
when he lies totally still and seems to merge with the earth of
Africa and the twilight sky. Samba Diallo is at prayer, and as
he prays he is not at the point of death but at the center of
life.

Through Samba Diallo flows the continuity of the Diallobe
clan. It is through him that the ancestors give voice in the night,
and it is at the moment of feeling their sap moving in his veins
that the Word finds its highest expression in him.

> . . . Slowly, he recited the prelude to the Night of the Koran
> . . . knowing that on this enchanted night . . . he was repeating
> for his father what . . . from generation to generation through
> centuries the sons of the Diallobe had repeated for their fathers,

from knowing that he had not failed in this respect and that he was about to prove to all who were listening that the Diallobe would not die in him . . . he was on the point of fainting.[18]

The scope and depth of the Word make Samba Diallo a part of infinite space and eternal time. In the cemetery, beside the grave of his friend, Old Rella, Samba Diallo reflects that what is lost in physical presence is gained in spirit. He is on the brink of ultimately realizing that to end the physical containment of the body is finally the only way to rid oneself of weight and substance—and to release the spirit, which may then unite with the One. Death is the end of weight and the birth of spirit.

At the Hearth of the Master, Samba Diallo feels a deeper sense of pride than he does in being the son of the chief. He desires nobility, but a nobility more discreet, more authentic than that of patrician birth. But the choice of spirit over body separates Samba Diallo to some extent from physical reality. When chided by a fellow disciple, Demba, at the irony of one of his noble birth not living the comfortable life, Samba Diallo becomes dark and angry, though as always restrained. Finally, something gives, and he strikes out: "The mutiny of his body was calmed somewhat with every blow, as every blow restored a little clarity."[19]

But for the Most Royal Lady, the nobility of the Diallobe lineage is of paramount importance. Samba Diallo, then, must go to the French school to learn "how to construct dwelling houses that will resist the weather."[20]

The Master agrees that the house must be strong, but he insists on a place for God within. A strong hand must defend the spirit, but he values inner force and the absolute over the Most Royal Lady's choice of physical and material triumph. She embodies the epic of the Diallobe in her haughty counte- nance. She reiterates and argues with the Master that: ". . . the time has come to teach our sons to live. I foresee that they will have to do with a world of the living in which the values of death will be scoffed at and bankrupt."[21] The newcomers have con- quered, and Samba Diallo must learn to resist conquest. The Most Royal Lady feels that even if losing a landmark means that men will not know which way to go, they can, after all, learn new ways as a baby learns to walk. Ironically, she says that one must be ready to die in order to be reborn. Flexibility enables the continuity of life; inflexibility in the face of new, more powerful invaders leads to destruction. The West has come first with cannon, and now with the school. It is the Master who asks the vital question: "But learning, they would also forget. Would what they would learn be worth as much as what they would forget? . . . can one learn *this* without forgetting *that*, and is what one learns worth what one forgets?"[22]

Samba Diallo cannot become an integral part of the Western school. He feels different, and others find him different. He seems to be a "break of peace" amidst the clatter and commotion of the accelerating West. The new school introduces him to Pascal and Descartes, and he is assailed by doubts as to the very nature of the totality of the Word and the continuity of tradition. He puzzles over the seeming incompatibility of work with God. Work is matter, God is force. But each one seems to demand its own distinct time. The omnipresence and omnipotence of the Word have been brought into question. The knight, Samba Diallo's father, points out that work is only an extension of prayer for the man of God. At this stage then, Samba Diallo's doubts are quieted.

The new education and new freedom of questioning and challenges cause Samba Diallo to move away from the first certainties of the Dark Child, the life within a drop of rain in *Tell Freedom*.

Yet a falling away has begun, and with it come recurring bouts of trembling, symbolic of the conflict and ambiguity he feels.

> . . . I am not a distinct country of the Diallobe facing a distinct Occident. . . . I have become the two. There is not a clear mind deciding between the two factors of choice. There is a strange nature, in distress over not being two.[23]

The conflict is dramatized by the play of colors in this twilight zone—the sun, the sunset, the moon, and the stars. The shadows of his home and hearth are warm and soft, and he feels comfortable. But the night of the Koran, pierced through with the "star-studded bolt" marks the end of an epoch before the new dawn. This brings with it a solar burst, which, the knight feels, is "the midday burst of an exasperated civilization. . . . Their sun is a mirage."[24] The blood-red of the sunset, death, bathes the white-flowing boubous and lends tints of the noble purple. All is color contrast and color afire.

Unlike those Africans who the French teacher Lacroix says, "turn their backs to the light but look at the shadow fixedly,"[25] Samba Diallo moves away from the Hearth's shadow into the glaring light of the West. Now he faces not the warm inner light of individual relationship to God, but the harsh reflected light of the mirror-surfaced West where all is turned outward, away from the heart and soul.

Samba Diallo now finds the moment is valued over the eternal. From the new school, he goes to Paris, where his sense of alienation deepens into anguish. In a conversation with an old African acquaintance self-exiled in France, Samba Diallo expresses his concern over the feeling of emptiness and absence in the streets of Paris, cluttered as they are with objects, machines, and events. There are only hard human shells. "Here, now, the world is silent, and there is no longer any resonance from myself. I am like a broken balafong, like a musical instrument that has gone dead. I have the impression that nothing touches me any more."[26]

Under these circumstances, Samba Diallo, who has been taught to live at the heart of things, is now torn away and made to live at a distance from himself and life, from the continuity and the soul of the universe. Like Camara Laye's Dark Child, Samba Diallo gradually feels a loss, lack of the presence and fullness of death and the dead, the continuity of tradition, and of life's cycle; the totality of dream and spirituality is shattered. Unlike the Dark Child, Samba Diallo returns to the land of Africa, after his movement away, not in memory, but in essence. For Samba Diallo, the past, the lived present, and the possibility of Being held out by the future in the flow of river and time are all ecstasies of temporality. In choosing death, his future existence becomes his past existence, and Samba Diallo is saved from a total falling away from Africa, a total wrenching from his past.

Like *L'Enfant Noir*, the book *Weep Not, Child* also presents a traditional African family, but the turbulent Kenyan political situation on which the author, James Ngugi, focuses, affects individual households and precipitates their disintegration. Early in the novel, the household of Ngotho seems well-ordered. He is honored in the community beyond his menial status—

that of clerk in an East Indian's town shop, later that of
trusted shamba-boy of the white overseer, Mr. Howlands, and
finally as a *Muhoi* (headman) in the pyrethrum fields of the
African, Jacobo. His wives—Njeri, the "elder mother," and
Nyokabi, are "two good women . . . who liked each other and
were good companions and friends."[27] Ngotho remains diplo-
matic, knowing one cannot quite trust women, and he is careful
to display no bias: when he buys meat, he bundles it into two
equal packages for each of the huts of his domain.

Njoroge, the youngest son, is a content schoolboy, cozy in the
security of the large family: his respected father, two loving,
pampering mothers, and three half brothers, almost a generation older, who treat him with a fatherly familiarity absent in
the more aloof and feared Ngotho. But in the lives of the
brothers, the workings of disintegration have already begun.
Although Kamau is the village carpenter's apprentice and
seems "to carry the family dumbly on his shoulders,"[28] keeping
the home together, buying food and clothes, paying school fees
for Njoroge; eventually he rarely slept at home. Kori has
taken a job in the city and seldom visits, then only to prose-
lytize the ideas of Jomo Kenyatta, the leader of the K.A.U.
black socialist movement. Boro, another half brother, has returned cynical and critical from the white man's war, permanently embittered by the death of Njoroge's only true brother,
Mwangi.

It is Boro's rupture with his father, who had passively accepted the appropriation of tribal lands, that begins the disaster, the breakup, the falling away.

At the fire one evening, Ngotho begins to talk:

> Then came the war. It was the first big war. I was then
> young, a mere boy, although circumcised. All of us were taken
> by force. We made roads and cleared the forest to make it
> possible for the warring white man to move more quickly. The
> war ended. We were all tired. We came home worn out but
> very ready for whatever the British might give us as a reward.
> But, more than this, we wanted to go back to the soil and
> court it to yield, to create, not to destroy. But Ng'o! The land
> was gone. My father and many others had been moved from
> our ancestral lands. He died lonely, a poor man waiting for
> the white man to go. Mugo had said this would come to be

. . . (that in the country where the hills and ridges lie together
like lions, a man will rise to drive away the white man). The
white man did not go and he died a *Muhoi* on this very land.
It then belonged to Chahira before he sold it to Jacobo. I grew
up here but working . . . working on the land that belonged to
our ancestors . . . waiting for the prophecy to be fulfilled.[29]

Boro listened to the story with growing anger. "In a whisper
that sounded like a shout, he said, 'To hell with the prophecy.' "[30] As Njoroge listened to his father and to Boro, his
drive for education was reinforced.

He instinctively knew that an indefinable demand was being
made on him, even though he was so young. He knew that for
him education would be a fulfilment of a wider and more
significant vision—a vision that embraced the demand made on
him, not only by his father, but also by his mother, his brothers and even the village. He saw himself destined for something big, and this made his heart glow.[31]

Boro's active revolt finds its first expression in alliance with
the K.A.U. strike movement. Ngotho, too, supports the K.A.U.
of Jomo, who is for him a Black Moses, one who stands "for
custom and tradition purified by grace of learning and much
travel."[32] When Jacobo, the richest Black in the district, is
brought by the police to pacify the strikers, to betray the long
years of waiting and suffering that culminated in the strike, it is
Ngotho who leads the demonstration against him. But the
K.A.U., with its moderate demands of higher salaries and the
abolition of the color bar, is easily broken by a coalition of
government, police, and Black landowners. Leaders are imprisoned, and agitators such as Ngotho simply lose their positions.
The failure of a rational approach sends Boro to seek revenge
solutions in extremism. He joins the outlaw Dedan Kimathi,
leader of the African Freedom Army.

Soon after the strike, Boro quarrelled much with the old
man. He accused him of having spoilt everything by his rash
action. . . . Boro clearly had contempt for Ngotho . . . Ngotho
as a result, had diminished in stature, often assuming a defensive secondary place whenever talking with his sons and their
friends. . . . Boro thought that he could make the old man

submit to his will. But Ngotho made a determined resistance. He would not take the Mau Mau oath at his son's hands or instruction.[33]

But the terrorism of the Mau Mau and the counter terrorism of the "Emergency Period" in Kenya exacted total involvement, even from the irresolute. In a time of senseless disciplinary killing of Blacks who were out after the sunset curfew or without their identity papers, the relationship of Ngotho and his family with a Mau Mau activist condemns them through association.

Ngotho's is the principal family studied in *Weep Not, Child*, but two others, those of the African landowner, Jacobo, and the English settler and District Officer, Mr. Howlands, also reflect the Kenyan situation. Three attitudes exist simultaneously in each family, determined by the generation to which a family member belongs. Ngotho, Mr. Howlands, and Jacobo, members of the World War I generation, incarnate the colonial situation: Ngotho, the disinherited awkward African, is united in an almost contractual amity with his dispossessor, Howlands, because of their joined, sincere love for the same rich soil. Ngotho fondles and tends the earth of the shamba as though it were still his own, although it is the life and soul of Howlands and is to be fiercely defended by him. Jacobo, outside this communion, is the profiteer. Both Howlands and Ngotho lose sons in World War II, and they watch with bewilderment the confusion of their older children. Howlands' daughter, in some obscure reaction, has become a missionary; Howlands considers her dead. Ngotho's older sons leave him, one by one, spun off by the centrifugal force of social chaos. "Could he now put his faith in the youngest of the sons?"[34]

A margin of hope is evident among the youngest of the three families. Njoroge maintains an affectionate relationship, despite the public dispute of their fathers, with Jacobo's youngest daughter, Mwihaki, a friendship that matures into love in the most desolate circumstances. At an interschool sports meet, Njoroge encounters Stephen Howlands and strikes up a strained but equal relationship. In Kipanga, their region, they had watched each other passing on the road, too shy to speak. Stephen explains:

I used to hide near the road. I wanted to speak with some of you, but I was afraid you might not speak to me or you might not need my company.

Strange . . . I suppose it's the same everywhere. I have heard many friends say they didn't like the way Africans looked at them. And when you are walking in Nairobi or in the country, though the sky may be clear and the sun is smiling, you are still not free to enjoy the friendliness of the sky because you are aware of an electric tension in the air. . . . You cannot touch it, you cannot see it . . . but you are aware of it all the time. . . . It's bad.

It's bad, agreed Njoroge. They felt close together, united by a common experience of insecurity and fear no one could escape.[35]

The failure of the strike and the declaration of the emergency shattered the peace of Njoroge's family. Though once strong, Ngotho no longer exacts loyalty and admiration from his family. Two of his sons had joined the resistance movement, and his wives no longer moved with the same ease and grace. Njoroge was deeply disturbed by the disintegration. Yet:

Through all this, Njoroge was still sustained by his love for and belief in education and his own role when the time came. And the difficulties of home seemed to have sharpened this appetite. Only education could make something out of this wreckage. . . . He would one day use all his learning to fight the white man, for he would continue the work that his father had started . . .[36]

The news that Njoroge passed his exams and would go on to high school served to sustain his family's hope that one day the difficulties would end.

For the first time for many years, something like a glimmer of light shone in Ngotho's eyes. He could even be seen making an effort to walk upright. Here at last was a son who might eventually be a match for the Howlands and the Jacobos and any others who at all despised him. Kamau too was pleased. He hoped he could go on helping Njoroge. Njoroge might do something for the family.[37]

Ngugi uses light to symbolize Njoroge's gradual movement away from certainty. Early in the novel, looking at the lights of Nairobi from a hill near his home, Njoroge feels the stir of a sense of mission. Even after the country is torn by the strike and the emergency declared, he feels an optimism which he tries to instill in Mwihaki's frightened soul.

> . . . 'Sunshine always follows a dark night. We sleep knowing and trusting that the sun will rise tomorrow.' . . . He was rather annoyed when she laughingly said, 'Tomorrow. Tomorrow never comes. I would rather think of today.' But her eyes dilated like a child's as she looked hopefully at him. An idea came to her. She held Njoroge by the neck and shook him excitedly.
>
> 'What is it?' asked Njoroge, startled.
>
> 'Something. Suppose you and I go from here so that we come back when the dark night is over . . .'
>
> 'But—' . . .
>
> Njoroge was very serious. He saw his vision wrecked by such a plan. And what would God think if he deserted his mission like this?
>
> 'No, No. How can we leave our parents alone?' . . .
>
> They moved together, so as not to be caught by the darkness. A bird cried. And then another. And these two, a boy and a girl went forward each lost in his world, for a time oblivious of the bigger darkness over the whole land.[38]

As long as Njoroge's progress in education continues, he continues to believe in the advent of "a sunny day, a warm sweet day after all this tribulation."[39] Yet, from the "Waning Light," which focuses on the beginning of disintegration of Njoroge's family, the author moves to "Darkness Falls."

Though darkness is all-pervasive, Njoroge clings to the light as an assurance that he will one day commit himself to decisive action for this country. Yet, the assurance is a naive one. While he believes education is the only means to succeeding in his biblical mission, his brothers and father turn to action. Each real participant in the struggle dies after committing an act of heroism. Ngotho, sure that one of his sons has killed Jacobo, assumes the guilt himself and is tortured and beaten to the point of death. His movement into the final darkness is a triumph: his life had finally been given an ultimate meaning. Only then could he succumb, not a shriveled, old man but a tough and proud warrior. Boro, too, moves to the darkness, but only after killing Howlands, the oppressor. Even the deaths of Jacobo and Howlands come only after they have committed themselves to—and followed—a course of action. They had taken decisive stands, and the force of the darkness pulled them to its center. It is only Njoroge who is not allowed to succumb to the darkness. Throughout the novel, the author has traced first his optimism and then his disillusionment in terms of light and darkness. Njoroge's decision to commit suicide comes after Mwihaki, in a second conversation on the hill, resists his plea to leave the land. The drama has shifted. It is now Mwihaki who stresses their responsibility to remain. Defeated, his last hope gone, Njoroge makes the journey to the hill, the same one on which he had sat so many times and spoken of sunshine and light to come. He longed to join the many "who were now beyond the call of the land, the sun and the moon . . ."

> He came to the bend of the road and instinctively looked up. It was there, there that she had left him after declaring her love. The plain was on his right. He moved from the road that had no beginning and no end and went to the slope that extended from the road to the plain. He sat on a rock. He took out of his pocket the carefully folded cord. He felt a certain pleasure in holding it. . . . he sat there waiting for darkness to come and cover him.[40]

But Njoroge is prevented from following those who had, each in his own way, committed an act of heroism before entering the darkness. Njoroge saw the light his mother was carrying and "falteringly went towards it." It is almost as if Ngugi is driving him back into the light, denying him the peace of darkness, because Njoroge has not yet accepted a responsibility, free of biblical and personal illusions.

Across the violence, Njoroge had once believed in the future. Murders on all sides, the meticulous massacre of his father and all his brothers, his disillusionment in leaving school, Mwihaki's refusal to leave Kenya with him, all create a despair. Yet he is saved from suicide, from abandoning his responsibility to the future for which he has prepared himself since childhood, by his mothers, Njeri and Nyokabi, who come out into the black night in search of a son.

The sense of guilt, the sense of having failed his mother, which is so acute in *Weep Not, Child*, is absent in *Kossoh Town Boy*. "If I had to live my life over again, I would not have it different,"[41] says Robert Cole in his autobiography. Yet, at the same time, the author wonders whether he might not have merely accumulated years, slipping imperceptibly into manhood: "All I know is that one day I woke up to find that that cocoon of a boy with which we started at Kossoh Town was gone."[42] The evolution has been a smooth one, and he can "see, somehow a continuing evolution."[43] In the novel, Cole recalls with fondness, though not with the nostalgia of Camara Laye, his growth and development from that cocoon. Laye's statement, "Ah, how happy we were in those days,"[44] is charged with a wistful *saudade*, for he has moved away from his tradition. There has been a break, and he can no longer feel the throb of his family's guardian snake. Robert Cole, on the other hand, says: "To think of those days brings a glow, a reinduction of that warmth which a whole youth full of tropical sun has burnt deep into my being."[45] Perhaps this is because his growth has been free from conflict and tension.

The Cole family had survived the transition from the traditional to the urban world without trauma. They had made use of the educational and professional opportunities provided by the British to the native population in the last century. By Cole's time, they were a second-generation *bourgeoisie*, comfortably blending European mannerisms and Ibo, Ijebu, and Egba folkways. "I use the term 'middle class' almost subconsciously," Cole writes, "because I have been conditioned by years of living in Britain and Europe, where these things matter. If my family were English, or what until recently used to be officially termed 'British subjects of pure European descent,' they would have been upper middle class folk."[46]

Like the household of the Dark Child, that of the boy of Freetown, Kossoh district, was internally well-integrated and structured. Externally, it was part of an extended kin group and secure in its social position because of the prestige of its titular head. Laye's father, in a more traditional frame, fulfills the ancient honored place as a blacksmith; Cole's father, in an urban context, is a "Civil Engineer, a Water Engineer; furthermore, he was head of his Department, the first African in the twentieth century to have that distinction."[47] The family was "in the fullest sense of the word a united family," where "Father's authority was ably backed by mother's loyalty."[48] But, though he exerted much control over his children's upbringing, the elder Cole also helped them develop confidence, wanting his children to look on their parents as friends. At the same time, "Home for us was mother. She was the center of our life, and was never far from us. Even when she was out of the house things were so smoothly run that we did not miss her long."[49]

The Cole family's social position depended, to a great extent, on education. Robert Cole had to live up to this tradition, so the principal theme of the autobiographical novel treats the educational growth of the boy of Kossoh Town. Though there is educational development, however, and the boy moves from class to class, we do not see his parallel growth in awareness. Unlike Samba Diallo of L'Enfant Noir, Medza of Mission Accomplished, and the heroes of other autobiographies, the Kossoh Town Boy seems to remain in the cocoon and avoid the shocks that would jar him from his comfortable nostalgia. There are many anecdotes from his school days, told with wry chuckling and banter, but there are few, if any, descriptions of more profound events in his life. The closest he ever comes to describing an "unsavory" situation is his account of a fight with Horace Chandler, the West Indian boy, who loses but then pulls out a clasp knife.

Robert, or Ageh, his native name, which is used in the book, gradually becomes aware of girls, too, but as with the rest of his development, it comes about without trauma, as part of the normal process of growing up. He is at home in his environment, and there is—as far as we can tell from the book—no anguish and no alienation. His life is serenely wrapped in the daily rhythms of home, church, and school. His family, with all its diverse beginnings, is now part of the urban landscape, as Western as it is "native," but the two seem to blend rather than clash. It seems as if the Cole family, with its Christianity, modern sanitation standards, and stress on education has taken the best from the native tradition and from the modern world. Thus, Ageh is never allowed to mix with the "bad boys" of Kossoh Town or to indulge in its more "pagan" pleasures.

He claims that the story is not just about himself alone but about a group of boys who grew up in Kossoh Town at that time. But, perhaps because of his family's position in the community and the strict schedule laid out for him, he does not participate fully in the ordinary life of the town. The Cole children often watch the different elements and patterns of Kossoh Town, but only from a distance. He and his brothers and sisters were forbidden even to watch the celebrations in the Santigi's compound at the end of the Ramadan season, much less participate in them, though they easily circumvented this by looking from the windows of their home as the procession passed by. Their father, a strict, orthodox Christian, watched over them anxiously; it worried him that they were the boon companions of children who went naked even in puberty.

The larger, colonial situation, too, did not seem to impinge on Cole's life, as it did on Njoroge's. He rarely mentions any harsh encounters, but when he does, as in his description of his first meeting with a white man, he does so wryly, with a certain deceptive urbanity. However, these do not affect the cocoon of security and nontension of his home life.

Though the family is bourgeois and modern, Ageh has his household duties; he joins the family in bedbug hunting, and he sells cocoa beans for his grandmother. Also, the old native customs, such as the grandmother's washing and feeding of the newborn baby, are not rejected. English is spoken in Sierra Leone, and well, according to Cole. But at the same time, the stories and jokes are all in the native Krio language. Although urban, Cole is yet close to the soil and to the forest, "dark, lofty, and cool," with its carpet of "thick brown, soft crumbly, downy leaves," near to where the family's new home is to be. But he is the town boy, and there are trees and fruits he has never seen before, though he is at once appreciative of this "veritable Garden of Eden" and of the "African nymph, her twin breasts shapely beyond compare, firm, dancing up and down with the motion of her arms, as she scrubbed and poured the crystal water over her shining brown body."[50]

Ageh expériences some of the tension of the colonial situation, but as far as one can tell from *Kossoh Town Boy*, he never suffers from it. At the end of the book, he admits that he has not yet been able to write an essay on the text his father had once suggested: "Ageh, one day when you feel you can do it, I should like you to write an essay on the text, 'He that increaseth knowledge increaseth sorrow, and much learning is a weariness of the flesh."[51]

Kossoh Town Boy spools out from a cocoon in an uninterrupted movement bereft of tensions and devoid of the problematic. It, therefore, lacks the dramatic intensity apparent in *Ambiguous Adventure* or in *Weep Not, Child*. The hero's dreams are consonant with those of his family; his movement is at one with the environment. The falling away in the previous novels—*L'Enfant Noir, Ambiguous Adventure,* and *Weep Not, Child*—is interrupted. Robert Cole remains, albeit without resonances and rhythms, in his homeland. The falling away is stopped in *Ashanti Boy*, too, where the hero's dreams are at one with the development of the society. In the novel *Ashanti Boy*, in which there is little representation of deeper social and political forces, where the only problems are basically superficial ones interrupting momentarily the sure progress of the hero, there is little tightening of tension or rhythmical intensity, few climaxes. Our hero, too, remains within his homeland and does not fall away.

Ashanti Boy, by Akosua Abbs, resembles *Kossoh Town Boy* in that Kofi's dreams of education will be realized, but it goes beyond this and the individualism of *L'Enfant Noir* in that it embraces the totality of the society. In *Weep Not, Child*, the turbulence of the Mau Mau uprising hinders the total flowering of the hero, whose education has prepared him for a vital role in Kenya. The political upheaval seems temporarily or even totally to interrupt his growth. The hero's hopes seem to dissolve in the shadows of the highlands. In *Ashanti Boy*, the political situation does not interrupt but rather impels the development of the hero. When, after a bout of malaria, Kofi is at a critical point and the difficulties confronting him make his education seem almost unattainable, he is renewed by the news of Nkrumah's recent victory.

Alienation is not a consequence of education for Kofi as it is for Peter Abrahams in *Tell Freedom*. Given the monolithic society of South Africa, education leads to deepening frustration and an increasing sense of alienation for the Colored boy, Peter Abrahams. In *Ashanti Boy*, society not only needs but will absorb its educated. This is a novel of statement, at times of overstatement, where the realities of school life and the educational system are often given symbolic overtones. Akosua

Abbs sees a combination of the old and the new, the African and the Western, as necessary for the full development of Ghana. For instance, she presents a headmaster, Asare Ikoye, as embodying this ideal:

> He realised that in many young African minds there was a struggle between orthodox Christianity as a symbol of civilisation, and pagan ceremonies as a symbol of deeply rooted and indestructible tribal life. When he resolved this struggle for boys of that middle school, he was helping to produce a dignified, integrated African boy in whom old religious instincts were harnessed to Christian ideals and the best principles of the West.[52]

Kofi himself accepts the necessity for synthesizing the native tradition with the European imposition. As he tells the missionary: "I want to know things . . . Like the Europeans."[53] At the same time, however, he realizes, as his uncle, the Dwamansahene tells him, "We have always had to learn how to . . . evade the rules of the white man . . . when they were silly rules and against our ways of life—our good ways that hurt nobody."[54] Thus, the novel, even while it concentrates on the need for education, also highlights Ashanti custom and lore.

Kofi is *an* Ashanti boy, but at the same time, as an embodiment of the hope of his country, he combines the best of the old and the new. He is, according to one hyperbolic statement, one of those individuals who are like "the great peaks of a mountain range . . . timeless and raceless, as if they had come out of some more nearly perfect mould, closer to the vision of the supreme artist."[55] At the age of nine, he is already very wise, conserving his energy, while missing nothing of importance. But "when his head was full of thoughts, he was quite oblivious of his surroundings."[56] Kofi pursues his goal of education with great, and even unnatural, seriousness and determination. Yet, the pursuit was not easy: "to an African boy, used to villages and small towns on the edge of limitless bush or savannah country, and to a day governed loosely by sunrise and sunset, the school's routine was extremely severe."[57]

His desire for education is born out of observation of his immediate circumstances, and it is pragmatic. He wishes to help his country and realizes that most of the professionals are

Europeans who always go home in the end. Besides, as he tells the missionary: "We will get self-government one day. . . . Then we must have as good a government as you,"[58] which, he adds, must also be recognized as equal by the Europeans. To accomplish this, he says he is willing to undergo exams and conform to their value system—money, nice jobs, and cars and homes.

Realizing the political and social moment, he sees the necessity for his generation to be educated and will instill the desire for education in his brothers and sister as well as in the lazy Kwaku. In addition, there are many models and incentives offered him. He has before him the inspiration of his Uncle Kofi, who is in America studying to be a doctor. Both his mother and grandmother help and encourage him. Comfort Boateng is fond of her son and, at the same time, gives him a sense of his maleness by listening to him. She leaves Kofi's books and notebooks around her husband's room as hints of Kofi's desire to go to school. His shrewd grandmother sees the total need for educating all the youth of the country, both girls and boys. She and her husband, contrary to Akan matrilineal tradition, had scrimped and saved to send their own son to school, and it is to her that Kofi turns during one of his periods of discouragement.

The major obstacle to Kofi's education is Osei Tutu, his father. He is a prosperous cocoa farmer, building a two-storied house, and the owner of a wireless and an old Ford. But he gives Kofi as little financial aid as possible, and he is, besides, loath to lose his son's labor. Being insensitive to his son's needs, he is stubborn and miserly where education is concerned, and like Asare Ikoye's wife, who later mistreats Kofi, he is seemingly unable to comprehend fully the historical processes at work in his country. Even Kwasi, Kofi's youngest brother, who also wants to be a rich cocoa farmer, realizes the usefulness of going to a technical school to learn modern, scientific ways. In the end Osei Tutu is appreciative of his son's qualities, so that Kofi, with his Uncle Nana's and his mother's help, is able to get around him. Later, too, Osei Tutu allows the other children to go to school, though not without a struggle.

Thus, throughout *Ashanti Boy*, Kofi consistently overcomes obstacles, often with the aid of different members of the community. Even some older people, who cherish material things as

much as Osei Tutu, can appreciate the need for education.
Mame Badu, whose first thoughts on seeing Osei Tutu's great
cocoa crop are of new clothes and furniture, and the
Dwamansahene, whose illiteracy, despite his shrewdness and
sagacity, shocks Kofi and reinforces his desire for an education.
Some of the more enlightened Europeans, such as the missionaries from Kofi's area, are interested and helpful, but their
assistance is often interrupted or terminated because of their
transfers from place to place. Father Patrick and David Wray
seem far more permanent, being more deeply involved in and
concerned with Ghana's future. They are impelled by love, and
they both agree: ". . . it's love that transforms a situation—even
impossible situations—not a sense of duty."[59] They are unlike
both Wallace, the young English master, and the first headmaster of the secondary school, who look down on the "natives," and it is the former, the author seems to say, who are
the real Christians, ideally suited to Ghana's needs.

At Akan Secondary School, some of the inner workings of
secondary school life in Ghana are revealed: the youthful
bigotry of many of the European masters, the lackadaisical
attitudes of many African masters, who are on their way to
further education. But here, too, we meet David Wray and
Major Hamer, the new headmaster, who insists that his assistant be African. Kofi, after his initial difficulties with the "endless rules and restrictions of a boarding school run on so-called
European lines,"[60] and with his financial problems somewhat
alleviated, later learns to give vent to his high spirits. A "bit of
an old man in his primary and middle school years, . . . his whole
appearance now seems changed." As Wray remarks: "He's
bright, cheerful, seems taller, and has a devil-may-care look in
his eyes."[61]

But Kofi remains serious in his dedication to his work. When
the political discussions regarding the Convention People's
Party or the National Liberation Movement, the two major
dissenting parties, get violent, he leaves "for the peaceful labo-
ratory to forget all strife in his work."[62] But Kofi is developing,
too, with regard to human relationships. Here, once again, he
embodies the ideal. His friends are Bukari, a northern territory
boy, and Struthers, a mulatto. Ghana needs unity, tribal and
racial as well as political. Here again, his Uncle Kofi, with his

hyphenated European-African name, Boateng-Baer, is a symbol and an example.

In the end, Kofi's success is the success of Ghana. He represents the flower of his country's youth, full of wisdom, knowledgeable in the realities and needs of his country, and dedicated to her welfare. It is no coincidence that his graduation from secondary school coincides with Ghana's independence; both are poised for progress, ready and armed to grapple with all the incidental difficulties.

The optimism and certainty of success evident in *Ashanti Boy* contrast with the oppressive weight of apartheid in South Africa. There, education is not necessarily a guarantee of success or escape. There, the darkness of the shanty towns encloses the shadows of people who answer to curfews, carry passes, and are always at the behest of an alien force. *Down Second Avenue* concerns a family exposed to the rawness of degradation and the possibility of final degeneration: the family of the South African, Ezekiel Mphahlele. When his father, a violent, vicious man with something "brutal and razor-like about the corners of his mouth . . ."[63] something menacing about his limp, refused to support them, Mphahlele and his two other siblings were fetched from the dark mountains of their grandmother's village to join their parents in Marabastad, a Black location in Pretoria. Their father fired his rages on the corn-malt beer the dressmaker-mother brewed in the evenings for extra cash. She attempted to still his rages by her long-suffering patience. "Probably every trickle of a thought was pain, but grumble she would not."[64] His temper explodes on a Sunday morning in a scene which will haunt the young boy:

> When he thundered in, we knew he had been chasing after my mother. She kept on her knees, clearly hurt.
>
> 'I'll show you who I am!' my father said.
>
> 'What is it with you, Moses? What are you standing up to do? . . .'
>
> 'This is the day you're going to do what I tell you!' He limped over to the pot on the stove. In no time it was done. My mother screamed with a voice I have never forgotten till this day. Hot gravy and meat and potatoes had got into her blouse and she was trying to shake them down.

He caught hold of her by the blouse and landed the pot in the middle of her skull with a heavy gong sound . . . An ambulance carried my mother to the hospital.[65]

She recovered, went off to live as a domestic servant, and deposited her children with her mother and her sister's family in a Second Avenue slum, which housed ten in two rooms.

My younger brother doesn't stir beside me. Nor the youngest uncle the other side of him under the same blanket as we. They say I am a bad sleeper. . . . I know the cold air coming through the hole in the flooring boards will whip us out of sleep as it plays upon bare flesh, else one's leg will rest on my neck and then I shall dream that some fiend is slitting my throat and I shall jump up with a scream. My sister also on the floor is kicking the leg of the table she's sleeping under. Grandmother and three of Aunt Dora's children are lying quiet on the old double bed.[66]

The household in which Mphahlele grows up is ruled neither by a father nor a mother; rather it is controlled by his Aunt Dora and a grandmother, two strong figures. Aunt Dora is physically strong, powerful, uncomplaining, resistant to the corrosive elements of Second Avenue: ". . . people spoke of her as 'Aunt Dora of Second Avenue'—that woman who throws a man over a fence. . . . a woman of strict discipline, who wanted things done to time and thoroughly."[67] She never spoke about the future, she simply grappled with the present.

Water taps were communal on Second Avenue: crowds lined up to catch the drops. "Tck, tck, so much water in the seas, but none in Marabastad."[68] "Dirty water and flies and dead cats and dogs and children's stools owned the streets . . ."[69] otherwise, the location seemed to be the property of the police.

The men in uniform may even now be sniffing about in the yard. Far to the west end of Marabastad a police whistle, the barking of dogs—no, it must be in Fourth Avenue, maybe because I hear heavy booted footsteps, it's sure to be a person running away from the law, the police cells, the court and jail. Saturday night and it's ten to ten, I can hear the big curfew bell at the police station peal 'ten to ten, ten to ten, ten to ten' for the Black man to be out of the streets, to be at home, to be out of the policeman's reach. Year after year every night the sound of the bell floats in the air at ten minutes to ten and the Black man must run home and the Black man must sleep or have a night special permit.[70]

Ten to ten: the police whistle blows and all Kaffirs enter their family shacks where rats play over the torn bedclothes, where people sleep the fitful sleep of the exhausted and dream of water dripping through leaks, where people shiver together and die uselessly.

Overlying the life of misery is the oppression of the white world. Any show of resistance to the police, to whites, can draw attention that will end in beatings, jail, or possibly death.

> A white and African constable came round the corner and focused that terrible blinding light on my face, so that I could only see the big shoulders of the white man on the sides. I became stupid with terror and I trembled.
>
> 'What are you doing here, my jong?' the big white man asked in Afrikaans. . . . 'What was that I heard when I came in?'
>
> 'I was throwing a stone at a dog,' I said. . . .
>
> 'Hold the bastard's arms, Jonas, and pin them behind his ass.' The Black constable had hardly reached my hand when the big white hand crashed full on my cheeks so that I seemed to hear my name called, and staggered and hit against a pole that was supporting a vine. . . . I got a backhand on the mouth and in an instant I tasted something salty. While I held my mouth the big white man caught me behind the neck and pressed my face against his other massive hand, so that I began to suffocate.
>
> 'Now this is for your bloody lies, you son of a stinking kaffir!' With the last word he thrust me away from him. I went down on the hard ground.[71]

Mphahlele's reality differs completely from the tranquility and flowing, easy lives that the Dark Child, or the Kossoh Town Boy experience. His situation is monolithic, unchanging, repetitious. There is little possibility for escape—only the cheap movies of the bioscope; the superstitious fantasies of black magic; the music of Siki, the tubercular guitarist, who coughed "like the twang of his guitar strings, and coughed and coughed until the blood came out of him and he dies." So strangling and corrosive is the environment that only a total physical escape can bring Mphahlele any relief or comfort. Education is held out as the means of this necessary escape.

The tone and mood of *Down Second Avenue* are gray and stark, and the social circumstances surrounding the boy's life are brutal and harsh. Only through education is Mphahlele eventually able to free himself from the oppressive nature of South Africa. His every moment at school is threatened by "harassing conditions at home," but with each new advance in his education, he feels "a great light of dawn" flashing into him, as the "obtuse shaft of light, was narrowing, sharpening and finding a point of focus."[72] But education, he learns, is not a sure escape. Always, the social conditions impose themselves into the personal dreams and desires of the Black world:

> Grandmother was most proud of her three sons who had gone to 'college' as she put it. The youngest of them went to a school in Natal for motor mechanics. He was very sorry after the three years because no garage employs Africans as skilled workers. European trade unions don't allow it, and then the government does not recognize African apprentices. He is now a bus inspector and does not hope to be anything more.[73]

Like Lee, in *Tell Freedom*, who feels peace at Grace Dieu, Mphahlele experiences a quiet and nonturbulent world at St. Peter's school. Yet, for him, too, the equation is incomplete:

> For the first time in my life, when I was at St. Peter's, an awareness was creeping into me: an awareness of the white man's ways and aims. There was complete harmony between us and the white teachers at school and between them and the African staff. And yet no one, Brother Roger or the Principal, or the Community fathers, ever said anything about the attitude they thought we should adopt towards whites and white authority outside school. Slowly I realized how I hated the white man outside the walls of St. Peter's.[74]

Had Mphahlele been willing to accept the Bantu Education Act and other restrictive decrees of the government, he could have continued his teaching career. But he felt that would be a connivance with the forces of a monolithic totalitarian society. Not wanting to be "Time's Eunuch," he resisted the system's attempt to drain him of his manhood. He could find no beauty, no sources of inspiration from his land. The author's style reflects his increasing bitterness:

> My longing search continued. Mind and heart stood still. It tormented me to feel so insufficient, and not to know the why and wherefore. At times thought and feeling would gush forth in torrents so that many things became jumbled symbols of my hope and yearning: the purple pink sunsets; the wasting bleached earth; the rock hanging precariously on the cheek of a hill; the muddy grey waters of the Caledon; the eternal streak of cloud lying stretched out like one of heaven's drunken sots. But alas, my dreams had long since taken flight and now hung dry in shining cobwebs to which my fermenting furies clung crucified . . .[75]

Like Ngugi, in *Weep Not, Child*, Mphahlele uses darkness to symbolize the condition of his people and his land. From Orlando:

> . . . comparative cleanliness and bigness blunt the edge of political discontent here, but you know you're in a ghetto and God, those lights are so far away, too far for you to reach. Between you and them is a pit of darkness, darkness charged with screams, groans, yells, cries, laughter and singing. They swell and reach a frantic pitch, only to be suppressed by the spirit of night.[76]

As a child, Mphahlele had drawn inspiration from the lights. Yet, as a man who had learned that his education did not give him a permanent place in the privileged society, the lights become a symbol. After he had applied for a passport for Nigeria, where he could escape the CID and develop his creative ability, Mphahlele uses the lights of the city as an integral part of the white machine: "That passport, will it ever come or is it wrapped up in those electric lights?"[77]

Somehow, he was able to hold on. The passport was obtained, but only through the aid of a valuable and trusted friend. The disillusionment that had led to bitterness is worked in images of lights and bird's wings. Mphahlele gradually realizes that if he stays in South Africa, his homeland, he will be drained of life. Like Abrahams, he is a writer, and he fights to save himself. The movement away is inevitable. It has come not only because of education, as in Samba Diallo's case, but also because of the white government's efforts to transform those searching and fighting for freedom of expression into mute machines, whose actions are determined by decree.

The striving for formal education described in *Down Second Avenue* and *Ashanti Boy* is satirized in *Mission to Kala*, by Mongo Beti, of the Cameroun. In his formulation, Beti sees the necessity for a natural rather than formal education. The prime motive of Medza, Beti's hero, is to enter into full living, to learn by participating and to exercise the sensory powers and social graces.

The hero Medza has just failed his exams at the French college. Yet, ironically, out of a high regard for the value of book education and shrewdly aware of its bargaining powers, his uncle selects Medza for the mission of retrieving a relative's wife who has run away to an upcountry village. It is old Bikololo, the elder of the village, who tries to cajole the unwilling Medza to undertake the mission by expounding in a kind of dialectic palaver style the values of education:

> My son . . . when the story is recited after my death, you will be its hero. *You* are that formidable man, *you* speak with the voice of the thunder, and have never suspected your own powers. Shall I tell you what your special thunder is? Your certificates, your learning, your knowledge of white men's secrets. Have you any idea what these upcountry bushmen will quite seriously believe about you? That you only have to write a letter in French, or speak French to the nearest District Officer to have anyone you like imprisoned, or get any personal favor you want.[78]

In Kala, the geographical center of his tribeswoman's wandering escapade, Medza is regaled and honored as a prodigy of learning, "educated *and* a city dweller," the conveyer of the white man's wisdom.

> 'Geography?' exclaimed someone, fumbling over the unfamiliar syllables. 'What's that?'

I gave them what must have been the most feeble, certainly the most arguable definition of geography ever presented to any audience . . . who hung on my every word. . . . I found myself telling these simple people about New York—an inconceivable city to them, with its seven million inhabitants and skyscrapers of anything up to seventy-five floors, soaring up for a thousand feet. . . . just as the other evening the young guitarist had switched his rhythms, and without exactly knowing why, I played suddenly a Russian chord, to which they at once responded.

'Russia?' they asked. 'Where's that?'[79]

Medza, for all his approximate scholarship, longs for the free, rollicking life he sees around him; yet, in order to perpetuate his own worldly wise stature, he refrains from joining unfamiliar activities. The sham provokes many bawdy scenes.

They then proposed that we should go for a swim: the proposal was carried unanimously, with only one absention—me. I don't happen to be able to swim. All the same, I went with them.

It was a broad stream, almost a full-sized river. They all stripped off in a flash and plunged into the water stark naked. At first I said I didn't think I would bathe. They insisted on my coming in with them, jollying me along, even saying that if I still refused they'd haul me in by main force. I knew that they were only joking and wouldn't really do it. Nevertheless I took off all my clothes, except a pair of brief pants. At the moment I entered the water—still wearing my pants—they all burst into shrieks of laughter.

'Why don't you undress properly?' Zambo asked.

'You haven't got a dose, by any chance, have you?' enquired the Boneless Wonder.

'Perhaps it's a real whopper and he doesn't want to show us,' giggled Son-of-God.

'Or a tiny shrimp of a thing.' This from Duckfoot Johnny, who was laughing himself sick.

'Him?' someone else said. 'Don't be funny. I bet it's twice as big as yours. I know these chaps from the city.'[80]

Medza wanted desperately "to eat, drink and be happy without having to bother . . . about the next term, or such depressing things as revision-work and orals." He begins to resent his scholar's aura. "I'd have given all the diplomas in the world to swim like Duckfoot Johnny or dance like the Boneless Wonder, or have the sexual experience of Petrus Son-of-God, or throw an assegai like Zambo. The very least I could do was to conquer my fear of women."[81]

Interspersed with Beti's more satirical scenes are Medza's serious reflections about what his education has done for him. Unlike the Dark Child he has not learned the wonders of the world; he cannot say, "How happy we were in those days"; he cannot even reflect on having lost his totem, since he is totally oblivious to a totem, to the sensuous and the spirit world around him. Unlike the heroes of *Weep Not, Child, Ashanti Boy*, and other autobiographical novels, Medza has never held fast to education as a means to a better life. He admits to himself that he had really been forced to go to school by his father, and had "turned the whole thing into a game, something to pass the time away and amuse me."[82] As he moves closer to the traditional life of Kala and feels the sting of his own inexperience compared to the boys his own age, Medza becomes more bitter about the system that had imprisoned him: "My resentment against schools and educational systems mounted steadily as the days passed by. I saw a school as a kind of giant ogre, swallowing young boys, digesting them slowly, vomiting them up again, sucked dry of all their youthful essence, mere skeletons."[83]

His confidence grows as he experiences more of himself, discovering that he could be more than a "mere skeleton." Medza's Tarzan of a cousin, Zambo, fortunately had some kind of Freudian bee in his bonnet about arranging appropriate meetings. Medza's first encounter, with Eliza, a proud, beautiful "good-time girl" sought after by all the village men, is fumbled in frightened frigidity, which Medza manages to pass off with supersophisticated disdain: ". . . as far as I'm concerned, in future you can count Eliza out. Oh, she's pretty enough, one of the best-looking girls I've ever seen in my life . . . but what I really want is a nice young girl who doesn't know her way about at all, if you get me. As long as she's young, sweet and innocent, I don't care a damn about her looks. I'm sick to death of experienced old bags."[84] Zambo promptly delivers the chief's youngest daughter, Edima. In a beautifully paced

scene Beti captures all the irony attendant on Medza's initiation
into love-making:

> Edima sat down on the bed, at a decent distance from me. I
> stared [at her] in dumb misery, while she returned my gaze
> half-smiling now, one finger in her mouth like a little child
> being introduced to a stranger . . . I bent down under the foot
> of my bed, pulled out my whiskey-bottle, and gulped down
> several mouthfuls without drawing breath. At once I became
> far more passionate and excited; it seemed as though this slight
> alcoholic stimulus had triggered off the dormant effect of all
> the stuff I had drunk earlier.
> 'Come here, baby,' I said, playfully.
> She shook her head. She wouldn't come any closer. I had to
> move over to her.
> When I was beside her, she turned her head away. I took her
> hand, and she snatched it away sharply . . . I seized both her
> hands at once, and she struggled savagely. I was a bit astonished
> at her violence, because normally she was such a gentle little
> creature; but I didn't let go. . . . Edima's main endeavour was to
> scratch me, as if she wanted not only to hurt, but also to mark
> me. I couldn't understand it. Driven on by whiskey and cir-
> cumstance, I had, as it seemed to me, become an actor in a
> strange, crazy comedy.[85]

Medza's initiation into riotous drinking comes when the village boys invite him to Duckfoot Johnny's palm-wine still:

> I took my courage in both hands, realizing that I was fairly
> caught in a drinking contest. I wondered how long it would be
> before I had to admit defeat, and whether it wouldn't be better
> to do so straight away. But to keep my end up, I decided at
> least to string along on the first round. We helped ourselves by
> plunging our [split coconut shell] goblets into a full jar.
> 'Now don't forget,' said Duckfoot Johnny, still handing out
> instructions, 'the first four rounds must be drunk at one go—
> no heel-taps.'
> 'Why?' I enquired, in some alarm.
> 'Why?' So that my house may always be blessed with plenty,
> of course. Don't you know *anything* in your part of the coun-
> try? . . .
> On the sixth round I showed all the symptoms of exhaustion
> and incipient surrender. My cousin, observing this . . . operated

a private sleight-of-hand manœuvre over the drinks. I would fill my own goblet and put it down beside him; he would replace it with the one he had just emptied. Right till the end of the party no one spotted this little dodge. . . .

A tiny grin quirked round the corner of Zambo's mouth, like a flower-bud unfolding. Duckfoot Johnny seemed totally impervious to alcohol; the only unusual thing he did was to fling one arm round my shoulders and tell me that henceforth I would be his closest friend, because, despite my shocking upbringing, I drank better than any of them.

'The first time I saw you,' he said, 'I wasn't too sure about you. I know these city slickers; they're a different kind of chap from us altogether. You must be the exception that proves the rule. I propose to *adopt* you, Jean-Marie.'[86]

In contrast to Laye's Dark Child and Kane's Samba Diallo, Medza must move into traditional life before he can begin the process of movement away. When his pseudoscientific answer of what "blood" means evokes peals of laughter from his uncle, Medza realizes how simple and uncomplicated his uncle's views are and how absurdly complex his explanations of simple things have become:

> For him it represented the keystone of all science, the ultimate word in every mystery, the foundation of his universal theory, his Euclidean hypothesis, his Fourth Dimension. Others might have invented relativity, the Quantum theory, and heaven knows what besides; but he had discovered, in blood kinship, a whole unique cosmogony, irreplaceable, undeniable.[87]

Beti's novel is a variation on the theme of the movement away. Medza can move away only after he has moved into the land. In the first part of the novel, he is presented as a somewhat rebellious schoolboy, a "mere skeleton" who is afraid of who and what he is and reluctant to take the responsibility for a brother's difficulties. In Kala he learns some of the wonders of the world, and this new education affirms that he is flesh as well as bones. When Medza mounts his well-oiled bicycle and heads down the red dirt road back to town he takes a sensory education with him. Also leaving the village with Medza are his brother's wife, sheep given to him in payment for the endless

circle of visits to villager's homes, his lover, Edima, whom the
chief has forced Medza to marry, and Zambo, who has decided
to string along. Medza tastes the best of both worlds and is able
to select pleasures out of the context of the traditional village
and carry them out to a cosmopolitan life—ultimately, to Paris,
where he and Zambo "led a life of endless wandering: different
people, changing ideas, from country to country and place to
place."[88]

Medza's education did not afford him the peace and appetite
for achievement that Kofi, of the *Ashanti Boy*, enjoyed. Nor
did it end in the ultimate return to the land by death, which
Samba Diallo made in *Ambiguous Adventure*. Rather, in his
endless peregrinations that drew him away from his land, he
grew to understand truths of which he had been unaware as a
mere school boy.

> Not least among these was the discovery—made by contact
> with the countryfolk of Kala, those quintessential caricatures
> of the 'colonized' African—that the tragedy which our nation
> is suffering today is that of a man left to his own devices in a
> world which does not belong to him, which he has not made
> and does not understand. It is the tragedy of man bereft of any
> intellectual compass, a man walking blindly through the dark
> in some hostile city like New York. Who will tell him that he
> can only cross Fifth Avenue by the pedestrian crossings, or
> teach him how to interpret the traffic signs? How will he solve
> the intricacies of a subway map, or know where to change
> trains?[89]

In many of the autobiographical novels, the protagonist is
caught in the middle of great social disorder: the Mau Mau
uprising in *Weep Not, Child* or the corrosive, monolithic
apartheid of South Africa in *Down Second Avenue* and *Tell
Freedom*. For such sensitive persons as Njoroge, Mphahlele,
and Abrahams, education would seem to be one of the principal means of coping with and even changing their circumstances; but instead, its acquisition merely alienates them from
the very reality that it reveals to them with increasing clarity.
First, while they are there, school is a way of life, protecting
them from the pressures of outside reality. Once outside the
school compound, however, the outer reality unmistakably, and

shockingly, confronts them. In turn, their reactions are conditioned by their educated awareness and aspirations.

All the protagonists in the autobiographical novels under discussion are searching for direction. Their new awareness often leads them into struggle or active conflict, embitterment, loss of hope, and finally, escape. Confusion and perplexity often assail them, and with the possible exception of Robert Cole in *Kossoh Town Boy*, they all suffer loneliness and alienation. In *Weep Not, Child*, Njoroge has been educated for a positive role in his country's evolution, but his role ultimately is a negative one. Education in *Down Second Avenue* assuages the dreadful fears of Mphahlele's earlier years, but at the same time, it alienates rather than prepares him for participation in South African life. An apartheid society has no place for an educated black man. The pattern is the same for Peter Lee Abrahams in *Tell Freedom*. The stifling lot of the nonwhite in South Africa finally becomes so intolerable that he is forced to seek freedom and life elsewhere.

Most of Abrahams' family remains rooted in and victim of the social circumstances of the Colored world in South Africa. Abrahams, with his sensitivity and educated awareness, cannot accept these circumstances; gradually, almost inevitably, he rejects them, and ultimately, despite his love for those who are inextricably caught in the system, he moves away from the circumstances also. Inevitably, he even moves away from his mother who, partly because of the acquiescence of those of her generation, is caught in the system and cannot give him the sustenance he needs. Young Lee trusts her completely, and his dreamy, poetic, seemingly hesitant nature does not make him doubt her protective instincts. Like Camara Laye's mother and many of the other mothers of these novels: "She was Mother. She belonged to me. With her I had no doubts, no uncertainties. With her everything was always all right."[90] Abrahams' mother, like all the other mothers, also suffers at every juncture of Abrahams' continuous movement away in his search for larger areas of expression. But unlike Laye's mother, she understands and accepts the necessity: "A mother always minds. But don't you think about that. You go, and I'll pray to God to look after you." Then, as they walk away from Vrededorp, "my mother said heavily: 'It is a bad place. I'm glad you are going out of it.' "[91]

His sister Maggie, on the other hand, cries. Warm and affectionate, she does not share her mother's resignation to his growing alienation and departure. She realizes that he is a dreamer, and she worries over what his education and awareness will lead to in South Africa. She senses his every change and wants to alleviate his loneliness. But although she is often defiant and resentful of her place as a Colored, Maggie, with Abrahams' sensitivity and perhaps larger sense of humanity, has learned to "cope" with the situation; she does not understand Abrahams' own need for something beyond South Africa.

Her brother Harry, like Abrahams himself, also shares the sense of individual dignity and worth that is the legacy of their deceased father. But this, perhaps, only compounds the tragedy, for Harry, once "dapper and neat in dress," with a "buoyant radiance"[92] has become both frustrated and defeated, swallowed up into the broken, useless living of most of his generation of nonwhites.

The corrosive effects of the grinding poverty and unremitting toil of the exploited nonwhite population is evident, too, in the stoic acceptance of Aunt Liza with whom Abrahams lives in Elsburg for a time after his father's death. Aunt Liza, who washes for the white folks, is still tender, though gruff, despite her perpetual weariness and "the thickness of her arms, and her big hands, which were pitted from being in water the whole day, white as a sheet and swollen to twice their size."[93] Aunt Mattie, on the other hand, "looked harshly, coldly, on a harsh cold world. She was harsh with herself as with anyone else. The only two people who ever seemed to pierce her coldness were my brother Harry and her daughter Catherine."[94]

This, then, is the world in which the young Abrahams grows up; but from the very beginning, his father's training and his own sensitivity cause him to question it and even to fight against it. In Elsburg, after some bullying from some white boys, he beats them up. But his uncle is later forced to beat him until the young boy apologizes to the white father and to the boys who stand by and jeer. This is his first lesson about his lot in South Africa.

He drifts into some sort of *modus vivendi* and lives the life of any young Colored boy in a South African township—stealing fruit from Indian traders with his gang, going to the bioscope, fighting, working. But he never ceases to question his lot. At thirteen, he is given his first book by a Jewish secretary at his job; he leaves to go to school so that he can learn to read the book, a copy of Lamb's *Tales from Shakespeare*. He now becomes aware of a world other than that which he has known, a world where dignity and equality are accorded all men. He begins to drift away from Dinny and his gang; he "felt lonely and longed for something without being able to give it a name."[95] He has been alienated from the Colored world and longs for:

> . . . what the white folk had. I envied them their superior, European lot.
> The familiar mood that awaits the sensitive young who are poor and dispossessed is a mood of sharp and painful inferiority, of violently angry tensions, of desperate and overwhelming longings. On these nightly walks, that mood took possession of me. My three books fed it.[96]

At the Bantu Men's Club, his longing for a better life is given more positive focus. For the first time, he encounters nonwhites who possess something of the dignity he has always longed for. These black men, the gentleness of their eyes seemingly common to them all, are men of education and culture, and "it was almost as if I had met a new kind of black person."[97]

Here, too, he realizes for the first time that in other parts of the world, men of color had achieved artistic prominence. While listening to the American baritone, Paul Robeson, he even experiences a momentary identity, though when the voice stops, "the moment that had given us a common identity was over."[98] But this is only the beginning of his realization of a nonwhite identity. With the discovery of the shelf of books marked "American Negro Literature," he is startled to discover that "These poems and stories were written by Negroes: Something burst deep inside me. The world could never again belong to white people only. Never again!"[99]

His growing sense of identity makes him even more acutely aware of what he is being denied and the possibilities that he can attain. Further education is a concrete step toward any higher kind of life for him, and he goes to the college at Pietersburg, in the valley of Grace Dieu. He has moved farther away from his family and the harsh reality of South Africa, and here, "in the peaceful valley, the equation worked out. The fathers who taught us lived up to their teaching. . . . Belief was translated into reality."[100] But Grace Dieu is only a temporary haven, and the only fault, if any, was that "they had taught us too well," for in the rest of South Africa, "the equation did not work out."[101]

On a holiday excursion to the nearby town with Jonathan, a Bantu boy, he is shocked into realization of this. A white man who bumps into him takes it lightly, until he realized that the boy is Colored. Afterward, young Abrahams asks himself: "Why did he look so sick with disgust? The other wouldn't have mattered if he had not looked so sick with it. Am I really like ordure to him? Only the touch of that could make him feel and look as he did."[102] This heightens the enigma and bitterness, and he remembers the difference between the treatment accorded his teacher and mentor—who is white—and himself.

He cannot remain at the school after this episode, and he transfers to St. Peter's secondary school in Johannesburg. There, he meets his first Christian socialist, Brother Roger. But he rejects Marxism because of its lack of humanism and the bitter division between its adherents. For him, Marxism fails, as does Christianity, for it cannot fill in the lack in the human equation and cannot bring social justice.

Abrahams the dreamer seems doomed to disappointment in South Africa. Even his love-making goes awry. He had, he says, wanted his first experience to be "an act of dedication. It had worked out as liberation without dedication, freedom without beauty."[103] His dreams and hopes have successively isolated him from his family and his society. At each juncture, his failure to find any satisfaction leads him on, rootless and wandering, and always alone. His discovery of Shakespeare and poetry had been the first steps on that long road. "I lived in two worlds, the world of Vrededorp and the world of these books. And, somehow, both were equally real. . . . Only the victory of one or the other could bring me peace."[104] He begins to look on his family and the world of Vrededorp with a "new, seeing coldness that had nothing to do with coldness of feeling."[105]

At St. Peter's, he had "first discovered the independent life possessed by a work of art and the strange loyalty art demands of those who would serve it."[106] He sees finally that he cannot reconcile the two divergent realities of art and the brutal, dehumanizing life of a South African Colored. He must leave, despite his family and friends.

> For me, personally, life in South Africa had come to an end. I had been lucky in some of the whites I had met. Meeting them had made a straight 'all-blacks-are-good, all-whites-are-bad' attitude impossible. But I had reached a point where the gestures of even my friends among the whites were suspect, so I had to go or be forever lost. I needed, not friends, not gestures, but my manhood. And the need was desperate.
>
> Perhaps life had a meaning that transcended race and colour. If it had, I could not find it in South Africa. Also, there was the need to write, to tell freedom, and for this I needed to be personally free.[107]

And so in spite of love of the land, in spite of nostalgia, in spite of Africa, Mother Africa, many move away—some inevitably through the process of growth and through the cycle of initiation into life, others because they are compelled by growing alienation and disaffection with the realities that surround them. Peter Abrahams, too, moves away completely from his land, and desirous of saving his land, he will never forget it.

> Is there a land with the compelling power of this African land? Can any other land be cold and austere and yet tender?[108]

Notes

1. Cheikh Hamidou Kane, *Ambiguous Adventure* (New York: Walker and Co., 1963), pp. 142–143.
2. Camara Laye, *The Dark Child*, tr. from French by James Kirkup (London: Collins Press, 1955), dedication.
3. Chinua Achebe, *Things Fall Apart* (New York: McDowell, Obolensky, 1959), p. 189.
4. Laye, *op. cit.*, dedication.
5–14. *Ibid*: 5. p. 12; 6. pp. 65–66; 7. pp. 134–135; 8. p. 175; 9. p. 174; 10. pp. 188–189; 11. pp. 188–189; 12. pp. 96–97; 13. pp. 184–185; 14. p. 187.
15. Kane, *op. cit.*, p. 31.
16–26. *Ibid*: 16. p. 161; 17. p. 4; 18. pp. 71–72; 19. pp. 19–20;

20. p. 11; **21.** p. 27; **22.** p. 34; **23.** pp. 150–151; **24.** p. 68; **25.** p. 78; **26.** p. 150.

27. James Ngugi, *Weep Not, Child* (London: Heinemann Educational Books, Ltd., 1964), p. 12.

28–40. *Ibid:* **28.** p. 54; **29.** pp. 29–30; **30.** p. 30; **31.** p. 44; **32.** p. 84; **33.** pp. 79–80; **34.** p. 84; **35.** pp. 124–125; **36.** pp. 92–93; **37.** p. 118; **38.** pp. 108–109; **39.** p. 121; **40.** pp. 152–153.

41. Robert W. Cole, *Kossoh Town Boy* (New York: Cambridge University Press, 1960), p. 11.

42–43. *Ibid:* **42.** p. 191; **43.** p. 11.

44. Laye, *op. cit.,* p. 54.

45. Cole, *op. cit.,* p. 11.

46–51. *Ibid:* **46.** p. 13; **47.** pp. 13–14; **48.** p. 59; **49.** pp. 43–44; **50.** pp. 131–134; **51.** p. 191.

52. Akosua Abbs, *Ashanti Boy* (London: Collins Press, 1959), pp. 99–100.

53–62. *Ibid:* **53.** p. 73; **54.** p. 180; **55.** p. 229; **56.** p. 26; **57.** p. 147; **58.** pp. 74–75; **59.** p. 197; **60.** p. 147; **61.** p. 171; **62.** p. 235.

63. Ezekiel Mphahlele, *Down Second Avenue* (London: Faber and Faber, 1959), p. 25.

64–77. *Ibid:* **64.** p. 26; **65.** p. 28; **66.** p. 44; **67.** pp. 76–77; **68.** p. 29; **69.** p. 33; **70.** pp. 44–45; **71.** p. 42; **72.** p. 86; **73.** p. 123; **74.** p. 126; **75.** p. 185; **76.** p. 204; **77.** p. 206.

78. Mongo Beti, *Mission to Kala* (London, Heinemann Educational Books, Ltd., 1958), p. 15.

79–89. *Ibid:* **79.** pp. 65–66; **80.** pp. 43–44; **81.** pp. 58–59; **82.** p. 79; **83.** p. 68; **84.** p. 76; **85.** pp. 136–137; **86.** pp. 114–115; **87.** p. 89; **88.** p. 180; **89.** p. 181.

90. Peter Abrahams, *Tell Freedom* (New York: Alfred A. Knopf, 1954), p. 4.

91–108. *Ibid:* **91.** p. 254; **92.** p. 113; **93.** p. 24; **94.** p. 112; **95.** p. 191; **96.** p. 193; **97.** p. 228; **98.** p. 224; **99.** p. 226; **100.** p. 280; **101.** pp. 280–281; **102.** p. 288; **103.** p. 294; **104.** p. 189; **105.** p. 268; **106.** p. 296; **107.** p. 370; **108.** p. 282.

TWO

DISILLUSIONMENT AND BREAKUP ... THE COLONIAL WORLD

A falling away from the kind of unity and certainty portrayed in the world of *The Dark Child* is always inevitable. This breakup of old beliefs may result from a natural and gradual growth of boy into man, or it may be thrust upon an individual by external forces. If the novels in Chapter I can be set apart by their autobiographical nature, the novels treated in this chapter may be grouped for their preoccupation with perhaps the most powerful of these external forces—colonialism. Colonialism is the force that has changed the lives of Africans, Asians, peoples of the Caribbean, and indeed of a large segment of the world's population. It is a fact of history, and its impact is now irrevocable.

The nostalgia and serenity of boyhood present in many of the novels of the first chapter here give way to chaos and agony as young men confront strange and threatening individuals and civilizations which they are not equipped to understand. The transposition of the center of gravity, consequent on colonial impositions, brings with it transposition of catharsis from simply that of moving away or falling away to that of breakup. In the course of this colonial imposition many native social structures were shattered, family groupings destroyed, and individuals plunged into disillusionment and despair. The reverberations of this breakup, this destruction, this increasing disillusionment resound in these novels. In *Ambiguous Adventure*, Kane describes the encounter in this way:

> Strange dawn. The morning of the Occident in black Africa was spangled over with smiles, with cannon shots, with shining glass beads. Those who had no history were encountering those who carried the world on their shoulders. It was a morning of accouchement: the known world was enriching itself by a birth that took place in mire and blood.[1]

The cannon shots are symbolic of one phase of colonialism: exploitation and physical cruelty. These novels often become an elaboration of the various kinds of brutality inflicted on the natives. The smiles and the beads have myriad variations, motifs attendant on the colonial imposition. Not only territorial conquest resulted from the clash of the two worlds, but also prostitution of the body and seduction of the mind were elements of the encounter. The naive African discovered too late that the smiles masked greed and that the beads were only of glass. The once naive native is awakened quite rapidly to the harsh realities of the colonial imposition, thus precipitating the disillusionment which also characterizes this particular group of novels.

The theme of colonialism is one of the most persistent notes in African literature and in fact in that of all newly emerging nations. It appears of historical necessity and will continue to be present in many literatures, for its effects on individuals and societies have been deeply wrenching, precipitating "the falling apart of things." Colonialism with its concomitant conflict between individuals and generations and confrontation between groups is the moving force in these novels—compelling the climax of action and the final denouement.

The intragroup conflict is at times even more destructive than the conflict with the outsider, the generational conflict being that which often breaks up the African way of life. Some of the older generation are resigned to the strangers' intrusion, still strong in their confidence that their tribal gods will right the wrongs for them; others having fought and lost are now disillusioned about their chances for success. Resignation and disillusionment produce the inaction and passivity that allow the foreigner to effect his conquest still more easily. The young men, however, are impatient, impulsive, and anxious to strike out against the intruders. They will reject tribal tradition and old beliefs if they think them ineffectual against the powers of the white man. This was apparent in Boro's damning of Ngotho's deep reliance on the prophecy in *Weep Not, Child*, a damning which hastened the breakup of Ngotho's well-structured household.[2]

Such a vast churning of society cannot but produce a sense of alienation and frustration in the individual. Meka, the central figure in *Le Vieux Nègre et la Médaille*, is one of the most tragic of those characters whom the conflict destroys and leaves with a loss of identity. Meka is to be awarded a medal by the white man as a reward for his cooperation. As he stands within the circle of chalk traced on the platform to receive his award, he becomes painfully aware that he belongs to neither group. He has stepped out of his tribal tradition, but he is being humiliated by the whites by being forced to stand apart from the true leaders. Meka is thus in a psychological void, a state of nonbelonging from which he grasps at one world and then another for assistance. When neither will support him, he sinks into despair and an aged resignation: "Je ne suis plus qu'un vieil homme."[3]

Inability to comprehend and thus to sympathize is perhaps the most significant cause of tension and conflict in any human relationship. A nearly complete void of penetration and understanding existed between Africans and Europeans, blacks and whites. Fear was spawned through the misinterpretation of appearances and actions, dread through lack of comprehension of differing words. Everything about the white man that was strange or different to the native caused unduly strong reactions of fear and distrust.

The physical appearance of the white man and his accouterments excited the natives' imagination. The stranger was first called a butterfly and a ghost because of his white skin.

On parlait de la présence d'un homme fantôme dans le pays. Il était blanc comme la chaux, avait des yeux de panthère et de longs cheveux comme la crinière d'un cheval.[4]

People spoke of there being a ghost abroad in the region. He was white as chalk, with the eyes of a panther and a long mane of hair like a horse.

His physical appearance—straight hair, red cheeks, ability to peel off his skin (i.e., remove his gloves)—at first perplexed and then amused the natives.

Et ceci, n'était-ce pas plus terrifiant encore? N'avait-il pas vu, ces jours passés, lors de l'arrivée du nouveau "commandant," n'avait-il pas vu celui-ci enlever la peau de sa main, une peau qui, ma foi, ne ressemblait que fort peu à toutes les peaux déjà connues.[5]

And wasn't this even more terrifying? In the last few days since the new "commandant's" arrival, hadn't he seen him remove the skin from his hand? And honestly, that skin resembled only slightly any skin he'd ever seen before.

Some speculate that the white man has no toes because his feet are covered by shoes.

"Is it true that one of their women in Umuru went outside without the white hat and melted like sleeping palm oil in the sun?" asked the other companion.

"I have also heard it," said Akukalia. "But many lies are told about the white man. It was once said that he had no toes."[6]

The white man's ability to add artificial limbs, teeth, and eyes (spectacles) is ascribed to the white man's magical powers. The unknown is always mysterious, frightening, and endowed with undue significance. Tales of the white man's powers are soon exaggerated to include the supernatural. In *Weep Not, Child,* Dedan, a black man and leader of a terrorist uprising, is said to have learned some of the white man's tricks through fighting in a war with him. "Dedan can change himself into anything—a white man, a bird, or a tree. He can also turn himself into an aeroplane. He learnt all this in the Big War."[7]

The white man is then at the outset regarded as a super-human and as such, not subject to human frailties or emotions. Eventually, as contact between the groups lengthens, the native begins to suspect that the white man is vulnerable. "He heard the big white man muttering something or other and he drew closer so as to hear better; he was curious to know what a white man said if he was frightened or hurt."[8] In *Arrow of God*, when the white administrator, Winterbottom, falls ill, Ezeulu, the priest of Umuaro, is shocked because he had believed him to be immune to death and sickness.

The myth of the physical powers of the white man is more easily torn down than the terror produced by his material possessions. Handcuffs and the police pickup van called the Snatcher in *Turn to the Dark* inject such fear into the natives that compliance is immediate and unquestioning. The reaction of the ignorant is thus completely out of proportion to the actual power of the object. "In the eyes of the villager hand-cuffs or *iga* were the most deadly of the white man's weapons. The sight of a fighting man reduced to impotence and helplessness with an iron lock was the final humiliation. It was a treatment given only to violent lunatics."[9]

The mechanized white man evokes the fear and curiosity and at times amusement of the natives. Here they dismiss the bicycle as another of the white man's odd creations:

> Tout cela était 'manières de blancs,' comme était 'manières de blancs' courir les routes juché sur l'un de ces deux objets ronds et élastiques qu'on propulse tantôt du pied droit, tantôt du pied gauche, et qui jouent à se poursuivre sans jamais parvenir à se rattraper.[10]

> All that was "white man's ways," just like dashing along the road perched on one of those two round, springy things which you move first with your right foot and then with your left, and which put on a show of chasing each other without ever managing to catch up.

Nor can the Africans think of reasons or justifications for many of the white man's actions. It seems to them the height of ridiculousness that he should build bridges over the streams that they and their ancestors had always waded across. "You really had to be white to have such outlandish notions. Honestly now, do you really need bridges on rivers that you can wade across?"[11]

To be sure, the transition from fear of the white man's magical powers to amusement at his seeming foibles clearly manifests the process of the natives' demystification. Yet, any form of incomprehension leads to misinterpretation, to distortion and exaggeration of values. The presentation of a medal to Meka in *Le Vieux Nègre et la Médaille* takes on a significance for him and his people that far exceeds its actual significance. In a grandiose speech, after he has been awarded the medal, Meka invites the Grand Chef to plunge his hands into the same pot of food in a tribal ritual of friendship. He is promptly rebuffed. The medal is symbolic only of his further subjugation to the white man. It was but an empty token for Meka's sons killed in the service of France and for his donation of his ancestral lands to the French church. Meka's entire tribe, with the exception of his wife who cries during the ceremony, also misunderstands the awarding of the medal. His reputation in the group is enhanced considerably by the honor, and many believe that some of his prestige will transfer to them. "From now on, your family, your friends, and your friends' friends will be privileged people. All they'll have to say is: 'I'm a friend of a friend of Meka's brother-in-law' for all doors to swing open for them. Even I feel a bit honored. . . ."[12]

Like the native, the white man, too, misrepresents and naively misinterprets the characteristics of those whom he is subjugating. Throughout the novels, the white man regards the native as subhuman, at the very best as a child and a simpleton worthy of tolerance and condescension. The physical qualities, the psychological attitudes, and the institutions of the native African are ridiculed, scorned, or simply misunderstood. Père Gilbert is one of the most sympathetically portrayed whites in these novels. He treats Toundi Joseph kindly but not as an equal, rather as a lovable but stupid pet. "He's a cheery fellow who used to think of me as a little pet when I was small. He liked to tweak my ears and he got a lot of laughs out of my frequent amazement during my long education."[13]

Most of the whites in these novels are not nearly so benevolent. Not only do they consider the African an animal, but also they attribute savagery and irrationality to him. Mr. Howlands, the white settler in Kenya in *Weep Not, Child*, ignored the natives as long as possible, but when awareness of their presence is forced upon him during an uprising, he says:

> Who were black men and Mau Mau anyway, he asked for the thousandth time? Mere savages! A nice word—savages. Previously he had not thought of them as savages or otherwise, simply because he had not thought of them at all, except as a part of the farm—the way one thought of donkeys or horses . . .[14]

Belief in the savagery of the African becomes a justification for the separation of the races. Père Hux in *Cœur d'Aryenne* believes he must prevent an interracial relationship from contaminating the purity of a young white girl, Solange.

> Ma petite Solange, mais tu es extraordinaire. Comment oses-tu te faire conduire en pirogue par un petit nègre tout sale? N'as-tu peur de te voir jeter à l'eau par ce sauvage qui se régalera ensuite de ta chair si tendre? N'as-tu pas peur de te contaminer de sa vermine? Il ne te comprends pas, mon enfant. . . . Oublies-tu donc que tu es une blanche, une maîtresse pour tous les nègres quels qu'il soient?[15]

> You really are something, my little Solange. How do you dare let some filthy little nigger take you out riding in a canoe? Aren't you afraid that that savage will throw you overboard and then feast on your tender flesh? Aren't you afraid of being contaminated by his vermin? He doesn't understand you, my dear child. Are you forgetting that you are a white girl, mistress over any and all Negroes?

The physical qualities of the native are repugnant to the whites, and to the African is attributed a characteristic stench by the colonists. The arrival of an African is even heralded by his odor. "Every morning, the first thing to reach me from the veranda is the smell of alcohol and filth. That's what tells me my boy is there."[16] Physical contact with an African native is also disgusting to the white man. Toundi Joseph notices that the Commandant recoils in distaste after a handshake. "He let go of me. In the darkness I could see his white hands making a gesture of disgust, as if he had touched something dirty."[17]

There is neither sympathetic penetration into the natives'

psychological reactions to the white imposition nor comprehension of the natives' defensive gestures. Laziness is attributed to the black man when he is reluctant to work on the white man's projects. Isabelle, the French girl living in Africa in *O Pays, Mon Beau Peuple*, admits that the French consider all Africans to be indolent. Mr. Wright, who is the foreman of a roadbuilding project in *Arrow of God*, describes his men: "Many of them were, of course, bone lazy and could only respond to severe handling."[18] One reason which white officials often give for suppression of the native is his lack of trustworthiness as evidenced by his continual lying. The colonists in *Arrow of God* are constantly frustrated because each native tells them a different story; they are unable to extract the truth from any of them. The colonist had not comprehended that lying or feigning ignorance was an effective means of protection. Lying is interpreted by the native chief Batouala merely as an embellishment of the truth—a good native custom.

> Les 'boundjous' ne valent rien. Ils ne nous aiment pas. Ils ne sont venus chez nous que pour nous faire crever. Ils nous traitent de menteurs! Nos mensonges ne trompent personne. Si, parfois, nous embellissons le vrai, c'est parce que la vérité a presque toujours besoin d'être embellie.[19]

> "Boundjus" are no good. They don't like us. They only came here to butcher us. They call us liars! Our lies don't fool anyone. If we sometimes embellish the truth, it's because the truth almost always needs a little prettying up.

The white man ascribed very little intelligence to the African. The white priest Père Hux in *Cœur d'Aryenne* is amazed that an African youth had the ability to learn to speak fluent French, and even more, to recite the Mass. The natives are frequently referred to as imbeciles and stupid fools. " 'Get back in your places, you morons!' shouted a white-skinned man whom the Negroes looked at fearfully."[20] In the introduction to *Batouala*, René Maran summarizes white attitudes as follows: "As a matter of fact, the Negroes of Equatorial Africa have no reasoning power. Lacking all critical faculties, they have never had, and never will have, any sort of intelligence."[21]

The conjunction of all these impressions forms the premise on which the white man bases his feeling of superiority. The

schoolmaster in *Weep Not, Child* is described as a kind person
who treated black and white alike, but:

> . . . he believed that the best, the really excellent could only
> come from the white man. He brought up his boys to copy and
> cherish the white man's civilization as the only hope of man-
> kind and especially of the black races. He was automatically
> against all black politicians who in any way made people to be
> discontented with the white man's rule and civilizing mis-
> sion.[22]

Given these mutual misconceptions and fears, conflict and
struggle between the two races could not be avoided. Since the
power in this case belongs to the colonials, it is the blacks who
must conform to the will of the whites. Thus, the application of
force by the white colonist to produce desired actions provides
the data of all of these novels. The whites who came from
Europe to Africa filled different positions in the colonial societies. They were governors, administrators, road builders, ministers of God, merchants, or landowners. The native turned
alternately to one group and then to another, but soon he discovered that with none of them could he escape brutality or
find relief from exploitation. The material exploitation of the
colonial administration was no harsher than the spiritual domination exercised by the missionaries.

Few fragments of the Africans' possessions remained intact
in the wake of the colonial administrator. The natives were
dispossessed of their lands and plantations. "We hadn't even
finished building our huts and clearing land for our plantations
when those blasted whites were on top of us."[23] Their wives
and sisters were also sexually exploited at the will of the administrators. In *Arrow of God*, the administrator Clarke is said
to be sleeping with native women, and there are hints in all
the novels that this practice is widespread and common. Heavy
taxes were levied on the property that remained to the natives,
further draining off their livelihood. Natives were forced to work
on their own land for wages much lower than the wages paid to
the Europeans or Indians. The discriminatory working conditions that prevailed provoked the state of emergency in *Weep
Not, Child*. In *Arrow of God*, the natives are forced to work

on the road with no compensation whatsoever. These impositions and inhumanities radically altered African tradition and
institutions. At the same time, the whites hypocritically pro-
claimed that they were doing the natives a favor by allowing
them to work. The "white man's burden" and the "civilizing
mission" excused any atrocity and justified any brutality. Batouala parodies the line of reasoning used by the white men to
justify their continuing exploitation: "We force you to work for
your own good. And we only take the tiniest part of the money
we make you earn."[24] But in many instances these roads
were of little use to the native and aided him but little. In
Arrow of God we read: "As the new road did not point in the
direction of a stream or a market, Ofoedu and Obika did not
encounter many villagers."[25] Many of the roads, too, were
often built for specific purposes that aided only the colonial—
either to facilitate conquest of the entire region or to withstand
invasion of his fellow Europeans, as in *Weep Not, Child.* "All
of us were taken by force. We made roads and cleared the
forest to make it possible for the warring white man to move
more quickly."[26]

Many native men were also lost fighting in white men's wars
that did not concern them. Meka in *Le Vieux Nègre et la
Médaille* had given his two sons for the service of France.
Ngotho had lost a son in *Weep Not, Child.* Whole families
were disrupted, and consequently, the motif of losses suffered
in war appears throughout these novels. "Her other son had
died in the Big War. It had hurt her much. Why should he
have died in a white man's war? She did not want to sacrifice
what was hers to other people."[27]

All these impositions were forced on the natives through
physical cruelty and brutality. Often the colonial administrator
communicated with the native only by using the whiplash. In *O
Pays, Mon Beau Peuple*, it is said: "The colonials are the worst.
They say, 'You can't do a thing with these lazy thieving niggers.
Flogging is the only way to get any work out of them.' "[28] When
Obika arrives late for work on the road in *Arrow of God*, he is
whipped by Mr. Wright: "He [Obika] made to pass Mr. Wright
who, unable to control his anger any more, lashed out violently
with his whip. It flashed again and this time caught Obika
around the ear and stung him into fury."[29] But whippings were

often the most minor of castigations. Many characters in these novels suffer jailings, starvation, torture, and even violent death at the hands of the colonial administrators.

> He would never forget his experience in the post. That particular homeguard post was popularly known as the House of Pain. The day following his arrival in the post he was called into a small room. . . . Njoroge lay on the dusty floor. The face of the grey eyes had turned red. He never once spoke except to call him Bloody Mau Mau. A few seconds later Njoroge was taken out by the two homeguards at the door. He was senseless. He was covered with blood where the hob-nailed shoes of the grey eyes had done their work.[30]

Of all the characters in these novels it is perhaps Toundi Joseph in *Une Vie de Boy* who most completely undergoes all these various forms of torture. He is psychologically debased by certain little sadistic cruelties of the Commandant. When Toundi is tying his master's shoes, the Commandant feints a stumble and steps on Toundi's fingers. The Commandant apologizes too profusely and leaves the room with a smile on his lips. He also kicks Toundi in the seat of the pants as he is bending over. But the kick was no surprise, for his previous master, Père Gilbert, had conditioned him to such attacks. "With that, the Commandant let fly a kick in the shins that sent me rolling under the table. The Commandant has more voltage in his kick than the late lamented Père Gilbert. He seemed very pleased with his performance."[31]

These subtle abuses from individuals are minor, however, when compared with the full-scale torture and starvation he must later endure at the hands of the police of the colonial administration. " 'Nothing to eat tomorrow, understand?' said Gosier d'Oiseau as he rolled me over with his foot. 'Bring him to my office the day after tomorrow. A full day's whipping, understand?' "[32]

Within the statement of the novels, the native heroes have nowhere to turn for protection and no redress for their grievances. In *Cœur d'Aryenne*, Mambeke, on hearing that his fourteen-year-old sister has been sexually abused and made pregnant by the white tyrant, Roch Morax, realizes with impotent frustration that his hands are tied and he can do nothing.

Oh! sa sœur . . . , sa pauvre petite sœur violée par cet homme. Et il ne pouvait rien, absolument rien contre lui, contre ce serpent venimeux. Il lui était interdit de toucher à lui, parce qu'il était de la race des Aryens, de la race des surhommes, parce qu'il était le Maître.[33]

Oh, his sister, his poor little sister, raped by that man! And there was nothing, absolutely nothing he could do to that poisonous snake. It was forbidden to touch him because he was of the Aryan race, the race of Supermen, because he was the Master.

In many instances the only recourse open to the natives is flight; only in this way can they remove their women from the white man's reach.

De nombreuses familles ont dû s'enfuir du pays pour mettre leurs femmes à l'abri. Des pères ont été obligés d'envoyer leurs filles à Epena, à Imphondo ou à Fort-Rousset pour les soustraire aux atteintes de l'homme blanc. Quelques-uns ont demandé refuge à la forêt pour fuir la colère du Blanc de la factorerie à qui ils avaient refusé une niece, une petite sœur.[34]

Many families had to flee the country to keep their women safe. Fathers were forced to send their daughters to Epena, Imphondo or Fort Rousset to keep them out of the white man's clutches. Some sought refuge in the forest to escape the wrath of the white man from the trading post after they refused to hand over a niece or a little sister to him.

Thus, this enforced migration of the natives along with the numerous deaths by torture, liquidation, and starvation lead to a decimation of the population of which René Maran speaks scathingly in the introduction to *Batouala*:

Ah! Monsieur Bruel, en une compilation savante, vous avez pu déclarer que la population de l'Oubangui-Chari s'élevait à 1,350,000 habitants. Mais que n'avez-vous dit, plutôt, que dans tel petit village, de l'Ouahm, en 1918, on ne comptait plus que 1,080 individus sur les 10,000 qu'on avait recensés sept ans auparavant?[35]

Ah, Monsieur Bruel, one of your learned statistics states that the population of the Ubangi-Chari rose to 1,350,000 inhabitants.

But why didn't you say instead that in 1918 some little village in the Ouahm numbered only 1,080 individuals out of the 10,000 counted by the census seven years earlier?

The physical destruction of native life and property by the white man is coupled with the psychological destruction of the African and his mode of being. Throughout these novels the white man imposes his own customs, religion, and values on the black man; native tradition and way of life are forcefully interrupted by proselytizers. In *Le Pauvre Christ de Bomba*, the missionary is horrified when he hears the beat of the tom-tom and realizes that the natives are holding a ceremonial dance on the first Friday of the month, a Christian day of penance. He rushes to the site, grabs the sticks from the drummer, and delivers a sermon against such "sinning." The sense of guilt that is integral to Christianity often bridles actions which were completely accepted in native society before the white man's coming. When the Chief orders a sacrificial murder to replenish the medicine horn against his enemies in *Turn to the Dark*, MaLira, who has been chosen to kill the old woman, feels a sense of guilt about it because she has been taught by the Christian missionaries that killing is wrong. "You mean that I—a Christian—must take my own friend and betray and kill her? . . . What a sin before the eyes of God! To murder an innocent soul—a friend who is at my door! You are bringing the most terrible evil on us all, and God will punish you!"[36]

Toundi Joseph, when asked whether he is a thief, answers "No!" because he doesn't want to go to hell. He refrains from stealing, not because he feels it is morally wrong, but because he has been taught by the priests that eternal damnation in hell is a consequence of such actions.

Après m'avoir longuement observé, mon nouveau maître me demanda à brûle-pourpoint si j'étais un voleur.
—"Non, Commandant," répondis-je.
—"Pourquoi n'es-tu pas un voleur?"
—"Parce que je ne veux pas aller en enfer."
Le Commandant sembla sidéré par ma réponse. Il hocha la tête, incrédule.
—"Où as-tu appris ça?"
—"Je suis chrétien, mon Commandant," répondis-je en ex-

hibitant fièrement la médaille de Saint Christophe que je porte
à mon cou.
—"Alors, tu n'es pas un voleur parce que tu ne veux pas aller
en enfer."
—"Oui, mon Commandant."
—"Comment est-ce, l'enfer."
—"Bien, c'est les flammes, les serpents et Satan avec des
cornes . . ."[37]

After observing me for a long time my new master asked me
point-blank whether I was a thief.
"No, Commandant," I answered.
"Why not?"
"Because I don't want to go to hell."
The Commandant seemed thunderstruck by my reply. He
shook his head in disbelief. "Where did you learn that?"
"I am a Christian, Commandant," I answered, proudly display-
ing the St. Christopher medal I wear around my neck.
"So you don't steal because you don't want to go to hell."
"Yes, Commandant."
"What's hell like, then?"
"Um, it's flames and snakes and Satan with horns . . ."

Ironically, the natives had often of their own volition gone to
the church, for at first it seemed to be a place of protection and
succor. Père Gilbert in *Une Vie de Boy* induced the young natives to come to church by giving them sugar cubes as he passed
through the streets. In *Le Pauvre Christ de Bomba*, the natives
turned to the missions hoping for a defense against the cruelty
of the whites, who forced them to labor on the roads. "The
father superior doubts that the people who live on the road are
sincere Christians. I doubt it too now, after what happened
yesterday and today. Because when you come right down to it,
women, those mission workers, are mostly people from the
roads."[38]

However, the natives were often exploited just as brutally by
the men of religion. The priest in *Le Pauvre Christ de Bomba*
exacted huge sums in tithes from the natives and refused to
exempt them on any grounds—even old age or extreme poverty. The Sixa was one of the worst forms of exploitation.
Young girls were forced to stay at the mission for three months
before marriage to prevent premarital intercourse if they were

to have a church wedding. Once in the Sixa, they were nearly starved and forced to do hard labor. It was common practice for them to be sexually exploited by the catechists. In the Sixa of *Le Pauvre Christ de Bomba*, syphilis and venereal disease were spread to the entire group by an infected catechist. The missionary schools were also considered a haven by many young boys, but their illusions were soon destroyed by the harsh treatment inflicted on them, and they became bitter because of discrimination. In *Turn to the Dark*, Lesiba asks:

> Why should we get the cane, when white scholars of our age never do? Why should they say we are receivers of charity when our parents have to pay for us, and white children go to government schools without paying a penny—even for books? Why should we take our bath in the cold dam in winter? Why should we have no liberty and learn inferior knowledge to that which white children learn?[39]

Neither did the native escape physical punishment by turning to religion. The reverend father in *Le Pauvre Christ* had the native girls whipped as cruelly as would any colonial administrator. "The assistant cook, brandishing his cat-o'-nine-tails, looked for just the right spot. He found it, and raised his switch very high before bringing it down across Marguerite's backside with a sharp, resounding noise exactly like the one a mango makes when it falls to the ground from a great height during a dry spell."[40]

It is evident that religious institutions provided little protection for the African. After the priest abandons the mission in *Le Pauvre Christ de Bomba*, Denis turns next to a Greek merchant for protection from the colonial administration.

> Oh! J'ai appris qu'ils venaient de commencer le creusement de cette route dont parlait si souvent M. Vidal, et qui doit traverser le pays des Tala. Il paraît que c'est terrible. On réquisitionne jusqu'aux femmes pour le chantier. Le bruit court même qu'il viendront chercher des gens jusque chez nous. Nous qui avons déjà creusé notre route! . . . C'est injuste! Ceux de chez nous protestent d'avance et affirment qu'ils ne se laisseront plus réquisitionner. Mais comment pourrons-nous résister aux

miliciens de la subdivision? Ils me prendraient certainement aussi, malgré mon jeune âge. Mon père dit que c'est dangereux pour moi de rester à Sogolo. Je pense à ce que me confiait un soir le cuisinier adjoint Anatole! . . . Aller à la ville et chercher une petite place de boy chez un commerçant grec . . .[41]

Oh! I've learned that they have just begun work on that road Monsieur Vidal talked about so often, and which is supposed to cut across the Tala country. It sounds terrible. They're going so far as to draft women for the roadwork. There's a rumor going around that they're even going to get people from our region. And we've already built our road! It's not right! Our people are protesting in advance and insist they won't allow themselves to be drafted any more. But what kind of resistance can we put up against the subdivision militia? They're sure to take me too, in spite of my youth. My father says it's dangerous for me to stay in Sogolo. I'm thinking of what Anatole, the assistant cook, told me one evening: Go into town and look for some work as a boy with a Greek merchant.

The book ends with these lines, and Denis is hopeful that he will find a position for himself with the merchant, but we can be fairly sure from the experiences of characters in other novels of this group that he will not find relief from abuse here. Merchants and landowners who had 'boys' working for them were usually as cruel as the colonial administrators and missionaries. In *Weep Not, Child,* the Indian merchant, Ngotho's employer, always withheld a month's pay from a worker so that when left, he had to forfeit recompense for a month's labor. Mrs. Howlands, also in *Weep Not, Child,* made a practice of beating her servants. As we have already noted, the Commandant in *Une Vie de Boy* played sadistic tricks on his houseboy, Toundi Joseph. In *O Pays, Mon Beau Peuple,* the Greek merchant is portrayed as a mean and boorish person who treats the natives like animals.

Batouala summarizes the feelings of most natives when he says that a profound sadness reigns over the land of the Africans. In short, their joy in living is gone.

"Notre soumission," reprit Batouala, dont la voix allait s'enfiévrant, "notre soumission ne nous a pas mérité leur bienveillance. Et d'abord, non contents de s'appliquer à supprimer nos plus chères coutumes, ils n'ont eu de cesse qu'ils ne nous aient imposé les leurs.

"Ils n'y ont, à la longue, que trop bien réussi. Résultat: la plus morne tristesse règne, désormais, par tout le pays noir. Les blancs sont ainsi faits, que la joie de vivre disparaît des lieux où ils prennent quartiers."[42]

"Our submission," resumed Batouala with more and more fire in his voice, "our submission hasn't earned us their good will. In the first place, it wasn't enough for them to work at destroying our most cherished traditions; they didn't rest until they had imposed their own customs on us.

"In the long run they succeeded only too well. Result: the bleakest sorrow now reigns throughout the black country. The way the white men are made, the joy of living disappears from wherever they settle."

In these novels we follow the natives through an awakening to the meaning of the white man's presence in their lands. The natives' reaction to the European changes from worship to fear to disillusionment as they become aware of the extent of his domination. At first, the Africans strive to emulate the white man, for they think that he must possess some kind of superior virtue. Later, however, the natives see only base qualities in the Europeans. They are nothing more than a race of thieves for Banda in *Ville Cruelle:* "It wouldn't do any harm. Doesn't everyone know that the Greeks are a race of thieves?"[43] Oumar's father in *O Pays, Mon Beau Peuple* warns him that no white man may be believed: "All white men are like that. Believe me, son, I knew them before you. Their words aren't worth chickenshit."[44]

The white man is growing visibly wealthy as time passes, and even the most naive cannot help but notice. The Greeks who arrived with one battered suitcase and rags on their backs in *Ville Cruelle* soon live in houses as big as churches; there they hid their fattened and protected wives. The white man was, in effect, in possession of the majority of the productive land (as Mr. Howlands in *Weep Not, Child*), and even more profitably, he controlled the export of goods and products from the African continent. He held the Africans in economic slavery.

The white man, by instilling a sense of guilt and the idea of damnation has, in effect, used religion to control the black man. This too, however, began to lose its effect as the native shed his naiveté. In *Ville Cruelle*, fear of the results of breaking the commandment, "Thou shalt not steal," no longer restrains him.

> En réalité, deux voix parlaient en lui. L'une criait très fort et formulait des assertions catégoriques; elle disait: "Tu fais mal. Cet argent ne t'appartient pas. Si tu le gardes, tu voles. A César ce qui appartient à César". . . . Mais Banda ne l'écoutait pas cette voix; il ne voulait pas l'entendre.[45]

> Actually, two voices were speaking within him. One shouted very loud and formulated categorical assertions. It said: "You are doing wrong. That money doesn't belong to you. If you keep it you'll be stealing. Render unto Caesar that which is Caesar's." But Banda didn't listen to this voice; he didn't want to hear it.

Banda also begins to look objectively at the religious service and parodies the Latin liturgy, which he is sure not even the catechist understands. He scorns the parable of the Good Samaritan, for in his culture to help an injured person would be taken for granted and hence requires no praise. Zacharie, the cook in *Le Pauvre Christ de Bomba*, points out that the symbolism of the parable of the Good Shepherd is meaningless for the natives in that region, because they have no sheep and do not know what sheep are.

Some natives take advantage of their knowledge of the white man's ways. The African middlemen in the roles of inspector, jailer, policeman, and catechist were sometimes even crueler to naive members of their own race than the white men themselves. Yet, a moment of crisis would produce a gesture of solidarity. The natives in *Une Vie de Boy* were warned by an African policeman before a raid on their quarters by Gosier d'Oiseau. They disappeared out the back door before he arrived, so he was unable to arrest anyone. He found only bananas, which he stole: "Gosier d'Oiseau didn't nab anyone on yesterday's raid. He ate bananas."[46]

The naive native, the resisting native, the native middleman, the newly arrived white, and the white who has learned of his power are all types that appear in this group of novels, their interaction providing the character conflict. The initial deceptions and subsequent development of knowledge are the moving impulses. Presentation of the clash inherent in the various exploitative situations gives structure to the novels. The novels all have a deep sense of the pathetic and a tragic inevitability about them. As the river flows on, clasped hands are wrenched apart, and friends, generations, and races are separated. No chance of a return to the order and tranquility of *l'enfant noir* exists, for "rivers do not flow upstream."[47] The movement away from a source is an unavoidable consequence of the clash of two worlds in which all the heroes seem to move from a certainty of effort and position to self-doubt and disillusionment.

Destruction of Self

Three of the novels, *Une Vie de Boy, Le Vieux Nègre et la Médaille,* and *Le Pauvre Christ de Bomba,* deal with the disintegration of single individuals who are confronted with colonial situations that they cannot control. The three principal characters, Toundi Joseph, the young uncircumcised native, Meka, a well-established community leader, and Reverend Père Drumont, a white missionary, all bring to their encounters with the other race an initially naive interpretation and optimism about the possibilities of communication and friendship between races. The attempts of all three end in failure.

Toundi Joseph in *Une Vie de Boy* is moved to leave home by his father's rigidity and his own gluttony: the Catholic priest Père Gilbert has attracted him with candy and sweets; when in a moment of anger his father denies him a dinner of succulent porcupines, Toundi runs away to the mission to learn the ways of white men. "J'allais connaître la ville . . . et vivre comme eux."[48] He leaves the day before he is to be circumcised, a ritual which would symbolize an entrance into his own culture. Thus he becomes a symbol of the young native seduced from the culture of his ancestors by the material wealth of the white man. He is completely isolated from his family and his tribe. They regard him as a traitor who has caused them evil by joining the white man's religion, and they blame him for his father's death. "They say in the village that I caused my father's death by running away to a white priest's on the day before my initiation, when I was to meet the famous serpent who watches over everyone of our race."[49]

Thus separated from his own culture by his irrevocable act of rejection, he finds himself in limbo—between two worlds and belonging in neither. The ambiguity of his position is skillfully reflected by Ferdinand Oyono in the style and essence of the novel. The tone is consistently ironic. When Père Gilbert dies, Toundi speculates that he will be named a Christian martyr because he died in Africa, which incisively satirizes with one deft stroke the European flavor of Christianity and the Europeans concept of "dark Africa." In the early pages Oyono cuts through the guises of the morally decadent European community in Dangan with a swift portrait of the surreptitious winks exchanged during the church service, thus presaging the action of the novel. Toundi's final suffering and torture are likewise foreseen in the pointless raid on native quarters by the police and their wanton stealing.

Oyono's imagery is consistent in his painting of scenes and descriptions. The accumulation and interweaving of references saturate his prose. Animal imagery is prevalent in this novel and used with subtle shades of meaning. The Europeans often refer to the natives in creatural terms. Père Gilbert is said to distribute sugar çubes to the young natives just as a farmer would throw out grain to his chickens. Toundi remarks that the priest treats him like a pet dog. He uses bird imagery, however, to grace the description of the lovely native woman Kalisia: ". . . then one morning Kalisia went away, just like that, with the departure of the birds at the end of the dry season . . . then she returned to Dangan as a bird returns to earth after wearing itself out in the air . . ."[50]

He creates caricatures of whites and blacks to emphasize a particular trait—Gosier d'Oiseau ("gullet of a bird") for the greedy police chief and Roi des Bagues for a native chief with a fetish for rings—and to add humorous notes. His use of metaphor can be equally as piercing. "Madame Gosier d'Oiseau's fat legs were packed into her slacks like manioc in a banana leaf."[51]

The process of disillusionment is dramatically presented in this novel by a countermovement of illusion and disillusion in Toundi Joseph and the Commandant's newly arrived wife. They are the only two characters whose perceptions of the other race change throughout the novel, for the supporting cast of natives (such as Sophie, the cook) and the colonists (the group of the *Cercle Européen*) are already fixed in their beliefs. Upon her arrival from Paris, the Commandant's wife is naively egalitarian toward the houseboy. She offers him her hand when they are introduced, an unprecedented gesture which Toundi receives with ecstasy, psalming her with flowery imagery. "My happiness knows neither day nor night. I was not aware of it; it was revealed to my inmost being. I will sing it on my flute, I will sing it beside the marigots, but no words can convey it. I have pressed the hand of my queen. I have felt that I am alive."[52]

At first she treats Toundi as a human personality, showing concern for his childhood and his parents. Soon, however, because she is the Commandant's wife and also a beautiful woman, she becomes the queen of European society and realizes her own position and power. When Toundi confides that he has not married because he could not afford to support a wife and children in the manner of the whites, she accuses him of having delusions of grandeur and warns him that he must stay in his place: "My poor fellow, you have delusions of grandeur. Let's be serious. You know that wisdom counsels everyone to keep in his place. You are a houseboy; my husband is a commandant. Nothing can be done about it. You're Christian, aren't you?"[53]

"Nothing can be done." She counsels Toundi to passivity in accepting his place. When she begins to feel threatened in her position, however, she asserts her authority with all possible force. The possibilities of power are learned not from her husband, whose Napoleonic tendencies have tempered to joviality as a result of her presence, but from her lover, the brutal Monsieur Moreau, governor of the prison, who instructs her in the properly harsh tone to use with the natives. Toundi accidentally learns of the love affair, and her attitude toward him completely changes. She coldly challenges him to keep her secret, transfixing him with narrow stares in a scene that he describes in reptilian imagery: "Madame didn't take her eyes off me. . . . Terror of Madame had nailed me to the spot. I had gone nosing around the citronella stalks, the favorite lair of the green snakes whose bite knows no mercy."[54]

When the Commandant learns of the affair, Toundi is accused of betrayal by both sides: by the Commandant because he abetted the liaison by carrying notes to Monsieur Moreau and by the Madame for having babbled to his native friends and thus spread the news so that it finally reached her husband's ears.

The Commandant then looks for an excuse to punish Toundi. When Sophie, the much nibbled dish of the agricultural engineer, robs him and runs away, Toundi is accused of having been her lover and of having planned the escape. He is arrested on this suspicion, which is usually ample cause for slow execution. Solidarity among the blacks protects him for awhile. Toundi is delivered to a gigantic Negro jailer, imported from the Coast, to torture him until he confesses. Toundi and the jailer play cards all day and then dribble animal blood on their clothes and the floor to lead others to believe the directions have been carried out. Black fraternity cannot shield him forever, however. In realistic scenes, Toundi is tortured personally by whites and forced to work until he collapses. In a belated gesture of solidarity, a native doctor allows Toundi to escape from the hospital, but it is already too late. He manages to leave French territory, but he is too weak to recover. While he is dying, a comrade from the Cameroun listens to his final question. "What are we, brother? Who are all these Negroes they call 'French'?"[55] He removes the boy's journals, which constitute the novel, from his clothing after he dies.

Le Vieux Nègre et la Médaille, a later novel by the same author, also treats an individual's loss of identity as a result of the colonial situation, but both style and leading character are more mature. *Le vieux nègre* is Meka, an old and established leader in his tribal structure. He presents a direct contrast to the juvenile Toundi Joseph, who was never fully integrated into native society because he deserted the day before his entrance ritual was to take place. Meka's situation is more complex than Toundi's, and the events of the novel are saturated with tragic implications. Toundi's plights may sometimes be written off to the foibles of the young, but Meka who supposedly acts with the judgment of maturity, also is broken by the colonial situation.

The plot of the novel is relatively simple, but Oyono gives depth and fullness to it through the structural symbolism of many situations. Meka's position between the native and white worlds is sketched rapidly through small incidents in the first pages. When Meka awakens, he takes a sip of palm wine and then regrets the action, for the whites had forbidden the distillation of all native liquors and he knows that if the government officials smell alcohol on his breath he will be sent to prison. The missionary Père Vandermayer had condemned drink as sinful. "He had decreed that all those Christians who drank were committing a mortal sin with each swallow." This decree places Meka in an ambiguous situation, for on the one hand he likes to take a small glass and on the other he is considered an exemplary Christian for having donated his lands to the church. "Cela avait mis Meka dans une situation dramatique. Meka était souvent cité en exemple de bon chrétien à la Mission catholique de Doum." In an irony that is reminiscent of *Une Vie de Boy*, Oyono says that Meka was considered by most Christians as a sure bet for reaching heaven. "For the Christians in Doum, Meka was a big favorite in the race for Paradise, one of the few mortals who would pay a fleeting appearance in Purgatory."[56] Meka clings to the ways of his ancestors when it is convenient for him to do so. He continues drinking native wine because it makes his rheumatism feel better. Yet at the same time he has symbolically accepted the white man's ways. This short scene, then, previews Meka's predicament in the rest of the novel.

When the announcement is made that Meka is to receive the highest possible honor, a medal from the white man, his position within the tribe is enhanced even further. Meka is truly an exalted person among them, one whom they expect will have the power to ask favors. "L'ami du chef n'est-il pas lui-même un peu chef? From a simple farmer, he was going to become a somebody among the whites."[57] In another ironic commentary, Oyono juxtaposes the excitement of the approaching July 14 celebration with that of the circumcision ceremonies: "Ce 14 juillet, qui égalait en animation et en fièvre les fêtes de circoncision . . ."[58] The rest of Part I of the novel involves the preparation of Meka's wardrobe for the event in scenes reminiscent of the classic arming of the hero. Only Kelara, his wife, has the nerve to say what the rest are thinking—that Meka looks ridiculous in his European suit and new vest. He has trouble with the shoes, and he decides to carry them and put them on at the last minute.

The second part of the novel is highly symbolic. Meka stands alone on the platform in the center of a circle delineated with

white chalk. For the first time he is alone between the two
worlds.

> Il réalisa qu'il était dans une situation étrange. Ni son grand-
> père, ni son père, ni aucun membre de son immense famille ne
> s'étaient trouvés placés comme lui, dans un cercle de chaux,
> entre deux mondes, le sien et celui de ceux qu'on avait
> d'abord appelés les "fantômes" quand ils étaient arrivés au pays.
> Lui, il ne se trouvait ni avec les siens ni avec les autres.[59]

> He realized that he was in a strange situation. Neither his
> grandfather nor his father nor any member of his immense fam-
> ily had ever found themselves in his present position: in a chalk
> circle between two worlds, his own and that of the people who
> had been called "ghosts" when they first arrived in the region.
> He belonged neither with his own people nor with the others.

The shiny medal which the great chief pins on his chest
assuages his discomfort, however, and restores his naive assurance about his position among the whites. Oyono, with rapid
strokes, paints an indicative picture of Meka's growing isolation, of his drifting away from his own people into the faceless
European crowd: "Meka was the only black and khaki spot amid
the white suits of Doum's Europeans on the porch of Monsieur
Fouconi's office." Some of the guests show polite curiosity about
his medal, and he thinks to himself that he has become quite a
guy. But when he approaches Père Vandermayer, whom he had
always respected, he is brusquely rebuffed: "Completely dumb-
founded, Meka raised his hand to his chin and opened his mouth
like a fish. No, it wasn't possible; Père Vandermayer couldn't
answer him like that."[60]

Yet, he continues to harbor naive illusions about his having
an eminent position among the whites. When Père Vandermayer finally speaks to Meka it is only to ask him to ride in the
back of his pickup truck to the Foyer Africain for the remainder
of the celebration. Riding on top of a case of wine, Meka finally
removes his shoes. Only when he has again been relegated to
his usual position can he be natural.

Under the effect of the whiskey, Meka exposes himself to
further abuse and rebuffs from the whites by inviting the *Grand
Chef* to his home to eat the goat that his brother-in-law is
preparing in his honor. His proposal is politely, but definitively,

rejected. Meka's naive enthusiasm is not dampened, but the interpreter's anger is aroused by the refusal. He challenges the native crowd: "What would your ancestors think if they saw you in your present state before these men from over the seas? You make me ashamed."[61]

A thunderstorm violently awakens Meka, who, forgotten in a corner, had fallen into a drunken sleep. Further, it symbolically dramatizes an awakening to the truth of his situation.

> Meka n'eut pas le temps de se réveiller lentement, progressive- ment, comme cela lui arrivait quelques rares fois dans sa case. Il s'était trouvé subitement rejeté sous le banc. Le Foyer Afri- cain plongé dans l'obscurité subissait les assauts de la première tornade de fin de saison sèche.[62]

> Meka didn't have time to wake up slowly and in stages, as he had in his hut on a few rare occasions. He suddenly found himself hurled under the bench. The African Home, plunged in darkness, was assaulted by the first tornado at the end of the dry season.

He tries to stumble home in the darkness, but losing his way in the white quarter, he is violently accosted by white policemen. In an ironic and pathetically comic scene with overtones of the Christian parable of the Good Samaritan, Meka says: "Don't shine the light in my eyes, oh heaven-sent stranger! Light the Lord's earth where I search my path . . . oh stranger! Just the path." When the policeman grabs him abruptly, he thinks he is being lifted to the heavens: "Meka felt himself raised above the earth. Was he in the grip of a heaven-bound eagle?"[63] Here again Meka's two-world standards make him plead for salvation from the white policeman in two ways. First, in the context of his own culture, he pleads with the policeman to accord him the traditional respect that is due an elder. Later, his plea is that of a supplicant begging a white man for Christian charity.

Jailing marks the beginning of Meka's self-confrontation, which brings with it a disillusioning understanding. "Never had he been face to face with himself in this way."[64] He is still naive, however, and plans how he, Meka of the grand line of Mekas, will make fools of the guards when they come to haul him before Gosier d'Oiseau. But his rage multiplies as he is further confined in the "animal cage," and he begins to defy the guards with oaths: Slaves of the uncircumcised. He recalls the days of his youth when his grandfather resisted the white man and hung a blonde scalp from a tree to show that he was not afraid of the intruders. With deft irony, Oyono juxtaposes Meka's real situation with his imaginary world of heroic bravado. Meka thinks about his powerful ancestors, the masters of yesterday, now slaves: "Who would have thought that yesterday's masters would be today's slaves? The 'Mekas' . . . , he murmured, 'Lion Men,' 'Men of Thunder,' 'Men of the Skies,' men who were power incarnate and ruled over heaven and earth in this region."[65]

His only statement in an interview with Gosier d'Oiseau is ". . . I am the last of the imbeciles who believed until yesterday in the friendship of the whites."[66] It is on his way home from the jail that Meka finds himself again. As he walks along the forest path through the morning mist, we watch his spiritual progress, his return to his own world. First he cleanses himself, using the means hallowed by his ancestors—brushing his teeth with crushed leaves of citronella, washing his hands in a puddle. He returns momentarily to his Christian training as he starts his morning prayer, but he is quickly deflected by stumbling over a rock. A passerby reminds him of the tradition that to fall is an omen that he will come upon a good meal. A bird brings him a blessing from the skies, and when this is repeated, Meka's cup is full. "All these superstitions had sprung up again in his mind, sweeping years of Christian instruction and practice away like a tidal wave."[67]

But Meka has been broken by the struggles. When he enters the village, a friend's dog, not recognizing him, snarls. He goes straight to his bed, and the natives gather around to drink his liquor and wait to seize his possessions if he should die. He has lost his position of respect in his tribe. There are hints that the young people are becoming aroused enough to try to withstand the white man. Essomba is furious at the treatment Meka has received and begins to realize that the natives and all their traditions are being submerged.

> Je ne sais plus où vont les blancs! poursuivit Essomba. Rien de ce que nous vénérons n'a d'importance à leurs yeux. Nos coutumes, nos histoires, nos remèdes, nos hommes mûrs, tout cela c'est comme les affaires de leur boy. . . . Et maintenant ils

nous tendent des pièges commes aux rats . . . je me demande où ils vont.[68]

I no longer know where the white men are heading, continued Essomba. Nothing we hold sacred has any importance in their eyes. Our customs, our tales, our remedies, our elders, it's all like some houseboy business . . . And now they're setting traps for us like rats . . . I wonder where they're heading.

But Meka's battles are over; he settles down on his blankets.

Le Pauvre Christ de Bomba by Mongo Beti is also a chronicle of an individual's breakup caused by the colonial situation—this time a white man. Père Drumont has been a French missionary in Africa for twenty years. The novel is constructed entirely around the diary of his native houseboy, Denis. Denis' naive irony, which characterizes Beti's style, is revealed early in the novel when he tries to justify his calling the priest Jesus Christ. Denis rationalizes that it is not really blasphemy because Père Drumont does embody the traits of the Savior.

> Jésus Christ . . . oh! je crois bien qu'il n'y a pas blasphème. . . . Il mérite bien ce nom, cet éloge innocent de petits enfants. Un homme qui a réussi à imposer la foi. A rendre les gens quotidiennement bons chrétiens. Souvent malgré eux. Un homme autoritaire. Un homme terrible. Un père . . . Jésus Christ!"[69]

> Jesus Christ . . . oh, I don't really think there's any blasphemy in it. . . . He does deserve that name, that innocent praise of little children. A man who succeeded in establishing the faith. In making people good Christians on a day-to-day basis. Often in spite of themselves. A man of authority, a terrific man. A father . . . Jesus Christ.

Early in the novel the basis for the action is set. Père Drumont learns that many of the natives whom he has supposedly converted have become cynical and have been neglecting Christianity and their tributes to the mission. The priest of Timo tells him that the natives have lost all respect for the missionaries.

> Mon Père, ils disent qu'un prêtre, ce n'est pas meilleur qu'un marchand grec ou tout autre colon. Ils disent que ce qui vous préoccupe tous, c'est l'argent, un point c'est tout: vous n'êtes

pas sincères, vous leur cachez des choses, vous ne leur enseignez rien.[70]

Father, they say a priest is no better than a Greek merchant or any other colonial. They say that all of you just care about money, period: you're not sincere, you hide things from them, you don't teach them a thing.

Late in the novel we learn of the heroic and messianic way in which Père Drumont conceived of his journey:

Je me suis élevé dans mon esprit au niveau de Napoléon traçant sur une carte ce fameux plan qui devait lui valoir la victoire d'Austerlitz. . . . voici mon stratagème. Il s'agissait tout simplement de laisser les Tala deux ans à l'abandon: ils éprouveraient comme une faim de moi, comme une fringale du Christ. Tout à coup, je surgirais et ce serait le miracle: ils accourraient à moi, m'embrasseraient, se réjouiraient de m'avoir retrouvé.[71]

I mentally raised myself to the level of Napoleon as he was mapping out the famous plan which was to bring him victory at Austerlitz. . . . This was my stratagem. Simply abandon the Talas for two years; they feel a sort of hunger for me, a sort of craving for Christ. Then suddenly I appear, and it's a miracle: they rush up to me, kiss me, rejoice at having me back again.

Three different but related progressions give structural movement to the novel: the geographic movement from village to village, the growth of awareness from ignorance to more complete revelation, and the consequent deepening disillusion from optimism to despair.

The Père, Denis (the naive houseboy who adores the Père), and Zacharie ("Ironique, irrévérencieux, insouciant") set out on a picaresque adventure to win back the natives. This contingent provides Beti with the opportunity to contrast views and interpretations of what the group encounters. Denis praises the priest's work in building the Mission singlehandedly and in instituting the Sixa, whereby native girls had to spend three months at the Mission in order to have a Christian marriage, and defends the Père against those who call him Le Malin—the malicious one. But Zacharie, who finds this arrangement ridiculous, merely sings a taunting ditty.

Beti forewarns us of the futility of the Père's mission and of his unpreparedness for the journey he is about to undertake by comparing his reactions to his environment with those of Le Guen, the vicar at Bomba. The vicar's familiarity with the language after one year's stay, his friendliness, and his understanding of the terrain contrast with the Père's inability to communicate with the people after twenty years, his aloof fatherly image, and his lack of understanding of his environs.

Le Guen's concept of the forest symbolizes the inimical nature of the area through which Père Drumont will travel: ". . . motionless bushes full of menace, static forest that seems nevertheless to ripple, huts clinging to the forest where wild beasts roam." The Père sees the forest as a series of isolated trees, without at first sensing its cohesive inimical strength, even when he has been forewarned: "The forest isn't just trees standing next to each other. It has a personality of its own, does the forest, independent of the personality of each individual tree."[72]

The three set out to bring the lost sheep back into the fold. In the village of Timbo, an incident occurs that reveals Père Drumont's insensitivity. A group of young natives greet him singing the *Marseillaise*. He is overwhelmed and begins a grandiose sermon in which he is the Good Shepherd and the natives are his sheep. He says he has left them alone for the past three years for their own benefit, but now he has returned to care for them. He is so moved by his own speech that he lowers his eyes and is close to tears. Zacharie's comments reveal that no one else was affected, and in fact, the parable of the Good Shepherd is completely irrelevant to the natives. They, who possess only a few straggly goats, do not even know what sheep are.

D'abord, dit-il, les gens ne comprennent évidemment pas ce que c'est un bon pasteur: ici, il n'y a pas de pasteur. Quand un homme possède trois ou quatre chèvres, il ne s'en occupe guère, assuré qu'elles broutent dans le champ du voisin. Ensuite, les gens ici, aiment bien éprouver de la pitié pour un étranger, mais ils supportent mal qu'on les prenne en pitié.[73]

In the first place, he said, people obviously don't understand what a good shepherd is; there aren't any shepherds here. A man who owns three or four goats doesn't bother much about them, confident that they're off grazing in a neighbor's field.

Then too, people around here enjoy feeling sorry for strangers but can't stand it when people feel sorry for them.

To the boy the whole affair was very touching. The priest continues to blunder through his contacts with natives in various villages. Even though he sees that the natives in areas with some material prosperity have turned away from the church, he remains relatively optimistic.

In Kota, we meet the young colonial administrator Vidal for the first time. He is used as an effective parallel to the priest, and in their conversation the innermost thoughts and aspirations of the Père are revealed and we first see the doubts that begin to assail him. Here, as in other places, Beti makes the physical appearances of the protagonist mirror his emotional state: ". . . the [priest] was grave and his sad, vague glance wandered over the domes of distant trees as if it searched after something—the answer to a problem, perhaps."[74]

The priest confesses that to missionize successfully necessitates undermining the foundations and shattering the basic structures of another's way of life: ". . . go take a vase that's already been fired, try to give it a form of your own and let me know what happens."[75]

The administrator, realizing that such doubts are sure signs of the Père's weakening faith in his mission, warns him: ". . . when a man begins to doubt his mission, doesn't it mean it's all over with him?"[76]

Later an incident in Evindi reveals the growing untenability of Père Drumont's situation and accentuates his dilemma. When he arrives in the village he hears the drums and xylophones playing pagan music a short distance away. He immediately becomes riled. Zacharie tries to calm him, but the beating of the drums in the background begins.

Père Drumont can no longer stand it and sets out with Denis against all Zacharie's warnings to break up the festivities. Unable to control himself when he sees the villagers dancing and playing xylophones, he rushes in and destroys the instruments. This action brings on a tirade from the Chief that expresses many of the natives' grievances against the white man.

Qu'est-il venu ficher dans notre pays, je vous le demande? Il crevait de faim dans son pays, il s'amène, nous le nourrissons, nous le gratifions de terres; il se construit de belles maisons avec l'argent que nous lui donnons; et même nous lui prêtons nos femmes pendant trois mois. Mais il n'est pas encore content; ne voilà-t-il pas qu'il se met à vouloir nous empêcher de danser?[77]

What the hell did he come to our country for, I ask you? He was starving to death back home, he blows in here, we feed him, we let him have land, he builds himself beautiful houses with the money we give him; and we even lend him our women for three months. But still he's not satisfied. Isn't he starting to try to keep us from dancing now?

The forces of disillusion, and the Père's intolerance, are working toward a loss of faith. But Denis notices a change. A non-Christian asks the priest what would have happened had the man with the instruments been white. Père Drumont replies that the whites cannot be saved; the blacks are closer to heaven. The fact that he does not automatically and dogmatically assert his own position puzzles Denis.

En entendant cela, [le Père] a eu un mouvement de nervosité. Je ne comprends pas d'où vient ce goût récent qu'il montre à écouter de telles niaiseries. Autrefois, il aurait tout simplement envoyé promener cet homme; mais, aujourd'hui il a sincèrement discuté avec lui.[78]

The [priest] gave a start upon hearing that. I don't understand where he gets his recent taste for listening to such nonsense. Before, he would simply have sent that man packing, but today he had a serious discussion with him.

And Denis bemoans this change, and laments this poor figure of Christ. Père Drumont from this point is on the defensive, constantly trying to justify himself to the natives as well as to his traveling companions.

The climactic confrontation of the reconversion journey occurs at Ekokot between the priest and the renowned sorcerer Sango Boto—"l'incarnation de Satan," as he is called by Père Drumont.

Ironically, Beti shows that Sango's method of gaining converts is not unlike that of Père Drumont: "They arrive just like that in the middle of a naive, superstitious population. They start speechifying at them, making a big whoop-de-do and shrouding themselves in mystery. After that they exploit the population . . . It is true that those people are giving a lot of gifts to Sango Boto?"[79]

But unlike Père Drumont, Sango Boto comes to an area fully armed with all pertinent data, which was collected beforehand by his informants. He is neither a quack nor a charlatan but a shrewd practitioner.

Initially, the contest is won by Père Drumont, who after brutally dragging Sango through the streets forces him to admit the error of his pagan practices and to confess the truth of Christian baptism and prayers. In the long run, however, Sango triumphs. He has been forced to leave the village, but on his way, he spreads the news abroad that the Père's fall into the river, prior to their confrontation, was of Sango Boto's doing and that only the goodness of his heart and fear of the white administrator Vidal's wrath had saved the Père from drowning. This story asserting the sorcerer's power gains credence and precedes Père Drumont's visit to every succeeding village.

The narrative begins to drag, however, suffering from repetition and the monotony of the unvarying structure of each episode. The main action is filled out with many secondary incidents such as the superb scene of Denis' seduction by Catherine, a girl from the Sixa.

Beti's irony is deceptively subtle; just when he seems most sympathetic to the Père, he is most accusing: by contrasting the brutal realism of the professionally successful administrator, Mr. Vidal, with the Père's idealistic incomprehension and one-dimensional interpretation of phenomena as well as events, he further emphasizes the Père's failings as a missionary of a colonial power.

Père Drumont's encounters with the colonial administration make him aware of the connivance between secular and spiritual colonialism; it is clear that the number of adherents to Christianity varies proportionately with the location of the administrators' brutal road-building program. His decision to leave the country is crystallized. He is confronted with one of the sad effects of his missionary work and laments that: "I know that you protect us, and that we clear the way for you by preparing their spirits and making them docile."[80]

Beti pushes his ironic statement about the Père even further, reemphasizing his amazing lack of awareness. On the Père's return to Bomba, he is confronted with the realization that right under his nose, but unknown to him, the women of the Sixa had for a long time been sexually abused by the catechist director of the Sixa and that many had contracted venereal diseases.

Beti reemphasizes that the Père's intolerance has turned into uncharitable, sadistic brutality as he exacts confessions of venality from the women of the Sixa. This final episode brings home to Père Drument the total failure of his life's work, and he laments to Vidal: "... I am a failure, a blasted failure. I don't think anyone has ever sunk further into defeat."[81]

But Père Drumont has gained some understanding. His thoughts on his errors in evangelizing the natives are phrased heroically:

> Ces braves gens ont bien adoré Dieu sans nous. Qu'importe s'ils l'ont adoré à leur manière . . . en mangeant de l'homme, ou en dansant au clair de lune, ou en portant au cou des gris-gris d'écorce d'arbre. Pourquoi nous obstiner à leur imposer notre manière à nous?[82]

> These good people had indeed worshipped God without us. What does it matter that they worshipped Him in their own way . . . by eating men, or dancing in the moonlight, or wearing greegrees made of bark around their necks. Why should we insist on making them do things our way?

It is this sudden understanding that leads Vidal to call him an exception among missionaries. This is the final irony, for even as cruel and ineffectual as Père Drumont is, he has been an exception for the good, as Beti has told us in the frontispiece.

> Il n'y a jamais eu de Révérend Père Supérieur Drumont; il n'y en aura probablement jamais, autant du moins que je connaisse mon Afrique natale: ce serait trop beau.[83]

> There never was any Monseigneur Drumont; there probably never will be, at least not as far as I know my native Africa. That would be just too good.

And so Père Drumont returns to France, abandoning his twenty years of work. His church and school are in ruins, and the native girls have deserted the Sixa—"un sacré vaincu."

Le Pauvre Christ de Bomba is a protest novel, but it transcends mere expostulation in the character of Drumont, who is, above all, a human, even tragic figure. The author severely satirizes him, but makes him at the same time the recipient of our pity and sympathy.

Disintegration of Society

Toundi Joseph, Meka, and the Père Drumont in the preceding three novels were placed in static situations; that is, the colonial situation was already a fact, and they, not understanding its meaning, end in disillusionment and despair. It is their own intransigence and naive interpretation of the realities of colonialism which brings their downfall—indeed seems to doom them almost from the beginning. In *Turn to the Dark* and *Arrow of God*, however, we witness entire societies in turmoil; both cultures are still struggling for dominance, and thus the characters are wrestling with problems of allegiance. No character, black or white, seems to be able to withstand the furies of either the internal or the external conflicts. Here we see not only man's life being destroyed, but society itself, the entire tribe. The group is splitting, and the characters are mirrors that reflect the cracks already visible in society.

Nearly all the characters in *Turn to the Dark* by Mopeli Paulus are ambivalent in their reactions to the white man's imposition. The white man in this novel is not a physical presence but rather a background, a psychological force that produces disruption, conflict, and change. The claims of tribal custom and loyalty are in conflict with the white man's religion and his laws. As he chooses his action, each character then is caught in the same dilemma. We meet the central figure, Lesiba, as he is returning from the white missionary school where he has just led a student strike. Lesiba is happy as he enters the small train station, for he is looking forward to his return home: "The lights of that small town meant much to Lesiba, whose mind had been locked in darkness for many days. He knew the next morning would see the end of his journey and the sun of peace shining above his own village, his home—Majoaneng."[84]

But Lesiba is not destined to enter peace and light. His return home marks a turn to the dark, for he is plunged into the controversies that are tearing the tribe apart. His own position

in the struggles is ambiguous, for even though he tried to reenter his tribe and assert himself as a man, he is rejected because he is uncircumcised and considered a traitor because he
has been to the white man's schools. The natives say he has
"one leg in the water and another on the land" and that he is
"brown-skinned and white-souled."

> Khanya's mouth hung open a moment, and then filled with
> words: 'But he is a boy—he is uncircumcised—his tail twists
> round the mountains! And how can the son of a Moruti—that
> half-cooked man with his nose buried in the white man's black
> Book—become one of us?'[85]

Lesiba's situation is further complicated by his family's
affiliations. His father is a Moruti, a preacher in the white man's
church. He disowns his son when he runs away to undergo
initiation ceremonies so that he can marry his childhood
sweetheart, Lineo, "a spark of a girl—brown and shining as a
seed of corn!"[86] Even his father's commitments are ambiguous,
however, for we learn that he sacrifices a black sheep to cleanse
Lesiba. This he did in secret so that the members of the congre-
gation would not see it. Lesiba's mother sides with his decision to move away from the white man, for her sympathies
are still with the native tradition, even though she practices the
Christian religion for her husband. His fiancée Lineo's family is
likewise split between the two worlds.

> Lineo's father, Kokong, was not a Christian, though her
> mother attended the Moruti's church. Lineo had more educa-
> tion than the other girls in the valley, but her parents did not
> seem to care whether she went to school or not, and the Moruti
> would have liked to see his son married to a teacher or nurse.
> And she was initiated, while Lesiba—a man in years—had not
> been allowed to go with his age-mates to *mophato*.[87]

The central incident of the novel, which forces all characters
to stand on one side or the other, is a ritual murder ordered by
the medicine man, Mafa. He aims to replenish the "horn" with
flesh, thus restoring the power of the Chief against witchcraft
and against his enemies, the whites. Chief Johannes asks for
Lesiba's help and approval, for he is one of the few in the tribe
who respect Lesiba's knowledge and schooling. Lesiba makes

a feeble attempt to stand against the murder (" 'Then is any
man an ox, to be slaughtered by the butcher?' said the young
man in a small voice."[88]), but he does not persist in the face of
opposition from the rest of the Chief's advisers. Lesiba stands
between two worlds, and he makes his choice.

> Like a hare that must choose between the flames and the
> spears of men when grass is burning: that leaps from the fire
> and sees men all about it and leaps again towards the scorching
> fire: Lesiba knew that he would choose murder rather than be
> rejected by the Chief.[89]

Lesiba's position is further complicated when the chosen
victim is a friend of Lineo's mother, a Zulu woman whose
presence in Basutoland is taken as an ill omen. Lineo's mother
is to lead her up into the mountains where she will be killed by
Kokong, Lineo's father. She objects to her role in the killing
but, as a woman, has no choice but to obey her husband.

> "You mean that I—a Christian—must take my own friend
> and betray and kill her? How often are these horns to be
> refreshed. Every year? Many, yes, many like you and this
> foolish husband of mine have hanged for them! So you want to
> hang, father of Lineo? I have no wish to, although I am only a
> woman, and no longer young. . . ."
> Kokong was ashamed that his wife should show him so little
> respect before the eyes of Makoa. "Your duty is to agree, not
> argue," he shouted weakly, but he knew in his heart that she
> spoke the truth.[90]

The killing ends Part I of the novel, and Part II opens with a
dry, dust-filled wind that chokes the entire region. The red wind
blows through the marriage of Lineo and Lesiba. Lineo dis-
covers the sacrificial victim's body a few days later. Her parents
squelch her inquiries about it, so she challenges Lesiba. He
reveals that both he and her parents were responsible. He
promises that he would go to jail himself rather than implicate
her parents, but she leaves him anyway. When the police come
to investigate, a direct confrontation between the white man's
laws and native tradition takes place. The European law condemns an act performed within the native tradition.

The white man's legal system soon seeks to ferret out the

guilty. Lesiba is accused and tried, as well as Lineo's mother and the medicine man. The society is breaking up physically as well as psychologically. The physical decline is etched on Lineo's face.

> The round milky eyes have taken on a different shade: they are red with spots of blood. They wear the frightening look of someone insane. Her beauty of a bird is gone. Lineo, daughter of Kokong, who used to walk with dignity among the young women, has forgotten herself, and roams the fields like a cripple, and lets the tears run down her cheeks like a river upon rocks.[91]

Even Chief Johannes is summoned to court. Everywhere there is talk that the old order is changing; the power is no longer with the Chief but with the white man. The breakup is complete when the Chief is sentenced to hang by the white judge. Lesiba was found guilty of being an accessory to murder and sentenced to seven years' imprisonment. A fellow prisoner summarizes the encroachment of the white foreigners at the end of the novel: "They will destroy us. They will take our land away from us. We sleep and dream while they take our cattle away. We run after the things they throw to us, and our children work on their farms . . ." Lesiba will be in a precarious position between the two worlds when he is released, for as Mopeli Paulus writes at the end of the novel, "A wind was blowing—a high wind—and Lesiba was a young bird, swaying on the twig of a tree."[92]

In Chinua Achebe's *Arrow of God* we also witness the collapse of tradition in the fall of a native priestly line and its titular head, Ezeulu, as a consequence of the white man's presence. This collapse ensures the establishment and growth of the Christian Church and further solidifies the British colonial administration. The cohesive force and thrust of colonial institutions and their pervasiveness and total impact on native life is observed by one of the early Christian converts:

> Yes we are talking about the white man's road. But when the roof and walls of a house fall in, the ceiling is not left standing. The white man, the new religion, the soldiers, the new road— they are all part of the same thing. The white man has a gun, a

machete, a bow and carries fire in his mouth. He does not fight with one weapon alone.[93]

Achebe implies that conflicts and rivalries within a native society facilitated British colonial penetration, for not only are there interclan land disputes between the villages of Umuaro and Okperi, but also jealous rivalries between the minor deities of the clans. Furthermore, within a single clan rivalries exist between the spiritual head, Ezeulu, the chief priest, and his half brother Okeke Onenyi, the medicine man, and between Ezeulu's sons, and between his wives.

To be sure Achebe suggests that within the British colonial order there are also tensions and rivalries, but the British officers, bent on projecting an unshakable image and loyal front, subordinate personalities to respect for authority and acquiesce to orders. The chief administrative representative in the district, Captain Winterbottom, the "Destroyer of Guns," as he is known to the natives, chafes under a command from head-quarters: ". . . but in this matter of Indirect Rule there did not seem to be any point in continuing his objection when people who until quite recently were with him in opposing had now turned round to blame him for not implementing it. He was now under orders to find a chief and his duty was clear."[94]

By alternating in consecutive chapters the events in the native community with those in the colonial order, Achebe seems to imply that although these two worlds touch, they do not in fact associate or come together. The novel moves slowly and is composed of many stories within the larger narrative. Native folklore and legends are also woven into the novel, often with not much relevance to the plot, but strengthening the total sense of traditional life. Yet it is the interaction of the new white order with the native traditional society that brings about the latter's collapse. The imminence and threat of collapse is skillfully restated in the proverbial refrain: ". . . a man who brings ant-infested faggots into his hut should expect the visit of lizards."[95]

Ezeulu's downfall is owing as much to his stubborn intransigence, uncommunicating aloofness, and destructive pride as to the progress of colonial administration. His eldest son, Edogo, recalled the words of his mother:

Ezeulu's only fault was that he expected everyone—his wives, his kinsmen, his children, his friends and even his enemies—to think and act like himself. Anyone who dared to say no to him was an enemy. He forgot the saying of the elders that if a man sought for a companion who acted entirely like himself he would live in solitude.[96]

Within the native community Ezeulu's prestige rises and falls according to the stand he adopts in his encounters with the white administrator. When he is suspected of connivance with white men his stature as head priest of the god Ulu wanes.

. . . no man however great can win judgement against a clan. You may think you did in that land dispute but you are wrong. Umuaro will always say that you betrayed them before the white man. And they will say that you are betraying them again today by sending your son to join in desecrating the land.[97]

It is this son, Oduche, who, desirous of proving his allegiance to the Christian Church, attempts to suffocate a sacred royal python. It is an action symbolic of the tenuous position of native converts to Christianity and one which further opens Ezeulu to the mockery of his enemies and the pity of his friends.

. . . his anger was not so much against Oduche as against all the double-faced neighbors and passers-by whose words of sympathy barely concealed the mockery in their hearts. And even if they had been sincere Ezeulu would still have resented anybody making him an object of pity.[98]

Another incident involving his son Obika further weakens Ezeulu's prestige. When, through the same sense of equity that he demonstrated in the land dispute, he fails to take action after the unprecedented whipping of his son, Obika, by a white man, he is suspected of betraying his own. Captain Winterbottom summarily orders Ezeulu brought before him; the proud priest at first refuses to go, then refuses to take counsel with him. He is detained in jail while the British officer recovers from a sudden and serious illness. This illness both raises Ezeulu's prestige, since he is credited with working a charm against the white man, and hastens his downfall. He realizes that an extended stay in jail would impress upon the people of Umuaro how vital to them he, the chief priest of Ulu, is: "Let the white man detain him not for one day but one year so that his deity not seeing him in his place would ask Umuaro questions."[99] It would also provide him with a direct method of exacting punishment from his detractors: "The rain was part of the suffering to which he had been exposed and for which he must exact the fullest redress. The more he suffered now the greater would be the joy of redress. His mind sought new grievances to pile upon all the others."[100]

The denouement is unraveled fairly rapidly. While Ezeulu was away he omitted the eating of one of the yams at the new moon. Since the Harvest of Yams may commence only after he has eaten twelve yams, the harvest is delayed, and the yams begin to rot in the ground. Native leaders beg Ezeulu to eat the remaining yam, even offering to take the total blame from Ulu if the god is displeased. But Ezeulu remains inflexible and instead of being the mediator between Ulu and Umuaro, he is accused of being an enemy. "But I should like to know on whose side you are, Ezeulu. I think you have just said that you have become the whip with which Ulu flogs Umuaro. . . ."[101]

John Goodcountry, a native Christian missionary, seizes the opportunity to intervene for the benefit of his church. He promises that the people will be protected from Ulu's wrath if they bring their harvested yams to the Christian church. Obika's sudden death while performing a ritual funeral ceremony is interpreted by the people as an omen of Ulu's displeasure with his headstrong and ambitious priest. The villagers, threatened with famine, turn away from Ezeulu and begin the harvest, sending their sons to the Christian church with the tribute of yams.

Ezeulu's mind cracks under the double strain of paternal grief and public humiliation, and in his demented state he is spared the knowledge of the final outcome. The novel ends with Achebe picking up the lizard motif to exemplify the destruction of the house from within.

> . . . Ulu had chosen a dangerous time to uphold this wisdom. In destroying this priest he had also brought disaster on himself, like the lizard in the fable who ruined his mother's funeral by his own hand. For a deity who chose a time such as this to destroy his priest or abandon him to his enemies was

inciting people to take liberties; and Umuaro was just ripe to do so.[102]

Degradation of Society

In *Batouala*, René Maran moves beyond Achebe's prophecy of disintegration of the native tradition to a picture of the degradation of native society. The native customs in this novel are still being practiced in spite of white occupation of Oubangui Chari. In the opening scenes, Batouala wakes up in his compound of eight wives, makes love to his favorite, Yassigui'nda, and beats out an announcement of a circumcision festival to be held in nine days. The native society is portrayed as an entity in itself, without physical intervention of the white man except for one commandant who appears briefly during the festival. Colonialism has done its work, however, for the native tradition has disintegrated internally and ends in debauchery and death.

The festival turns into a sex orgy; males interrupt the traditional dances to carry the women off to make love: "Sexual intoxication, coupled with alcoholic intoxication. An immense animal joy, free of all control. Insults roared, blood spilled. In vain. Desire alone was master."[103]

Batouala's father drops dead suddenly from the excesses of alcohol and sexual activity. In accordance with native custom, his body is allowed to lie unburied for eight days to make certain that he will not come back to life. Some of the younger generation begin to resent this tradition when the stench, carried on the evening breezes, permeates the village: "Tradition! People were tending to forget it a little too easily of late, the elders remarked bitterly. The young people and, in general, everyone who's been working for the white men, were making a mockery of it."[104]

The degradation in this novel goes beyond the events in this village or the black-white conflict. Maran's bitterness and pessimism extends to all of humanity. Men are portrayed as being without control over their actions and animal appetites: "Everyone's fate is settled in advance. You cannot appeal its decisions."[105] Animal imagery expressive of competition for survival is prevalent in the novel. Batouala's father likens the white's treatment of the natives to a cat that is slowly torturing a mouse:

". . . it doesn't escape me that they are having fun with us just like Paka the wildcat does with a mouse."[106] Again he puts the conflict in animal terms when he counsels his son to resignation toward the white intervention: "Resign yourself. Once Bamara, the lion, has roared, no antelope would dare utter a sound nearby. We're like the antelope. Since we aren't the stronger ones, all we can do now is keep quiet."[107] Animals are named and treated like human characters, further bringing man down to the animal level. Even in his descriptions of the native existence before the coming of the white man, Maran depicts a society based on the satisfaction of animal desires.

> On vivait heureux, jadis, avant la venue des "boundjous." Travailler peu, et pour soi, manger, boire et dormir; de loin en loin, des palabres sanglantes où l'on arrachait le foie des morts pour manger leur courage et se l'incorporer—tels étaient les seuls travaux des noirs, jadis, avant la venue des blancs.[108]

> One lived happily formerly, before the coming of the "boundjus." Worked a little, and for oneself, ate, drank and slept; at long intervals bloody parleys where the livers of the dead were snatched so that their courage could be eaten and absorbed— such were the tasks of the blacks, formerly, before the whites came.

The novel ends in naturalistic hunt scenes. A diviner accuses Yassigui'nda of being responsible for the death of Batouala's father. Bissibi'ngui, the tribe's young Adonis, promises to run away with her to Bangui to shield her from punishment. He persuades her to wait until after a big hunt on which he and Batouala go together, each intending to kill the other and make it appear accidental. Moureu, the panther, rips open Batouala's stomach just after Batouala has thrown a spear that narrowly misses Bissibi'ngui. Batouala lies dying an agonizing death in his hut. Bissibi'ngui and Yassigui'nda begin to make love a few feet away from him when they believe he is dead. He staggers to his feet, seeing them together, and drops dead beside them. They flee into the night, and Batouala is left in the silence.

Maran states in his introduction that the novel is objective, a reporting of the facts. But his own philosophy of life has been projected over the events so that the novel condemns humanity rather than merely the white perpetrators of the crimes he reports. His own comments are often thinly disguised as Batouala's thoughts. His philosophy of life is best stated at the end of a short novel, *Youmba, La Mangouste,* which accompanies *Batouala.*

> . . . l'homme, pour peu qu'il ait faim, n'hésite pas à tuer son meilleur ami pour s'en repaître.
> Tuer pour ne pas être tué: telle est la grande loi de la vie et de la brousse. Toutes les autres lui donnent raison et la justifient. C'est pourquoi la faiblesse est le pire des crimes.[109]

> . . . man, if he were hungry, does not hesitate to kill his best friend to feast on him.
> Kill in order not to be killed: This is the great law of life and of the bush. All others build on it and justify it. That is why weakness is the worst of crimes.

Batouala seems to be constructed in four movements, with two contradictory but complementary voices running throughout producing a harmonic counterpoint. One voice represents the native philosophy of life and the other, the white man's.

In the first movement, the voices are muted modulations that announce daybreak and tell of a life of simple, instinctual natural pleasures and their pursuit before the coming of the white man. The native voice is droll and slyly bantering: "To scratch oneself is an excellent exercise . . . There isn't a living creature who doesn't . . . scratch himself on awakening. Well then, a good example to follow, since it is natural."[110]

Time and the progress of the day is marked by a series of short stacatto phrases which break the longer rhythmical sentences and pinpoint the changing scene, as at the end of the first chapter: "Day has come . . ."[111] Or later: "The sun has arrived at the height of its course."[112] All is accompanied by myriad voices of the animal world. The movement is climaxed by a clear expression from the voice of Batouala who represents the traditional mores: "Guardian of archaic ways, he remains faithful to the tradition that his ancestors bequeathed him, but he plunges no further."[113] He summons the tribes from far and wide on the tam-tams to a great ritual feast: "And now down there, over there, further away and further yet, from everywhere, to the left, to the right, behind him, before him, like noises, identical drumrolls, similar tom-toms were rumbling . . ."[114]

The second movement is more strident as the voices of the celebrants wildly join together in an orgiastic bacchanal, the culminating expression of the instinctual. The contrasting voice in this movement is not bantering but becomes a harsh condemnatory diatribe by Batouala of the destructive and disruptive presence of the white man. And the second movement comes to an abrupt halt with the arrival of the commandant and the summary imposition of a fine: "An overwhelming, abrupt stupor succeeded the indescribable clamor and hubbub. Then a shout suddenly rose from the silence: 'The commandant! . . . The commandant!' "[115] Symbolically, the happy life is ended, the orgy is ended as Maran comments: "Not every day is a holiday. After the dry season comes the rainy season, songs of joy give way to dirges, and tears follow laughter."[116]

The end of the orgy had been heralded by a fierce tornado whose build-up paralleled the rhythmical increase of the tempo of the bacchanal:

> Les nuages obstruent le ciel bas et, stationnaires, dominent la Bamba, la Déla, la Déka; dominent les villages de Yakidji et de Soumana, de Yabi'ngui et de Batouala . . . dominent toute cette verdure que leur ombre étouffe, suppriment la vue quotidienne et, pleins d'une menace imminente, attendent un signal qui ne vient pas. . . .
>
> Ouhououou! . . . Enfin! Un grand vent chaud se lève, venu on ne sait d'où.[117]

> Clouds choke the lowering sky and, stock-still, tower over the Bamba, the Déla and the Déka. They tower above the villages of Yakidji and Soumana, of Yabi'ngui and Batouala . . . they tower above all that greenery which is suffocated by their shadow. They block the usual view and, full of imminent menace, await a signal which doesn't come. . . .
>
> Woo, woo, woo! At last! A great hot wind is rising, coming from heaven knows where.

The second movement had announced or foretold the conflict between Bissibi-ngui and Batouala, and this becomes the principal motif of the third movement, whose atmosphere is heavy, brooding, silent. Its mood is ominous with thoughts of animal vengeance. This is the scene of the animal hunt, the hunt for the panther. The motif of the panther, which had

appeared throughout, now swells. The elephant motif introduced earlier in a folk tale is now picked up. Bissibi'ngui becomes the elephant who trumpets and crashes through the
bush. Batouala, the stalking panther, is himself stalked by the
real panther. In this movement the voice of Batouala, the great
Morungo, sings for the last time the legends of the tribes.

In the final scene Batouala lies dying. The mood is darker
and the gloom of night is setting in. The dying man reflects on
humanity: "He added . . . that there were neither Bandas nor
Mandjias, neither whites nor blacks;—there was nothing but
men—and all men were brothers."

But this momentary tone of conciliation with the white man
is followed by a deep note of pessimism: "Marche, sale nègre!
Marche, et crève!" Night closes over the dying chief.

> Peu à peu les rumeurs s'apaisent. Le sommeil gagne les
> animaux. Il n'y a plus que le silence qui te veille, Batouala, et
> que la solitude. La grande nuit est sur toi. Dors . . .
> Dors . . .[118]

> The noises gradually die down. Sleep comes over the animals.
> There's nothing but the silence watching over you, Batouala,
> silence and solitude. Night lies deep upon you. Sleep . . .
> Sleep . . .

In *The River Between* the clash between the colonial order
and a traditional way of life is presented through the play of
color contrasts, contradictory emotions and allegiances, antagonistic oppositions of phenomena, and conflict situations
within a single character, between characters, and between
representatives of opposing ideological approaches to life.
Those who attempt reconciliation between the ancient way of
the hills with its legends and myths and the new practices of
Christianity merge with the mist and flow away into the darkness. Such had been the fate of Muthoni, who fled the intransigence of her father, Joshua, to be initiated into the beauty and
mystery of the hills:

> I am still a Christian, see, a Christian in the tribe. Look. I
> am a woman and will grow big and healthy in the tribe. . . .[119]
> Then he saw that it was Muthoni, and she was thrown into the
> river and she was saying, "I am a woman now." The river

carried her with it into a darkness which no one could fathom.[120]

The hills, standing in opposition to one another, meet at the banks of the river, which both unites and divides them but which flows on, a symbol of life and cure. Ngugi charges all phenomena with symbolic content, gives historicity to landscape and qualitative time to the flow of the Honia River:

> A river flowed through the valley of life. If there had been no bush and no forest trees covering the slopes, you could have seen the river when you stood on top of either Kameno or Makuyu. . . . The river was called Honia, which meant cure, or bring-back-to-life. Honia river never dried: it seemed to possess a strong will to live. . . . And it went on in the same way, never hurrying, never hesitating. People saw this and were happy.[121]

It is on the banks of the Honia that circumcision ceremonies are performed, the observance of which becomes the pivotal conflict between those who follow Christianity and those who continue in the ways of the tribe, for through it man is linked to his past, to the earth: "Blood trickled freely on to the ground, sinking into the soil. Henceforth a religious bond linked Waiyaki to the earth, as if his blood was an offering."[122] The Honia River murmurs an unknown song and symbolically offers to Waiyaki and Nyambura—to those who seek reconciliation between the old and the new—peace, comfort, and a bank for the consummation of their love. But even this river awakens contradictory effects: "Nyambura did not feel at peace. The river no longer soothed her."[123]

All is color contrast, color symbol. Muthoni's death, which totally affects the hills, is marked by an orange countryside: "The sun seemed to have set early. The country was dull, pale orange; everything seemed strangely quiet."[124] Through the play of darkness and light, Ngugi dramatizes the conflict that engulfs the land and suggests, through illumination, the possibility of resolving this conflict. Overcome by a sense of his inability to bridge the gulf between his people, "guilt weighed on him. The darkness terrified him."[125] And it is Waiyaki's eyes that appear sad, contemplative, but "they seemed to burn bright. A light came from them, a light that appeared to pierce your body, seeing something beyond you, into your heart."[126]

Contradictory emotional reactions to the same situation by many of the characters, especially those of the younger generation who are seeking a way out, are clear indications of their tension and inner conflict. The older generation, however, the white missionary Livingston and his stubborn follower Joshua, Waiyaki's father Chege (interpreter of the legend of the hills), and Kabonyi (self-appointed guardian of these legends), are rigid and unswerving in their determination and beliefs and, consequently, are not torn between any contradictory emotional reactions. Yet there is contradiction throughout the land, even in the rain:

> The rain carried away the soil, not only here but everywhere. That was why land, in some parts, was becoming poor. . . . The racing drops of water had turned to filth and mud. . . . Even here in this natural happening, he could see a contradiction. The rain had to touch the soil. That touch could be a blessing or a curse.[127]

Fusing the legends of the Gikuyu people and elements from the biblical narrative, Ngugi makes a savior come from the hills. It is only when viewed from the sacred grove where Waiyaki is taken by his seer father, Chege, to be told the prophecy that the hills unite, that contradictions and conflicts cease: "The ridges slept on. Kameno and Makuyu were no longer antagonistic. They had merged into one area of beautiful land, which is what, perhaps, they were meant to be. Makuyu, Kameno and the other ridges lay in peace and there was no sign of life, as one stood on the hill of God."[128] It seemed that the old antagonism of the hills had been deepened, the former peace shattered, with the coming of the white man; the people of the ridges had been alienated from their land: "There is something unexplainable in the coming of the white man. He had found no resistance in the hills. Now he had penetrated into the heart of the country, spreading his influence. This influence could be disruptive."[129]

Even the prophecy brings with it conflict: who is its interpreter? "Who is the savior of the land?" becomes the central question, the conflict situation that controls the action of the novel. Will peace come to the ridges from Joshua and the Christian church, from Kabonyi and the Kiama formed to preserve the traditions of the hills, or from Waiyaki and his school, Marioshoni, which brings a new awareness to the people of these hills?

In *The River Between*, James Ngugi treats the problem of how the African reacts to the clash between his own culture and religion and that of the white man. Several alternatives are presented in the lives of the main characters of the novel. Joshua represents total acceptance of the white man's customs. When he was converted to Christianity, he completely renounced tribal tradition. "He had clothed himself with a religion decorated and smeared with everything *white.*" But by rejecting the truths of the tribe he also rejects his pre-Christian self, and estranged from himself and his tradition, Joshua "had nothing to rest upon, something rich and firm on which to stand and grow, he had to cling with his hands to whatever the missionaries taught him promised future."[130] He becomes the leader of the Christian community, damning all native customs, especially the rite of circumcision. When his youngest daughter, Muthoni, runs away to make herself beautiful in the eyes of the tribe through circumcision, he disowns her. She dies soon afterward of an infection, and Joshua is further reinforced in his condemnation of the rite.

Kabonyi, who also attended the missionary school with Joshua, eventually rejects everything about the white man and returns to traditional customs with the fervor of a convert. He would reject the Western-inspired schools, force the Christians to be circumcised, and drive the Europeans from the country. In this novel, Kabonyi triumphs, thus seemingly tightening the hold of reaction, but Ngugi makes it clear that this victory is only temporary. In one of his frequent foreshadowings of coming events, Ngugi asks: "How could he understand that the people did not want to move backwards, that the ridges no longer desired their isolation? How could he know that the forces that drove people to yearn for a better day tomorrow, that now gave a new awareness to the people, were like demons, sweeping the whole country."[131]

Ngugi shows that both the Christian converts and the traditionalists who fanatically try to advance their causes become dehumanized and lose all perspective and sense of value. This becomes clear in the reaction of both sides to the death of Muthoni. Compassion for the loss of life is snuffed out. Joshua sees her death as "a warning to those who rebelled against their parents and the laws of God," while the traditionalists regard it as a "warning to all to stick to the ways of the ridges, to the ancient wisdom of the land, to its ritual and song."[132]

Waiyaki, the protagonist of the novel, the last of a line of prophets who had warned against the European culture, had been sent to a missionary school by his father Chege to "learn the wisdom and all the secrets of the white man."[133] When, as a result of Muthoni's death, the missionary school is closed to all who took part in the circumcision rites, Waiyaki begins a Gikuyu independent school where the young could receive a Western education while continuing to observe tribal customs. Waiyaki thus finds himself between the two disputing factions of his tribe. He devotes himself completely to education as the compromise that would allow each individual to find some expression of his own reconciliation of the native and the European mores. Still the division within the tribe deepens. Waiyaki falls in love with Joshua's eldest daughter, Nyambura, which further complicates his position as between these two worlds. He concludes that although there is good in the ways of the Europeans, one must clear away the inessential to reach the eternal, which then may be reconciled with native tradition.

> A people's traditions could not be swept away overnight. That way lay disintegration. Such a tribe would have no roots, for a people's roots were in their traditions going back to the past. . . . If the white man's religion made you abandon a custom and then did not give you something else of equal value, you became lost.[134]

The novel is also the personal tragedy of Waiyaki. His tragic flaw seems to be his indecisiveness. At the first big gathering of the people about the new school, he had planned to speak out for unity of the tribe. In the heat of the debate with Kabonyi and in the flush of success over the popular support he gets for his school policy, he forgets to mention it. The missed opportunity haunts him increasingly throughout the novel. He had been too involved in education to feel the growing demand for political action; when he responds it is too late.

In the final confrontation of the novel, Kabonyi calls on Waiyaki in front of the entire tribe either to reject the Christian

Joshua's daughter or to take the oath of loyalty to the traditionalists. Both he and Nyambura are to come to trial before the Kiama, founded by Kabonyi to administer oaths and secure compliance to maintain the purity of the tribe. Waiyaki's faith in education has failed him for the moment, but Ngugi hints that his kind of education and reconciliation will eventually triumph. The people are intimidated only for the moment by Kabonyi, and life and progress will go on.

> The land was now silent. The two ridges lay side by side, hidden in the darkness. And Honia river went on flowing between them, down through the valley of life, its beat rising above the dark stillness, reaching into the heart of the people of Makuyu and Kameno.[135]

Notes

1. Cheikh Hamidou Kane, *Ambiguous Adventure* (New York: Walker and Co., 1963), p. 48.
2. James Ngugi, *Weep Not, Child* (London: Heinemann Educational Books Ltd., 1964), p. 30.
3. Ferdinand Oyono, *Le Vieux Nègre et la Médaille,* (Paris: René Julliard, 1956), p. 209.
4. *Ibid.,* p. 170.
5. René Maran, *Batouala* (Paris: Editions Albin Michel, 1938), p. 39.
6. Chinua Achebe, *Arrow of God* (London: Heinemann Educational Books, Ltd., 1964), p. 23.
7. Ngugi, *op. cit.,* p. 76.
8. Eza Boto (Mongo Beti), *Ville Cruelle* (Paris: Présence Africaine, 1954), pp. 49–50.
9. Achebe, *op. cit.,* p. 189.
10. Maran, *op. cit.,* p. 40.
11. *Ibid.,* p. 60.
12. Oyono, *op. cit.,* p. 50.
13. Ferdinand Oyono, *Une Vie de Boy* (Paris: René Julliard, 1956), pp. 25–26.
14. Ngugi, *op. cit.,* p. 87.
15. Jean Malonga, *Coeur d'Aryenne* in *Trois Ecrivains Noirs* (Paris: Présence Africaine, no. 16, 1954), p. 170.

16. Oyono, *Une Vie de Boy*, p. 78.
17. *Ibid.*, p. 67.
18. Achebe, *op. cit.*, p. 94.
19. Maran, *op. cit.*, p. 96.
20. Sembene Ousmane, *O Pays, Mon Beau Peuple* (Paris: Amiot-Dumont, 1957), p. 13.
21. Maran, *op. cit.*, pp. 9–10.
22. Ngugi, *op. cit.*, pp. 129–130.
23. Maran, *op. cit.*, p. 93.
24. *Ibid.*, p. 97.
25. Achebe, *op. cit.*, p. 100.
26. Ngugi, *op. cit.*, p. 29.
27. *Ibid.*, p. 19.
28. Ousmane, *op. cit.*, p. 121.
29. Achebe, *op. cit.*, p. 101.
30. Ngugi, *op. cit.*, pp. 130–132.
31. Oyono, *Une Vie de Boy*, p. 38.
32. *Ibid.*, p. 171.
33. Malonga, *op. cit.*, p. 211.
34. *Ibid.*, p. 210.
35. Maran, *op. cit.*, p. 10.
36. A. S. Mopeli-Paulus and Miriam Basner, *Turn to the Dark* (London: Jonathan Cape, 1956), p. 133.
37. Oyono, *Une Vie de Boy*, p. 34.
38. Mongo Beti, *Le Pauvre Christ de Bomba* (Paris: Robert Laffont, 1956), pp. 323–324.
39. Mopeli-Paulus, *op. cit.*, pp. 22–23.
40. Beti, *Le Pauvre Christ de Bomba*, p. 307.
41. *Ibid.*, pp. 369–370.
42. Maran, *op. cit.*, pp. 93–94.
43. Eza Boto (Mongo Beti), "Ville Cruelle" in *Trois Ecrivains Noirs*, p. 57.
44. Ousmane, *op. cit.*, p. 85.
45. *Ibid.*, p. 128.
46. Oyono, *Une Vie de Boy*, p. 41.
47–55. *Ibid:* 47. p. 88; 48. p. 24; 49. p. 18; 50. p. 137; 51. p. 76; 52. pp. 73–74; 53. p. 87; 54. p. 103; 55. p. 12.
56. Oyono, *Le Vieux Nègre et la Médaille*, pp. 19–20.
57–68. *Ibid:* 57. p. 55; 58. p. 62; 59. pp. 109–110; 60. p. 123; 61. p. 138; 62. p. 147; 63. p. 153; 64. p. 161; 65. p. 169; 66. p. 168; 67. p. 177; 68. p. 188.
69. Beti, *Le Pauvre Christ de Bomba*, p. 11.
70–83. *Ibid:* 70. p. 40; 71. p. 266; 72. pp. 17–18; 73. p. 49; 74. p. 61; 75. p. 62; 76. p. 66; 77. p. 99; 78. p. 103; 79. p. 123; 80. p. 268; 81. p. 260; 82. p. 260; 83. frontispiece.
84. Mopeli-Paulus, *Turn to The Dark*, p. 60.
85–92. *Ibid:* 85. p. 60; 86. p. 28; 87. p. 21; 88. p. 124; 89. p. 23; 90. p. 133; 91. p. 244; 92. pp. 276–277.

93. Achebe, *op. cit.*, p. 105.

94–102. *Ibid:* 94. p. 71; 95. p. 178; 96. p. 114; 97. p. 162; 98. p. 63; 99. p. 198; 100. p. 225; 101. p. 261; 102. p. 287.

103. Maran, *op. cit.*, p. 111.

104–108. *Ibid:* 104. p. 118; 105. p. 63; 106. p. 90; 107. p. 99; 108. p. 98.

109. Maran, "Youmba, La Mangouste" in *Batouala*, p. 250.

110. Maran, *Batouala*, p. 29.

111–118. *Ibid:* 111. p. 33; 112. p. 40; 113. p. 30; 114. pp. 41–42; 115. p. 113; 116. p. 116; 117. pp. 75–76; 118. pp. 187–190.

119. James Ngugi, *The River Between* (London: Heinemann Educational Books, Ltd., 1965), p. 61.

120–135. *Ibid:* 120. p. 138; 121. p. 1; 122. pp. 52–53; 123. p. 132; 124. pp. 60–61; 125. p. 139; 126. p. 12; 127. p. 76; 128. p. 19; 129. p. 83; 130. p. 163; 131. p. 166; 132. p. 62; 133. p. 24; 134. pp. 162–163; 135. p. 175.

BRIDGE

THE FALLING AWAY

The movement away leads to the falling apart of things, and when things fall apart the rhythms of life are broken, so the rhythms of an Ibo clan of Umuofia are broken when an outside force, in this instance a white colonial order, jails its six most prominent men and by abusing them threatens its very structure and existence.

> It was the time of the full moon. But that night the voice of children was not heard. The village *ilo* where they always gathered for a moon-play was empty. The women of Iguedo did not meet in their secret enclosure to learn a new dance to be displayed later to the village. Young men who were always abroad in the moonlight kept to their huts that night. Their manly voices were not heard on the village paths as they went to visit their friends and lovers. Umuofia was like a startled animal with ears erect, sniffing the silent, ominous air and not knowing which way to run.[1]

And some individuals, such as the hero of *Things Fall Apart*, Okonkwo, will run to an ironic death; some, such as his son Nwoye will run to the white man's religion and church and bring about the breakup of a family; some, maybe the majority, will accommodate to the ways of the conqueror and slowly move away from many of their traditions. The novel *Things Fall Apart* symbolizes this triple movement away.

In his novel, Chinua Achebe exposes the whole panorama of Ibo life in all its multiple layers. This life is viewed from many different sides and angles; its material phenomena and sensory elements are captured in a language and style whose inner imagery and basic rhythm correspond completely to the rhythm of the life described. By an exposition of Okonkwo's character, Achebe captures the essential genius of this Ibo society. It is an agricultural society, and its economics and life rhythms are expressed in images of yams and kola nut.

Okonkwo is the regenerative force of his line. He is the hard center between two weaker halves: his father Okoye, who did not accept the premises on which success was achieved in Ibo society, and his son Nwoye, who drops away from the clan to embrace Christianity. Okonkwo is the vital force of his group; when he is destroyed, the clan's force is destroyed too.

The tension of this novel is the interaction of Okonkwo with the vital forces of the clan, the "things." When these "things" begin to "fall apart," Okonkwo, who is a supreme expression of these "things," also falls apart. But the reverse may be true: things fall apart because Okonkwo, or people like him, do not adjust to the changes which take place in the "things," which are accelerated by the coming of the white man, with his church, missionaries, and administrators. When he begins to fall apart, the clan too commences to fall apart. Does the clan weaken man, or is it the opposite?

Throughout the novel we are presented with the quiverings of tightened bows whose tautness will eventually cause them to snap. The "tightened bows" are presented in the characters of the hero Okonkwo and his son Nwoye and in the structure of Umuofia and the Ibo clan. Two things cause Nwoye to snap: Okonkwo's killing of his adopted son Ikemefuna, which results from a flaw in Okonkwo's personal character, and second, the tribal practice of leaving twins to die in the evil forest. This same dualism—character and society—runs throughout the novel.

As the man who had cleared his throat drew up and raised his machete, Okonkwo looked away. He heard the blow. The pot

> fell and broke in the sand. He heard Ikemefuna cry, "My
> father, they have killed me!" as he ran towards him. Dazed
> with fear, Okonkwo drew his machete and cut him down. He
> was afraid of being thought weak.[2]

This fear of being thought weak tightens the tension of
Okonkwo's "bow." His every action becomes a compulsive
rejection of any show of weakness, his every gesture is high-
strung and unrelaxed.

The bow begins to snap when Nwoye hears the crying of
twins in the forest.

> Nwoye had heard that twins were put in earthenware pots and
> thrown away in the forest, but he had never yet come across
> them. A vague chill had descended on him and his head had
> seemed to swell, like a solitary walker at night who passes an
> evil spirit on the way. Then something had given way inside
> him. It descended on him again, this feeling, when his father
> walked in, that night after killing Ikemefuna.[3]

But Okonkwo tries to explain and excuse his action, that is, the
killing of Ikemefuna, by a proverb. For among the Ibo "proverbs are the palm-oil with which words are eaten."[4] Okonkwo
says: "A child's fingers are not scalded by a piece of hot yam
which its mother puts into its palm."[5]

The Earth, the ancestors, the clan had decreed that Ikemefuna, who had been given as a hostage by another tribe and
who had been placed in Okonkwo's care, eventually calling him
father, should die. Okonkwo, because of his desire not to show
weakness, designates himself a messenger of the Earth. "The
Earth cannot punish me for obeying her messenger," Okonkwo
had said, but obeying her messenger and becoming her messenger are different things. Obierika, Okonkwo's friend, had
said, "if the Oracle said that my son should be killed I would
neither dispute it nor be the one to do it."[6] However, Okonkwo,
because the cord of his bow has been drawn so tight, becomes
the executioner of his son, who is actually the communal property of the clan. He makes himself the executor of the tribe's
will and the messenger of the Earth—the Earth who is Mother,
who brings forth yams to feed the clan. Sometimes the decrees
of Mother Earth are harsh and can burn the mouths and hands
of those whom she feeds. And so it is paradoxically part of

Okonkwo's character not always to execute but sometimes to disobey the decrees of Mother Earth. He will beat his wife during the week of Peace: "Okonkwo was not the man to stop beating somebody half-way through, not even for fear of a goddess . . . [even though] it was unheard of to beat somebody during the sacred week."[7]

It is this constant interaction between the evolution of Okonkwo's character and the practices, customs, and beliefs of an agricultural community—for such was Umuofia—that gives *Things Fall Apart* its dramatic tension. Okonkwo's beating of his wife during the week of Peace can bring destruction to the whole clan because the clan is intradependent and still tightly knit. It is an Ibo clan, dependent on yams for its livelihood, dependent on rain for good harvests—harvests that will bring to a man happiness, the ability to feed his family, and by extension, stature within the community. For in this community it is a man's individual worth which counts most.

Okonkwo is at the center of the novel. The tribe's strength reinforces his strength. Thus the main elements of the novel are the dissolution and falling away of those "things" that were well-ordered and tightly strung together and the rise and fall of Okonkwo.

Achebe paints for us the picture of an Ibo clan, its daily life, its customs, its beliefs, its ceremonies. A wedding ceremony and a warrior's funeral are described. The protocol inherent in the breaking of the kola nut is often exhibited. This picture of the bargaining for the bride price introduces the reader to many of the social rituals of Umuofia:

> As the men drank they talked about everything except the thing for which they had gathered. It was only after the pot had been emptied that the suitor's father cleared his voice and announced the object of their visit.
>
> Obierika then presented to him a small bundle of short broomsticks. Ukegbu counted them.
>
> "They are thirty?" he asked.
>
> Obierika nodded in agreement.
>
> "We are at last getting somewhere," Ukegbu said, and then turning to his brother and his son he said: "Let us go out and whisper together." The three rose and went outside. When they returned Ukegbu handed the bundle of sticks back to Obierika.

He counted them; instead of thirty there were now only fifteen. He passed them over to his eldest brother, Machi, who also counted them and said:

"We had not thought to go below thirty. But as the dog said, 'If I fall down for you and you fall down for me, it is play.' Marriage should be a play and not a fight; so we are falling down again." He then added ten sticks to the fifteen and gave the bundle to Ukegbu.

In this way Akuke's bride-price was finally settled at twenty bags of cowries.[8]

In this Ibo society, a man's position is judged by the number of wives he can support. But the position of each wife is clearly demarcated, and the husband pays assiduous attention to this polygamous social hierarchy. The first wife will wear round her ankles her husband's signets of honor, and at mealtime her dish will be tasted first. This controlled, well-defined, ethical pattern of behavior is also evident in funerals. The extent and magnificence of a man's burial is relative to the number of titles he has taken. The whole clan will participate at the funeral of a warrior who has taken many titles. He will be paid homage by other warriors who will come and go according to their age groups.

From the preceding excerpts one can see that Achebe deftly weaves the Ibo social customs into the fabric of his story. Style and content fuse and Achebe distills an African essence through the use of proverbs, a particular imagery, and also the images that are engrained in the natural background. Almost every element of style draws upon the very substance, on the earth of Umuofia. After nights of sleeplessness and restlessness after having killed Ikemefuna, Okonkwo's state of being is depicted in a succinct yet dramatic image: "He felt like a drunken giant walking with the limbs of a mosquito."[9] Indeed, most of the successful images are regional: "Okonkwo's fame had grown like a bush-fire in the harmattan";[10] and Ikemefuna "grew rapidly like a yam tendril in the rainy season, and was full of the sap of life."[11] Not only are they successful, not only does the author use an image functionally, but, as a poet, he will develop or repeat an image.

When the rain finally came, it was in large, solid drops of frozen water which the people called the "nuts of the water of heaven." They were hard and painful on the body as they fell, yet young people ran about happily picking up the cold nuts and throwing them into their mouths to melt.[12]

Later in the novel the way in which Nwoye accepts Christianity is compared to the eating of the frozen nuts: "The words of the hymn were like the drops of frozen rain melting on the dry palate of the panting earth."[13]

Not only is poetic time marked by the continuity of an image such as that of food and water, but spatial time is marked by the moon's cycle or by the rhythm of the harvest or by market days. Unoka, who cared little for work or the acquisition of titles, "was very good on his flute, and his happiest moments were the two or three moons after the harvest when the village musicians brought down their instruments, hung above the fireplace."[14]

The depiction of Okonkwo's daughter Ezinma is based on the belief that she is an "ogbanje"—a spirit-child who does not grow to adulthood but visits and revisits its mother's womb in a cycle of births and deaths.

> At last Ezinma was born, and although ailing she seemed determined to live. At first Ekwefi accepted her, as she had accepted others—with listless resignation. But when she lived on to her fourth, fifth, and sixth years, love returned once more to her mother, and with love, anxiety. . . . Everybody knew she was an ogbanje. . . . Some of them did become tired of their evil rounds of birth and death, or took pity on their mothers, and stayed.[15]

Ezinma gladdens the heart of her father Okonkwo, although he continuously regrets her not having been a boy—a boy whom he could train to be strong in the ways of the clan, to be a warrior, to be the continuum of the clan. Regrets will turn into grief because the continuity of his family will be interrupted when his heir and eldest son Nwoye, snapping like a bow drawn too tight, turns his back on the customs and beliefs of his clan and accepts Christianity, for Christianity helps to bring about the falling apart of this well-ordered society. Okonkwo will mourn for his clan: "Okonkwo was deeply grieved. And it was not just a personal grief. He mourned for the clan, which he saw breaking up and falling apart, and he mourned for the warlike men of Umuofia, who had so unaccountably become soft like women."[16]

Okonkwo's actions are guided by two basic principles: a hatred of everything his father stood for and, unlike his father, a desire to become one of the lords of the clan. On a personal level his hatred of his father's weakness conditions his every gesture: "And so Okonkwo was ruled by one passion—to hate everything that his father Unoka had loved. One of those things was gentleness and another was idleness."[17] On the group level his sole intention is to become a dominant figure in Umuofia ("His life had been ruled by a great passion—to become one of the lords of the clan. That had been his lifespring."[18]) These two powerful drives merge together and become his operational weapons.

Because of his hatred of gentleness and fear of appearing weak he frequently explodes in fits of anger. He hides any feeling of tenderness for wife or children, and he runs the household with a harsh hand. Because of his unswerving determination to become a great lord of the clan he unflinchingly drives himself, toils hard, and shuns no exertion:

> Okonkwo was clearly cut out for the great things. He was still young but he had won fame as the greatest wrestler in the nine villages. He was a wealthy farmer and had two barns full of yams, and had just married his third wife. To crown it all he had taken two titles and had shown incredible prowess in two inter-tribal wars.[19]

He had all but achieved his aim to be great:

> Then everything had been broken. He had been cast out of his clan like a fish onto a dry, sandy beach, panting. Clearly his personal god or *chi* was not made for great things. A man could not rise beyond the destiny of his *chi*. The saying of the elders was not true—that if a man said yea his *chi* also affirmed. Here was a man whose *chi* said nay despite his own affirmation.[20]

His affirmation, however, had been an uncompromising and unswerving desire to always act the strong man. Yet his very act of strength in killing Ikemefuna seems to have brought with it retribution, that is, the accidental killing of the son of the man who had warned him not to take part in Ikemefuna's death. For this act Okonkwo will suffer seven years of exile, during which time a stranger arrives and men defecate in his house. Given the irascible nature of this strong man, it is obvious that the man who defiles his house, and by extension, his clan, will be severely punished.

The chain of circumstances that leads to Okonkwo's downfall thus has its beginning in Okonkwo's guiding principles. From the killing of Ikemefuna, he not only kills his legitimate son's will and spirit, but he is made to kill a son of the clan. The vital force not only of his family but of the whole clan is thus weakened. For this female crime, or "female ochu," he has been sent into exile for seven years during which time white missionaries and white administrators are establishing themselves in and around Umofia, destroying many ancient rituals and beliefs. The functional nature and the symbolic relationship of a seemingly irrelevant folk tale become apparent: ". . . how Sky withheld rain for seven years, until crops withered and the dead could not be buried because the hoes broke on the stony Earth."[21] Okonkwo, a strong man who at first thinks only of personal prowess, personal achievement, who shuns weakness or womanly qualities, and who exalts force, manliness, and power, finally sublimates his egotism through a grief that is climaxed by an act of strength and personal tragedy. On his return from exile he no longer mourns for himself, even though during the first part of the novel his eyes seemed to be focused more on himself and his personal achievements than on the clan which mirrored his ascendancy.

The clan is falling apart, the mirror is cracking. Okonkwo's reflection changes. The good old days are gone, the warriors are gone.

> Okudo sang a war song in a way that no other man could. He was not a fighter, but his voice turned every man into a lion. "Worthy men are no more," Okonkwo sighed as he remembered those days.[22]

Personal striving becomes a striving to recapture those good old days, even in the face of the outside threat—the arrival of the white man, his missionaries and his religion. But the cracked mirror falls to pieces and the reflected figure is obliterated. At this point of weakness the clan can be easily assailed by the white man's presence, and the ancestral mask and guardians can be exposed. Okonkwo, who is the embodiment of the clan, also is assailed. Yet even as he is threatened, his stature as a character rises. No longer is his striving a personal one; his actions, his desire to break the skull of the stranger who defecates in his house and who then builds his own house on the sacred grounds of the clan, now have as their only purpose the holding together of the clan. For he will attempt to help his ancestors cease their weeping by wiping out the abomination which has come to the clan: "All our gods are weeping. Idemili is weeping, Ogwuwu is weeping, Agbala is weeping, and all the others. Our dead fathers are weeping because of the shameful sacrilege they are suffering and the abomination we have all seen with our eyes."[23] His last defiant action will be to kill one of the court messengers who is in the service of the white man. But even this gesture is tragically ironic since at the point of killing the stranger Okonkwo realizes that Umuofia will not rise up to rid itself of the abomination. He realizes that things have indeed fallen apart. His final act of suicide gives the last ironic twist to Okonkwo's character. He will be called a great man; yet his act, a brave personal act, is one that in the context of the clan defiles the Earth goddess.

> Obierika, who had been gazing steadily at his friend's dangling body, turned suddenly to the District Commissioner and said ferociously: "That man was one of the greatest men in Umuofia. You drove him to kill himself; and now he will be buried like a dog . . ."[24]

. . .

Such a burial is the consequence of breakup; the consequence of alienation will be the burying of their men by lonely widows of the reserves.

Notes

1. Chinua Achebe, *Things Fall Apart* (New York: Mc-Dowell, Obolensky, 1959), pp. 202–203.

2–24. *Ibid:* 2. p. 63; 3. p. 64; 4. p. 7; 5. p. 69; 6. p. 69; 7. p. 31; 8. p. 75; 9. pp. 65–66; 10. p. 4; 11. p. 54; 12. pp. 134–135; 13. p. 152; 14. p. 5; 15. p. 83; 16. p. 189; 17. p. 15; 18. p. 135; 19. pp. 8–9; 20. p. 135; 21. p. 56; 22. p. 206; 23. p. 209; 24. p. 214.

THREE

ALIENATION AND
FLIGHT . . . APARTHEID

> Alone they bury their babies one by one and lastly their
> unknown lovers—their husbands, whose corpses alone are sent
> back to the Reserves.[1]

These lines from Phyllis Ntantala's essay, *Widows of the Reserves,* evoke the deep tragedy that has befallen native South
Africans. Pathos is effected merely through statement, for the
total situation of this land breeds the pathetic. In such circumstances, works of fiction need not rely upon highly imaginative
processes, for the outward features of South African reality
seem in themselves to be fiction; it is a reality that breeds the
solitude of which Phyllis Ntantala writes, a system which brings
about fear, degradation, disgust, anger—untold states of emotional upheaval—the combination of which produces a deep
sense of alienation. Men become strangers to their families, to
their homes, to their land: ". . . strangers in a strange land—
but equally strangers at home to their wives and children."[2]

It is not surprising, therefore, that the works treated in this
chapter on alienation are almost all South African.

There, native traditions have long been broken, shattered by
an imposed system. There, the rhythms of the Dark Child can

no longer be understood or felt; for symbolically, the huge, vast voices of the men are absent, and the harmonies are broken: "For now the women sing and dance alone, with but the aged men, the blind and the cripples to join in the dance and song, and all miss the rich deep bass chorus of the men."[3]

The process of movement away from the first certainties of the Dark Child continues. The sense of loss deepens. The literary and realistic dehumanization of peoples proceeds with monotonous inevitability. The realism is not shot through with historical analysis; rather it becomes a contemporary representation of immediate social situations wherein the writer is actor, moving through the total environmental presentation of his work of art. This total environment reflects and reacts to the total controlling system that prevails throughout South African life. It is a system that worms its way into the lives of all the inhabitants of that country, both black and white, a system "that has demoralized and dehumanized a whole people" with the result that "A black man in South Africa cannot forget."[4]

The recalling of the system, and its effect on the black man, bringing with it this overriding alienation, is the essential subject of the works under consideration. Two realities exist: a large, all-pervading, all-controlling outer society, which chokes and strangles an inner society. The play of the former on the latter and the total reactions of the latter constitute the essential elements of this chapter. The consequences of this interaction bring about the literary tensions in their various formulations and manifestations.

The larger world presented in the works treated is the white world, a world which operates within a political framework based on racial separation and inequality, the world of apartheid. This political monolith appears in various socioeconomic dimensions; it is reinforced by legal institutions whose executors are the police and whose tacit supporters are some of the middlemen—themselves natives—and the large majority of the white population. This larger society has a corrupting historical legacy, which the writers implicitly or directly blame for the alienation that dominates their works. The larger society is presented in two essential ways: directly, through statements of the authors and by implication, through impressionistic scenes. This larger society is omnipresent and pervades every segment of the inner, black world, by controlling, exploiting, and oppressing it. The larger world is the agent and the smaller, the object. Thus, all sensations, impressions, and reactions of the more numerous—but less powerful and therefore qualitatively smaller—world stem from and are controlled by the larger world.

It is important first to present the expressions of both groups and second to show their interaction within the works themselves. To be sure, given the complete and thorough mingling of relationships between the two groups, even under the system of apartheid, the presentation of the first part will embrace cause and effect—that is, the social institutions and the results and emotional effects of these institutions.

> I have learned that in South Africa the law is white, its legislative and executive authority is white . . . I have also learned that the law may be manipulated—by the process of the law, not to conform to principle—not only to protect the interests of the few, but to maintain and perpetuate them in positions of arbitrary authority.[5]

Here Bloke Modisane apprehends the nature of the legalized "democratic" institutions, which, even as they operate from a seemingly democratic process, result in a prefabrication of that very process. The due process of law perpetuates a basically unjust, illegal system that by its very nature creates the element against which all laws are promulgated—violence. By a converse application of justice, violence becomes a "given" in South Africa, and all the institutions of that country sanction this violence. Modisane puts it this way: "Violence exists in our day-to-day relationships, the expression of the public conscience; it is contained in the law, the instrument of maintaining law and order."[6]

In such circumstances, the Church seems to have defaulted from its societal position as director of the spiritual and moral well-being of the total community. The very fact that the Church continues to function as an institution means that the precepts on which Christianity is founded are being betrayed. It is not surprising, therefore, that many of the authors reject the Church as an institution, regarding it as yet another example of a distorted ethic, another support of a basically perverse social system.

Perhaps the fact that the 'greatest faith in the world' should have to be divested of its spiritual nobility and to be thus shaded with such fearful overtones, is probably the most un-Christian act of all. . . . By acceptance and association, the Christian Church in South Africa is white—its authority and symbols are white. . . . The Church has become a symbol of everything that is white in a country where white is the symbol of political domination and racial superiority.[7]

It is not surprising that the larger society exploits and seems, at times, to enslave the smaller society. Economic control is ensured by a brutal system of migratory labor, with all its consequent disruptive forces and suffering. In this literature, which is primarily situated in an urban complex, migrant workers, effectively controlled by Pass and Influx Laws, are brutalized even though they carry the work burden of the society. It is this system of economic exploitation that supports the white population and simultaneously enfeebles and ultimately destroys the blacks. ". . . The world of grinding machines has no use for men whose lungs are riddled with t.b. and miner's phthisis."[8]

Enfeeblement and destruction, however, may also result from imprisonment or from the brutality of the police. The police, who are the executors and carriers of the legally unjust social system, are a constant motif in all of this literature and are drawn by all of the authors with unsympathetic slashes. Curfews and raids, peremptory jailings and beatings, cold, truculent calculations and the use of weapons, make the police agents of the larger society, the hunters of the smaller society, which is sought out and destroyed like an animal. Thus, the police seem to control every gesture, every action, even every thought process of many of the characters. "The presence of the police beat upon me."[9] Phrases such as this abound, for during a time of protest marches which created solidarity "the police wanted them to ride and not walk, so that there should be no strength of will and so that they should be without a voice."[10]

And the little girl in *Chocolates for My Wife* . . . is surprised to find that a London policeman "isn't wearing handcuffs or revolvers, and . . . he's got such soft hands like he never has to catch people with them."[11] She had known only "men who wore their guns like appendages of their bodies and whose faces had the hard metallic look, and whose hearts and guts were merely valves and wires which operated robots."[12]

The cold, brutal police officer is the middleman between the white world and the black, the agent by means of which the corrupt society visits its brutality and oppression upon the native South Africans. And yet, the white civil element thus supported is presented in stark contradistinction to the hard, robot-like quality of its policemen. The white South African is almost invariably characterized as weak, flaccid, and intensely suspicious ("weak blue eyes peering through strong lenses"[13]) for the white man is, paradoxically, highly dependent upon and therefore often fearful of the black man:

> . . . they won't understand simple things like kaffirs swarming over our suburbs, living there, gambling there, breeding there, drinking there and sleeping there with their girls. They won't understand, these stupid fools, until the kaffirs enter their houses and boss them about and sleep with white girls. What's to happen to white civilization?[14]

Even those whites who are not presented as having this fear of being haunted by blacks, even those "liberal" whites who "know" the blacks, are ironically presented. A prime example of this appears in the story, "We'll Have Dinner at Eight," by Ezekiel Mphahlele. Here, the well-meaning white who professes to "know" the blacks, with whom she has been in contact in a supervisory capacity, cannot escape the tendency to cast them in stereotypes.

> She liked to say to her cronies, "My knowledge of the African . . ." or "after working with Africans for many years . . ." or "when I led a deputation to the Minister to ask him to instruct the police to be more considerate with Africans . . . all my life I've been working with Africans . . . So much more fun working with Blacks than Whites, anyhow. Too independent— that's the way with Whites."[15]

Few truly liberal whites appear in these works, and when they do, an all-pervasive stereotyping of one group by another is operative. Everyone is suspect and true feelings are not easily perceived. All members of the opposing group become faceless and become "they": the "they" who persecute or the "they" who fear. On the point of death after being shot by a police-man, Willieboy, one of the characters in A *Walk in the Night* by Alex La Guma, states with resigned impotence, "They's always kicking a poor bastard around."[16]

It is this sense of persecution, this sense of "they," that is reiterated and clearly reflected in statements such as the following, where the speaker can condone the stealing of a sheep by emphasizing the total exploitation which "they," the white world, have perpetrated.

> Do we not cut coal so that they become rich? Do we not build roads so that they can drive on them, while we must walk? Has not everything that they have been taken from us? You worry because we take this sheep. They have taken all from us—even our strength.[17]

In consequence, an apparently total fatigue and weariness possesses the young and a feeling of resigned sadness grips the old. Looking at his young countrymen who are like bewildered orphans, the old man can only exclaim, "The white people are troubling the children . . ."[18]

"They," however, are not only the whites. Often, the black policeman or attendant or simply the black man who is marginal to both groups, but in the employ of the larger, is even more brutal than the whites. In his role, where he attempts to cater to the establishment, he carries out his duties with alacrity and brutish force, with an inhumanity to his own kind. He, too, like the white "liberal"—indeed, like all the members of the society—is caught in the clutches of that society, despised by the whites and hated by the blacks. These men are often presented as dull, slow-witted, dumb oxen ("their faces dull and cow-like"[19]) who are goaded by a sense of inferiority to the white world into brutal action against their brothers, who ask, bewildered, "Why do you do this, brother? Why do you do this to your own people?"[20]

So far, we have presented some of the elements that go into the making of the larger group and some of the effects derived from the imposition of the larger group on the smaller. Since these works are written by black and Colored Africans, the emphasis and insistence will be on the world which they know best, that is, their own immediate milieu. This they will present in all its diversification: its unsavory outer material aspects, its corrosive and cramping emotional stresses, its atmosphere of abandonment and decay, all of which induce an immense alienation and compel a desire to flee. For the smaller society feels that the larger seeks its total absorption, seeks to suck its very marrow and matter. "They stood above me, all around, with large sharpened steel straws that they put to your head and the brain matter seeped up the straws like lemonade up a playful child's thirsty picnic straw."[21]

The smaller group, however, remains and perseveres in spite of the hostility of the larger group; it continues to survive, in spite of the decay and abandonment in which it lives. The authors all present as a "given" of the smaller group a total sense of the material and physical horror brought on by an ever-present, inimical exterior, omnipresent also in its hostile advances. Thus all elements of nature, of society, of man, seem to be enemies of the smaller group. We are given, then, a total realistic interpenetration of cause and effect and all of their extensions.

The realism is of two kinds: in the foreground are the lives of the characters and often of the authors themselves; at the same time, a realistic material presentation reveals the outward circumstances controlling these lives. The outward features are ugly, the lives often creatural. The presentation is a baroque compilation of unwholesome elements, a continous repetition of degrading incidents, to the point where the canvas becomes a total exposition of stark horror.

It is seldom, however, that the reader feels this horror, for even as a moral condemnation of the society that produced this animalism and ugliness is implicit in the realism, the realism is presented with an objective, literary intellectualism that fails to produce a subjective emotional involvement.

Let us examine, then, the outward circumstances and the lives of the smaller group: the apparent hostility, even of the elements, to the lives of this group; the poverty and decay in many of the living quarters; and the shabby communal gathering places of a low class of society. The examples cited come from the writings of Alex La Guma, whose narrative talent lies in the powerful construction and flowing movement of his depictions. In all of his scenes, the passage of time corresponds to the growth of decay, thereby producing works which in themselves have an inner dynamic flow. In his novel, *And a Three-fold Cord*, the total phenomena intermingle to produce saturated scenes wherein the lives of the poor are washed away. And yet, life always continues.

> The rain scrabbled at the side of a house, groping at a weak overlap, a loosened seam, found a hold and clung on, tugging and jerking, until rusty nails and bailing wire surrendered and the rain and the wind ripped away a great flap of tin and wood, and left the interior of the shanty exposed like the side of a shrapnel-sheared face, showing all the bloody convolutions of brain, ear and muscle which were drenched furniture, huddled people and slapping pieces of sacks. . . . The house groaned and winced in agony under the whip of the rain, and the floor sagged, but held on.[22]

The obvious motifs here are the hostility of the elements that, like the larger society, tear away at the lives of the natives. The motif of attack has an obvious progression, leading to the point of destruction. The movement is from the outer to the inner, from the exterior of the house to the interior of the bodies of its occupants. The houses are poor hovels where there are rusty nails and loose seams, and the people are exposed, huddled powerlessly together to offset the attack. Some of the houses are lifted and yet others persist, continuing to hold in spite of the destructive brutality of the rain.

A second scene, taken from *A Walk in the Night*, also by La Guma, shows not hostility and violent movement in a quick moment of time but rather the accumulation, over a period of years, of grease and dust and ash that blur the exterior of the tenement house which once had been dignified and almost beautiful. The corrosive power of time is presented in stages. At first, the "Victorian plaster around the wide doorway was chipped and broken and blackened with generations of grime." Then the anonymity and blurred grayness came about with the incessant movement of innumerable tenants.

> The floor of the entrance was flagged with white and black slabs in the pattern of a draught-board, but the tramp of untold feet and the accumulation of dust and grease and ash had blurred the squares so that now it had taken on the appearance of a kind of loathsome skin disease.

Final decay and decomposition ensue: "A row of dustbins lined one side of the entrance and exhaled the smell of rotten fruit, stale food, stagnant water and general decay."[23] In addition, the social gathering places are stained and chipped with "ancient strips of flypaper." It is in such a place that the down-and-out, the wrecks, the bums, the homeless, and the petty-criminal elements of the underworld gather. In his description of the café, the author gives us a select presentation of the random pursuits and the variety of livelihoods of many communities in South African townships.

The outward material circumstances are reflected in the physiognomies of the characters, which are also broken and chipped. Indeed, in some stories and novels, the features of the people are unattractive, and even where some handsome quality might have existed, it is distorted by anger, suffering, or uncomprehending pain. Many features reflect the drift and vagrancy, the uselessness of the lives of the people. Joe, in *A Walk in the Night* is described:

> [He] was short and his face had an ageless quality about it under the grime, like something valuable forgotten in a junk shop. He had the soft brown eyes of a dog and he smelled of a mixture of sweat, slept-in clothes and seaweed. . . . His shoes were worn beyond recognition.[24]

Some of the faces reflect the criminality of the characters' intention. Again, in *A Walk in the Night*:

> Willieboy was young and dark and wore his kinky hair brushed into a point above his forehead. He wore a sportscoat over a yellow T-shirt and a crucifix around his neck, more as a flamboyant decoration than as an act of religious devotion. He had yellowish eyeballs and big white teeth and an air of nonchalance, like the outward visible sign of his distorted pride in the terms he had served in a reformatory and once in prison for assault.[25]

Still other faces reveal the distortion of actual physical crippling —almost invariably as a result of police brutality:

> Lopsided body . . . Pathetic, beautiful lips . . . Steady eyes, almost expressionless. The paralyzed flank of his body looked

as if it might curve in any moment and bring flesh and bones down to the ground in dismantled pieces.[26]

Some characters are worn and calloused from simple hard work: "hands . . . muscular, with ridges of vein, the nails . . . rimmed with black from handling machine oil and grease . . . the palms . . . pink with tiny ridges of yellow-white calluses."[27] And finally, there are those characters who are simply abandoned wrecks.

> The purple-veined, greyish skin had loosened all over . . . and sagged in blotched, puffy folds. With his sagging lower eyelids, revealing bloodshot rims, and the big, bulbous, red-veined nose that had once been aquiline, his face had the expression of a decrepit bloodhound. His head was almost bald, and wisps of dirty grey hair clung to the bony, pinkish skull like scrub clinging to eroded rock.[28]

It is among such people that many of the short stories and novels are set—except, perhaps, for such works as *Chocolates for My Wife, Slices of My Life* and *Road to Ghana,* where emphasis is placed on a professional middle class, which nonetheless is subjected to that total pressure, that ever-present pall, —the larger society. Even where material circumstances are not palpably oppressive, where members of the smaller society are professionals, the larger society still is inescapable, exercising a pervasive and corrosive psychological hold. Thus, almost all emotional and mental attitudes of the smaller society are reactions to the larger.

Many of the characters seem continually to be haunted by fear of being beaten, being jailed, being brutalized, to the extent where they are almost paralyzed by it. Fear in its various forms runs throughout the works. Indeed, in the personal narrative, *Road to Ghana,* the narrator's every mood, every reaction, is one of dread. Having suffered imprisonment for protest action and all that goes with long hours of treason trials, his instinctive reaction becomes one of apprehension, of shrinking backward. The immanence of fear brings on cowardice, which leads to irresolution and inaction.

Fear, resignation, hopelessness: these contiguous emotions are constant motifs in this literature (though other motifs that differ, and are antithetical to fear and resignation, are also present). Perhaps anger and criminality, with their ensuing violence, stem from and arise out of fear and hopeless resignation. Or perhaps they are the end result of a deep frustration that grips so many of the characters. Frustration comes from active resignation, frustration being active and resignation, passive. Criminality and violence are the active components of hopelessness and fear. In their search for some form of conscious being in a totally negative society, many characters strike out blindly, even when afraid, thereby gaining some form of identity through action. Thus, the gratuitous criminal action is everywhere present in this body of literature.

Indeed, it may be said that criminality and amorality become the ethic of this society. Many stories are structured around criminal action. There is no judgment by the authors, no moral condemnation. There seems only to be an acceptance of a fact of life. In a society where one group is faceless, a criminal action gives corporate stature to anyone who has the courage to perpetrate it. Performance and other people's knowledge of the action are essential, to the point where Michael Adonis in *A Walk in the Night*, having accidentally and gratuitously committed a crime, feels equal and indeed superior to the gangsters who walk throughout the night. Though he has achieved identity inwardly, he ironically cannot display or make apparent this new criminal accomplishment.

Criminal actions, such as petty thievery, are also linked to a desire for an identity of a different sort. At times the criminal action is motivated by a desire to gain the outward accouterments, the trappings and material possessions of the larger society. This search for identification through criminality, this quest for otherness, is the highest point of alienation experienced by the characters. To be other, to want to identify with the group which oppresses and which is hated, is certainly one of the most paradoxical effects of the play of the larger society upon the smaller.

This desire for otherness has as its corollary a sense of nonbelonging, a sense of rootlessness, which is everywhere present in the works under consideration. In all of these, the sense of nonbelonging, so common to many of the characters, caught up as they are by fear, resignation, frustration, and gratuitous criminality, creates a total atmosphere wherein a man is essentially alienated from himself, from the larger group, and from the total society.

Yet the single man can be saved from this total alienation. This can be achieved by a shared participation, by communal action, by that communicity which music and song evoke, which resistance to oppression fortifies. Often, survival seems possible only through communal action.

Two are better than one; because they have a good reward for their labor.

For if they fall, the one will lift up his fellow: but woe to him that is alone when he falleth; for he hath not another to help him up.

Again, if two lie together, then they have heat, but how can one be warm alone?

And if one prevail against him, two shall withstand him; and a threefold cord is not quickly broken.[29]

At times, however, the cord may be broken, as the larger society stamps itself on the smaller, as individuals of the smaller are brutalized, and as the community is uprooted.

It is the play of the larger on the smaller and the analysis of all of the motifs outlined above, together with an examination of the style in which this play is presented, that will form the basis of our exploration of these stories and novels. We will attempt to show the insistent feeling of alienation that enshrouds the various types and characters. In the short stories selected, the development will follow an ever-increasing interaction between the larger and the smaller groups, eventually effecting a sense of strength through the communal. In the first group of stories, the larger group—the white world—is a point of reference, always and ever present, controlling and goading reactions that ultimately end in alienation from self, from group, or in that larger alienation—death.

Perhaps "Resurrection," by Richard Rive, best exemplifies the bitterness and total horror brought about by the racial policies of South Africa. "Resurrection" is a story of the unrelieved hatred, and the expression of that hatred, by a dark-skinned daughter for her mother who is black but who has spawned other, fair-complexioned children. Hatred consumes the daughter, Mavis, who has been rejected by the rest of her family and who blames her mother for having made her black, for the complete rejection that they both experience. The mother had suffered life-long relegation to the kitchen along with her dark-skinned friends. Even now during her funeral they are separated from the family's Colored or white relatives and friends. The story line lapses momentarily and is enacted through Mavis' thought processes; they flash back, revealing the total emotional relationship that had existed between mother and daughter and the present relationship between Mavis, her mother's corpse, and the mourners. Mavis' hatred had been naked, venemous, and sadistic. Her mother's reactions, on the other hand, had been those of uncomprehending bewilderment, momentary flashes of maternal sympathy, and steadfast resignation, which derived strength from the memory of her childhood and the land of her upbringing.

The material circumstances of the story exude a sense of decay. The physical features of the people, grotesquely caricatured by the author, give off a derisive, distorted image.

> Only Mavis sat silent, staring at her hands and noticing that the left thumbnail was scarred and broken . . . the room was overcrowded, overbearingly overcrowded. Hot, stuffy, crammed, overflowing . . . the priest from Dadda's church stood at the head of the coffin, sharp and thin, clutching his cassock.[30]

And the mother's friends, the black people, "sat in the kitchen, a cowering, timid group around the fire.[31]

The irony of the story lies in the life to which Mavis aspires, the life led by her "white" sister and brothers, which is far from desirable. Yet it is the very wanting of this kind of life that brings on Mavis' bitterness. The ridiculous is further underscored by the author's juxtaposition of the real and the fanciful, the mourners' scornful rejection of the mother when she was alive and the trumpery of their grief.

The play of Mavis' deep emotions and the superficial hypocrisy of the mourners, the interaction of past and present reactions, evoke the pathetic as well as the ridiculous, blending dark tones with light ones and ending in the resurrection of the mother, whose strength in death flows into her daughter. Only now can Mavis shout out the hypocrisy and the lies of the Colored and white mourners. The end of the story echoes the emotional reverberations that had tensely and angrily vibrated in Mavis.

The second story to be treated, "Echoes," by Alf Wannenburgh, also reverberates—but in this instance, with a shot that kills a native mine worker on his way home from the city. The pathos of this story is softer, less vibrant than that of "Resurrection," receiving the overtones from the land, rather than from a societal situation. There is irony in the story. Of the three men who are homeward bound after having narrowly escaped death in a mine disaster because of the carelessness of the white man, the one who has most completely preserved his ties to his home, his land, and his family, who has been the least corrupted by the immorality of the city, is the one who undergoes final alienation in death. To steal a sheep seems wrong to him, even though his two companions, who have learned to use the very weapon of the larger group, the "other," validate the stealing by citing the prostitution and the exploitation of the blacks by the whites.

In this story, "they" are always present and in fact bring about the denouement of the story, which seems a tragic pastorale, the interruption of a beautiful homecoming. In "Out of Darkness," by Alex La Guma, a similar pastorale or love relationship comes to an end through the tragic act of criminality. Again, the end is brought on by the encroaching societal values that are based on color lines. Here "they" represent the constant intrusion of a presence for whom the jailed protagonist, the perpetrator of the act of violence, the lover, is waiting. His alienation from society is a derangement brought on by his loss of love and by his killing of a friend who had informed him that his loved one had left him for another who is lighter-skinned. In this deranged state, he continually awaits Joey, the friend whom he has murdered, and also awaits his own death, for he is fast decaying in the filth, the stench, and the darkness.

In an accumulation of detail, La Guma not only captures the decay of the prison but also presents us with a useless, tucked-away individual—broken, creatural, and decrepit. Phrases such as these abound: "the dim shapeless bulge of his body curled up on the mat . . . neither staring mad nor violent . . . he was clamped up tight and retired, like a snail withdrawn into its shell."[32]

In all three stories, simple human events such as birth, love, and a return home become incidents because of the ever-present encroachment of "they" upon the smaller group. In "Resurrection" and "Out of Darkness," the incidence of color and its interrelationships are the motivating forces for hatred and anger in one instance and for criminal action, leading to mental derangement and imprisonment, in another. In "Echoes," there is simple presentation of the incident, of the total disregard of one man for another, of the white man for the native.

In the stories "The Park," by James Matthews, and "The Master of Doornvlei," by Ezekiel Mphahlele, another element is introduced: the white man exists not only as a foil or a symbol but as a distinct personality. In "The Park," the whites appear not as inhuman perpetrators of evil but as carelessly oblivious observers of the natives and their living conditions. They have absolutely no desire or interest in concerning themselves with blacks, but neither do they regard these blacks with active malice or hatred. In "The Master of Doornvlei," Sarel Britz, the white man, plays an active and vigorous part in the story. He is at once fearful and contemptuous of the tenant laborers on his farm, both sensitive and blind to the natives' needs and desires. But above all, he prides himself on his "knowledge" of and "decency" toward the blacks, while he simultaneously becomes more and more dependent upon them.

> He leant more and more on his foreman, who realized it and made the most of it. . . . Britz had discussed . . . his father's theory about allowing the Black man a few rungs to climb up at a time, because he was still a child. Most of his colleagues had laughed at this. Gradually he accepted their line of thinking: the White man must be vigilant.[33]

The white man's counterpart in these stories, his link to the world of the natives, is the middleman, the black who has made his peace with the way things are, who attempts to ingratiate himself with the larger society by becoming the agent of its brutality toward the smaller. This man is perhaps the most alienated of all the characters who appear in these works. He is nowhere at home, despised by whites and blacks alike. Because of his peculiar position, he is unable to come to terms with either side, unable to identify with either.

In a number of stories, however, members of opposing groups do attempt, at times, to come to terms with one another, albeit through accepting the misconceptions of the stereotype. In such instances, it is the inability to free oneself from the suspicion of the "other" that brings about still further stereotyping, increasing suspicion and rejection or even the perpetration of violence on the other. Therefore, confrontation of the groups brings about conflicts which often end in violence. The suspicion in one group of another is well demonstrated in the following excerpt from the story, "The Living and the Dead":

> "They keep letters there many months, baas, and no-one comes for them." His tone suggested that Stoffel should surely know that.
> *The cheek he has, finding fault with the way the white man does things.*
> "You lie! You wanted to open it first to see what's inside. When you found no money you sealed it up and were afraid your boss would find out you had opened it. Not true?"
> "It's not true, baas, I was going to bring it here whatever happened."
> He fixed his eyes on the letter in Stoffel's hand. "Truth's God, baas," Lebona said, happy to be able to lie to someone who had no way of divining the truth, thinking at the same time: *they're not even decent enough to suspect one's telling the truth!*
> *They always lie to you when you're white*, Stoffel thought, *just for cheek.*
> The more Lebona thought he was performing a just duty, the more annoyed the white man was becoming.[34]

"The Living and the Dead" is essentially a statement of the white men's fears of the possible social uprising of the blacks. It vividly demonstrates the lack of knowledge of one social group about the other in South Africa and the defenses that both groups set up.

It is this not-knowing, accompanied by the curiosity to know and to share, that is the motivating force for the story, "Debut," by Alf Wannenburgh. Here the white man, the boss, has invited himself to his native employee's home for a party. The black guests immediately stereotype him as a white "baas," and in spite of his good intentions, the white man is excluded from the party, becomes intoxicated, and behaves quite shamefully (that is, for a white man). The disdain of the blacks is summed up in the phrase of a member of the party: "these whites always got to show off!"[35]

The white man is not entirely innocent, however. He has brought to the party many preconceptions about the blacks; and because of his inbred inability to react naturally to a new situation, he jeopardizes his chances for entry into that situation and arouses the equally inbred stereotyping instincts of the blacks. Again, "Debut" is a story of statement, which, like its counterpart, "The Party," by James Matthews, presents the play of stereotype on behavior.

In "The Party," members of the opposing groups (blacks and whites) find themselves in a social situation where they are forced to visit with one another and interact on a superficial, but polite, level. Again, preconceived notions are reinforced on both sides of the color line, and stereotypes replace reality in the minds of the whites and the blacks alike. In this story we are introduced to a wide spectrum of types: there is the "liberal" white, overanxious to demonstrate his open-mindedness; the typical black middleman, willing to go to all ends in order to ingratiate himself with the whites; and a friend of this man, a former admirer of his who ultimately rejects the sham and hypocrisy of the "liberal" whites but who, in so doing, also falls prey to the tendency to stereotype, even as he has been stereotyped. Thus, he is unable to sense the real liberalism of one of the white women at the party. In rejecting his middle man friend for his studied ability to move easily among the whites, he rejects all whites as well.

In "Debut" and "The Party" the superficial, peripheral relationships between groups are always coated with suspicion. In "The Party," the end result of interaction between the groups is the destruction of a friendship between two men and the angry departure of one from the party:

His anger brought a flood of blood to his head, making speech impossible as he glared at Ron. He got up from the couch and blindly pushed his way through the animated throng, not aware of the approval evident in Margo Pearce's eyes.[36]

Margo is a white woman who has genuine regard for the young man and not for his friend. But the boy's suspicion of the motives of white extends to her, as well.

It is this very suspicion that swells and hardens into a vicious act of murder in the story, "We'll Have Dinner at Eight." Here, the crippled figure of Mzondi, a native boy, festers not only with suspicion but also with memories of having been shot and permanently deformed by a white policeman. His crippled figure evokes the protective feelings and inquisitive sympathy of a white do-gooder who finally persuades him to visit her at home, in spite of the prevailing Immorality Laws. The story is really the play of the ever-increasing inner brooding of the suspicious cripple and of the thoughts and stereotyped actions of the "liberal" woman. The play ends in the cripple's brutal murder of the woman. The act of murder releases the pent-up fury and anger of the black man and gives him a sense of self, a feeling of accomplishment, however short-lived.

Thus, release from frustration and anger comes through a criminal action. As we previously noted, criminality is accepted as a natural part of human events. Therefore, the story "Nocturne," by Alex La Guma, which is posited on the planning of a criminal action, makes no moral judgment about the act but rather shows how the natural event (the robbery) is suspended by an aesthetic experience. One of the criminals hears music being played by an ethereal, other-worldly young woman, briefly enters the mood of the music and remains momentarily suspended in an aesthetic hiatus from his criminal intent.

This suspension of the everyday through the act of listening to music and the possibility of the release of anger through a criminal act go into the making of the story "The Portable Radio," by James Matthews. Here there is another element, however: the seeking for otherness through the great need to possess the material prerequisites of the richer, larger, outer society, the white world. The protagonist here is not physically crippled, but he is completely outside the society—jobless,

friendless, and completely alienated. The purchase of a portable radio with money he accidentally finds gives him a sense of
self, brings him into contact with society through its music. He
can float along and identify with a song; he can touch a button
and command many and varied voices. But here too, a life of
poverty, rooted in decay and filth, circumscribes and effectively
limits his enjoyment. His aunt, who is not asocial, considers
work a necessary part of life and can not understand the vicari-
ous pleasure her nephew derives from this escape into otherness. This story, too, ends on an impending criminal act, the
killing of the aunt by the nephew, an act that will offer momentary release from the cruelty of society.

This society breeds criminality and immorality by impos-
ing its Immorality Laws and un-Christian social concepts in an
atmosphere of oppression, distress, and brutality. And so the
young woman in "Slipper Satin," by Alex La Guma, who has
been jailed for an act considered immoral in the society of
whites and those blacks who have accepted the ethical standards of whites, who has had a love affair with a white man,
accepts the verdict imposed upon her by both groups: that she is
a loose woman, a whore. As a result, she is alienated from both
the larger and the smaller, the black and the white, elements of
society. Her acceptance becomes a beautiful act of generosity,
for eventually she uses her body to acquire a dress for her
younger sister who is about to be married. The dress in this
story can be equated with the portable radio in the preceding
one. It is a material prerequisite, an acquisition giving a certain
middle-class stature to the indigent.

Even within a society founded on immoral standards, a
"criminal" act alienates the perpetrator from the group and
from society. The society breeds suspicion, and suspicion, by its
very nature, prohibits genuine intercourse and forestalls deep
relationships, hindering a sense of community. Thus, suspicion
also brings about alienation. Displays of fear and anger which
stem from a feeling of having been rejected, only increase that
sense of exclusion. Here, too, many of the characters in the
stories become alienated from a group or groups by their very
emotional reactions. Thus, a solution offered by some of the
authors lies in communal action, in a shared suffering and in-
justice.

These are the elements prevailing in two of the short stories,

"Azikwelwa," by James Matthews, and "Awendgesang," by Alf Wannenburgh. The dominant chords are these:

> Looking at her and with the people swarming around him, Jonathan felt a surge of love sweeping through his body and he raised his mug to the woman.
> "Azikwelwa! My sister," he said.[37]

> There is no promised land for us alone, and we cannot find it alone. Things are changing. But if we stand together and show these others that we shall not be moved from our plan, then there must be a day when they will join us and together with them we shall make this the Promised Land.[38]

Destruction of Individuals in South African Society

The two novels by Alex La Guma, *A Walk in the Night* and *And a Threefold Cord*, are enlargements of two principal motifs already discussed: criminality and communality. The walk that takes Michael Adonis through the night leads him relentlessly and unswervingly toward a life of crime. The hand that leads him is the hand of society, the police hand that searches him, his own hand that commits a gratuitous criminal action, and finally, the hand of the gangster who also walks through the night like a vulture, waiting for the societal carrion, which Michael Adonis becomes. The criminal element appears at every turn in the book.

The second novel, *And a Threefold Cord*, describes the destruction of members of the Pauls family, the chief protagonists of the story. But here the compassionate, easy-going character Charlie Pauls is able to withstand tragedy after tragedy for his burden is lightened by the communicity already noted. The reiteration of the message is that "people can't stand up to the world alone, they got to be together."[39]

Since the naturalistic prescription for survival in the South African society is not the same in both of La Guma's novels, the basic treatment of the works also differs. To be sure, the books have many stylistic similarities in their detailed use of minute description, capturing all of the tiny essentials of each scene. Even in a larger sense, the books have structural similarity in that the outward action in both novels takes place along a short strip of asphalt road. Yet the lives led by the people along these roads, the nature of the communities, the treatment of temporality, and the descriptions of phenomena, are divergent and veer away from one another.

The scene of *A Walk in the Night* is District Six, an urban area in South Africa where life is multifarious, quick-moving, and blotched. It is an assorted jumble of lights that are hard blue and dirty yellow, of harsh noises, of smells of decay, of thick-layered grime that is the deposit of useless lives. Dinginess has set in. The characters live in fetid, decaying tenements. Their hangout is a café where fly-studded strips of flypaper drip down over the habitués, and the plates are chipped, even as the customers are chipped, cracked, and soiled. The floor is coffee-stained and the characters, too, seem stained. Time is recorded by the waxing and waning of daylight and the ever-decreasing crowds in the streets.

In *And a Threefold Cord*, the characters are not cracked and stained as much as beaten by life and by the elements. They are not a random assortment of people who walk through the night. There are no tenement houses here; rather, there are run-down, squalid shacks, pressed together by the hostility of the outside environment. Time is marked not by the dimming of lights or the lessening of crowds but by the constant, inimical falling rain, which tears away at the shacks and at the lives of the people. We do not see the happenings of one single night as in *A Walk in the Night*, where emotion and anger lead to criminality in one character. We see instead the playing-out of the lives of a whole family: the death of the head of the household and the birth of a grandchild.

To be sure, in *A Walk in the Night* many total existences are quickly unfolded for us through the process of flash back. But we are not presented with the crescendo of a single emotion, eventually erupting into action and reaction. Yet the characters are individuals who have no real connection with one another, whereas in *And a Threefold Cord*, the characters are members of one family whose fortunes are pursued throughout the novel.

Again, in *A Walk in the Night* it is the social phenomena that interplay and release descriptions. In *And a Threefold Cord* a larger world is embraced, and human, social, physical, and elemental phenomena are all brought into the picture. There is a complete interplay of all of the natural forces that affect men's lives. Naturally, the societal dimension looms large, as it does in almost every work of South African fiction. The police and the outer world are omnipresent, affecting the characters, leading to the denouement in *A Walk in the Night* and offering a structural link in *And a Threefold Cord*.

In *A Walk in the Night* the outer world, the larger society, is the cause of Michael Adonis' seething and blinding anger. He has once again been fired from his job. He has attempted to live as a societal creature but has been thwarted in his efforts by the hostility of his white employers. His anger is further increased by an act from the outer world, the wanton search of his person by two white policemen. His frustration and anger against the white world finally explodes in a gratuitous, unpremeditated act of violence against a poor white derelict whose skull he bashes in with a wine bottle. His criminal action gives him a feeling of belonging at last, and he enters the world of the gangsters. In addition, the outer world, represented by the white policeman, is the one which kills the antisocietal character, Willieboy. He refuses to work because, after all, "where does it get you?" when he knows, "Always there's somebody to kick you around."[40] He refuses to play the game of society. Willieboy has lived his entire life in asocietal alienation, and he undergoes final, total alienation when he is hunted down and shot by the force or rule of law, by the larger society, which had brought about his original alienation.

Thus it is that the outer world of the whites plays a powerful and direct part in the novel, *A Walk in the Night*. It controls the destinies of the chief protagonists and controls the very movement of District Six, their immediate environment. Here, the police are the hunters. Often corrupt, brazen, and unprofessional, they exercise an unremitting control over the native living areas. Perhaps yet another difference between *A Walk in the Night* and *And a Threefold Cord* is that the former explores, to some extent, the human elements delineating, and yet further distorting, the characters of the two police officers:

> There was a girl in the town who he liked very much, and to whom he now wrote occasional letters. He had not decided whether he was in love with her, for he considered himself a very serious young man and did not wish to fling himself headlong into marriage unless he was absolutely sure.[41]

Raalt had been thinking morosely about his wife again and the sight of the crowd pleased him a little with its relief from his gnawing thoughts.[42]

In this instance, the police are not portrayed as monolithic stereotypes. Rather, they are two distinct individuals, members of the same racial group who have been haphazardly thrown together and are basically antagonistic toward one another. The older one, the leader, is Raalt. He thinks only of unleashing his pent-up anger against the blacks and carelessly allows his shot victim to die while he indolently goes off to buy a package of cigarettes. The other police officer is a young constable, totally imbued with his superiority of stock vis-à-vis the natives and abjectly concerned about Raalt's destruction of the white man's image before the blacks.

In *And a Threefold Cord* there is no such differentiation in the portrayal of the police. Here they act as a unit: the whites and the middlemen, the black police, act as one monolithic group. They come in the night, rip things apart, and leave again. The structure of the last section of the novel is a series of vignettes that depict various members of the Pauls family as the police investigate their township, ferreting out and raiding their dwelling places.

The group of policemen comes upon the very dismal scene of the Pauls' daughter, Caroline, in childbirth as she is assisted by her mother and a neighbor, whose ministrations are crude but practiced. Another contingent of policemen barges into one of the shacks, oblivious to all who live there, intent only upon checking for papers, hoping to find the narcotics which they suppose to be hidden there. They find Charlie Pauls in the home of his girl friend, Freda, whom they accuse of being a "black whore." And Charlie's brother, Ronald, is apprehended in the act of murdering Suzy, a girl who has been unfaithful to him. Finally, there is a scene in which the police have rounded up some of the Pauls' neighbors and friends, and Charlie, in an impulsive but completely gratuitous act, unleashes his long-smoldering anger and knocks down one of the policemen. Thus, the police officers become a device, similar to that of the street in *A Walk in the Night*, through which the author presents a series of short scenes, yet another view of the already familiar characters.

Although the police are actively present in *And a Threefold Cord*, they do not seem to influence the lives of the people of the community. They are simply one more, among the many hostile forces that burden and overwhelm the characters to the point where time stands still, and the life cycle is the only point of continuity. Birth, a life of desolation, and death—these are the only sure events, the only points of reference.

In *A Walk in the Night*, however, time does pass, things happen, individuals change, and there is a structural dynamic in the novel. It is not simply, as *And a Threefold Cord*, a series of canvases depicting the lives of one family and its community at different stages of life. Rather, there is a sense of the possibility of change, of movement through criminality. Yet both novels exude the hopelessness of both continuity and change, of the linear progression in individual lives, or in the unbroken cycle of the community.

The characters in *A Walk in the Night* are all reflections of the milieu, reactions to the circumstances of the society. None of them possesses individual emotional idiosyncrasies. A quick glance at the people who walk through the night is all that is needed to see the characters and their societal dimensions. Perhaps the overwhelming presence of the white society prevents the development of the idiosyncratic, the individualistic. Many of the characters in South African fiction are reactions and not primary agents, resultant states, not operative forces.

Michael Adonis has no given characteristics. We know that he would like a good, steady job, someone "with soft hair you can run your hands through" who will "have your diet ready" every night.[43] We may have glimpsed a certain generosity in his friendship with Joe, the derelict (who is yet another happening and whose figure also awakens our sympathy), but we know nothing of Michael Adonis' emotional or intellectual qualities. The totality of his character is the ripening and festering of his anger, derived from his rejection by society.

Willieboy's antisocial attitudes are a result of his brutal upbringing and the harshness of the society around him. He is a resultant condition, with a philosophy of life that stems from this society. His insouciance, his assumed disregard for social ethics, make him an object of envy for Michael Adonis. Yet both are completely alienated. Michael Adonis is friendless; of his family we know nothing. Willieboy's harsh upbringing arouses our sympathy, and that of a whore who knew him as a boy. But he too lacks affection, is friendless, and when he is dying after having been shot by Constable Raalt, he can only recall the drunken brutality of his father and the lack of concern of his mother, both of whom appear to him in his painful delirium.

> His father's leather belt crashed against the sides of the van and snapped through the air, its sharp edge ripping at his legs and buttocks, the pain jumping through him. . . . Once his mother woke up and turning her head shouted at him to stop complaining.[44]

The mother and the father in *And a Threefold Cord* are quite different from Willieboy's parents, for in *And a Threefold Cord*, the family unit is intact at the beginning of the novel. Of course, Dad Pauls is very ill, Caroline is with child, Ronald is petulant and an angry, truculent young man. Yet Ma Pauls is strong and resistant, and by her hard toil, she manages to keep the family together, above water and relatively happy. Charlie, too, is a good person—sweet-natured, optimistic, kind, and jovial. The characterization in this novel differs from that of *A Walk in the Night* in that the qualities of the protagonists are directly and at times shrewdly delineated for us. The characters' relations to the community sustain them or bring about their downfall.

To be sure, the society of the whites exercises a total control over the life of the black community in *And a Threefold Cord*, yet all of the characters have their peculiar idiosyncrasies— even if these may have been adopted as defense mechanisms against the society. Perhaps Charlie's optimism is his way of expressing an inner strength, of resisting his complete ruin, of suppressing the rage that controls the gestures and thoughts of his younger brother, Ronald. Dad Pauls has worked hard and dies as a broken, pathetic man; nevertheless, he ends his life respectably.

> He just lived and worked and didn't do nothing that was wrong in the eyes of the Lord. He worked for his family and when he couldn't work no more, he lay down and waited for the Lord Jesus to take him away.[45]

Ma Pauls' evident faith in the essential goodness of the Lord gives her the strength to continue in the face of the inimical, tragic circumstances of her life.

What happens to the characters at the end of *And a Three-fold Cord* seems to result from their own attitudes to life. For instance, Ronald will kill the flirtatious coquette for whom he has had a jealous passion, and the good-natured Charlie will marry Freda, for whom he has had a long and unexpressed liking. Freda, like Ma Pauls, is industrious, virtuous, and very womanly; she shares Charlie's optimism toward life, in spite of the fact that she is essentially a tragic figure, having lost first her husband and later all of her children, in terrible accidents.

And a Threefold Cord proceeds by introducing its characters in a series of scenes. We are given their family relationships, their idiosyncratic gestures toward one another and toward members of the community. Then we see them playing out their roles opposite those with whom they have relationships or rapport, after which we are shown the results of these relationships, results brought about partly by society and partly by their own inner qualities.

This does not apply, however, to all of the characters in the novel. Some are simply living statements of alienation. There are, for instance, George Mostert and Roman.

> A common labourer, Roman had drifted from one mean job to another, earning a few shillings here, a few shillings there. Finally, despairing, perhaps, about the upkeep of his offspring, he took to petty thieving, robbing the weaker ones around him. Now and then he robbed out of bounds, and found himself in jail.[46]

> Life was there, no matter how shabby, a few yards from George Mostert's Service Station and Garage, but he was trapped in his glass office by his own loneliness and a wretched pride in a false racial superiority, the cracked embattlements of his world.[47]

La Guma's vision of society is demonstrated through his imagery, which he spins throughout his novels. In this he is masterful, as he relays the various levels and layers of meaning by the differing and distinctive intonations which resonate from his images. He picks up smells and sounds; he endows the visual with incisive action. The pace of A Walk in the Night is quickened by verbs of movement. Its tone is made hard and flat by the use of words without curves, which conjure images of harshness. La Guma is a master of atmosphere, his words creating moods that presage the occurrences in his novels. For example, a murder in A Walk in the Night is presaged by indications of death:

> The room was hot and airless as a newly-opened tomb . . . [the old man] was a deserted, abandoned ruin, destroyed by alcohol . . . and waiting for death, trapped at the top of an old tenement, after the sweep of human affairs had passed over him and left him broken and helpless as wreckage disintegrating on a hostile beach.[48]

The sense of the latent and evident hostility in the society is everywhere present in the imagery of And a Threefold Cord. Everything seems to be embattled; everywhere, the destructive images of war-torn scenes are presented in their stark materiality. Thus, such words and phrases abound: "a chin as curved and hard as the toe of an army boot . . . the morning was sneaking carefully past the sentries of drizzle . . . Overhead the sky erected its fortresses of granite-grey clouds . . ."[49]

Creatural images of decay such as creeping insects abound in A Walk in the Night. In And a Threefold Cord, images of animal bestiality cut through the pages of the novel; even as the outside world is embattled, many physical features and characteristics are canine:

> The rest of the group slithered and shuffled in the mud, watching with the sharp, alert eyes of crows. Everybody felt Roman had to fight. It was like a mongrel snarling over a bitch against a rival.[50]

> A smeared mouth smiled up at him, showing a gap in her upper gum, flanked by small, yellow canines, like the fangs of a puppy.[51]

In this world of the poor and bewildered presented by La Guma, no escape is possible. In the lives of slush and slime there is solace only in communality. And so, even the slushy pools of water along the road, formerly separated puddles, are linked together at the end of the book, forming a cord. There is no escape: these people cannot, like Alfred Hutchinson and Todd Matshikiza, flee to Ghana or to England.

Individuals in Exile

In the two novels just treated, the material effects of the social circumstances of South Africa are evident in the day-to-day existence of the characters. The next novels, the novels of exile, *Road to Ghana* and *Chocolates for My Wife, Slices of My Life*, deal essentially with the dilemmas facing middle-class, professional South African natives. It is not their daily life that is the most affected. Rather the concern here is with the psychological omnipresence of domination. Even physical movement away from the scene of domination cannot obliterate the constantly controlling presence from the minds of the protagonists. Even after they have physically escaped from South Africa, their reflexes are so conditioned that they react as though they were still under the oppressor's heel.

It must be stressed, however, that in these novels, the characters are uniformly of the professional, intellectual, middle class, with enough standing in the community to take part in treasonable associations, to have as their friends and associates professional people of all races, to move with a certain amount of ease through the controlling legal forces. Yet in spite of it all, the hold that South African social forces exerts on them is again and again demonstrated and becomes a variation on a single motif. In this respect, the domination is not materialistic and seemingly total, as in the La Guma novels and most of the short stories.

Even men of training and some talent, however, are unable to free themselves from the omnipresence of domination. This domination must, indeed, be of a binding and pervasive nature. The protagonists of the novels of exile are beset by fear: fear of police, fear of summary arrest and incarceration, and fear, too, of demonstrating any sign of weakness when exposed to brutality. Both *Road to Ghana* and *Chocolates for My Wife . . .* present movement away from an unhealthy social situation.

Road to Ghana is a statement of the problems encountered

in attempting this movement away from South Africa, set as it is against the background of the treason trials. This background is rooted in historical fact, and many real people move in and out of the pages of this autobiographical work. *Chocolates for My Wife* . . . depicts the arrival of one of these fleeing exiles; it is the end result of the movement away. Here, Matshikiza and his family have already arrived in England, have already physically escaped from the clutches of South African society. But the background is still that of South Africa; ironically, the South Africans who have congregated in London are presented by Matshikiza as adrift, unsettled, thirsting for news of the country that is still home. They were alienated from the society which they fled, but they are equally alienated from the surroundings to which they have come.

Physical separation brings psychical alienation from the land of one's birth, but the incongruity is heightened when old social conditions continue to dominate the actions of those who have removed themselves from their immediate control. Indeed, the situation seems futile, for even as Hutchinson succeeds in his flight, the end result of his travels to Ghana will most probably be his alienation from his own country, as well as from his immediate, newly adopted surroundings.

Not surprisingly, therefore, many scenes in these two novels are recaptured through flash back, through a present situation that gives birth to thoughts of a somehow similar situation in South Africa. This gives the authors an opportunity to present the social workings of the South African scene by juxtaposition with the "free" surroundings in which they now find themselves.

There are essentially two parts to *Road to Ghana*. The first tells of the treason trials and the attempts of Hutchinson to flee from South Africa; the second is a travelogue of his flight by train—"a hissing, creaking, runaway" creature—which takes him to Tanganyika, and by plane, which eventually brings him to Ghana. The first part of the novel is more engaging, since the latter is largely a documentation of a trip, with descriptions of various social elements in the areas traversed. The entire novel is linked together by Hutchinson's observations, his emotional reactions, the constant alternation of exhilaration and hope with futility and despair. This movement from hope to despair gives structure to most of the chapters, which begin on a high note of the possibility of achieving a goal and end on a note of dejection.

Like *Chocolates for My Wife . . . , Road to Ghana* is episodic, a novel of statement rather than analysis, wherein events are presented, not explained or examined in depth. (Something happens, Hutchinson records it. If the incident involves him personally, he adds his own reactions and then moves on.) Emotion, then, becomes objective and the tones flat, the mood of many events lost by overintellectualization.

The constant desire to display intellectual prowess and cultural knowledge, so prevalent in many South African writers, may be another method of acquiring self, of identifying with the other. The tendency is there in Hutchinson, in Matshikiza, and in Modisane. Their search for cultural identification is perhaps a direct result of cultural rejection suffered by these professional men of South Africa. It is but another method of flight from the social circumstances of their homeland. This intellectual display of men who reiterate that they are cultured in spite of prevailing circumstances, that they were able to absorb culture in the face of adverse situations, often obtrudes, lessening the pace of many scenes within their works.

Hutchinson is at his best when he is describing crowds of people who are either huddled together, such as mine workers, or are striving together, such as treason suspects. He has an acute ability to capture faces and the qualities that radiate from them, giving to them a definite presence. Indeed, his best-developed figure is that of Moses Banda, who is imbued with the qualities of the mask of Africa. Banda is strong, silent, and derives his strength from the certainty of his relationship to the earth.

> It was a wonderful face he had. It was strong and calm and deeply compassionate. . . . A knot of pain overlooked his spreading nostrils. He had strong hands, hands that could hold things firmly. And I thought I saw the compassion of his face in his hands also. . . .
> I turned to the coal-black man . . . and steadied in the calm of his face.[52]

Hutchinson often derives strength from the presence of Banda, but at times he regains his feeling of confidence even when alone. The constant, vertical movement of hope and despair seems to weaken him more and more as the novel progresses, to the point where we are given nothing more than quick glimpses of rapid emotional responses in the latter pages of the book. The forboding and fears of isolation are expressed in phrases such as ". . . terror rose like a miasma."

In spite of this, however, we are not made to feel the drama of his escape, nor do we feel the poignancy of his relationship with the white Englishwoman, Hazel. We do feel the clutching hold of South Africa upon the lives of its citizens, however. In Ghana, Hutchinson recovers his strength and regains his identity, feeling a deep sense of pride in his own Africanness and in the possibility of African development.

Chocolates for My Wife . . . also presents myriad examples of the hold which South Africa exerts on many characters, most of whom have suffered the double alienation of exile and of remembrances of a home in which their lot had been rejection and nonbelonging. As Matshikiza says, he was but a number to many people—and but a first name even to his closest liberal friends. Matshikiza is exiled in England so he never seems to experience that throb of Africanness which Hutchinson feels on his arrival in Ghana. Matshikiza's "homecoming" to England and his meeting with most of his South African compatriots there is devoid of warmth; it is noisy but not deeply affectionate. On one or two occasions, however, we are made to feel a sense of *camaraderie* in a shared African heritage. One such instance is the first meeting on English soil of Matshikiza and his old friend, Anthony Sampson. Sampson seems to be the least alienated of the exiled South Africans—black or white—who have congregated in London. Sampson has retained some of the vigor which comes from the African soil.

> Anthony Sampson was there to meet us. He was all there. Bigger, stronger. Blue and bright in the eyes as ever. . . . Here he was talking and walking as upright as ever. Warm and comfortable as the central heating in London. Bright and cheery as the sun in Africa.[53]

As he relates every incident in England to a similar one in South Africa, Matshikiza is himself an alien in exile. When he recalls parts of his father's life in Queenstown, his involvement

in the production of the musical, *King Kong,* his sneaking in to
parties after bribing black elevator men, there is a sense of self,
an identification. But even these references are overshadowed
by the social impositions of life in South Africa, and the novel
becomes a constant juxtaposition of his sense of freedom in
England, which is realized but not deeply felt, with a sense of
the unethical social system of South Africa.

The style of *Chocolates for My Wife . . .* is impressionistic,
the structure episodic, the imagery at times contrived and over-
worked. As in *Road to Ghana,* an animal image, that of the
powerful African elephant, occasionally appears.

> Africa will trample you underfoot, Verwoerd. Africa will hurt
> you. The hurt that the African elephant visits on its foe.[54]

> The big steel door . . . yawned like this: hmm, hmm, hmm.
> Swallowed us like the elephant swallows little peanuts, pushing
> them with its tough unescapable trunk through its mouth into
> its big elephant.[55]

One obtrusive element of Matshikiza's style is his use of per-
sonification. Hutchinson does this also, although to a lesser
degree, in *Road to Ghana.* Phrases such as these abound in
both works: "trousers looked like Saturday gone shopping in
Johannesburg . . . my gasp found words . . . My curiosity
tiptoed behind."

Both Matshikiza and Hutchinson tend to caricature rather
than portray many of the minor characters who appear in their
narratives. Hutchinson employs this method throughout his
novel. He draws them with a few rapid strokes, fastening upon
a single idiosyncratic or material aspect of a person which
comes to stand for the whole. It is a kind of impressionistic
shorthand, which is at times effective but at others a bit facile
and specious.

Total Destruction of the Individual

Both *Road to Ghana* and *Chocolates for My Wife . . .* are
novels of exile, but the land of the authors' birth remains a
constant presence for them. Points of reference are still rooted
in South Africa, and so Todd Matshikiza and Alfred Hutchin-

son are not able to experience the total destruction which Bloke Modisane tries to present in his historical expository novel, *Blame Me on History*. From Modisane's point of reference, the things that bind him to the earth and to his country are all a part of his township, Sophiatown. Here reside a multitude of associations and memories, but here, too, destruction has occurred. Sophiatown has been bulldozed out of existence and with it the history of Modisane's own self, his past existence. His flight and eventual exile, combined with the eradication of self through the material destruction of his place of birth and upbringing, give him a doubly intense alienation, powerful and total.

Society has made Bloke Modisane what he is; it has destroyed him, recreated him, and given him ideals which in essence are valueless. It has prostituted his emotions and deprived him of an inner self. A certain negative historical continuity has been imposed on Modisane by the societal norms, a certain positive material destruction by the liquidation of the township, Sophiatown. But neither liquidation of the township nor physical removal from the scene of South Africa frees the protagonist of the total presence of oppression. Like Hutchinson and Matshikiza, who also have fled South Africa, he cannot enjoy freedom and is forever bound to the land of his birth.

> South Africa and everything I had known, loved and hated remained behind me. I was out of South Africa. But it was no victory or solution, the compulsive agony was still with me, the problem was still with me; only its immediacy was removed, like an orgasm in bed; the tension was released but the filth slimed down my thigh dripping on to the sheet.[56]

Unlike Matshikiza and Hutchinson, who present the encroachment—and continuous presence—of the larger society on their own group, Modisane attempts a sweeping, panoramic historical penetration into the interplay between the larger and the smaller societies. The confrontation of these two groups can give rise to a dramatic, epic style, and indeed it is such a style that Modisane attempts, using the devices of grand statement and gesture to their fullest—and even, at times, to extremes. Yet embracing as it does so many motifs peculiar to the whole South African situation, presenting so many personal effects and reactions and analyzing the historical dimension of apartheid, *Blame Me on History* is an overly ambitious undertaking. It treats a question that is worthy of our fullest consideration—and perhaps of a fuller, more subdued, less strident literary effort.

The book has two parts. The first is the ruthless destruction of a symbolic representation of the smaller, black society, Sophiatown, by the larger group. The slumlike features and corrupt atmosphere of Sophiatown evoke for the author the realities which he has lived and experienced and which indeed he believes to be a part of himself. Thus, its destruction is a destruction of an essential element of the author's psyche.

> Something in me died, a piece of me died, with the dying of Sophiatown. . . . In the name of slum clearance they had brought the bulldozers and gored into her body, and for a brief moment, looking down Good Street, Sophiatown was like one of its many victims; a man gored by the knives of Sophiatown, lying in the open gutters, a raisin in the smelling drains, dying of multiple stab wounds, gaping wells gushing forth blood; the look of shock and bewilderment, of horror and incredulity, on the face of the dying man.[57]

The second part of the novel is the historical analysis of apartheid, its institutions and its effects on the total behavior of the author and on the general morality of the public. History—in this instance, the total South African society—has destroyed Sophiatown, a past which belonged to Modisane and to many others. It is there that the author's father was bludgeoned into anonymity by a show of that violence which is one of the results of history and a component of the present social order. Not only does Sophiatown reek with violence, but, as noted before, the total society provides a spawning ground for it. Here, too, are spawned cowardice and fear, a fear which Modisane feels and which curtails action, which prevents him from attempting to offset the violence that errupts around him.

His nonparticipation leads Modisane to the self-accusation that he is basically a coward. Yet this cowardice, this fear of implication in violent social situations, permeates the entire society. Its effect is an inertia that breeds separation and from which Modisane attempts to free himself through another kind of violence (self-abuse), through sexual promiscuity, through drunkenness, and through a seeking for otherness.

These patterns of behavior are direct results of historical forces at play in South Africa. The present is rooted in violence, criminality, and amorality. This amorality, which derives from the total society, is essentially an alienating experience. This seeking for otherness is a direct cause of immorality, of criminality. In some of the short stories and the La Guma novels, this desire for otherness manifests itself in a desire for possessions, for the material trappings of the white world, and leads, therefore, to stealing. In Hutchinson and Matshikiza the desire for otherness becomes the desire to flee the entire situation and leads to the forging of papers and passports and the assumption of false identities. In *Blame Me on History*, Modisane's desire is for intellectual association with white men and romantic association with white women, both of which are crimes in the rule of law under which he lives.

Even if the law inherent in the Immorality Acts were not exercised, the very existence of the act would serve to further alienate all those who entered into black-white relationships, separating men from their own group. Modisane is unable to relate to or exist in either the black world or the white; he is rootless and suffers a deep sense of in-betweenness.

> I was to become an alien situated between the scorn and the hatred of both the white and the black world; the white world wanted to fasten a noose around my neck for soiling that purity which is white, the blacks were distrustful, eager to spit on me for thinking and loving white, which is the symbol of their oppression. The whites could not see me as a man, and the blacks could not see her as a woman.[58]

So the loneliness which the widows of the Reserves are made to suffer, those women who bury their children and their husbands alone besets most of the characters in these works of fiction. It is an aloneness which brings with it a deep, gashing alienation, wounding the members of the society to the bone. "I felt too much, alone, and bled too deeply, alone, the being alone is unbearable. I am the eternal alien between two worlds."[59]

If we accept the final statement of *Blame Me on History*,

then the motifs resident in the literature we have examined, the instances we have adduced and the thorough pervasiveness of alienation which we have attempted to examine, can only be rooted out by a further and larger alienation—total destruction:

> Only South Africa the country is worth preserving, her attitudes must be destroyed even unto a destruction of physical South Africa; the attitudes are bigger than we are and perhaps we might have to destroy ourselves if we are to get at them.[60]

Notes

1. Phyllis Ntantala, "Widows of the Reserves," *An African Treasury*, ed. Langston Hughes (New York: Crown Publishers, Inc., 1960), p. 21.

2–4. *Ibid*: 2. p. 20; 3. p. 23; 4. p. 22.

5. Bloke Modisane, *Blame Me on History* (New York: E. P. Dutton and Co., Inc., 1963), p. 217.

6–7. *Ibid*: 6. p. 59; 7. pp. 184–185.

8. Ntantala, *op. cit.*, p. 21.

9. Alfred Hutchinson, *Road to Ghana* (New York: The John Day Co., 1963), p. 63.

10. James Matthews, "Azikwelwa," *Quartet: New Voices from South Africa*, ed. Richard Rive (New York: Crown Publishers, Inc., 1963), p. 38.

11. Todd Matshikiza, *Chocolates for My Wife, Slices of My Life* (London: Hodder and Stoughton, 1961), p. 31.

12. Alex La Guma, *A Walk in the Night* (Ibadan, Nigeria: Mbari Publications, 1962), p. 55.

13. Richard Rive, "Strike!" *Quartet*, p. 31.

14. Ezekiel Mphahlele, "The Living and the Dead," from *The Living and the Dead and Other Stories* (Ibadan: Ministry of Education, 1961), pp. 6–7.

15. Ezekiel Mphahlele, "We'll Have Dinner at Eight," *ibid.*, pp. 20–21.

16. La Guma, *op. cit.*, p. 87.

17. Alf Wannenburgh, "Echoes," *Quartet*, p. 94.

18. Hutchinson, *op. cit.*, p. 81.

19. Alex La Guma, *And a Threefold Cord* (Berlin: Seven Seas Publishers, 1964), p. 136.

20. *Ibid.*, p. 133.

21. Matshikiza, *op. cit.*, p. 123.

22. La Guma, *And a Threefold Cord*, p. 166.

23. La Guma, A *Walk in the Night*, p. 19.
24–25. *Ibid:* 24. p. 8; 25. p. 3.
26. Mphahlele, "We'll Have Dinner at Eight," *op. cit.*, p. 21.
27. La Guma, A *Walk in the Night*, p. 2.
28. *Ibid.*, p. 21.
29. La Guma, *And a Threefold Cord*, inscription preceding p. 9.
30. Richard Rive, "Resurrection," *Quartet*, pp. 72–73, 84.
31. *Ibid.*, p. 78.
32. Alex La Guma, "Out of Darkness," *Quartet*, pp. 59–60.
33. Ezekiel Mphahlele, "The Master of Doornvlei," *The Living and the Dead and Other Stories*, p. 33.
34. Mphahlele, "The Living and the Dead," *op. cit.*, p. 11.
35. Alf Wannenburgh, "Debut," *Quartet*. p. 189.
36. James Matthews, "The Party," *Quartet*, p. 161.
37. Matthews, "Azikwelwa," *op. cit.*, p. 44.
38. Alf Wannenburgh, "Awendgesang," *Quartet*, p. 51.
39. La Guma, *And a Threefold Cord*, p. 168.
40. La Guma, A *Walk in the Night*, pp. 4, 79.
41–44. *Ibid:* 41. p. 75; 42. p. 55; 43. p. 43; 44. pp. 86–87.
45. La Guma, *And a Threefold Cord*, p. 107.
46–47. *Ibid:* 46. p. 103; 47. p. 67.
48. La Guma, A *Walk in the Night*, p. 22.
49. La Guma, *And a Threefold Cord*, p. 22, 36, 53.
50–51. *Ibid:* 50. p. 48; 51. p. 129.
52. Hutchinson, *op. cit.*, pp. 65–66.
53. Matshikiza, *op. cit.*, p. 10.
54. Hutchinson, *op. cit.*, p. 9.
55. Matshikiza, *op. cit.*, p. 95.
56. Modisane, *op. cit.*, p. 311.
57–60. *Ibid:* 57. p. 5; 58. p. 229; 59. p. 218; 60. p. 230.

FOUR

THE LOST GENERATION . . .
URBAN POLITICAL REALITY

Mother Africa! Oh, Mother Africa, make me strong for the work I must do! Don't forget me in the many you nurse. I would make you great. I would have the world respect you and your children. I would have the sun of freedom shine over you once more. It was for this I left you for so long and lived in strange lands among strange people and suffered and was abused and was cold and hungry. It was in order to come back to free you, to free all your children, and to make you great among those who now look down on you. They do not understand your dark ways. For them you are something to be exploited, and your children creatures to be held down. Now this must end. I will end it if you help me. I cannot see you, but I can feel you out there in the dark. Tomorrow, I will be with you, in you. Do not let me get lost in your many.[1]

Unlike the Dark Child, who reminisces nostalgically about Africa: "Black woman, woman of Africa, o my mother . . . how I should love to be beside you once again . . . to be surrounded by your loving warmth again . . ."[2] Michael Udomo in Peter Abrahams' *A Wreath for Udomo* invokes Mother Africa to help him in his task of political reformation. He, too, had moved away, had lived a long exile, but now he returns, strong in his resolve to end the reason for exile, a supplicant fully aware of the formidable problems that await him. Conscious too that the heart throb of Africa is unsteadied by historical upheaval and wavers in the midst of political uncertainties, Udomo pleads for sustenance from his homeland.

In the above quotation, we have the play of Mother Africa: exile from Africa and return to Africa, but the return is not to the nostalgically recreated wonders of the world of *L'Enfant Noir*; rather it is a partial return to the vast problems of civic unrest and political convolutions in which the son of Africa is caught and for which he has to seek moral and practical resolutions. Udomo, like so many of the other characters, wishes to work for the political independence of Africa and desires, in a climate of full freedom, to achieve an exuberant development of the continent. But in this quest many are lost, many desires are thwarted, and often, ideals are twisted in the chaos of changing historical circumstances. Death may ensue, but Africa's heartbeat belongs to her sons; if her breath is stifled theirs will be stilled: "Africa? She is a little like a heart. You've seen the shape of her. It's like a heart. Africa is my heart, the heart of all of us who are black. Without her we are nothing; while she is not free we are not men. This is why we must free her, or die. That is how it is."[3]

Africa is the problem of her sons; they are the problem of Africa: "You don't understand my friend. Look, it's simple. I'm black; my friend Mike, here, is black. We don't have to be on our side. We are our side. We don't have to understand the problem: we are it."[4]

The portrayal of the social and political dilemmas becomes a shifting, all-pervasive background. The resolution of problems, economic or moral, that beset the characters of these novels, becomes the action, and the characters who are coincidental with the convoluted social circumstances often, in their search to bring about that total freedom of Africa, become convoluted and twisted themselves. Dialogue is often a discussion as to the expediency of action, the morality of an act: do the ends justify the means? Must racialism be used to counter racialism? For

instance, the central debate of the novel *Emergency* is evident
in the following discussion:

> ". . . Where do we go from there? Do we sit on our back-
> sides discussing the finer points of political theories?"
> "Don't underestimate the importance of political theories."
> "Very fine phrases. But exactly how does one translate your
> views into practice?"
> "By educating people."
> "In classrooms?" Braam interjected.
> "No, in life. Education, not learning. On the level of ideas
> firstly. A people that wants to bring about its own emancipa-
> tion must understand that the acceptance of racialism is a
> negation and a repudiation of our common humanity."[5]

In the majority of the novels under discussion, the authors'
vision pierces the problematic, cuts through the overwhelming
pessimism of the present, and extends to a hopeful future. It is
for this concrete future that most of the characters strive: "And
the wonderful feeling that came over him when he felt his
oneness with Africa. The Africa of the future. Glimpses of the
vision splendid. More than a vision, the feeling of inevitable
realization."[6]

The bases for a firm future have been made apparent; they
have become visible. The search is for rapidly evolving forms,
rejecting a formless chaotic ferment, recalcitrant to orderly evolution.

The works are rooted in contemporary history; man attempts
to apprehend the current reality of heterogeneous societies by
exploring current problems and searching for moral solutions in
a transitional world. The political and social emanations of this
transitional world, caught in upheavals and cataclysms, bring
with them violence and moral decay. To explore contempora-
neous history is to enter the historical dynamics of new units
that have come into being through dynastic and political con-
tingencies. The newly created urban units, amorphous and
formless, regurgitate characters, equally formless, who are
pulled between old traditional ways and new, as yet unfelt,
urban realities. On the political level, the exploration of historical dynamics becomes the novelistic presentation of the inner
workings of political parties, a searching for political kingdoms,
a dream of Pan-Africanism.

In three of the novels, *God's Bits of Wood* by Sembene Ousmane, *Emergency* by Richard Rive, and *A Night of Their Own* by Peter Abrahams, we see the inner mobility and the disorder consequent on political emergencies and crises. In *God's Bits of Wood*, Ousmane attempts to show the total effect of a strike on both a whole community and the individual members of that community. We note the reactions of these individuals who become political activists without fully realizing the grave consequences of the calling of the railway strike. In this novel Ousmane dramatizes the Dakar-Niger railway strike of 1947.

Emergency also dramatizes a real situation, that of the Sharpeville riots in South Africa in 1960. There, friends question the validity of one another's actions, and friendships between the central characters are destroyed by the external social circumstances. In both novels, the external social reality totally impinges on the individual; the tension of the novels stems from this interplay between the individual character and critical social-political circumstances.

A Night of Their Own by Peter Abrahams does not dramatize a real historical situation. Instead, the author, through the novelistic process, creates an emergency that is quite probable and, given the South African situation, might easily become a reality. In this novelistic emergency, characters are symbolic of political beliefs, which are polarized between the blackman myth symbol Nkosi and the upper-class Indian woman Dee; the Colored school teacher Mildred and the high-ranking Afrikaner Karl Van As. Here, too, all the characters, buffeted by external political circumstances, rapidly traverse a night of their own, which brings with it disillusionment, death, and separation.

The characters in these three novels are searching for an escape from the problematic consequence of social-political disorder. More often than not, they do not find an escape; the social convolutions seem to twist them. Yet, amidst the chaos, they are exploring ways of creating stable, free political orders.

A Wreath for Udomo presents on a large scale the search for political freedom: independence for Africa and viable development after the gaining of this independence. We note the deep allegiances that bind a group of friends working for independence, as well as the divisive factors that sever these allegiances once individual members are confronted by the practical realities of development after independence. Political idealism and dreams are often shattered in the quest for the political kingdom. This novel presents the inner mobility of different political epochs—working for independence abroad, return, the fight for independence and the postindependence developments.

In the preceding four novels the exigencies of the political search result in a state of unease. The same resultant condition occurs in Chinua Achebe's novel, *No Longer at Ease*, set in Nigeria just prior to independence. This is a time not of critical emergency but of flux, transition, and social restratification as administration of the country is taken over by local native personnel. The initial idealism of its main character, Obi Okonkwo, is destroyed in a social context where the economic substratum is built on an acceptance of bribery and corruption. The hero falters, caught between residual traditional ties and the social pressures accompanying an administrative position formerly held by colonial officers. He lives in a state of unease, unable to contend with a social ethic as yet unformulated, one that is shifting and pervaded by immorality.

The characters in *People of the City* and *Jagua Nana*, both written by Cyprian Ekwensi, also live in a state of unease, bobbing up and down in the same shifting, unformed social circumstances. The urban realities are amorphous and chaotic, and the central figures who live these realities seem equally amorphous and disturbed. The traditional exerts its force on the people of the city as they search for luster and transient pleasures within the throb of city life. Values, ideals, and dreams are lost in the crowded city masses, and when violence erupts it bludgeons all social and political activities. The political situations presented in these two urban novels, though peripheral to the main concern of the author, which is the corrosive influence of the city on the people, take place in an arena fraught with corruption, violence and death.

The chicanery, folly, corruption, and violence of a changing political order are at the center of the novel, *A Man of the People*, by Chinua Achebe. Practical politics on the local level, its inner workings and functions, are all presented through the central figure, Chief Honorable M. A. Nanga, M.P., a satirical portrait of one of the many new ministers who control the reins of government in many of the developing countries. The Minister is juxtaposed with a seemingly idealistic young man who, although quite venal, attempts to correct the unethical political practices of such ministers.

In *Beautiful Feathers* by Cyprian Ekwensi we move from the presentation of circumscribed local politics as expressed in *A Man of the People* to a wider political concern that preoccupies all African leaders—Pan-Africanism. The ironic statement central to the novel is that Wilson Iyari, who dreams of the solidarity of the continent and idealistically, if somewhat immaturely, attempts to bring about this solidarity, seems unable to foster this unity in his own marital life. This central character, too, lives a life of constant self-doubt, caught in the play of forces inherent in the mobility of evolving social and political phenomena. In all of these novels, principles and problems collide, ideals and dreams strike against practicality and expediency. In the incomparability of the shifting social and political phenomena and in their unique centrifugal pull, man flounders even while seeking new approaches.

Coming of the Political Kingdom

In their search for approaches to the political kingdom, many characters are imbued with the poetry of action; when they see the need and feel the compulsion for action, they idealize it. At the beginning, action itself possesses its own poetry; it invests some characters with the will to succeed. In *A Wreath for Udomo*, the articulator of freedom and the theoretician, Lanwood, had inspired the future political activist, Udomo, with the following words:

> In order to be free we must marshal our forces and husband our resources for the coming struggle. Our young men must ceaselessly prepare themselves for the fight. All their strength, all their energy, all their talents must be devoted to preparing themselves for the fight that will result in the liberation of their country and the freedom of their continent. There is no nobler task on earth.[7]

The freedom of Africa is here an all encompassing goal; action has been made the *raison d'être* of the young African. Michael Udomo accepts completely the vivifying force inherent in action that leads to freedom. Action infuses him with the lyricism of life.

> I never had a chance to read poetry, like you and Mabi, but I know it is beautiful for both of you. Well, for me the freedom of my people and the dream of that freedom is as beautiful. I know you think I think of nothing but politics. But it's not really politics. It's my people, Lois. That is my poetry.[8]

For Udomo, then, politics has its own inner dynamic, the freeing of his people, its own poetic essence.

Richard Nkosi in *A Night of Their Own* also accepts the existential altruism of political action, extending it into a simple question of personal belief:

> "And it is for this fairy story that you take these risks?"
> "No, sir. It is for the people of this country, but primarily it is for what I believe. I think this is the difference between ourselves and other animals."[9]

Liberating action is not always sheer idealization; at times it derives from a simple need to survive. Sammy Naidoo, an Indian political activist in *A Night of Their Own*, realistically expresses why he acts: "Whether we like it or not, we must work our passage into the movement and into the future. If we fail, we'll have no future here. This, whatever we feel or think of it, is the hard reality of the Indian situation."[10] For without action the search for political freedom, justice, and social equality is but trumpery and a farce. To expel prejudice requires a change of order, a change that can only be brought about by social and political action. Thus, Dee Nunkhoo reiterates to a young Indian who, in spite of himself, had shown a strong resentment against the idea of an Indian upper-class woman falling in love with an educated black man:

> "But it come up, like you say, like a sickness. How can I stop it, Miss Dee? Honest I want to."

"The only way to stop it," she said, "is by changing our world."

"But for now so I don't get these thoughts?"

"I don't know, Dicky. I don't know. I don't think it can be done without changing the society and the control of power in the society."[11]

Social action is a necessity; it is mandatory if human interrelationships are to be devoid of prejudice. Thus, social action may be raised to the level of the humanistic:

> Ours is not the first generation called upon and I don't think it will be the last. This is our responsibility now, because in our time the greatest ugliness in the world and the greatest danger to the human spirit is here in our land. And this has nothing to do with race or colour. . . . But the sense of it is that the great South African adventure, that intense and special dialogue between the people and the earth which shapes and fashions and nurtures them, can only begin when the land is rid of this racial ugliness. This must be done before there can be any real beginning.[12]

The morality of an action is its justification and repels the fear of its consequences. Tiomoko in *God's Bits of Wood*, caught up in the moral dilemma of the strike, expresses it in the following way: "It's not a question of dying, cousin. It's a question of learning, and of winning. It's a question of doing what is right, and of doing it as men should."[13]

In the search for the political kingdom the consequences of political action, even if rooted in morality, are fraught with danger; yet these dangers must not curtail action. The situation created by such action becomes the responsibility of those who undertook the action. To act is to be responsible:

> The question that we must consider here is whether we intend to be responsible for what we have undertaken in this strike. We have made some mistakes, and doubtless we will make others, but is that any reason why we should abandon now those who have followed us and trusted us, those who have gone hungry, and those who have been imprisoned or killed?[14]

And so Joe, a young Indian political leader, will continue to act, knowing full well that even if he encounters death because of his political actions there will be others who, sharing his beliefs in the cause of freedom, will replace him: "When the time comes and if I'm lucky, I might be able to slip away an hour or so before they come for me. In that case, I will join the band of exiles fighting from elsewhere. If I'm not lucky, then they get me. But whatever happens there'll be someone to take my place because our work must go on."[15] And Richard Nkosi will continue to act even if his action may spring from idealism, chimera, and dream: "I still think it is dreaming, but at least I see the sense of it. You'll never really change the world, but I think I understand now that you must try . . ."[16] The end result of all action rooted in the sincere belief that the cause is righteous will be, in spite of all obstacles, the consummation of a wish, final success. The essential thing is not to falter: "It is not necessary to be right to argue, but to win it is necessary both to be right and never to falter."[17] Indeed, any action, whether springing from necessity or from a moral undertaking, compulsion or dreams, is more valuable than no action. Inaction is to be dreaded, especially when it is impelled by doubts as to the ethics of action. The situation that confronts those who search for the political kingdom may advocate its own justification and, by creating its own ethic, give validity to all action. At times, therefore, the argument of means and ends disappears in that of causal situation and resultant action. Ethics is not a given objective; it is merely relative to the factors prevailing in the situation. One can only hope that an action is ethical. In the quest for political freedom, to act is to hope, to exist.

The means-and-ends argument is pretty wonderful as long as it remains an argument: it assumes that issues are either right or wrong, that the choice is always a straightforward one between good and evil. But the moment you enter the field of action this simplification of values falls away. Nearly always, in situations like this one, an action is at once both right and wrong, is enlarged with the possibility of both good and evil. The real problem here, the real gamble, the real hope is that our judgment has been sufficiently sound, our faith in the phantasies sufficiently strong for our actions to tip the scales in favour of good. That is the limit of our guarantee: a mere hope that out of our action will come good rather than evil. Because this has not been enough for many people they have chosen inaction. One does not risk being wrong or doing evil if one does nothing.[18]

To be sure, to act is often to be alone. Many of the protagonists in these novels feel the weight of aloneness when called upon to arrive at decisions leading to involvement. Often, however, communal action seems to have its own rewards, by providing an objective solidarity minimizing the dangers and maximizing the possibility of resistance. Personal endurance is strengthened by the communality of action.

> "We have to hang on," Samba said. "We have to know what we want, and we have to stand together."[19]
> "You know that there is support for you everywhere—from Kaolack to Saint-Louis, from Guinea to Dahomey, and even in France itself. The time when we could be beaten by dividing us against ourselves is past."[20]

Fully aware of the thrust and efficacy of communal action, Michael Udomo acts with expediency to maintain it. Here the end justifies the compromise:

> The secret is always to find a point on which all feel the same and build on it. The one thing stronger than all the points that divide tribal and clan loyalties, is the will to be free of the foreign oppressor. The thing then is to play down the divisions, to ignore them as far as possible, and to play up the foreign oppressor.[21]

Sometimes, unfortunately, this unity of action may prove transitory and ephemeral, dissolving once the immediate obstacle has been surmounted: "Briefly, the common danger, the common enemy, and the common objective of outwitting him, had brought them together in a special and intimate relationship. The end of the danger meant, also, the end of the intimacy."[22]

The achievement of solidarity is the culminating desire of Wilson Iyari in *Beautiful Feathers*. It is the basis of all his actions. He demands of his leaders that they strive for this solidarity: " 'Africans must come together,' Wilson said. 'My

movement is dedicated to the abolition of disunity.' "[23] For
Wilson the vision of Africans acting in unity, harmonizing their
efforts for the good of all Africa, is awe-inspiring.

> Wilson looked about him and immediately the burning hope
> of Africa was here evident. These men were all black and they
> carried brief-cases and looked as if the future of the world was
> tucked away under their armpits. Brotherly love glowed on
> their faces, and patriotism, loyalty and, above all . . . fight.
> African Solidarity. African Unity. Wilson heard the phrase
> over and over. African Solidarity.[24]

Expediency of Action

It is evident that as the novelists explore the contemporary
political and social circumstances of the continent, their preoccupation with action, methods of acting, and performance
gives an actuality to their writings. The immediacy of the situation gives larger significance to the analyses of action, to the
discussions of methods of approach, to the realization of political goals. What, for instance, is the most effective way to begin
a political party? Is it the task of the trained professional to
mobilize the masses?

> "I must say that I find it somewhat odd that a party calling
> itself the Common People's Convention should be made up of
> only professional men and women . . ."
> "That is not entirely accurate, Odili. What you see here is
> only the vanguard, the planning stage. Once we are ready we
> shall draw in the worker, the farmer, the blacksmith, the car-
> penter . . ."[25]

Such planning, such attempted organization is clearly advo-
cated by most of the writers, who are fully aware of the need to
fill the vacuum that came with takeover and independence.
Such planning is necessary to offset a political situation that
might, in its newness, produce an inherently destructive power
struggle.

> The trouble with our new nation was that none of us had
> been indoors long enough to be able to say 'To hell with it.' We
> had all been in the rain together until yesterday. Then a hand-

ful of us—the smart and the lucky and hardly ever the best—
had scrambled for the one shelter our former rulers left, and
had taken it over and barricaded themselves in. And from
within they sought to persuade the rest through numerous
loudspeakers, that the first phase of the struggle had been won
and that the next phase—the extension of our house—was
even more important and called for new and original tactics; it
required that all argument should cease and the whole people
speak with one voice and that any more dissent and argument
outside the door of the shelter would subvert and bring down
the whole house.[26]

Here Achebe clearly reveals the problems that are liable to
arise with the coming of independence; how to circumvent
these difficulties is the question posed in many of the novels.
Thus the novelists debate the expediency of action and often
discuss the process of development: Is gradualism acceptable to
a newly independent people eager for immediate growth and
gratification? What is the place of Africanization prior to political independence and its role after independence? To be sure,
the novels, though they pose these and other questions, are not
structured around a series of polemical dialogues. Rather, the
questions give direction to the actions of the characters. At
times the pace of the novels is slowed by discussions of these
questions; yet as the novelists attempt to seize the historical
dynamics of a continent in the process of political and social
evolution, they give an inner contemporary mobility to their
works.

In *A Wreath for Udomo,* one of the climaxes of the novel
centers on the expediency of cooperating with colonial technical assistance, thus aiding the development of a country and
preserving the gains achieved, a step that is needed but resented: "I've had a chance to see some of their technicians at
work on this tour. They're certainly the people we need here.
They're getting things done. Pity it has to be them, but they're
damned good."[27] Udomo is presented with an agonizing decision: should allegiance and friendship to one person be
bartered for this technical assistance? Such a question as the
one that Udomo asks Mhendi continually besets these characters, the present generation of African leaders: "Now tell me, if
you were in my position—or even in your own position—and
you were forced either to sacrifice one person to consolidate a

gain and perhaps gain more, or else lose all you've gained and a
lot more perhaps, which would you choose?"[28]

The present leaders realize that the coming generations will
judge them for actions that seemed necessary at the time, logi-
cal and expedient, but in the future may appear heartless. The
future generation will wonder about the humanity of an expedient action; yet the novelists, pushing the characters through
the immediate problem of political action, continually
confront them with choices. How does a leader act in order to
consolidate gains that will lead to the realization of political
ideals? In this situation Udomo sells his friend Mhendi. In later
situations he is obliged to fight against the same groups with
which he had allied himself and which had brought about his
political ascendancy. Confronted with the larger question of the
functional validity of tribalism, Udomo at first utilizes tribalism
in his fight against the colonialists, but later, believing himself sufficiently strong, he attempts to crush it. Here the expediency of a prior action eventually creates a larger problem.

Udomo, in his fight for the development of Africa, recognized three enemies: the white man, poverty, and the past. He
temporarily compromises with one enemy, capitalizing on the
political expedient of working with one enemy in order to
liquidate another.

> When I first came back I recognized only one of the three,
> the white man. But the moment I defeated him I saw the
> others and they were greater and more dangerous than the
> white man. Beside these two the white man was easy, almost
> an ally. Well, I turned him into an ally against poverty. He
> works for us now builds for us so that those who come after us
> will have bread and homes. There are schools and hospitals in
> the land. The young men and women are waking up. Why do
> you think I spent so much money sending them abroad? I will
> tell you. Because I need them as allies to fight our third enemy,
> the worst enemy we have: the past. I've paid lip-service to the
> ritual of ju-ju and blood ceremonies and worshipping at the
> shrines of our ancestors. Now I don't have to anymore. There
> are enough liberated young people now for me to defy all that
> is ugly and evil in our past. We can defeat it now.[29]

In this search for the political kingdom most of the novelists
seem to suggest that each and every ally is acceptable, that all

sectors of the population may be mobilized to achieve political ideals. Thus, in the novel *God's Bits of Wood*, contrary to their traditional role in the society, that of being wives, the women of the area are affected by the strike; they not only become involved in it but, in alliance with their men, become leading political activists. Contrary to tradition, a woman is allowed to address a public meeting, and further, the women demand that they be allowed to take an active role in the strike.

> "I speak in the name of all of the women, but I am just the voice they have chosen to tell you what they have decided to do. Yesterday we all laughed together, men and women, and today we weep together, but for us women this strike still means the possibility of a better life tomorrow. We owe it to ourselves to hold up our heads and not to give up now. So we have decided that tomorrow we will march together to Dakar."[30]

Again, contrary to tradition, they are accepted as allies by the men: a traditional way of life has been compromised to achieve political success. The question posed by the novelist is this: does a situation of emergency and violence breed its own expedient action, necessitate compromise, bring with it a parallel destructiveness? On another level, the question remains as it was stated before: Must racialism be fought with racialism?

In the following excerpt from *A Wreath for Udomo*, Lanwood, leader of the African Freedom Group, seems to say that violence bequeaths violence:

> "We are in the arena of naked imperialism, of divide and rule. Divorce the leadership from the mass of the people, create hostility towards the leadership in the minds of the people, that is her policy. . . . We must be negative and destructive until we are free. You ask for our cooperation. Good! Here is the one and only condition for our cooperation: when you are ready to discuss with us the date of your withdrawal from the colonies, then, and only then, will you get our willing cooperation! The slave does not cooperate with the slave-owner! We spurn your invitation! We give you warning, frankly and publicly, that we intend to break our chains! The battle is joined!"[31]

These novels are constantly caught in the dialectic of action, between choice of action and effect, decision and result. The characters are often involved in a historical moment, socially and politically indeterminate but which can be determined through action. Through all the novels we are presented with a sense of historical causation and social determinism that dictate the progress of the novel and the formation of its characters. The political moment has its own inner dynamic, its own vitality that seems to control and guide the dynamics of action. Preindependence action, of necessity more destructive and violent, is distinguished from postindependence decisions, by nature more constructively problematic. Both historical times, however, abound with the problematic: " '. . . they've all changed. . . . Only I am still the same. And now they are more like me. But they have power. Their problems are problems of how to build, of how to create. Only mine are still those of how to destroy. That's the difference between us now.' "[32]

Often, the trajectory described by the characters moves from the idealization of action, where action is poetry, to action compelled and brought about through the necessity of pure survival, and finally to action guided by sheer expediency. Often, too, the resolution of the problem dictates the kind of action taken; the reaction is consonant with the outward social circumstances. It is not simply that the characters are social or political refractions; rather they are people caught in the violent flux of social and political forces that contemporary Africa faces. The outward social circumstances are not simply contributing factors: they become controlling forces in the lives of the main characters. The political scene is not simply political; it pulses with life. The urban scene is not simply urban; it, too, throbs with a life of its own.

Corruption

The political climate within these novels, the game of practical politics, is cynically delineated. There is little idealism in this starkly presented portrayal where greed, corruption, and violence prevail. In *Jagua Nana,* an erstwhile idealistic youth, on his return from England, enters politics primarily for easy money.

"I wan' money quick-quick; an' politics is de only hope."[33]

Many of the characters and types presented in the urban political novels enter politics specifically for its lure, for the momentary glitter and glamor that accompany it, for the prestige and power it gives them. Entry into politics seems to destroy morality of any kind, transforming the politician into a self-seeking and unscrupulous activist.

> She was thinking how . . . ordinary people she knew became transformed by this strange devil they called politics. When so transformed a man placed no value on human life. All that mattered was power, the winning of seats, the front-page appearance in the daily papers, the name read in the news-bulletins of the Nigerian Broadcasting Corporation.[34]

Politics abound with mediocrity and charlatans, with ministers completely unqualified for their ministerial posts. For instance, in A Man of the People, the Minister of Culture is completely ignorant of the name of the president of the Writers' Society: "I had expected that in a country where writers were so few they would all be known personally to the Minister of Culture. But it was clear Chief Nanga hadn't even heard the man's name before."[35] Yet a modicum of political altruism persists. Some enter politics to counteract the fraudulence and inanity so glaringly revealed in some new ministerial systems: "Max and some of his friends having watched with deepening disillusion the use to which our hard-won freedom was being put by corrupt, mediocre politicians had decided to come together and launch the Common People's Convention."[36] Writers depict the world of politics as a jungle in which violence erupts and in which violence is fought with violence: "It is an ugly world. But you were wrong to rebuke me for what the Africans did to your people. This is the jungle, remember."[37] The harshness of the nature of politics is constantly reiterated. Even for the urbane, sophisticated Indian doctor Nunkhoo, entry into politics is entry into a state of war. "We have paid dearly for our former transparently honest methods of struggle. When they were ready they pounced and destroyed the movement, because we had all declared ourselves from public platforms all over the country. We have now learned that this is bitter war, no platform game."[38] Participation in politics exposes one to danger and often brings with it a brutal end. The politics of Lagos,

says Jagua Nana, is a filthy business, as she attempts to prevent
her young lover from entering it. "No, Freddie. I no wan' you
to win. . . . Politics not for you Freddie. You got education.
You got culture. You're a gentleman an' proud. Politics be
game for dogs. And in dis Lagos, is a rough game. De roughest
game in de whole worl'. Is smelly an' dirty an' you too clean an'
sweet."[39]

A political hireling echoes Jagua Nana's contention that politics is a rough business, not to be entered into by "gentlemen,"
that success in politics is achieved only by those who accept
and use its underhanded rules. The thug justifies his demands
for additional pay in the following way:

> "This no be matter for joke; we wan the money to pay
> certain porsons wey go go him house for night and burn him car
> . . . Look my frien I done tell you say if you no wan serious for
> this business make you go rest for house. I done see say you
> want play too much gentleman for this matter . . . Dem tell
> you say na gentlemanity de give other people minister . . . ?
> Anyway wetin be my concern there? Na you sabi."[40]

And so the political scene is surfeited with corruption and
bribery, heavy with threat and violence, reeling under the
debilitating effects of opportunism. Thus, the tone adopted by
the novelists is critical and, even when satirical, conveys a sense
of undirected social and political chaos. We can gather from
the following statement that opportunism is rampant:

> I knew very well and needed no reminder that we were not
> in Britain or something, that when a man resigned in our
> country it was invariably with an eye on the main chance—as
> when a few years ago ten newly elected P.A.P. Members of
> Parliament had switched parties at the opening of the session
> and given the P.O.P a comfortable majority overnight in return
> for ministerial appointments and—if one believed the rumours
> —a little cash prize each as well.[41]

If opportunism propels one into politics, self-interest can also
prevent one from entering the field of politics or from participating in political action. Thus those who achieved some measure of status through compromise even within an oppressive

political reality, either do not act at all or attempt to hinder the political action of others. In *Emergency* many of the Coloreds who have fairly decent jobs and have achieved and live moderately comfortable lives refuse to participate in any of the political action. Political action creates an emergency that would disturb their nonvital, inactive, comfortable existence. More specifically in *God's Bits of Wood*, Bachirou, who is on the junior staff of the European-run railroad and not a simple workman, attempts to forestall this fight: "Why are you trying to discourage them, Bachirou? Because you are on the staff, and the idea of any of the rest of us being on it, too, is enough to make you piss in your pants? Because you're jealous of everyone, and think only about yourself?"[42]

Those who enter politics do so mainly out of self-interest; those who actively comment on the political scene, the journalists, are also clearly seeking their own interests in their manner of reporting political incidents. The mass of the people who are caught in the turbulence of politics are easily swayed and as easily erupt into violent action. The press is resented but has to be stilled by bribery. Ironically, this is stated by a corrupt politician:

> "You see what it means to be a minister," said Chief Nanga. "If I don't give him something now, tomorrow he will go and write rubbish about me. They say it is the freedom of the Press. But to me it is nothing short of the freedom to crucify innocent men and assassinate their character. . . . I don't say they should not criticize—after all no one is perfect except God—but they should criticize constructively . . ."[43]

Political silence and apathy concerning inept, corrupt political parties easily becomes political gossip when such parties are bounced out of office: "Overnight everyone began to shake their heads at the excesses of the last regime, at its graft, oppression and corrupt government: newspapers, the radio, the hitherto silent intellectuals and civil servants—everybody said what a terrible lot; and it became public opinion the next morning."[44] Electioneering in such a political climate is hazardous: gangs of supporters of one party confront and attack supporters from the opposing side, in most instances wounding or killing some of their opponents. In the following excerpt we get a sense not only of electioneering fraud, but of its accompanying violence. Here the leader of a newly formed party is killed.

> Max had been informed by our party intelligence that Chief Koko's resourceful wife was leading the Women's Wing of the P.O.P. in an operation that one might describe as breast-feeding the ballot, i.e., smuggling into the polling booths wads of ballot paper concealed in their brassieres. Max immediately investigated. But as soon as he alighted from his car, one of Chief Koko's jeeps swept up from behind, knocked him over and killed him on the spot.[45]

Scenes of political violence are evident in all the novels whether they be set in Senegal, South Africa, or in the imagined country of *A Wreath for Udomo,* but they are most graphically and assiduously presented by Cyprian Ekwensi and Chinua Achebe in their political-urban novels, set for the most part in Lagos, Nigeria. Violence pervades not only politics, but the total atmosphere of the urban reality presented in the latter novels. This urban reality, like politics, has its lure and luster, its quick and transient glitter and success; it abounds with corruption, and is corroded by social immorality. The unethical is the normative. And yet the city pulses with life and movement and rhythms, even while it gasps and seethes with violence.

The following scene, like many in *Jagua Nana,* is one of the many lurid pictures of violence and death in *People of the City:*

> I have just witnessed the most grueling murder since I became crime reporter for the *West African Sensation.* In Magamu Bush, I saw her, a woman of twenty-five, lying with face twisted. And beside her lay her child, condemned in all its innocence by a gang of drunks. I saw also the two brutal clubs with which she had been done to death. The question I must ask the people of the city is this: Why? . . . And why the child too? The answer is simple: greed.[46]

The same phenomenon present in the political reality is repeated in the urban social reality; the possibility of violence deters few people from coming to the city, which lures them on with its promise of excitement, gaiety, and quick economic reward. The urban circumstances are presented in their stark reality, sometimes in description but at other times through characters symptomatic of the total corrosive malaise of the overcrowded cities. Money is master, dominating people's thoughts and actions, distorting their senses and sentiments: It is work that brought them four hundred miles to Lagos. " 'It is money, not work,' said the man. 'We left plenty of work at home. . . . Anyone who likes work can return home, take up his matchet and go into that bad bush between Umuofia and Mbaino. It will keep him occupied to his last days.' "[47]

In order to escape from the prospect of such unremunerative and dulling work many men and women flock to the city where their traditional mores are stifled. All the people in *People of the City* come like Aina, to live a life of luxury and glamor: "The glamorous surroundings, the taxis, the quick drinks. This was one reason why she had come to the city from her home sixty miles away: to ride in taxis, eat in fashionable hotels, to wear the *aso-ebi* . . . to have men who wore white collars to their jobs as lovers, men who could spend."[48] The majority of such women are swallowed up in the city without even having lived a moment of glamor. Others, in search of this excitement, finally end up compromising their desires and morals.

> Beatrice . . . made no secret of what brought her to the city: 'high life.' Cars, servants, high-class foods, decent clothes, luxurious living. Since she could not earn the high life herself, she must obtain it by attachment to someone who could. But she was not so well, and having found Grunnings, who did not quite satisfy her, she had to stick to him.[49]

In the urban political reality corruption has become a way of life, all pervasive, all encompassing, and totally acceptable. People do not question the ethics of accepting or not accepting a bribe; rather, they cynically admire those who know how to take a bribe and conversely consider a man such as Obi Okonkwo in *No Longer at Ease* a fool for being caught: " 'It is all lack of experience,' said another man. 'He should not have accepted the money himself. What others do is tell you to go and hand it to their houseboy. Obi tried to do what everyone does without finding out how it was done.' "[50] This cynicism is further compounded by the irony of language, for at times the proverbial turns of phrase that were traditionally used as moral dictums are now used to support immorality: "They were not only ignorant but cynical. Tell them that this man had used his position to enrich himself and they would ask you . . . if you thought that a sensible man would spit out the juicy morsel that good fortune placed in his mouth."[51] Not only proverbial idioms but also specious arguments are advanced to support the prevalence of bribery. Prior to independence the colonial administration made bribery a way of life and should the new Nigerian administrator not follow the example? Here, independence becomes a farce when colonial modes of conduct are made exemplary.

> " 'Let them eat,' was the people's opinion, 'after all when white men used to do all the eating did we commit suicide?' Of course not. And where is the all-powerful white man today? He came, he ate and he went. But we are still around. . . . The great thing, as the old people have told us, is reminiscence; and only those who survive can have it. Besides, if you survive, who knows? it may be your turn to eat tomorrow. Your son may bring home your share.[52]

In all the novels, both the political and the urban-political, bribery, corruption, blackmail, and payoffs are constantly repeated motifs. Indeed, often they are more than motifs, becoming, as in *No Longer at Ease*, the central construct around which the action revolves. When Obi Okonkwo returns to Nigeria from his study abroad he is full of resolve to act scrupulously and morally for the betterment of his country. On his arrival he is immediately confronted with a petty proposition:

> A young man, almost a boy in fact, was dealing with Obi's cabin. He told him that the duty on his radiogram would be five pounds.
> 'Right,' said Obi, feeling his hip-pockets. 'Write a receipt for me.' The boy did not write. He looked at Obi for a few seconds, and then said: 'I can be able to reduce it to two pounds for you.'
> 'How?' asked Obi.
> 'I fit do it, but you no go get Government receipt.'[53]

The young customs officer is surprised at Obi's refusal, for such proposals are automatic. All offers of bribery seem to be made directly and blatantly, even though the preliminaries may be a bit circuitous. In the following instance money is offered to the idealistic Wilson Iyari, who is searching for Pan-African solidarity, in exchange for a seat in the house and the murder of a political antagonist.

> "Listen, I am prepared to give you fifty thousand pounds. It's not much, but it will tide you over a few months till you have established . . ."
> Wilson said: "Wait. What are the conditions?"[54]

In *God's Bits of Wood*, an idealistic, stubbornly persevering leader of the strike, Doudou, is tempted by the French administrators to end the strike.

> "This strike is really annoying," Isnard was saying. "The appointments for the new positions on the staff have come in, and I saw your name on the list. Of course I knew it would be there because I proposed you for it a long time ago, but I wanted to keep it as a surprise. . . . The appointments are effective as of four months ago. That means you would get the pay raise for the whole time all at once—a nice little bundle. You could afford a new wife! . . . you almost made me forget the most important thing. Monsieur Dejean told me that I could put three million francs at your disposition right away. . . . This strike isn't doing anyone any good—you or me or the company or your comrades. You're the secretary of the strike committee, and as soon as the men go back to work it will be you who will work things out with the management."[55]

And even Afrikaner Karl Van As in *A Night of Their Own*, who is presented as having a high standard of ethics, stoops to offer the very dedicated Indian political leader safe conduct for himself and his group, in exchange for the betrayal of the man his group fights tenaciously to protect.

> "This is my proposition. You give me Nkosi and we'll leave you and Nunkhoo and all your other people on our list alone. In other words, give me Nkosi and I'll arrange to have the slate wiped clean for your group. The alternative is a clean up of all your leading people."[56]

It is clear, therefore, that the political and social realities in which action is to be carried out are completely subversive to ideals and actions that stem from poetry. Dreams are inevitably lost; goals are obliterated by the overpowering presence of a formless ferment. Some of the characters in the novels resist bribery, refuse to sink into corruption, persist in their search for the political kingdom. Disillusionment or heroic death often awaits them, even as disillusionment and violent death confront those overwhelmed by the force of politics and the city. At times the pull of tradition and the peace of rural circumstances are romantically presented by the novelists as a point of rest—a hiatus before the final disillusionment. But tradition becomes nostalgic and the movement back to it, illusory.

Of all the novelists, Cyprian Ekwensi reminisces most nostalgically about the restfulness and peace of traditional life. Ekwensi's characters often return to the village where momentarily they achieve a sense of peace, a feeling of freedom from the problems that beset them in the city.

Ol' Man Forest in *Beautiful Feathers* is a creation of Ekwensi who epitomizes love for the rural pastoral life. This old man has refused to go to the city or even to the nearest village and remains alone within the little kingdom he has carved out of the forest for himself. There he finds total freedom: "This is my kingdom. Every man has his own kingdom. Here I am free. I have no problem. I am happy. I have land, I have food, I have water. I am free."[57] To this forest, to this kingdom, the daughter of Ol' Man Forest flees from her marital problems, her infidelities, her loneliness in the vast city of Lagos: "Yaniya inhaled the damp scented air of the forest. In the distance she saw the roof-tops of the three huts that comprised the village Ol' Man Forest. . . . Built of mud and thatch, the three huts were like a discovery in the jungle. Yaniya's heart bounced with joy as she set eyes on them." In this forest Yaniya's mother lies buried and, symbolically, Yaniya's son, the grandson of Ol' Man Forest, dies and is buried. "It was home, the earth of motherland."[58]

The earth, the forest give a different perspective to problems that in the city seemed vast and overwhelming. Tempers are softened and thoughts are purified.

> She wandered in the forest all day, listless. She stopped by the river and bathed Jomo and Pandhit. She fed them forest

fruits that reminded her of her own childhood. She thought of Wilson Iyari, her husband. In this forest atmosphere his personality had become invested with a wholesomeness it had lacked when they were together in Lagos.[59]

For Jagua Nana, the "good-time woman" of Lagos in the novel *Jagua Nana*, village life brings serenity and a feeling of freedom, for the life is wholesome there and the waters of the river cleansing, the air soft, the earth restful. Going to the country was going home.

> She was singing gently now and enjoying the very rare luxury of being free. This was what the city women [sic] meant when she told her friends, 'I am going home.' No men ran after her in Ogabu, none of them imbued her with unnecessary importance. Here she was known, but known as someone who lived with them and grew up with them. She was not known as a glamourite, someone to be hungered after for sheer diversion. . . .
>
> How many years now, since she had had the time to look up at the night and see the moon? In Lagos the street lights were so bright that no one ever really saw the moon. She surrendered herself to the idleness and voluptuous feeling of laze. The hard earth bruised her body with all the fervour of an ardent lover. She was too lazy to care and too deeply asleep to feel anything.[60]

Yet wholesome village traditions, the restfulness and peace of life there, are unable to bind most of the characters to the villages. The characters seem to come for a whiff of clean air and then plunge backward to the turbulence of the city. To be sure, some of the novelists are aware of many defects in an unchanging traditional life that is deaf to the changing values of the total society. Obi Okonkwo in *No Longer at Ease*, caught between continuing traditional ties and new social attitudes, meets his downfall. He returns with dread to his village and does not encounter the same serenity, wholesomeness, and freedom that Yaniya and Jagua Nana found. He returns to a grasping bunch of relations, members of an extended family: "Although he had two weeks, he proposed to spend only one at home for reasons of money. To home people, leave meant the return of the village boy who had made good in the town, and everyone expected to share in his good fortune. 'After all,' they argued, 'it was our prayers and our libations that did it for him.' They called leave *lifu* meaning *to squander*."[61]

In *People of the City*, the milieu of the city, its social forces, becomes the principal agent, the most powerful force in the novel. The city is not a background; it is the central revolving stage on which spin shadowy and, in many cases, insubstantial characters. Perhaps the city is the character, and the people of the city are disembodied figures deriving substance from and endowed with a presence by their jostling with the city.

The novel is not formulated on a large scale, and consequently the inner workings and inner mobility of the city are presented in a series of superficial incidents and surface narrative with little in-depth treatment of the forces that make the city what it is. Episodes and incidents take the place of exposition and analysis. Melodramatic presentations are substituted for dramatic interplays of character and narrative climaxes. Yet, we feel the throb of the city in some of Ekwensi's descriptions, and by the very shadowyness of the figures presented, we grasp the insubstantial nature of the city. The city transforms or destroys people, and the depiction of this transformation becomes the depiction of the characters. Early in the novel we are introduced to "a girl, ebony black with an eager smile. She smiled not only with her teeth and her eyes, but with the very soul of her youth." She is young and full-blooded, and Amusa Sango, the chief character, "felt the vitality of the girl and it tantalized him."[62]

This girl, Aina, undergoes humiliating experiences; she is jailed for theft and in prison she changes: "But she was also bitter against everybody, against the very city that had condemned her. She had become hardened. Where previously Aina might have stalled or hesitated, or used a tactful word, she now spoke bluntly. Amusa was shocked by her cynicism."[63] She suffers a miscarriage and nearly dies after being slapped in a fit of temper by Sango whom she was trying to blackmail into submission and to whom she had become a "seductress." By the end of the novel Aina, who seems to have lost that buoyant vitality which once tantalized Sango, turns away from him with resignation: "Still pale, her coming here showed that she was a sport, a good loser. Perhaps life had taught her that: perhaps she still hoped . . ." and finally with defeat: "Aina stood there, crestfallen. There were genuine tears in her eyes and hint of rebuke. She had broken down at last."[64]

Perhaps it is Beatrice the First who best exemplifies the decadent and debilitating force operative in the city. The decline of her character is swift; her transformation brutal and tragic. She arouses the passions of many men of the city who become genuinely enamored of her. Grunnings, a British engineer she wed by custom and then deserted, searches for her in the night pits of the city; he "actually loved [her] more than she knew or cared."[65] Lajde, an unscrupulous landlord with an insatiable lust and eight wives, made "money and more money to consolidate his position with her."[66] Zamil, a rich Lebanese merchant and crook, maintains her in his house. Kofi, an affable Ghanian lorry driver, was her last man, "the helping hand had come too late."[67] Amusa Sango, once caught up by her petiteness and delicacy, found at their last meeting that "something had gone out of Beatrice the First. This could not be the same girl who had set his blood aflame."[68]

In spite of her many loves Beatrice dies alone and is buried as a pauper, fulfilling the prophecy that "She get some bad sick inside her. When them tell her, go home, she no go. One day she go die for this city."[69]

Ekwensi marks the spiritual degeneration of his character by outward physical decay, and conversely, he manifests growth of awareness and sophistication by improvement in physical appearance. Thus, Elina develops from a timid gawky-looking girl to a kind of "poster" girl: "No one advertising the Girl Guide Movement or the Women's this or that service could afford to overlook her. She had an air of calm response and confidence that put one at ease."[70]

Yet, Ekwensi does not let this erstwhile convent girl win Sango's love. The author seems to imply that underexposure to the country is just as bad as overexposure to the city. It is Beatrice the Second with whom Sango falls in love. She has lived in the city but has not been exposed to its corruption and idealistically speaks of starting a hospital in the remote interior with her doctor fiance: "No city life for us! . . . We'll go to the bush where we are needed. . . . I agree [we won't make money]. But that's not all there is to it. We will be doing something, giving something."[71]

Beatrice the Second reawakens the failing ambition of Sango

who, in spite of his noble intentions, was slowly being engulfed by the city. Sango, the chief protagonist and the narrator of the story, had been a successful and rapidly progressing journalist, the leader of a popular "high-life" band, and "a most colorful and eligible bachelor," who felt "that beneath his gay exterior lay a nature serious and determined to carve for itself a place of renown in this city of opportunities."[72]

But Ekwensi in delineating Sango's character only states, does not really show, this deep serious concern he attributes to Sango. He does show us Sango's attachment to his mother as demonstrated by his guilt at not having made a place for himself in the city.

> What had he achieved? Where was he going? Was he drifting like the others, or had he a direction? Whatever that direction was, he did not feel at this moment that he was progressing along it. Certainly his mother would not be proud to see how he was making out. . . . The old woman would think he was lost. . . . Something must have happened to his noble resolutions.[73]

In quick succession he is dispossessed of his apartment and almost arrested in a drug swindle; he goes from being leader of his own band to meagerly paid stand-in and finally loses not only his well-earned editorial promotion but his job as well. During this decline he meets Beatrice the Second.

> There is the girl for you, Sango. If you could win her, you would find a foothold in this city and all your desires would focus on a new aspiration. How different she is from them all: Aina, Elina, Beatrice the First. Have you ever felt anything like this beautiful feeling before? But it's hopeless.[74]

The meeting does not prove to be hopeless; Sango wins out and marries Beatrice the Second. They leave for the Gold Coast to start anew, hoping eventually to return to Nigeria and find a better life there. Sango is saved from total degeneration largely through Ekwensi's obvious desire to write a happy ending. Many other people of the city do not end so happily; they are relentlessly pulled into its quagmire.

Ekwensi uses the reporting of crime reporter Sango as a

vehicle for his presentation of the sordidness of the city, its prostitution, its crimes, its suicides, and its murders.

Many people are presented in *People of the City*, and many die brutally or senselessly. Yet, people continue to be attracted to the city: to its vitality, its music, and its easy glitter: "L-A-G-O-S Lagos! The magic name. She had heard of Lagos where the girls were glossy, worked in offices like men, danced, smoked, wore high-heeled shoes and narrow slacks, and were 'free' and 'fast' with their favours."[75]

Jagua Nana, in Ekwensi's novel *Jagua Nana*, cannot live without the Club Tropicana from which she derives momentary, yet deeply sensed pleasure, excitement, and thrills.

> The *Tropicana* to her was a daily drug, a potent, habit-forming brew. Like all the other women who came here, alone or with some man, Jagua was looking for the ray of hope. Something will happen tonight, this night, she always told herself.[76]

> Now an aging woman of 45, she is still sensuously attractive.

> She knew that, seen under the dim lights of her favourite night spot, the *Tropicana*—and from a distance—her face looked beautiful. In any light she was proud of her body, which could model for any painter or sculptor. When she walked down a street, male eyes followed the wiggle of her hips which came with studied unconsciousness.[77]

Aware of her aging, she desires a young man not only as lover but husband, and she finds him in the ambitious but poor Freddie. She longs for motherhood, which would fulfil and give authenticity to her womanhood. She also wanted Freddie "because only a young man would still be strong enough to work and earn when she would be on the decline."[78] Through prostitution she can generously support Freddie and offer to finance his education abroad. Still she yearns for lavish living and belittles Freddie by continuing to offer herself to other men who can satisfy this yearning.

> "I goin' to send you to Englan'; and you goin' to return and marry your Jagwa. Yes Freddie. I wan' me own man now.

Dem insult me too much. But as you is only a poor teacher you no reach yet for marry Jagwa woman. You mus' go train youssef to be proper man. . . . Den I kin born chil' for you. An' you kin look after me, in me old age.'"[79]

These contradicting desires for motherhood, for security that manifests itself in her love for the traditional rural life, and for the pulsating glitter of city life give credibility and humanity to Jagua Nana, a volatile, jealous, quick-tempered yet generous woman. She fears that she will lose Freddie: " 'I done old,' she sighed. 'Sometimes I tink say Freddie he run from me because I done old. God 'ave mercy!' she sighed again."[80] Her fear is crystalized in her jealousy of the glowing young Nancy. Her mounting feud with Nancy runs throughout the novel, becoming temporally obscured when Freddie departs for England. Jagua turns to Dennis, an arrogant young man who mirrors her own desire for wild thrills, for the life of careless abandon. Yet, when she realizes that he would be about the same age as her dead son, her maternal instincts are aroused, and she attempts to dissuade the young man from his fatal course.

> Somehow she felt that this young man's philosophy was intricately bound up with hers. He lived for the moment, intensely, desperately. He had no use for the conventional methods of thinking. . . . With her elderly woman's heart, she could not bear to see this young boy who could well be her son, sacrificed on the altar of recklessness.[81]

Dennis is but one of the casualties of the city; Uncle Taiwo is another. The epitome of the shrewd, ruthless politician, the elderly Uncle Taiwo is very protective of Jagua Nana. He becomes her agent of revenge against the politically ambitious Freddie, who eventually rejects her by marrying Nancy. Jagua continues to entice Freddie; and Nancy, aware that Freddie is yielding, publicly slashes Jagua at her most vulnerable point, her childlessness: "Harlot, you got no shame! So you use to run after man who you can born. I don' blame you, your womb done dried up. You old hag! You kin never born anymore."[82]

Jagua is now determined "to turn Freddie against his wife, to make him loathe the very sight of her, to break up his home if only to repay Nancy's humiliation of her."[83]

The urban political reality with its immorality, brutishness, and filth becomes an arena in which jealousies, hatreds, and political aspirations are enacted. The interlocking threads spool out in violent and tragic succession. Freddie is killed in a political clash between roving gangs of opposing parties, leaving Nancy a widow with two children. Uncle Taiwo is brutally murdered for having broken faith with the party and having lost the election.

> The body was lying there twisted and swollen; one knee was drawn up against the chest, the arms were clutching at the breast, rigid like a statue. . . . Some dogs [were] circling too. Perhaps they were waiting for nightfall to feast on the body of the famous man. This was in Lagos, nowhere else.[84]

Dennis is hanged, and Jagua Nana, fleeing from party henchmen, is driven into the worst squalor of Lagos: "Jagua looked at the degradation. Rosa had become like many women who came to Lagos, like Jagua herself—imprisoned, entangled in the city, unable to extricate herself from its clutches."[85]

The appearance of Jagua's brother, "to her the Day of Judgment, the silent symbol of torture,"[86] emphasizes the futility of her city life, and she leaves Lagos for her village home, Ogabu: "Not that she preferred the quiet life, but she gradually ceased to picture the riotous life. It had become an echo too distant to touch her."[87]

Unlike People of the City where the social situations are statically represented, in Jagua Nana they interplay with the development of the characters. Nor is Jagua Nana built around episodic incidents; rather a series of plots and subplots crisscross and carry the novel forward. The incidents arising out of character interplay and create their own motive power. The dialogue seems more spontaneous and less contrived than in People of the City. The prose descriptions and dialogue relating to the city are blunter and more strident than the soft easy evocative prose and dialogue of the rural areas. Although at times Ekwensi attempts to make his prose too fast and compelling, upbeating it too much, in general the tone seems consonant with the environment, a flashy, quick-beating, vibrating milieu.

In People of the City and Jagua Nana characters shift and

are caught in urban-rural polarity. In *No Longer at Ease* the character Obi Okonkwo is caught in the polarity between the values of a changing traditional order and the functions of a new social administrative class. Chinua Achebe introduces us to this young man whose tragic downfall slowly manifests itself in the untidy environment of Nigeria prior to independence. For Achebe "Real tragedy is never resolved. It goes on hopelessly for ever. Conventional tragedy is too easy. The hero dies and we feel a purging of the emotions. A real tragedy takes place in a corner, in an untidy spot. . . . The rest of the world is unaware of it."[88] Achebe attempts to make the world aware of the chain of events leading to Obi Okonkwo's downfall: how this young man of education and promise, who returns to Nigeria full of ideals, slowly but surely sinks into error, eventually employing the very unethical practices he had previously vehemently condemned. The novelist plots a series of minor incidents that together create a totally oppressive situation, a resultant state of unease for the character, Obi, who is unable to comprehend the seemingly formless social environment where he has been cast adrift.

Obi, having inherited a European post, is expected to behave according to European standards; however, he is still bound by native traditions and is expected to conform to them. Thus he becomes the center of a larger conflict. The European-educated professional Nigerian is called upon to conform and pay allegiances to two social orders which are not coextensive, being fundamentally at odds.

Because of the ineffectualness of Obi's character he is unable to extricate himself from the pull of these opposing forces and flounders in a state of unease. Perhaps Obi's friend Joseph touches the source of Obi's trouble when he says "that Obi's mission-house upbringing and European education had made him a stranger in his own country—the most painful thing one could say to Obi."[89] Obi seems not only to have forgotten the nature of communal traditional groupings such as the Umuofia Progressive Union, and the extent of its influence on the son of such a group, but also the allegiance it gives and demands in return. The Umuofia Progressive Union is a traditional extension of the communal village grouping in an urban situation: "Those Umuofians (that is the name they call themselves) who leave their home town to find work in towns all

over Nigeria regard themselves as sojourners. . . . No matter
where they are in Nigeria they start a local branch of the
Umuofia Progressive Union."[90]

This group had raised eight hundred pounds so the first of
their sons could be educated abroad, for study abroad brings
many privileges to the individual.

> A university degree was the philosopher's stone. It trans-
> muted a third-class clerk on one hundred and fifty a year into a
> senior Civil Servant on five hundred and seventy, with car and
> luxuriously furnished quarters at nominal rent. And the dis-
> parity in salary and amenities did not tell even half the story.
> To occupy a 'European post' was second only to actually being
> a European. It raised a man from the masses to the elite whose
> small talk at cocktail parties was: 'How's the car behaving?'[91]

But the Umuofia Progressive Union also expects to harvest
privileges and benefits accruing to its first chosen son.
" 'Thanks to the Man Above,' he continued, 'we now have one
of our sons in the senior service. We are not going to ask him to
bring his salary to share among us. It is in little things like this
that he can help us. It is our fault if we do not approach
him.' "[92]

Joseph, who had not been educated abroad, understood the
nature of communal obligations. He was aware, too, that young
men and women of his generation were pioneers who, even
when rejecting certain rules, were still bound by them. However, Obi, insisting on his individualism, makes mistake after
mistake in his treatment of this group. Achebe is aware of the
consequences of these initially trivial mistakes and accentuates
them at the beginning of the novel:

> Everybody was properly dressed in *aghada* or European
> suit except the guest of honour, who appeared in his shirt-
> sleeves because of the heat. That was Obi's mistake Number
> One. Everybody expected a young man from England to be
> impressively turned out.[93]

> Obi's English, on the other hand, was most unimpressive. He
> spoke 'is' and 'was.' He told them about the value of educa-
> tion. . . . When he sat down the audience clapped from polite-
> ness. Mistake Number Two.[94]

Nor does Obi realize the nature of traditional belief, its continuity, its strength. In spite of the objections of his friends, his
family, and his clan, Obi insists on continuing his romance with
Clara, an *osu*, traditionally regarded as an outcast among the
Ibo community. His friend Christopher, who like Obi holds a
"European post" tells him: "You may say that I am not broad-
minded, but I don't think we have reached the stage where we
can ignore all our customs. You may talk about education and
so on, but I am not going to marry an *osu*."[95] His father, a
devoted Christian, one who himself had defied tradition, refuses
consent to Obi's marriage to Clara: "*Osu* is like leprosy in the
minds of our people. I beg of you, my son, not to bring the
mark of shame and of leprosy into your family."[96] Obi dis-
misses the persistence of tradition as ignorance: "What made
an *osu* different from other men and women? Nothing but the
ignorance of their forefathers. Why should they, who had seen
the light of the Gospel, remain in that ignorance?"[97]

In the end, Obi's stand stems not so much from his convic-
tion about the rightness or wrongness of the matter but from a
stubborn, seemingly contrary individualism.

> His mind was troubled not only by what had happened but
> also by the discovery that there was nothing in him with which
> to challenge it honestly. All day he had striven to rouse his
> anger and his conviction, but he was honest enough with him-
> self to realise that the response he got, no matter how violent it
> sometimes appeared, was not genuine. It came from the
> periphery, and not the centre.[98]

This habit of remaining at the periphery instead of going to the
center of the matter is one of the traits in his character that
leads to his downfall. Obi is loathe to face things squarely. At
first the strength of his idealism, his deep nationalism, and his
sincerity make him reject any type of corruption, any connivance with bribery, makes him long for an ethical social
order.

> 'Where does one begin? With the masses? Educate the
> masses?' He shook his head, 'Not a chance there. It would take
> centuries. A handful of men at the top. Or even one man with
> vision—an enlightened dictator. People are scared of the word

nowadays. But what kind of democracy can exist side by side with so much corruption and ignorance?'[99]

The initial insistence on these virtues obscures the defects in his character, which later become apparent as he confronts an ever-increasing number of economic problems in a society where corruption is woven into its fabric. Obi succumbs to accepting bribes. The defects in his character and his inability to apprehend the historical and social forces at work in the society lead to his catastrophe.

Within this transitional moment Obi has to face not only the resentment of the older civil servants who have arduously worked their way up through the ranks, but also derision and scorn from the colonial administrative hierarchy. Obi condemns the former group for its corruption: "But take one of these old men. He probably left school thirty years ago in Standard Six. He has worked steadily to the top through bribery —an ordeal by bribery. To him the bribe is natural. He gave it and he expects it."[100] He resents the colonials for the disdain so clearly evident in the supercilious counsel they offer: " 'It is, of course, none of my business really. But in a country where even the educated have not reached the level of thinking about tomorrow, one has a clear duty.' He made the word 'educated' taste like vomit."[101]

As he uneasily shifts between these two groups, Obi's problems accumulate. Strapped by the repayment of his loan to the Umuofia Progressive Union, he is unable to maintain his government house and car; he must pay his mother's medical bills and his brother's school fees. In debt to the bank and Clara, and victim of a robbery, he is faced with the grim realities of abortion for Clara and the death of his mother.

Neither the old colonial administration nor the traditional communal group can comprehend the strength of the forces at work on members of this young professional elite. Mr. Green, the epitome of the colonial administrator, ascribes the financial difficulties of Obi's class to an inherent defect in the national character: "There is no single Nigerian who is prepared to forgo a little privilege in the interest of his country. From your ministers down to your most junior clerk. And you tell me you want to govern yourselves."[102]

The traditional group, the Umuofia Progressive Union, blames the individual: "What the Government pays you is more than enough unless you go into bad ways. . . . We are pioneers building up our families and our town. And those who build must deny . . . many pleasures."[103]

Essentially, *No Longer at Ease* is an implicit reproach of those unable to grasp the dynamics of a transitional social moment. In an effort to capture the continuity of the traditional in the present evolving society, Achebe overuses traditional expressions, maxims, and proverbs to qualify and further explicate often already obvious statements and events.

Everywhere the author's hand is evident. He carefully selects a number of random or chance occurrences that inexorably lead to his character's downfall. Thus, in a series of intertwining demonstrative incidents, Achebe succeeds in showing how ironic are the circumstances that lead to human failing and how tentative must condemnation of such failure be.

Obi Okonkwo is a mishap of the social order in which he finds himself. He succumbs to corruption, and his subsequent downfall is its consequence. Similarly, protagonists of the novels *God's Bits of Wood, Emergency,* and *A Night of Their Own,* which deal with an emergency political situation, also become mishaps of that situation; individuals undergo rapid change, some die. Friendships develop quickly and as quickly change, and as groups attempt to confront these political emergencies their traditions undergo vast alteration.

> In the old days, the singing of the pestles had begun even before the morning star disappeared in the first light of dawn. From courtyard to courtyard the women had exchanged their unceasing, pounding rhythms, and the sounds had seemed to cascade through the smoky air like the song of a brook rushing through a deep ravine . . . and the same echoes which announced the birth of the day presaged a peaceful day. . . .
>
> But now the mortar was silent, and the only sound to be heard was the whispering of the trees, announcing a sorrowful day. Deprived of the oils from the pounded grain, the mortar and the neatly aligned pestles lay baking in the sun, from time to time emitting a little crackling sound, as a split appeared in the dry wood. And the women could only watch helplessly, as fissures ran up from the base of the stump and zigzagged toward the rim.[104]

The days were no longer peaceful; the men were on strike; there was hunger and suffering, but the workers of the railroad were united, hoping to obtain for themselves that which made the difference between poverty and well-being, indignity and hope. The people Sembene Ousmane has depicted in *God's Bits of Wood* were struggling to gain a living wage that would lift them out of the abyss of poverty, provide them with compensation when they were sick and unable to work, a retiring pension for their aged. They were demanding what the white worker doing the same job received, but which the black man was denied because of the color of his skin. Ousmane has described the five-month struggle that took place in Senegal in 1947–48; the bitter fight was won, but a price was paid in suffering, fear, privation, and for some the heavy toll was death.

Ousmane shows how traditional life underwent changes, how many traditional beliefs were swept aside by the turbulence of the strike. Remembering the suffering they had incurred once before, Old Niakoro ponders:

> In her time the young people undertook nothing without the advice of their elders, but now, alone, they were deciding on a strike. Did they even know what would happen? She, Niakoro, knew; she had seen one. A terrible strike, a savage memory for those who had lived through it; just one season of rains before the war. It had taken a husband and a son from her, but now no one even came to seek her advice. Were the ways of the old time gone forever? Ibrahim Bakayoko, her own son, had told her nothing![105]

Niakoro was to be one of the victims of this strike. In protesting the arrest and mistreatment of Fa Keïta, the Old One, she:

> . . . hurled herself at the man, but a violent blow of his elbow directly over her heart left her stunned and breathless. She fell back against the wall, gasping, her eyes opened wide in terror. . . . When at last she fell, the light of morning from the open door lay coldly across the wrinkled, half-lifeless face. . . . Beneath the faded cloth, the old legs grew suddenly rigid, and her forehead cracked against the beaten earth.[106]

Violence was to become an everyday occurrence as the declaration of a strike was met with countermeasures. The most necessary provisions were cut off; the water was stopped and rice could no longer be bought. Not only were the people deprived of the necessities, they had to endure the brutality of soldiers and police. A group of workers was met by charging soldiers: "The battle was joined in an instant, and with every available weapon: the butt ends of muskets, the tips of bayonets, the soles of heavy boots, and tear-gas bombs. Cries of rage, of pain, and of fear mingled in single clamor, rising to the morning sky."[107] It was thought certain by the railroad employers that this combination of brutality and privation would force the strikers back to work, but the fight ahead was to be long and misery-laden, with the strikers determined to achieve their demands.

Ramatoulaye, who had always been quiet, unassuming, polite, became strong, violent through the upheaval caused by the strike. When she killed Vendredi, the ram, after he had overturned the pots in the kitchen, scattering the rice on the ground, "There was neither pride nor arrogance in her attitude but just a kind of satisfaction as if what she had done had been only a duty she would not avoid." The ram had destroyed the only hope for the evening's meal, and in killing it, Ramatoulaye was able to provide food for the hungry mouths around her. Perhaps Ramatoulaye was the first to taste the new awareness that the strike had wrought:

> When you know that the life and spirit of others depend on your life and your spirit, you have no right to be afraid—even when you are terribly afraid. In the cruel times we are living through we must find our own strength, somehow, and force ourselves to be hard. If Vendredi had not destroyed the only hope we had for today he would still be alive; and if he had killed me, you would have wept—but in weeping you might have forgotten your hunger, at least for today. Oh yes, God knows that these times are hard and strange![108]

At first the secretary-general of the union, Doudou, experiences excitement, euphoria; but slowly the sight of the hungry children and the other miseries endured because of the strike weigh heavily on him, and he begins to wonder "if he was right in urging them to stand firm and go on with the struggle." He realizes that the actions he has helped forge into actuality will entail deep pain and suffering for those he loves. But his vision, like that of the other leaders of the strike, outstretches the moment, advancing into the future with a dream of the noble life. "The men were growing restless and nervous from the constant spectacle of their hungry families."[109] Pressure to give up the struggle is keenly felt, but their determination to fight is reinforced by the miseries they have already experienced —to surrender after the fight had begun would be to negate the justness of their claims. Throughout the novel Ousmane implies that strength comes to those who fight, to those who believe in that for which they are fighting.

Doudou is offered a bribe of 3,000,000 francs to get the men to return to work. He rejects Isnard's offer, and the white supervisor is then forced to acknowledge that "the structure of ideas on which he had based his life and his conduct in all these years had been shaken."[110] The portrait of the African as a tractable child was one that Isnard could no longer reconcile with this man Doudou upon whom he had previously flaunted every indignity.

As the agonies of the strike begin to mount, the women at first begin to lose pride, sinking into apathy; their best clothes and headdresses are rejected by the merchants, and they turn homeward, scavenging amidst the litter in vacant lots with the hope of finding the smallest morsel to take home; but there was no lot that had not "already been scoured by the bands of emaciated children."[111] Soon the women become aroused with a sense of the indignities they have endured and are determined to fight with their men. For instance, Penda, a whore who had previously hated men, works by their side during the strike and gains a semblance of dignity and pride: she keeps the women in line as she gives them their rations, and the men respect her. Penda leads the women on their march from Thiès to Dakar in support of the strike; she is the symbol of strength that prevents a stranglehold of chaos from undoing the unity that will lead the marchers to success. But Penda is killed by police bullets as the women reach the outskirts of Dakar.

Not all of Ousmane's characters are heroic. This is seen in the personality of Sounkaré, the watchman. Crippled, lonely, bitter, he is almost jubilant over the bad fortune that has befallen his fellow workers. He is grateful to the white man who gave him his job. But the strike intensifies his loneliness and soon hunger gnaws at him: his fall into the pit, with only the company of scuttling rats, ends a pitiful life. His death foretells the end of an old way of life, a life of degradation, prey to pity, which had presaged the emergence of a new breed of men. Soon the strikers themselves sense the coming of something new:

> For the strikers and their families, life became more difficult with each succeeding day. Their bodies grew weaker and the lines in their faces were etched more deeply; but for many of them the ordeal they were passing through was taking on an even greater significance than the rites of initiation to manhood that they had undergone in their youth.[112]

Bakayoko was the man with "the soul" that infused the men with the courage they needed for their plight. He had heard enough of the adage "turn the other cheek"; he was lonely, angry, determined to win the battle before him; he was the leader others respected and were jealous of but who was always listened to. It is Bakayoko who remarked: "The kind of man we were is dead and our only hope for a new life lies in the machine, which knows neither a language nor a race." The men heard his words, but "They said nothing though, and only their eyes betrayed an inner torment brought on by the mounting terror of famine and an inconsolable loneliness for the machine." The strike makes the workers aware of their closeness with the machine: it is an undeniable part of their lives from which they can not turn. The strength of this "fellowship" was "stronger than the barriers which separated them from their employers, stronger even than the obstacle which until now had been insurmountable—the color of their skin."[113] Realizing how important the machine is to their lives the opposing groups are forced to strive for understanding.

Bakayoko had completely identified with the smoking train traveling over the savanna. He was dedicated to his people, to the salvation of their future and to their cause. So firmly committed that he would not and could not temper his dedication, he was a man to be admired and feared. Ousmane shows how this dedication had matured Bakayoko. The ordeal of the strike enables him to appreciate the loyalty and faithfulness of Penda,

the scorned prostitute; and he becomes more sensitive to the
needs of his wife, who is touched by his thoughtfulness,
feeling a warmth and joy in her heart that she had never known
before. It is Bakayoko who reads the telegram: "Conditions
accepted. Strike terminated." The struggle was waged, people
endured in spite of the brutality and privation forced upon
them by their European employers.

Ousmane relates in his story the experience of three generations. Fa Keïta, the Old One, was hesitant, almost reluctant, to
be connected with the strike. Even after having been in the
detention camp where he had been brutalized, where he had
been forced to watch helplessly while others were senselessly
and maliciously tortured, Fa Keïta returned home without bitterness, cautioning those around him not to hate. His son
Bakayoko wondered, however, if it is possible to fight without
hating; he had hated and so he had fought to erase the disparity
of opportunity that had prompted his hate. Unlike his father he
had not been hesitant and reluctant. Ad'jibid'j, Bakayoko's
daughter, is poised for the future; she will receive the legacy
created by her parents. As a woman she will not be confined to
the hearth like her mother; she will have the opportunity to
sense the power lurking within her, an opportunity which Penda
and the other women who fought in the strike made possible.

Through the use of differing symbols Ousmane implicitly
states his ideas of historical movement, of generational change.
The mortar and the pestle symbolize the strength of the traditions of the older generations, "But now the mortar was silent
. . . pestles lay baking in the sun."[114] The second generation
placed its reliance on the machine, which brought about a
change in the old order; it is the machine that is tracking a path
into the future. The third generation, as epitomized by the
granddaughter of Fa Keïta, liberated through education, will derive fuller benefit from the rails, which symbolically extend into
the future.

No such sanguine prospect is held out in Peter Abrahams' A
Night of Their Own or in Richard Rive's Emergency. Only
through a leap of faith or a belief in historical evolution can
Peter Abrahams even foresee an end to the dark night; in
Emergency Richard Rive forecasts no solution to the oppres-
sive South African situation that brought about the emergency.
In the continuing struggle, in the ever-present emergency, per-

haps the only sanguine note is the novelistic presentation of interracial love affairs. In *Emergency* the Colored Andrew finally seems to commit himself to an emotional relationship with the white Ruth in spite of the obvious and pressing dangers of such a relationship. In *A Night of Their Own*, love is consummated between the black Nkosi and the Indian Dee Nunkhoo.

To hammer and hew a novel out of the monolithic social situation of South Africa is to apprehend a reality in which man is beset by fear, isolation, loneliness, is plagued by doubts and indecision. For South Africa is a society whose members live under the constant corrosion of dehumanization and the possibility of swift death:

> Naidoo's eyes opened. He stared up vacantly, then he recognized Van As. And with recognition came a hatred so strong and forceful that Van As saw and felt it. Naidoo worked his mouth as one working up saliva to spit. Then he died. . . . And there was something especially shocking about this man's death. This man did not have to die, did not have to suffer even. If only . . .[115]

But the "if" does not apply; the conditions for its fulfillment are absent in the polity of South Africa. Here man is at odds with his social environment, a conflict that is manifest in *Emergency* and *A Night of Their Own*.

Emergency is rooted in the political reality of apartheid. Rive, using a cumulative style, often enumerates the legislation that created the atmosphere of ever-growing tension which erupts in bloody violence and death.

> The spate of apartheid legislation poured out unabated. The Nationalists were determined to make segregation work. Entrench white domination for at least another three hundred years. Legislation and more legislation. The Group Areas Act: complete residential segregation. Whites, Africans and Coloureds must by law live in different areas. Suppression of Communism Act: the Minister of Justice is the sole arbiter of whether a person is a Communist or not. Population Registration Act: all people in the Union of South Africa are to be classified into racial categories. Every person must be ticketed, photographed and identified according to race. Immorality

Amendment Act: any sexual relationship between Europeans and any variety of non-white becomes illegal. And still legislation poured out. Entrenching apartheid.[116]

Against a background of inflammatory speeches, organized resistance, and strikes protesting such legislation, Rive details the violence, brutality and death that culminate and explode in the Sharpeville riots.

The open space in front of the police station at Sharpeville resembled a battleground. Sixty-nine people including eight women and ten children were killed. One hundred and eighty were wounded, including thirty-one women and nineteen children. Ambulance-loads deluged Vereenigning Hospital and some patients had to be treated on the grass. . . . Women covered their heads with their arms as they wailed over dead relatives. As the news spread, tension built up and Saracens rolled in.[117]

The emergency regulations, and the scenes of bloody rioting are not merely a backdrop; they directly chart the motions of the characters:

Then the situation exploded. It happened so quickly that the police were caught off their guard. Like an enraged beast the crowd charged. . . . With a splintering crash the patrol van was overturned. Pistol shots rang through the air. . . . Angry shouts and roars. Screams of terror and uncontrolled fury. Hundreds of feet trampling everything underfoot. Stones crashing into the window of the shop. Heavy breathing and running feet, then the shop also went up in flames.

Andrew felt himself being dragged and carried across the field. Willing hands helped him through the fence. Abe's face a misty haze. The last thing he remembered as he was pushed into the back of the car was seeing the black pall of smoke over the shop and the police van, and hearing the sharp whine of bullets whistling through the air. Then he fainted.[118]

The novel is one of situation: essentially the political situation, but the private situations of the individual characters run parallel to the political. Public and private, with their respective moralities, intertwine, producing a statement not only of politi-

cal emergency but also of personal crisis. The personal crises
manifest themselves in the lives of three young Colored men,
Andrew, Abe, and Justin—members of the Modern Youth Association, a politically active group which ferments resistance
to the repressive political laws—and in their relationships with
one another, their families, and their friends, as they search for
a *modus operandi* within the South African polity of Cape-
town.

The poverty of Andrew's early youth continually haunts him,
often blunting him to the point of inertia, hopelessness, and
loneliness. He is divided by conflicting loyalties: loyalty to himself and his ambitions and loyalty to a larger action that would
mean social and political commitment. But real action is hindered by memories of his environment and by his continued
sensitivity to it. He would obliterate the memory of District Six
and, with it, that of his family, but he never succeeds in leaving
them behind. He carries with him a memory of his mother's
death, a fear of his brother James, and, from his many years in
his sister's house, the hostility of his politically unconcerned
brother-in-law Kenneth.

Andrew's school companion Abe, who has never known this
poverty, can rationalize the social reality that has trapped
Andrew. But Abe, who seems to be the voice of the author, is
hindered by his continuous rationalization; he is unable to act,
even though he says: "The answer is to fight situations, not
retreat into cynicism and petty personalities."[119] Thus Abe is
constantly at odds with a third young man, Justin, who gives
himself to action, enters the public political arena, and often
pays the price of imprisonment for his commitment.

In the social reality of the emergency, most of the characters
suffer from loneliness, "friendless nights, hostile and woman-
less,"[120] as Braam, one of the characters, defines it. After a police
search from which Abe is forced to flee, his mother dies a
lonely, unloved woman. Justin's wife, Florence, abandons herself to tawdry pleasures when left alone by her imprisoned
husband.

In order to convey three sets of facts—the political history
leading to Sharpeville, the history of his characters, and the
actual events of only three days—Rive relies heavily on flash
backs. At times, the flash back is carefully interwoven and
artistically successful; at other times, the flash back destroys

the novelistic moment and its continuity. Often the flash backs take the form of direct statements by the author through his characters, most especially through Andrew's recollections. Such statements tend to be cumulative listings of book titles, records, examination questions, and so on, as the author shows off the range of intellectual pursuits of his characters. Rive relies heavily on dialogue; his style at times becomes dialectical debate interspersed with witty and specious conversation.

Yet, the author does succeed in presenting a sense of the emergency and the consequent convulsions. Friendships are strained to the point of breaking. Andrew and Abe, operating from different political and personal credos, go their separate ways: Abe leaves the country to seek refuge in Basutoland, and Andrew becomes emotionally caught up in the hysteria of the moment. The strained love affair between him and the white girl Ruth, which he tries to seal by not running away, becomes his act of defiance, providing him at last with a sense of inner security.

Interracial love affairs play a large part in Peter Abrahams' novel A *Night of Their Own*. Nkosi, a black South African who has been away from his homeland for many years, returns as a courier with money for the underground movement. Upon return, he falls in love with an Indian, Dee Nunkhoo, saving her from a deep skepticism brought on by an earlier love affair and reenforced by the antlike existence of the Indian community. A second part of the novel relates to the problems besetting, and the eventual breakup of, a love affair between a young, high-ranking Boer police officer, Karl Van As, and a Colored, demure school teacher, Mildred.

The novel brings into conflict two systems, the hunters who dominate and the hunted who oppose this domination. The hunters have an amazingly complex and efficient system of records: "birth registration, school registration, the old-time pass registration, the old-time travel permits. . . . we have carbon copies . . . in our files. So we can tell you not only when and where a Native was born, but also . . ."[121]

The hunted are equally well-organized and resistant.

> But we do live like ants, you know. All the warning systems
> of the ants too. We would know an hour before any hostile
> force reaches here. And as in the ant world, there will always

be those who are ready to be sacrificed for the good of the mass.[122]

The larger statement of the novel derives from the clash inherent in these systems. As proof of its allegiance to the black South Africans, the Indian community has to save Nkosi from the hunters, who would like nothing better than to divide the two dominated groups, the Indians and the Africans.

All the characters represent one or more facets of these two forces, which, pressing close upon them as individuals, cause depression, resentment, or fear. A closed morality impinges upon individual action and the love affairs of the characters. Karl Van As is aware that the conflict inherent in the society, if prolonged, can only end in a blood bath. Yet, continuing to work in the system that spawns this conflict, he too becomes a hunter and will attempt to destroy the symbol of freedom.

> We want that man, Karl! We want him badly! . . . A myth is being created and that is always dangerous. At illegal meetings in Pretoria and Johannesburg and all up and down the Reef there has been talk about a new underground hero who cannot be captured and who cannot be killed because he is the spirit of freedom and is therefore invincible. . . . And his name is Richard Nkosi. . . . We've got to destroy the myth before it spreads. . . . And I want you to do that for me, for the nation![123]

Having made such a choice, Van As must bring his love affair with Mildred to an end; symbolically, he turns to Anna de Wet, who seeks to maintain total Boer domination: "Karl Van As stopped at the first bar, downed two double brandies very quickly, then looked up the telephone number of Anna de Wet. When she answered, her eager invitation filled him with dismay. And as he drove to her place, he wept inside for the man he would have liked Karl Van As to be."[124] Has the society done this to Van As or is it inherent in his character? Abrahams does not make this explicit. Like Van As, Nkosi resents the system which protects him and momentarily turns from "the woman and her people, and the terrible notion of antlike existence";[125] but unlike Van As, he remains faithful to a personal open morality that permits him to love and return to the crippled

Indian, Dee. But she sees realistically the horrible truth of social circumstances in South Africa. The outer world is always present, impinging upon an individual's more idealistic, romantic notions. Moments of tenderness between individuals are often invaded by the corrosive nature of the outer reality. Dee is at peace with herself when with Nkosi; a new South Africa seems possible as one dreams:

> But you know as well as I do that all we have to do is go outside this garden for all your fine ideals to become meaningless. . . . Here, sitting in this garden, it feels as though it is possible. But I know it is an illusion brought on by you. We are at war, my friend. It is wonderful to have, even for a moment, the illusion of being at peace.[126]

Symbolically, moments of tenderness and human intimacy take place in little gardens that shut off the outside world. Inner truth and outside reality, tender interludes and violent moments, common interiors and hostile exteriors all follow one another in dramatic sequence throughout the novel, which is like a play. Most of the scenes are set in interiors, with expository dialogue and debates between two or more people who argue the validity of social action and commitment in South Africa. There are three parts, three acts: the first focuses upon the love affair between Dee and Nkosi; the second shows Van As' dilemma and his relationship to Mildred; and the third presents the dialogue between Old Man Nanda, a rich Indian merchant, who has bribed his way through the system, and his son, who fights this system:

> "I've shown I'm a friend. I've given money. I give them presents. I've expressed my opposition to all your political nonsense. They'll believe me, you'll see!"
> "They won't father; I'll see that they don't." . . .
> "What kind of a son are you?"
> "One who had to stand up because he was a man, and who had to try and make up for his father."[127]

Abrahams draws his characters with compassion and with a sense of romanticized humanity. The world which he depicts is less immediate and vibrant, more inventive and imaginative than the world of Rive and Ousmane. All three novels may suffer from too much direct statement, wherein the authors seem to control too consciously the action and development of the plots. Yet given the nature of the political emergencies, it is hardly possible for any author not to state his convictions and not to postulate a solution to a harsh social situation.

The state of unease evident in the political emergencies is once more elaborated in Achebe's *A Man of the People*. The novel mirrors the unhealthy political climate present after four years of independent rule, where fraud and corruption are ethical norms and flagrant political deals transpire, where incompetent and greedy ministers reign and seemingly idealistic men are, in fact, self-seeking opportunists. Indeed the novel is a cynical presentation of the prevailing license and seeming hopelessness of newly independent countries: "Poor black mother! Waiting so long for her infant son to come of age and comfort her and repay her for the years of shame and neglect. And the son she has pinned so much hope on turning out to be a Chief Nanga."[128]

Politics is a game whose prize is the eating of the national cake, whose rules are dirty and uncompromising. Most people do not enter politics to serve the newly independent country; Odili's father believed that "the mainspring of political action was personal gain, a view which, I might say, was much more in line with the general feeling in the country."[129] Throughout the novel Achebe reiterates the gains and privileges that accompany political office, underscoring the great power wielded by ministers. These gains may be won in a variety of ways: through the taking of bribes, through corrupt economic arrangements with foreigners, and through patronage. It seems the whole society accepts the all-pervasive corruption through which many politicians acquire great wealth.

> As he gave instance after instance of how some of our leaders who were ash-mouthed paupers five years ago had become near-millionaires under our very eyes, many in the audience laughed. But it was the laughter of resignation to misfortune. No one among them swore vengeance; no one shook with rage or showed any sign of fight.[130]

The resulting mood is one of apathy and cynicism: "The people . . . had become even more cynical than their leaders and were apathetic into the bargain. 'Let them eat,' was the people's opinion, 'after all when white men used to do all the eating did we commit suicide . . . it may be your turn to eat tomorrow.' "[131]

It is in this political arena that Chief Nanga operates. Nanga is sketched for us by Odili Samalu, his former student who later becomes his social and political rival. At the beginning of the novel, Nanga is making a political visit to the school where Odili teaches. During this visit we glimpse the elaborate welcome reserved for a visiting minister.

> She was now praising Micah's handsomeness, which she likened to the perfect, sculpted beauty of a carved eagle, and his popularity which would be the envy of the proverbial traveler-to-distant-places who must not cultivate enmity on his route. Micah was of course Chief the Honourable M. A. Nanga, M.P.

Achebe ironically underlines the lavishness of the welcome by shrewdly injecting into his descriptions a note about the rising cost of living.

> The arrival of the members of the hunters' guild in full regalia caused a great stir. . . . Most of the hunters reserved their precious powder to greet the Minister's arrival—the price of gunpowder like everything else having doubled again and again in the four years since this government took control.[132]

Odili experiences intense disgust at such a welcome arranged by the headmaster of the school, who himself was seeking political preferment. In a flash-back sequence Odili recalls the figure of his former teacher.

> I remember him then as a popular, young and handsome teacher, most impressive in his uniform as a scoutmaster. . . .
> Nanga must have gone into politics soon afterwards and then won a seat in Parliament. (It was easy in those days—before we knew its cash price.)[133]

In detailing the economic crisis that catapulted Chief Nanga into his ministerial post, Achebe extends the purely local, domestic, and problematic setting of *No Longer at Ease* into the international scene, attempting, albeit superficially, to show how external economic forces affect internal political problems.

> Then came the slump in the international coffee market. Overnight (or so it seemed to us) the Government had a dangerous financial crisis on its hands.
>
> The Minister of Finance at the time was a first-rate economist with a Ph.D. in public finance. He presented to the Cabinet a complete plan for dealing with the situation.
>
> The Prime Minister said "No" to the plan. He was not going to risk losing the election by cutting down the price paid to coffee planters at that critical moment.[134]

The expulsion of professionally trained ministers from the cabinet and the vicious attack against the university-trained politicians introduces a bit more specifically a point of conflict hinted at in *No Longer at Ease.* Men such as Chief Nanga, who with the limited education possible under colonialism had achieved high political and social positions, resented those younger professionals newly returned from the university.

> Let us now and for all time extract from our body-politic as a dentist extracts a stinking tooth all those decadent stooges versed in text-book economics and aping the white man's mannerisms and way of speaking. . . . Away with the damnable and expensive university education which only alienates an African from his rich and ancient culture and puts him above his people . . .[135]

This conflict does not become the center of conflict between the two main protagonists in the novel. The conflict arises after Chief Nanga seduces a girl friend of Odili, about whose virtues Odili had not only spoken disparagingly but also in whom he had disclaimed any deep interest. Odili vows revenge and determines to do combat with the Chief on the personal level as well as the public stage.

> What mattered was that a man had treated me as no man had a right to treat another—not even if he was master and the other slave; and my manhood required that I make him pay for his insult in full measure. In flesh and blood terms I re-

alized that I must go back, seek out Nanga's intended parlour-wife and give her the works, good and proper. . . .

I must say that I was immediately taken with the idea of the Common People's Convention. Apart from everything else it would add a second string to my bow when I came to deal with Nanga.[136]

The contrast between Odili's fine utterances and ethical pronouncements about public morality and political probity and his own selfish and egotistical behavior emphasizes the deep irony of the situation. Further, the fact that Achebe puts forward Odili as a substitute and possible replacement for the by far more colorful and honest rogue Chief Nanga clearly shows the author's deepening cynicism.

Chief Nanga is a ruthless politician who is not averse to blackmail and violence for his own ends, yet shrewd and smooth enough to be "a man of the people": "Chief Nanga was a born politician; he could get away with almost anything he said or did. . . . He had the rare gift of making people feel—even while he was saying harsh things to them—that there was not a drop of ill will in his entire frame."[137]

He is a politician ready-made for the permissive amoral political environment Achebe has painted for us. Achebe's cynicism seems to give way to pessimism when it is not Odili but Max, the idealistic and practical founder of the Common People's Convention, who is killed during the election campaign. Achebe brings an end to the political chaos and a denouement to his novel by a *deus ex machina*, a military coup.

In *A Man of the People*, Achebe presents a kaleidoscopic view of the many elements at work in the newly independent Nigeria. For international color he adds a sprinkle of foreign stereotypes. A modicum of historical depth is given in the figure of Odili's father, a retired District Interpreter: "In those days when no one understood as much as 'come' in the white man's language, the District Officer was like the Supreme Deity, and Interpreter the principal minor god who carried prayers and sacrifice to Him . . . So Interpreters in those days were powerful, very rich, widely known and hated."[138]

Yet many of the incidents are but superficially treated, revealed through Odili's semi-ironic interpretion of incidents and events. Too many situations seem derived from college bull sessions. Too often there is confusion in our minds as to whether the voice is Odili's or the author's. Indeed, Achebe, with his casual tone and impressionistic style, portrays and delineates an endless variety of sketchily drawn female and male characters who are reflections of political incidents. The novel abounds with a variety of social and political motifs, yet does not penetrate the dynamic political convolutions at work in a newly independent country.

Cyprian Ekwensi deals with another political problem in his novel *Beautiful Feathers,* that of Pan-Africanism. The political question posed is this: how should an African nation-state attempt to implement the concept of continental unity? Achebe had failed to portray fully the vast political forces in motion in a nation-state; in *Beautiful Feathers* Ekwensi is no more successful in presenting the complex subject of Pan-Africanism with all its multilayered possibilities.

But *Beautiful Feathers* is concerned with more than Pan-Africanism. Ekwensi emphasizes the social immorality at work in society not only by presenting many scenes of infidelity but by making the wife of a young, idealistic, and highly respected Pan-African leader, Wilson Iyari, unfaithful to him. Thus, the second problem posed in the novel is this: how is it possible that a man who is working for and stands as a symbol of African solidarity cannot achieve the same solidarity in a much smaller unit, that of his family?

> Solidarity, where does it begin? Here, in my own home? I am the leader of the Nigerian Movement for African and Malagasy Solidarity. Wilson Iyari, good looking, famous outside. At home I am nothing. I am like a fowl with beautiful feathers on the outside for all to see. When the feathers are removed the flesh and bones underneath are the same as for any other fowl. I am not really different from other men. In fact, if only they knew how I am spited in my own home they would despise me. They would never again listen to me talking about solidarity.[139]

Yet, in spite of "beautiful feathers," Wilson Iyari persists in his dream and continues to work toward a Pan-African ideal. Together with a group of idealistic young men, he seizes every opportunity to demonstrate the need for African unity. Thus, he dramatically challenges the Prime Minister on his return from a trip abroad: " 'What are we doing about African and Malagasy Solidarity?' The question came out of the blue. The Prime Minister stared at him then smiled . . . Iyari felt uncomfortable, but stood his ground. He wiped his face. A spotlight had been swung around so that it shone full in his face."[140]

Later on Iyari and the Nigerian Movement for African and Malagasy Solidarity climax their demands with a protest march, which ends in riot. The organization of this march, the many hours of planning, take Iyari away from his wife Yaniya with whom he wants to live happily and from his profession of pharmacy in which he wants to excel. The many debates as to the efficacy of the march among the eager members of the Nigerian Movement for African and Malagasy Solidarity shows us how inflamed many were by the prospect of African unity.

As a result of the march Iyari is called upon to represent Nigeria at the Conference on African Unity by the Prime Minister, whom Ekwensi presents as being serenely wise: "At first Wilson did not notice the Prime Minister reclining self-effaced and barefooted on a 'catifa.' He was reading the Koran. Seeing him at home, Wilson felt a warm admiration for the man. There is still a belief in God, he thought."[141] Wilson Iyari realizes that this serene, benevolent man is completely sympathetic to the idea of Pan-Africanism but is not sure of the method. He says, "Yes, your help. Or do you think a Prime Minister does not need the help of his distinguished citizens. . . . We all feel as you do. It is merely a question of method."[142]

Full of optimism and zeal, Iyari goes to Senegal to the conference, where many fine resolutions are made. Then Ekwensi demonstrates the difficulty of implementing these fine ideas, and the divisiveness of material goods, through the use of an allegorical folk sequence: "Some of the hunters wanted the horns, some wanted the whole beast preserved in a museum and immediately an argument arose and voices became loud. Nobody knew who squeezed a trigger. There was the sharp crack of a shot and everyone ran for cover. Confusion spread."[143]

The moral of the story is told by the President of Senegal who presents Wilson with a medal for his efforts: "You know . . . it is like the struggle for African Unity. While Africa burns, interested parties carry away the loot. We must be on our guard, must be ready to give and take."[144]

Characterization is simple and uncomplicated. There is the idealistic Chini who has suffered the loss of the man she loved and who had sired her child. She could easily fall in love with Iyari but nobly refrains from it to reunite Iyari, his wife, and his family ("Now she could be a friend of the family, openly so because her conscience was clear. He watched her, trim and smart as always, and so selfless."[145]). Kwame is an idealistic Ghanaian who, like Max in *A Man of the People*, dies for his beliefs: "I am sure there was something about him we never knew. He hid it so well from all of us. I think he *knew* his fate was sealed even before he left. Yet he went and got killed."[146]

Ekwensi, characterizes the Minister of Consolation, and describes thereby chicanery and political incompetence of many men in public office ("He is vain, conceited, stupid, empty, illiterate, a thorough fool, but shrewd enough to take everyone in."[147]).

Beautiful Feathers is a slight novel where minor incidents are related in language more suited to a weightier, denser treatment of the subject of Pan-Africanism. *A Wreath for Udomo*, however, is a full-scale treatment of the fight for national independence and of the problems consequent on winning such independence. The many themes and motifs that have appeared in most of the preceding novels resonate through this work. Its chief characters move away and suffer exile abroad, fleeing colonial regimes; others flee countries ruled by white segregationist minorities. Abroad they plot the liberation of a continent; they move back to meet death and disillusionment, to be reabsorbed into tribalism or, with shattered dreams, leave again for a second exile.

For Michael Udomo, the central figure of the novel, movement away from Africa is no different than it is for many other Africans.

It was made up of the common experience of most colonial students. The missionaries had picked out the brightest boy in the little village in Africa and set about educating him. Education had brought awareness. The boy had then examined the world in which he lived and found it wanting by the very standards the missionaries had given him. He had turned against them then and struck out on his own.[148]

However, Udomo returns to Africa imbued with a powerful sense of nationalism and Africanness, vowing to give his life for the liberation of his continent.

> Mother Africa! Oh, Mother Africa, make me strong for the work that I must do! Don't forget me in the many you nurse. I would make you great.
> "I will die for my people!"[149]

Thomas Lanwood left Africa and lived abroad in England for thirty years, passionately theorizing about the freedom of the continent in writings that inspired young men such as Udomo: "He had spent his life in the fight and he knew his influence was at work all over Africa, but it was good to meet this young man who was the living proof of it."[150]

While in England, Lanwood founded and led for many years the Africa Freedom Group with Mhendi, Mabi, and Adebhoy. Lanwood's return to independent Africa turns to bitter disillusionment, culminating in a tragic departure back to England.

Mhendi had led an unsuccessful and bloody revolt in his own country, Pluralia, against the brutality of a monolithic segregated society. Later he returns to fight against this society and meets his death in the process.

Adebhoy, a medical doctor, is the first to return to Africa, and there he completely reenters the tribal system, answering the call of his totem.

Mabi, the artist, returns to his mountain people, the most traditionally tribal of Pan-Africa. Unable to meet the vast challenge that return poses to his generation, he flees back to England, lonely and crestfallen.

For all these characters, movement away is fraught with problems stemming from that morning of "ACCOUCHEMENT," return, with deep tragic consequences. The constant interplay of the members of this group, their planning for and dreams of political freedom, and when finally that is won, the full implementation of such freedom give width and depth to the novel.

The characterization derives its fullness and variety from the changing, fluctuating fortunes of the protagonists, the fleshing out of their personalities. A roundness is given to the novel by Abrahams' easily integrated conceptualizing about tribalism, imperialism, and industrialization; a lyrical pathos through the contrasting of allegiances to a cause with allegiances to a friend or to a lover.

On a cold blustery night, Michael Udomo, thinly dressed, meets a lonely thirty-six-year-old widow, Lois Barlow in a bar. She is instantly drawn to Udomo by his "haunted and lonely eyes," his compressed inner force. Lois, who had been friend and mentor to Lanwood, Mhendi, Adebhoy and Mabi, presents the excited Michael Udomo to the group:

> ". . . his excitement was so great that he felt unnaturally limp and calm . . . Lanwood came in and filled the room. Udomo saw only him. Those behind were like shadows."[151]

Eventually it was Udomo, through his inner strength and smoldering passions, who infused new purpose into the group: "He was the real force. His coming had affected the whole of the group. Before he came they had been a group of wishful dreamers. Now an organization had come into being. And they had plans rather than dreams. And all in the space of six months."[152] The *Liberator*, a magazine begun by Udomo, becomes an organ through which he and the others are able to work for the liberation of Pan-Africa.

Lois Barlow, attracted by Udomo's passionate energy and drive, is warned by Mabi: "Don't forget what I've told you, Lois. He frightens me a little too . . . And . . . he has the kind of muted violence that appeals to your peaceful sophisticated mind."[153] Nevertheless she falls in love with him and finds an unexpected tenderness: "Gentle Michael. What had she been afraid of, she and Mabi? Not of this utter peace. That violence she sensed must have been imagination. There'd been nothing violent about him. And now this quiet."[154]

As in his portrayal of so many other incidents, Abrahams uses comparative poetic structure in developing the love affair between Lois and Udomo; the changing moods are mirrored in shifting images of nature. When they first meet the night is cold and chilly: "The moon was in the first quarter. The stars were coldly bright. A sharp wind travelled across the earth."[155]

Before their first act of love the sun is gay and all of nature is about to burst out: "The warm afternoon sun shimmered in through the french windows, filled the room with a gaiety and light. . . . And on the trees, . . . the buds were choking fat to bursting-point. The period of blossoming was at hand, and earth and air held a gentle tenderness." Through an image of entry Abrahams further captures and draws out the act of love: "A chink of sunlight filtered in through the tiny gap at the top of the drawn curtains and played on the foot of the bed . . ."[156]

As in so many of his novels, Abrahams' lovers go to a house in the hills where they find complete peace and calm before the coming of the gale that destroys their love. Then, "all the world seemed calm." The sun images continue until Udomo's unfaithfulness with Jo Furse, Lois' attractive corn-haired roommate and motherless protégé. Then the night is cold, and "Outside, the snow came down steadily, no longer wafting but falling, thick and fast."[157] The brutally fierce end of the love affair between Lois and Udomo leads to the first real break in the group. On the political level, Mabi will continue to cooperate with Udomo, but on the personal level he spurns all advances. In the meantime, plans and schemes have gone relentlessly forward, and Adebhoy goes home to prepare the way for Udomo's movement back. Seeking traditional support for their fight, Adebhoy approaches the Council of Chiefs and Elders on Udomo's behalf, but his overtures are summarily and snobbishly rejected.

> . . . it is not the policy of this Council to give hearings to any unknown persons simply at their own request. Furthermore, Council directs me to inform you that there is no record of any family by the name of Udomo ever having held any position of authority either as chief or elder in any of the major tribes of Panafrica. . . . Your information of what he did in Europe is of no interest to the Council."[158]

Udomo's return to Africa is told in moon images aboard ship when darkness still hovered over the land: ". . . the moon is a woman comforting her children against the dark terrors of the night. Then he thought: no, a woman is near and touches you; the moon is far. Then again: but it does comfort. Be brighter, moon! Then I'll see Africa again."[159]

His arrival is unheralded but watched with deep interest by the influential market woman Selina, whom he had met aboard ship. "Do not forget the women, then, Mr. Udomo . . . When you have started, and when I can see what it is you are doing, come to me and I will speak for you with the women of the market. My name is Selina. Remember it. And do not forget the women."[160] He turns to her when after six months of frustrating work he is unable to break the stranglehold of the merchants, who, having financed the *Liberator*, control its voice. Together Adebhoy, Selina, and Udomo form the Africa Freedom Party. While the others organize a protest, Udomo goes to prison for his rallying editorial: ". . . I will write a call to our people to rise against the foreigners and demand the freedom to rule themselves. I will say that the Council of Chiefs and Elders and Dr. Endura are the tools of the British . . . that the time has come for us to fight and to go on fighting until we and our land are free."[161]

So far the common enemy outside has served to unite them. They win self-government for Pan-Africa and Udomo becomes Prime Minister. The task of building a nation, of fusing together the tribal groupings into a viable modern society, is Udomo's dream and overriding ambition and brings him into conflict with Adebhoy and Selina ". . . there's some opposition among our own people. Not to industrialization as such—I've convinced them at last that that is the only way we can become strong in terms of world power. The opposition is to the fact that we need European technicians and European capital to do it."[162] Udomo tells Mhendi, whose return to Africa he has arranged in spite of the protest of the neighboring white minority government of Pluralia.

Lanwood too has returned, but here in the real practical arena of emergent-nation politics he and his theoretical slogans seem jaded, dated, and out of place. Slowly and skillfully Abrahams captures and traces the decline and tragic disillusionment of a son of Africa who has fought all his life for her liberation but who has been away too long. In Pan-Africa it was clear to Mhendi that Lanwood was out of place: "he's going on as though he's still in England. He's been away from Africa too long. He's lost touch and could mess up things for himself."[163] Selina, too, quickly realizes that Lanwood has moved away, that he can no longer sense the rhythms of his land: "All day I

have watched him. And it was like watching a white man with a
black skin. He is too old to change. . . . He will never come
back to us. He is lost to us." Then she symbolically demonstrates this:

> First she took Lanwood and ushered him into an empty room.
> Then she led Mhendi to the room where she had taken Udomo
> the night before he went to prison. . . . "For you, there is
> someone to make your sleep more restful," Selina said. "You
> are of us, so there is no need to explain."
> "And my friend?"
> "That one is white for all his black skin. He would not
> understand."[164]

In that room Maria waits, the image of Mhendi's first wife, who
was killed leading a demonstration in Pluralia. A parallel
movement is developed by Abrahams: the increasing emptiness
of Lanwood on the one hand and a sustaining love between
Mhendi and Maria on the other.

All the members of the group try to save Lanwood from the
despair and anguish that overwhelms him. In a very touching
scene Mabi tries to console the lonely and aging Lanwood.

> How he's aged! Mabi thought. He felt a sudden rush of
> compassion.
> "What's it, Tom? You're not happy."
> "There's no room for me here, Paul . . ."
> "Nonsense, man!" He leaned sideways and put an arm about
> Lanwood's bulk. "It's just that it's all strange to you. Give
> yourself time. You've been away a long time. It takes time to
> adjust."[165]

Even Udomo, who himself has become a calculatingly cold,
lonely leader, ponders how best to funnel the somewhat useless
Lanwood and his theories into the practical political arena of
national development: "You talked about a book. The party
will publish it. Let that be a beginning. Get to know your people
again. Go about it carefully. Our people are not like the people
of Europe. You can make a place for yourself here."[166]

Another structural movement is at play in the novel: even as
we follow the decline of the aging theoretician Lanwood
through the eyes of the group, so do we view the vital strength

that comes with Udomo's political maturing and ascendancy. Mhendi perceptively observes "there are no flags in his eyes now, they're all about him; and how it's relaxed him, how he's grown!"[167] And later: "So Udomo had discovered the loneliness of those who would lead men. The odd thing was it had made him strong. He seemed to thrive on it."[168]

On his return, Mabi reflects on the effects of power on Udomo: "He's cold now, and deliberate, and he hides it all under the successful mask of easy friendliness."[169]

In one respect, Mhendi too has changed: now he feels a deep sense of peace; the brooding sadness of his lonely exile in England has been sanctified by the love of Maria. Since he has not gained the political kingdom nor the power consequent on it, however, he has not changed fundamentally. Mhendi nostalgically notes the changes that have taken place in the group. Its total disintegration is imminent.

> Then they had been young men nursing dreams . . . then there had been happy recklessness in the bold plans they dreamed. Now they were the rulers. . . . Men marrying the burden of state . . .
>
> Only I am still the same. And now they are more like me. But they have power. Their problems are problems of how to build, of how to create. Only mine are still those of how to destroy. That's the difference between us now.[170]

Mhendi undertakes his work of destruction. Accompanied by Maria and aided by the organizational skill and network of Selina, he returns to his home, Pluralia, through a jungle which was said to be impassable, though legend held a path existed. Abrahams is perhaps at his most lyrical in his description of this jungle: "The jungle is more than trees grown tall as towers; more than darkness darker than night; . . . It is time stood still and mocking man. It is the darkness in man's heart. It is the frontier of man's fear. The jungle is older than the days of man."[171]

From this jungle Mhendi carries on his daring acts of sabotage aimed at crippling the Pluralian government. There he meets death, betrayed by Udomo, who had placed the natonal good above personal loyalties, ambitious national development above the total liberation of all Africa, which he had vowed.

Mabi too had moved back to Africa, temporarily laying aside personal feeling in answer to the call, pulled back by the cause that had once united the group. "There is something compelling in this African cry for light. Perhaps it is because they don't even know they cry for light."[172]

Returning, he sees the change in Udomo, the deepening frustration of Lanwood, the inimical force of tribalism: "The real evil of tribalism in this day and age was that its ritualistic code of fear and authority had robbed man of his individual manhood."[173] Yet return to Africa, to his mountain people is also return to the embrace of a mother who thought that she had lost him to Europe:

> "My son . . . Oh, my son," she sobbed.
> He wrapped his arms around her, held her tight.
> "Oh, Mother . . ." he whispered in English.
> A long, long time afterwards she pulled away and wiped her eyes quickly.
> "I feared—That the white people may have taken you from me."
> "And now?"
> "My fears were foolish. You are still my son; a big man, but still my son."[174]

But even the tender embrace of his mother, of Africa, cannot hold him.

All the sons of the land had returned seeking the political kingdom, but they are "lost in the many." Udomo, ruthless in his pursuit of building a nation, fights the tribalism of Adebhoy and Selina and dies at their instigation, his body "hacked to pieces in true tribal fashion."[175] Mabi finally realizes how great a price has to be paid in the search for the political kingdom and confesses: "I think he and Mhendi were the only two who knew the price of what had to be done. And he was the only one among us prepared to pay it."[176]

Throughout the novels we can feel, can totally grasp the transitoriness of power, the ephemeral nature of pleasure in new urban complexes, the state of unease attendant on shifting social patterns, the turmoil and breakup resulting from political struggle, and the deep sense of disillusionment of a generation of Africans living at a moment of accelerated historical change. Many of the characters do not comprehend the nature of this historical moment. This generation seems lost, beset by problems, confronted by dilemmas, as all are called upon to make great sacrifices as they move away.

> And so our men must leave us. Some to die; some to go into prison; some to hide; some to go to far lands. And we must be alone in the land, waiting and working and fighting and scheming for the day of reunion, the day that must follow this terrible night.[177]

Notes

1. Peter Abrahams, *A Wreath for Udomo* (New York: Alfred A. Knopf, 1956), p. 135.
2. Camara Laye, *The Dark Child* (London: Collins, 1955), dedication.
3. Abrahams, *op. cit.*, p. 56.
4. *Ibid.*, p. 31.
5. Richard Rive, *Emergency* (London: Faber and Faber, 1964), p. 182.
6. *Ibid.*, p. 203.
7. Abrahams, *op. cit.*, p. 7.
8. *Ibid.*, p. 102.
9. Peter Abrahams, *A Night of Their Own* (New York: Alfred A. Knopf, 1965), pp. 218–19.
10–12. *Ibid:* 10. p. 43; 11. p. 105; 12. pp. 220–221.
13. Sembene Ousmane, *God's Bits of Wood* (New York: Doubleday and Co., 1962), p. 121.
14. *Ibid.*, p. 240.
15. Abrahams, *A Night of Their Own*, p. 196.
16. *Ibid.*, p. 221.
17. Ousmane, *op. cit.*, p. 119.
18. Abrahams, *A Night of Their Own*, pp. 69–70.
19. Ousmane, *op. cit.*, p. 36.
20. *Ibid.*, p. 254.
21. Abrahams, *A Wreath for Udomo*, p. 47.
22. Abrahams, *A Night of Their Own*, p. 82.
23. Cyprian Ekwensi, *Beautiful Feathers* (London: Hutchinson and Co., 1963), p. 46.
24. *Ibid.*, p. 125.

25. Chinua Achebe, A Man of the People (New York: The John Day Co., 1966), p. 88.
26. Ibid., p. 42.
27. Abrahams, A Wreath for Udomo, p. 287.
28–29. Ibid: 28. p. 318; 29. p. 348.
30. Ousmane, op. cit., pp. 254–255.
31. Abrahams, A Wreath for Udomo, pp. 76–77.
32. Ibid., p. 320.
33. Cyprian Ekwensi, Jagua Nana (London: Hutchinson and Co., Ltd., 1961), p. 103.
34. Ibid., pp. 116–117.
35. Achebe, op. cit., p. 69.
36. Ibid., p. 87.
37. Abrahams, A Night of Their Own, p. 45.
38. Ibid., p. 18.
39. Ekwensi, Jagua Nana, p. 103.
40. Achebe, op. cit., p. 128.
41. Ibid., p. 93.
42. Ousmane, op. cit., pp. 35–36.
43. Achebe, op. cit., p. 74.
44–45. Ibid: 44. p. 166; 45. p. 160.
46. Cyprian Ekwensi, People of the City (London: Heinemann Educational Books Ltd., 1963), p. 24.
47. Chinua Achebe, No Longer at Ease (New York: Ivan Obolensky, Inc., 1960), p. 79.
48. Ekwensi, People of the City, p. 88.
49. Ibid., p. 68.
50. Achebe, No Longer at Ease, p. 6.
51. Achebe, A Man of the People, p. 2.
52. Ibid., pp. 161–162.
53. Achebe, No Longer at Ease, p. 30.
54. Ekwensi, Beautiful Feathers, p. 85.
55. Ousmane, op. cit., pp. 204–206.
56. Abrahams, A Night of Their Own, p. 163.
57. Ekwensi, Beautiful Feathers, p. 102.
58–59. Ibid: 58. pp. 94–96; 59. p. 97.
60. Ekwensi, Jagua Nana, pp. 54–55.
61. Achebe, No Longer at Ease, p. 125.
62. Ekwensi, People of the City, pp. 4–5.
63–74. Ibid: 63. pp. 88–89; 64. pp. 154–155; 65. p. 141; 66. p. 101; 67. p. 145; 68. p. 129; 69. p. 42; 70. p. 143; 71. p. 115; 72. p. 3; 73. p. 58; 74. p. 116.
75. Ekwensi, Jagua Nana, p. 126.
76–87. Ibid: 76. p. 11; 77. p. 6; 78. p. 6; 79. p. 20; 80. p. 5; 81. p. 93; 82. p. 112; 83. p. 113; 84. p. 139; 85. p. 124; 86. p. 131; 87. p. 136.
88. Achebe, No Longer at Ease, p. 39.

89–103. *Ibid:* 89. pp. 71–72; 90. p. 4; 91. p. 92; 92. p. 80; 93. p. 31; 94. pp. 32–33; 95. p. 144; 96. p. 133; 97. p. 134; 98. p. 137; 99. pp. 43–44; 100. p. 21; 101. p. 95; 102. p. 153; 103. p. 82.

104. Ousmane, *op. cit.*, p. 137.

105–114. *Ibid:* 105. p. 12; 106. pp. 143–144; 107. p. 39; 108. p. 100; 109. pp. 198–201; 110. p. 207; 111. p. 188; 112. pp. 278–279; 113. pp. 109–110; 114. p. 137.

115. Abrahams, *A Night of Their Own*, p. 167.

116. Rive, *op. cit.*, p. 125.

117–120. *Ibid:* 117. p. 16; 118. p. 243; 119. p. 116; 120. p. 196.

121. Abrahams, *A Night of Their Own*, p. 116.

122–127. *Ibid:* 122. p. 28; 123. p. 136; 124. p. 208; 125. p. 27; 126. pp. 34–35; 127. p. 190.

128. Achebe, *A Man of the People*, p. 91.

129–138. *Ibid:* 129. p. 128; 130. p. 119; 131. pp. 161–162; 132. pp. 1–2; 133. pp. 2–3; 134. pp. 3–4; 135. p. 4; 136. pp. 86–88; 137. p. 73; 138. p. 32.

139. Ekwensi, *Beautiful Feathers*, p. 20.

140–147. *Ibid:* 140. p. 46; 141. p. 107; 142. p. 108; 143. p. 135; 144. p. 136; 145. p. 158; 146. p. 153; 147. p. 86.

148. Abrahams, *A Wreath for Udomo*, pp. 15–16.

149–177. *Ibid:* 149. p. 135; 150. p. 15; 151. p. 13; 152. p. 121; 153. p. 36; 154. p. 61; 155. p. 8; 156. pp. 60–61; 157. p. 122; 158. pp. 147–148; 159. p. 135; 160. pp. 141–142; 161. p. 170; 162. pp. 233–234; 163. p. 217; 164. p. 219; 165. p. 274; 166. p. 231; 167. p. 216; 168. p. 160; 169. p. 273; 170. p. 320; 171. p. 251; 172. p. 262; 173. p. 270; 174. p. 272; 175. p. 356; 176. pp. 354–355; 177. p. 237.

CODA

THE SEARCH

And so many of those who have moved away return, bent on resolving problems and dilemmas consequent on that movement away. Often their search condemns them, their deliberations ostracise them.

> I hear many voices
> like it's said a madman hears;
> I hear trees talking
> like it's said a medicine man hears.
>
> . . .
>
> Maybe I'm mad,
> for the voices are luring me,
> urging me . . .[1]

These voices urge and lure Okolo in Gabriel Okara's novel *The Voice* to seek for the essence of things, for *it*, in Amatu where "fear has locked up the insides of the low and the insides of the high are filled up with nothing but yam."[2] His search brings him into conflict with Chief Izongo who has the Elders and the townspeople at his back, and who counsels Okolo that "asking the bottom of things in this town will take you no place."[3] Before Okolo, only the woman Tuere, eventually ostracized as a witch, had dared to confront Izongo. Chief Izongo, Tuere, and Okolo represent forces in a changing Africa: Izongo represents the old, resistant political order; Tuere shows discontent with the old, but he is uneducated and inarticulate; Okolo comes as a voice which bids the people to seek the "straight thing" in their new society. In an interior monologue Okolo wonders: "Is his meaning of life then to plant *it* in people's insides by asking if they've got *it* . . . ?"[4]

Satirically Okara shows that in an evolving society *it* has many variant forms and many differing interpretations. The carver, a prototype of the artist, seems to have found his form of *it*: "It is to believe in everything or believe in nothing. The carver believes and puts even his shadow into creating faces out of wood and his inside is sweeter than sweetness."[5] A group of people whom Okolo meets in a surrealistic scene in an eating house believe that "the people who have the sweetest insides are the think-nothing people and we here try to be like them."[6] A white man, archetype of a modern administrator, advises Okolo: "Be sensible and be a good lad. This country will need men like you, if only you learn to shut your eyes at certain things."[7]

Okolo, strengthened by Tuere's advice, "Let the words that have grown take root,"[8] had persevered in his search for *it*, and his spoken words had entered the insides of many people. But his search first brought about his exile, later his death.

. : .

In *Ambiguous Adventure*, Samba Diallo, after searching to resolve his own individual ambiguity, had returned to the softness of the shadows, symbolically to a time before ambiguities. But "la rivière ne remonte jamais à sa source," and so Samba Diallo can only refind the past in the flow of the river, can only achieve softness of being within the moment, in an infinity where time is absent. Lyrically, he gives himself up:

> The moment is the bed of the river of my thought. The pulsations of the moments have the pulsations of thought; the breath of thought glides into the blowpipe of the moment. In the sea of time, the moment bears the image of the profile of man, like the reflection of the *kailcedrat* on the sparkling surface of the lagoon. In the fortress of the moment, man in truth is king, for his thought is all-powerful, when it is. Where it has passed, the pure azure crystallizes in forms. Life of the moment, life without age of the moment which endures, in the

flight of your élan man creates himself indefinitely. At the heart of the moment, behold man as immortal, for the moment is infinite, when it is. The purity of the moment is made from the absence of time. Life of the moment, life without age of the moment which reigns, in the luminous area of your duration man unfurls himself to infinity. The sea! Here is the sea! Hail to you, rediscovered wisdom, my victory! The limpidness of your wave is awaiting my gaze. I fix my eyes upon you, and you harden into Being. I am without limit. Sea, the limpidity of your wave is awaiting my gaze. I fix my eyes upon you, and you glitter, without limit. I wish for you, through all eternity.[9]

And in *The River Between*, even after Nyambura and Waiyaki die, the ". . . Honia river went on flowing through the valley of life, throbbing, murmuring an unknown song."[10] Even as Tuere and Okolo are swept aimlessly to their death:

Down they floated from one bank of the river to the other like debris, carried by the current. Then the canoe was drawn into a whirlpool. It spun round and round and was slowly drawn into the core and finally disappeared. And the water rolled over the top and the river flowed smoothly over it as if nothing had happened.[11]

". . . thought is all-powerful. . . . Where it has passed, the pure azure crystallizes in forms."[12] The lost generation is not lost, for after the search a symbolic return is possible.

Notes

1. Gabriel Okara, "Adhiambo," *Modern Poetry from Africa*, eds. Gerald Moore and Ulli Beier (Baltimore: Penguin, 1963), p. 96.
2. Gabriel Okara, *The Voice* (London: Andre Deutsch, Ltd., 1964), p. 24.
3–8. *Ibid*: 3. p. 29; 4. p. 134; 5. p. 96; 6. p. 95; 7. p. 101; 8. p. 112.
9. Cheikh Hamidou Kane, *Ambiguous Adventure* (New York: Walker and Co., 1963), pp. 177–178.

10. James Ngugi, *The River Between* (Heinemann Educational Books Ltd., 1965), p. 173.
11. Okara, *The Voice*, pp. 156–157.
12. Kane, *op. cit.*, p. 177.

THE MOVEMENT BACK

INTROIT

HOMECOMING AND REENTRY

HOMECOMING, by Lenrie Peters
The present reigned supreme
  Like the shallow floods over the gutters
Over the raw paths where we had been,
  The house with the shutters.

Too strange the sudden change
  Of the times we buried when we left
The times before we had properly arranged
  The memories that we kept.

Our sapless roots have fed
  The wind-swept seedlings of another age.
Luxuriant weeds have grown where we led
  The Virgins to the water's edge.

There at the edge of the town
  Just by the burial ground
Stands the house without a shadow
  Lived in by new skeletons.

That is all that is left
  To greet us on the home coming
After we have paced the world
  and longed for returning.[1]

FIDÉLITÉ À L'AFRIQUE, by Bernard B. Dadié
Afrique des tam-tam
Afrique des jeunes filles rieuses sur le sentier des rivières,
Je te demeure fidèle.

Afrique des paysans joyeux travaillant à l'unisson,
Afrique du diamant et de l'or,
Afrique des nuits sereines pleines de chansons,
Afrique de l'hospitalité
       Je te demeure fidèle.[2]

ALLEGIANCE TO AFRICA
Africa of the tom-toms,
Africa of laughing girls on the river bank,
I am true to you.

Africa of joyous peasants working in unison,
Africa of gold and diamonds,
Africa of serene, song-filled nights,
Hospitable Africa,
       I am true to you.

Peters' poems "Homecoming" and "We Have Come Home"[3] are not jubilant songs celebrating the homecoming; but ones in which, through the contrast of exile and return, of deception and promise, the poet evokes the pathos of homecoming, the resilience of the spirit that comes back to the "green foothills" of Africa. The reiteration of the refrain "We have come home," echoing Dadié's "Je te demeure fidèle," sings the certainty of the return. To be sure

    After we have paced the world
      And longed for returning

return may be to "the house without a shadow/Lived in by new skeletons." Yet there are past memories that vivify the house without shadows, and even though the memories of youthful love when "we led The Virgins to the water's edge" are wind-swept by time, within the growing "luxuriant weeds," they still persist. Even though pestilence, drought, and the sodden spirit linger on, even though the poet and his people return in the faltering dawn singing songs of other lands with sad hearts and massacred souls, the spirit of dignity still supports "the tortured remnants Of the flesh."

After the long exile, the return is to freshly sprouting lands and to seas where there is plenty. Lyrically the poet restates his faith that:

> We have come home
> To the green foothills
> . . . .
> Where boats go out to sea
> Threshing the ocean's harvest
> And the harassing, plunging
> gliding gulls shower kisses on the waves.

But for a long time even these waves forestalled return and hindered the symbolic entry into the sensuous landscape of Africa, postponed the spiritual merging with the dark radiance of the king. For in *The Radiance of the King*, Camara Laye symbolically tells of the mystical cleansing that someone coming from Europe must undergo before being able to move with the rhythms of the red earth of Africa.

Only through persistence can one cross the reef and land in Africa:

> Each time the rolling wave was about to reach the shore, it was lifted up; it would lift its head, and glimpse, for a second, the red earth of Africa; . . . It would lift its head and look, but it was careful not to look too long or to approach too closely to the shore! . . . It did not forget to draw the bark away from the shore, for it knew that once their curiosity was satisfied, the crew of the bark had nothing more to expect from the red earth of Africa. . . . But the crew of the bark would by no means be content with this one far-off glimpse. . . . They would bend to their oars with greater force and stronger determination; and finally, they would triumph over the reef, and touch land![4]

Once on this land emphases are different, thought processes undergo change, and the possibility of love with the essence of blackness becomes actual and immediate: "Yes, it seemed that it might be possible to love this frail adolescent, yes, it would

be possible, despite the pitch-black night of his skin. . . . Perhaps the midnight of these limbs would help to lift love to its
purest peak . . ."[5] Yet, before that love may be realized the
senses must be set free and soaring, must be intoxicated by all
that is sensuous:

> . . . a seductive perfume, or rather the seductive mingling of a
> thousand perfumes, almost too many perfumes, yes, far too
> many perfumes, all of them far too heady, disturbing, caress-
> ing, far too . . . far too delectable. . . . It's not quite the right
> word . . . it is certainly the right word to describe the outer-
> most reaches of this perfumed gulf that is like a real sea . . .[6]

The tightening rope that led to exile must be cut, the degradation, humiliation, and shame that one has suffered must be
jettisoned; only then is spiritual return consummated:

> Did you not know that I was waiting for you? asked the
> king.
> And Clarence placed his lips upon the faint and yet tre-
> mendous beating of that heart. Then the king slowly closed his
> arms around him, and his great mantle swept about him, and
> enveloped him forever.[7]

Notes

1. Lenrie Peters, "Homecoming," *Modern Poetry from
   Africa*, eds. Gerald Moore and Ulli Beier (Baltimore:
   Penguin, 1963), p. 69.
2. Read by the author at the 35th International P.E.N.
   Congress held at Abidjan, Ivory Coast, July–August, 1967.
3. Lenrie Peters, "We Have Come Home," *Modern Poetry
   from Africa*, ed. Gerald Moore and Ulli Beier (Baltimore:
   Penguin, 1963), pp. 70–72.
4. Camara Laye, *The Radiance of the King*, tr. from French
   by James Kirkup (London: Collins Press, 1956), pp. 304–
   305.
5–7. *Ibid*: 5. p. 25; 6. p. 109; 7. p. 319.

FIVE

EXILE AND RETURN . . . NEGRITUDE

The movement away and the consequent loss of cultural identity that have been discerned in the first four realities are catalogued in the poets of Negritude, but the very nostalgia that sets the mood for the dedication of Camara Laye's *L'Enfant Noir*, that attempts to remember the "wonders of the world," becomes the *raison d'être* of the Negritude poets. The loss consequent on colonialism and the alienation deriving from the movement away from rural traditions to urban political realities are reflected in one way or another in the thesis of the Negritude poets. To return symbolically to the source, to abnegate the loss, the alienation, the confusion, will be the prime intention and motive of the Negritude poets as they search through their single selves for a communal African authenticity. Thus things remembered, that had been lost—the entry into infancy, something long past—will link them, even as they seek a rebirth, to the beginnings of things. And since the child is, in African ontology, akin to the ancestor, the recalling of ancestors will be but a short step away from the plunging into those elements that lie at the beginning, at the birth. Infancy and ancestry, recalling and reidentifying, exile and return, will all color the poetry of the Negritude poets.

Negritude becomes a ceremony ritualizing the earth and life, its poets grasping the external world. They revitalize life through the cogency of pure memory, through the power of the poetic word: what was tense or dammed up flows, what lay dormant or shrouded in past times becomes present and dynamic. The belief in the primacy of life, in its enduring quality, leads the poet of Negritude to offer his poetic power to the service of all mankind.

> c'est pour la faim universelle
> pour la soif universelle
>
> la sommer libre enfin
> de produire de son intimité close
> la succulence des fruits.[1]
>
> it is for universal hunger
> and universal thirst
>
> to summon up, free at last
> from its inner depths
> the succulence of fruits.

Yet the poet, driven by his own black blood across time and space, celebrates mankind by a celebration of his race:

> Elle me force sans répit jamais, à travers les grands espaces du Temps.
> Me poursuit mon sang noir, jusqu'au coeur solitaire de la nuit.[2]
>
> It drives me without a single pause across the wide spaces of Time.
> My black blood pursues me straight into the solitary heart of the night.

In the search for the poetic absolute, time and space for the Negritude poet must be uninterrupted and continually flowing. The river and the rainbow must remain. It is the desire of all poets to seek the absolute in the midst of chaos, when the river flows in broken rhythms and when "seven rivers with lost waves flowed away into the distance."[3] To show the quality of endurance of a person, a people, is to show the quality that abides in all things, to show that all things are in a constant state of becoming, that time flows, detoured yet never interrupted. To accept the duration of all things is to capture the essence of all things. Thus the Negritude poets, Léon Damas, Léopold Sédar Senghor, Aimé Césaire, Felix U'Tamsi, and David Diop, in attempting to capture the essence of their people, release a rhythmic flow, delving deep into their furthest beginnings, into the nearer past, the immediate present, and the future of tomorrows unwinding to an infinite.

The past will be recalled with the music of a kora or bala-fong. The nearer past or present, the time of exile or anguish, will be harshly drummed out on the tam-tam and played in the sad notes of the bamboo flute; the return and future, prophesied by the magic of the sorcerer-poet. And so, in the Negritude poets, time, space, and memory flow together in the rhythms of the elements or in the rhythms of life. Timelessness becomes a constant motif, symbolizing the duration of a race, a people. The African masks for the poet Senghor have the qualities of things that are impervious to change, that persist in spite of lived time, enigmatic and wise. For Senghor, the mask seems never to age: it contains the perennial wisdom of the ancestors, the fixity and eternity of the dead who nourish the living. The masks belong to the primordial, far removed in time yet immediate and present:

> Vous distillez cet air d'éternité où je respire l'air de mes Pères.[4]

> You give off that air of eternity where I breathe the air of my Fathers.

The mask recalls immediate time, but it opens out backward, touching the point of eternity and then moves even further backward to that time before memory created eternity. And so, the poet in his poem "Masque Nègre" pushes the bounds of the black mask into the beginnings of all time and sings its praises:

> Visage de masque fermé à l'éphémère, sans yeux sans matière
> Tête de bronze parfaite et sa patine de temps
> Que ne souillent fards ni rougeur ni rides, ni traces de larmes ni de baisers

O visage tel que Dieu t'a créé avant la mémoire même des âges

. . . .

Je t'adore, ô Beauté, de mon oeil monocorde![5]

Mask's face, eyeless, without substance, closed to the ephemeral
Perfect bronze head and its patina of time
Which no cosmetic, flush or wrinkle,
No trace of tears or kisses soils.
O face such as God did make you, even before the memory of
    ages.

. . . .

I worship you, oh Beauty, with my monochord eye!

The adoration of the mask is the poet's ceremonial to the
guardian symbols of his race. They are eternal, and so the poet
must, through the poetic word, attempt to endow the black
woman with the same eternity. The beauty of the mask is unchanging; the beauty of the black woman celebrated by the poet
flows and vibrates with the sap of life, for in celebrating the
black woman, the poet is celebrating his earth. She is:

Fruit mûr à la chair ferme . . .
Savane aux horizons purs, savane qui frémis aux caresses
    ferventes du Vent d'Est . . .
Gazelle aux attaches célestes

Ripe, firm-fleshed fruit . . .
Savannah of pure horizons, savannah trembling beneath the
    fervent caresses of the East Wind . . .
Gazelle with the fine bones of heaven

She is living flesh, she is the present who must be captured for
all time for she has made the poet's mouth lyrical:

Femme nue, femme noire
Je chante ta beauté qui passe, forme que je fixe dans l'Éternel,
Avant que le Destin jaloux ne te réduise en cendres pour
    nourrir les racines de la vie.[6]

Naked woman, black woman,
I sing your passing beauty, a form I fix in Eternity
Before jealous Fate reduces you to ashes, to feed the roots of
    life.

The black mask and the black woman, the past and the present are commingled in timelessness through the poet's celebration. He celebrates them in the sounds of shadows that slither across space, and the unwrinkled old mask sings with a new voice. It is a firm, living creature, preserved by a voice that is as old as the youth of worlds:

> Je te chante ce chant d'ombre d'une voix nouvelle
> Avec la vieille voix de la jeunesse des mondes.[7]

> I sing to you this chant of the shadows with a new voice
> With a voice as old as the youth of the worlds.

Through the play of opposites and dualisms, the poet captures the contingency of youth and age, life and death, the correspondences between them, their mergings and their flow. The poet constantly reiterates:

> *Je ne sais* en quels temps c'était, je confonds toujours l'enfance et l'Eden
> Comme je mêle la Mort et la Vie—un pont de douceur les relie.
>
> . . . .
>
> Je ne sais en quels temps c'était, je confonds toujours présent et passé
> Comme je mêle la Mort et la Vie—un pont de douceur les relie[8]

> *I do not know* from when it was, I always confuse childhood with Eden
> As I confuse Life with Death—the bridge between them is a tender one.
>
> . . . .
>
> I do not know from when it was, I always confuse past and present
> As I confuse Life and Death—the bridge between them is a tender one.

Essentially, then, the seeming oppositions and dualism between life and death, present and past, infancy and old age, do not exist; rather they all flow together through uninterrupted time and space.

The movements of time and space are counter but the same,

one a spiraling upward and the other downward; together they are vertical in duration:

Précipice et altitude[9]

Awakening touches sleep, sleep touches death, the living touch the dead. The same woman whom the poet had preserved for eternity cushions him into learning the relationship between the living and the dead, preserves him until he has entered living and before he descends into the precipices of space-time:

... que j'apprenne à
Vivre avant de descendre, au-delà du plongeur, dans les hautes
    profondeurs du sommeil.[10]

... that I may learn to
Live before descending further than a diver into the lofty
    depths of sleep.

But the poet will not be lost in the depths of space/time for:

Mon enfance, mes agneaux, est vieille comme le monde et
    je suis jeune comme l'aurore éternellement jeune du
    monde.[11]

My childhood, lambs, is as old as the world and I am as young
    as the world's perpetual dawning.

and because entry into the extensions of space, into the center of time, is at the heart of the poetry of Negritude.

For the poets, time moves according to the pulse of the earth; time flows according to the rhythms of the river. For Senghor, the flow of the river Congo is timeless and must be celebrated in praises equally immemorial:

Oho! Congo oho! Pour rythmer ton nom grand sur les eaux
    sur les fleuves sur toute mémoire
Que j'émeuve la voix des kôras Koyaté! L'encre du scribe est
    sans mémoire.[12]

Ho, Congo, ho! To weave your name into generous rhythms
    over waters, rivers and the whole of memory

Let me wake the voice of the Koyaté koras! The scribe's ink has
no memory.

This Congo stands at the center of the poet Felix U'Tamsi's
Brush Fire.[13] For the Congolese U'Tamsi, the flow of his river is
synonymous with the flow of his life, with the movement of his
people. Time is flow. In showing the constant flow of the
Congo, the poet celebrates the continuity of his country, the
enduring qualities of his people:

> only to you I said around the fire
> my race
> it flows here and there a river

The poet leaps over waves and takes us across time and river.
The poet endures because the river flows in him, because all the
parts of his body move with the rhythms of the elements, with
the rhythms of the river:

> the fire the river that's to say
> the sea to drink following the sand
> the feet the hands
> within the heart to love
> this river that lives in me repeoples me

The potency of the river is clearly accepted; the quality of
endurance is reiterated by restatement of time's duration.
Throughout the long poem the poet presents time, that is, river,
being dammed—present time is cut off by obstacles that have
been brought there through colonialism and exploitation. Yet,
since all things endure, the river can melt away the obstacles
and pass on. The river will bring with it peace and silence and
life:

> the funeral bell rings the hour
> over time and river
> time fords the funeral bell
> on its mounts of silence
>   and passes
> my soul is ready
> peace on my soul
> light this fire that washes away my shame.

The ceremony to time and life has taken place. The black man, the poet, has been ritually saved through the ablutions of the river's flow. And in the center of the flow of the river, he and all men will be brothers:

> ordain my human flesh
> I am the brother of man
> join me
> where the river flows

The poets of Negritude ascribe force and curative strength to rivers and waters, accepting the rhythmic pulsations of all elements, each force concatenating to another force, forming an essential unity. They accept the unbroken convergencies of all things and give a total primacy to the strength which comes from that convergence. Organic and inorganic phenomena, restorative, cleansing, and abiding, move through their poetry. And so the poet hymns with rhythmic cadences the purity, eternal motion, and power of waters:

> Je vous invoque, Eaux du Troisième Jour
> Eaux murmures des sources, eaux si pures des altitudes, neiges!
>   eaux des torrents et des cascades
> Eaux justes, mais vous Eaux de miséricorde, je vous invoque
>   d'un cri rythmé et sans dédit.
> Eaux des grands fleuves et de la mer plus vaste et de la mer
>   plus faste.
> Et toi Soleil toi Lune, qui gouvernez les eaux du mouvement
>   contraire en qui se confond l'Unité[14]

> I invoke you, Waters of the Third Day
> Murmuring spring waters, flowing so purely from the heights
>   and snows! torrential waters, cascading waters
> Righteous waters, but you, oh Waters of mercy, I invoke you
>   with a rhythmic and constant cry.
> Waters of the great rivers and of the wider, brighter seas.
> And you, Sun, and you, Moon, who rule the contrary movements of the waters and who mingle them into Unity.

Man is united to the elements, transformed by them, invigorated by them; from the earth mother he receives life:

Tête debout, qui me perce de ses yeux aigus.
Et je renais à la terre qui fut ma mère.[15]

Head held high, her sharp eyes going through me.
And I am born again to the earth which was my mother.

From the earth also he receives the rhythmic vigor of dance:

Nous sommes les hommes de la danse, dont les pieds
    reprennent vigueur en frappant le sol dur.[16]

We are men of the dance, whose feet
    find renewed vigor as they strike against hard ground.

To live to the compass of earth, to its movement, ennobles:

Ma noblesse est de vivre cette terre, Princesse
    selon cette terre.[17]

My nobility resides in living this earth, Princess,
    in accordance with this earth.

The earth, waters, rivers, all elements conjoin, become rhythmic explosion and give a seismic power to Aimé Césaire's long poem *Cahier d'un Retour au Pays Natal*.[18] The poet summons the forces:

Et voici soudain que force et vie m'assaillent comme un taureau et l'onde de vie circonvient la papille du morne, et voilà toutes les veines et veinules qui s'affairent au sang neuf et l'énorme poumon des cyclones qui respire et le feu thésaurisé des volcans et le gigantesque pouls sismique qui bat maintenant la mesure d'un corps vivant en mon ferme embrasement.

And now suddenly life and strength assail me like a bull, and the swell of life swamps the papilla of melancholy, and now every vein and every veinlet is pulsing with new blood and the cyclone's enormous lung draws breath and the hoarded fire of the volcanoes and the gigantic seismic pulse which now keeps time with a living body as I burst into steady flames.

Through his poetic will, Césaire conjures up all elements, bursts into them and ignites them in an ever-exploding chain reaction.

The poet searches for that which is the essence of the earth, garnering it and establishing the primacy of earth:

> davantage la terre
> silo où se préserve et mûrit ce que la terre a de
> plus terre

> even more the earth
> silo that preserves and ripens what is of itself
> its very essence

He plunges in vertical movement through the precipices and altitudes of space and time to carve from the red earth his Negritude:

> elle plonge dans la chair rouge du sol
> elle plonge dans chair ardente du ciel
> elle troue l'accablement opaque de sa droite patience

> it plunges into the earth's red flesh
> it plunges into the glowing flesh of heaven
> it pierces the opaque gloom of its upright patience

Negritude for the poet explores only essences, seeks only essentials, but essence and rhythms move together, bringing with them abandon and freedom, the power to put into dance all things, "caught up in the movement of all things," and perform a ceremony to life: ". . . jouant le jeu du monde." And in this ceremony to life, the poet can chart out the emotions that lie at the center of life:

> Eia pour la joie
> Eia pour l'amour
> Eia pour la douleur aux pis de larmes réincarnées

> Eia! for joy
> Eia! for love
> Eia! for sorrow with udders of reincarnate tears

Suffering and joy, like infancy and age, life and death, present and past, are not opposites. Through the belief in the duration of things, the poet of Negritude weaves them together, demonstrating the essential unity and harmony between them. One exists because of the other, since to plunge into the essence of one is to plunge into the essence of the other. To know the essence of suffering is to know the essence of joy. To experience the passion of hatred is to know the force of love. To know that death is, is to know that life is, also, and that it must be lived:

> car la beauté est nègre
> et nègre la sagesse
> car l'endurance est nègre
> et nègre le courage
> car la patience est nègre
> et nègre l'ironie
> car le charme est nègre
> et nègre la magie
> car l'amour est nègre
> et nègre le déhanchement
> car la danse est nègre
> et nègre le rythme
> car l'art est nègre
> et nègre le mouvement
> car le rire est nègre
> car la joie est nègre
> car la paix est nègre
> car la vie est nègre[19]

> for beauty is Black
> and wisdom Black
> for endurance is Black
> and courage Black
> for patience is Black
> and irony Black
> for charm is Black
> and magic Black
> for love is Black
> and hip swinging Black
> for dance is Black
> and rhythm Black
> for art is Black
> and movement Black
> for laughter is Black
> for joy is Black
> for peace is Black
> for life is Black

Thus, Negritude has established the harmonious relationships of things. The continuity and flow of time, the rhythm of essences and elements, a *raison d'être* for life and endurance.

But one morning, one clear morning, this rhythm of life and endurance was broken and with its interruption came years of exile, loss, destruction, and degradation.

> one morning
> one clear morning
> no more totems and their parrots
> one morning
> one clear morning
> no more leaves anywhere[20]

This defoliation and barrenness ensued from the coming of the Europeans. The interruptions of rhythms, of the music of emotions, of ritual worship took place in the evening, and Damas describes the stoppage in a series of alliterative r's; in the circular movement of his poem "Ils Sont Venus Ce Soir" he repeats the loss consequent upon their coming.

> DEPUIS
> combien de MOI MOI MOI
> sont morts
> depuis qu'ils sont venus ce soir où le
> tam
>   tam
>   roulait de
>   rythme
>   en
>   rythme
>   la frénésie

> des yeux
> la frénésie
> des mains
> la frénésie
> des pieds de statues[21]

> SINCE THEN
> how many of ME ME ME
> have died

since they came that evening when the
tom
    tom
        rolled
            the frenzy
                from one rhythm
                    to
                        another.

Frenzy
of eyes
Frenzy
of hands
Frenzy
of the feet of statues

The poet of Negritude will speak of the interruption, of the ensuing absence, of the creative word broken at its point of beginning.

he came to deliver the secret of the sun
and wanted to write the poem of his life
. . . .
his soul was ready
when someone called him
dirty wog[22]

Such a naming is no mere happening; it becomes charged with a deeper significance, with presentiment that produces illusions, contorts ideas, leads to drugged nights and years of exile:

Dix ans mon amour
Et les matins d'illusions et les débris d'idées
Et les sommeils peuplés d'alcool
Dix ans et le souffle du monde m'a versé sa souffrance
Cette souffrance qui charge le présent du goût des lende-
    mains[23]

Ten years, my love,
And mornings of illusion and the rubble of ideas
And sleep peopled by alcohol
Ten years and the breath of the world has poured its suffering
    into me

This suffering which weighs down the present with the taste of
tomorrows

The exile becomes too long, too arduous, and so a countermovement takes place: the return. Senghor will return through
steeping himself in the earth of Africa: "Here I am trying to
forget Europe in the pastoral heart of Sine."[24]

Aimé Césaire at mid-juncture of his long poem, *Cahier d'un
Retour au Pays Natal,* pleads for his country's embrace to
cleanse him from his years of exile:

> . . . je dirais à ce pays dont le limon entre dans la composition
> de ma chair: "J'ai longtemps erré et je reviens vers la hideur
> désertée de vos plaies."

> Je viendrais à ce pays mien et je lui dirais. "Embrassez—moi
> sans crainte . . ."[25]

> . . . I would say to this land whose mud is part of my flesh: "I
> have long been wandering and am coming back to the deserted
> horror of your wounds."

> I would come to this land of mine and say to it, "Embrace me
> without fear . . ."

Of all these poets it is Léon Damas who suffers most deeply
the anguish of exile from self, exile from natural instincts of
childhood, exile from homeland, exile of his race. The mood
that dominates the poetry of Damas as he sings of these various
exiles is one of unending sadness. A sense of fatigue and weariness evoked by memories and regrets for what could have been
is ever-present in his poetry. The truncated life is the life of
exile, unbroken and continuous; wearily the poet says:

> Les jours inexorablement
> tristes
> jamais n'ont cessé d'être
> à la mémoire
> de ce que fut
> ma vie tronquée

> The days inexorably
> sad

> never ceased
> to remind me
> of my stunted life

But memory also brings with it bitterness and rancor as deep as the pervasive mood of sadness, shame as oppressive as the ever-present weariness:

> Mes aujourd'hui ont chacun sur mon jadis
> de gros yeux qui roulent de rancoeur
> de honte[26]

> Each of my todays looks on my yesterdays
> with wide eyes that roll in rancor
> and shame.

Exploitation in all its various forms had fed this bitterness: exploitation of the body as well as that of the mind. Throughout *pigments* the poet enumerates for us the many shapes of exploitation: the physical brutality, the verbal degradation, the forcible imposition of western bourgeois values and mediocrity. So thorough was this process that

> nous avons tout foutu de nous-mêmes
> tout foutu de nous-mêmes en l'air

> we threw away all that was ours
> simply threw it away

The repetition of the refrain

> Ils ont si bien su faire
> si bien su faire les choses
> les choses[27]

> They really knew how to operate
> really knew how to take care of things
> things

underscores the extent of the demeaning impositions.

The identifying *nous* of *nous avons tout foutu* is picked up by the repetition of *moi aussi, moi aussi* in "Un Clochard M'A Demandé Dix Sous," a poem which tells of the misery, the horror of poverty and of the mockery suffered while living a life of exile in Paris. Damas identifies bitterly with the hobo who requests ten sous of him:

> Moi aussi j'ai eu faim dans ce sacré foutu pays
> moi aussi j'ai cru pouvoir
> demander dix sous
> par pitié pour mon ventre
> creux[28]

> I too have been hungry in this damn worthless country
> I too thought I could
> ask for ten cents
> out of pity for my empty
> stomach

Again while in exile in France, the sight of the hooves of beasts of burden pounding the streets reminds the poet of the misery and drudgery suffered by peasants in his own land:

> Et les sabots
> des bêtes de somme
> qui martèlent en Europe
> l'aube indécise encore
> me rappellent
> l'abnégation étrange
> des trays matinaux
> repus
> qui rythment aux Antilles
> les hanches des porteuses
> en file indienne[29]

> And the hooves
> of beasts of burden
> hammering out Europe's
> still uncertain dawn
> remind me
> of the strange abnegation
> of morning trays
> loaded and
> set to rhythm by the hips
> of Antilles bearer women
> walking single file

Memory for Damas serves a double function, evoking images of what might have been, but also recalling sharply the degradation that is. And so the poet lives in a daze of yesterdays, a daze brought on by shocks from the cruelties that he has experienced.

> Va encore
> mon hébétude
> du temps jadis
> de coups de corde noueux
> de corps calcinés
> de l'orteil au dos calcinés
> de chair morte
> de tisons
> de fer rouge
> de bras brisés
> sous le fouet qui se déchaîne
> sous le fouet qui fait marcher la plantation

> Still there
> my stupor
> from bygone days
> from blows with the knotted cord
> from bodies charred
> from toes to back, all charred
> from dead flesh
> from embers
> from red-hot irons
> from arms broken
> beneath the lashing whip
> beneath the whip which moves the plantation

Here Damas uses the explosiveness of the sequence of hard initial c's (*coups, corde, corps,* and *calcinés*) to evoke the force used on the bodies of the exploited; the whistling f's in the repeated *fouet* is picked up in *fait* and brings out an onomatopoeic hiss of the whips that ruled the plantation; the plosions in *bras brisés* suggest the cracking of bones. Then with poetic skill Damas momentarily stops with a series of sighing liquid s's, the breaking and hissing sounds, which he continues and strengthens in the b, ff, and repeated hard c's of the poem's final line:

et s'abreuver de sang de mon sang de sang la sucrerie
et la bouffarde du commandeur crâner au ciel[30]

This technique of ending the poem on a hard, harsh note is
found not only in "La Complainte du Nègre" but is common to
the majority of the poems in *pigments*, reinforcing and emphasizing the harsh bitterness that characterizes Damas' attitude
toward his exile. Unlike other Negritude poets such as Senghor
and David Diop, who often end their poems on a note of reconciliation softening the tone of exile, Damas relentlessly maintains and reinforces a harsh note. The poem "S.O.S." is a good
example of this poetic technique. Here too we see at work
another of Damas' stylistic devices, that of repetition, reduction, and further repetition of the reduced fragments, a device
that reinforces the predominant mood or attitude in the poem.
In "S.O.S." this repetitive reductive movement builds up to an
explosive climax in which all the poet's venom at religious
exploitation bursts forth:

vous les verrez
vraiment tout se permettre
ne plus se contenter de rire avec l'index inquiet
de voir passer un nègre
mais
froidement matraquer
mais
froidement descendre
mais
froidement étendre
mais froidement
matraquer
descendre
étendre
et
couper leur sexe aux nègres
pour en faire des bougies pour leurs églises[31]

you will see them
really stop at nothing
no longer content to laugh with restless forefinger
when they see a Negro going by
but coldly beating up
coldly knocking down

  coldly laying out
  coldly
  beating up
  knocking down
  laying out
  the blacks and cutting off their genitals
  to make candles for their churches

As the last two lines clearly demonstrate, physical exploitation (*couper leur sexe*) is closely linked to moral degradation and to the deprivation of the essentials of life. In the poem "Limbe" Damas' rancor finds expression in the enumeration of all conceivable forms of this moral thievery: the loss of one's plot of land, of one's songs and labor, of one's home and hearth, of the wisdom inherent in tradition, of the very rhythms of life itself.

  Le sauront-ils jamais cette rancune de mon coeur
  A l'oeil de ma méfiance ouvert trop tard
  ils ont cambriolé l'éspace qui était mien
  la coutume
  les jours
  la vie
  la chanson
  le rythme
  l'effort
  le sentier
  l'eau
  la case
  la terre enfumée grise
  la sagesse
  les mots
  les palabres
  les vieux
  la cadence
  les mains
  la mesure
  les mains
  les piétinements
  le sol[32]

Will they ever know this rancor in my heart?
From beneath suspicion's eye that opened all too late

they have robbed me of the space that once was mine
tradition
days
life
song
rhythm
effort
pathway
water
cabin
the gray, fertilized land
wisdom
words
palavers
the aged
cadence
hands
measure
hands
footbeats
soil

Another constant theme in Damas is that of a childhood limited by the imposition of false cultural standards and stifled by unnatural, stilted social patterns. Time and time again the poet rages against these impositions, which from his very cradle choked his natural growth:

Ma haine grossit en marge
de la culture
en marge
des théories
en marge des bavardages
dont on a cru devoir me bourrer au berceau[33]

My hatred grew fat on the fringes
of culture
on the fringes
of theories
on the fringe of the prating
which they thought I should be stuffed with in my cradle

Often, however, this feeling of rage is siphoned off into a chuckling bantering comic irony. The best example of this is perhaps the witty, biting, sarcastic poem "Hoquet,"[34] in which Damas skips and gambols through the disaster of childhood. Memories of this childhood well up in a fit of hiccups, recalling all the absurd attempts of his mother to bring him up as a fine colonial gentleman:

> me revient mon enfance
> dans un hoquet secouant

> my childhood comes back to me
> in a fit of hiccups

The poet is sternly admonished at table for not complying with the rules of etiquette and good breeding. He scoffs at these rules, especially when they are uttered in the name of piety, and in mock seriousness he repeats his mother's utterances:

> Les mains sur la table
> le pain ne se coupe pas
> le pain se rompt
> le pain ne se gaspille pas
> le pain de Dieu
> le pain de la sueur du front de votre Père
> le pain du pain

> Hands on the table
> break your bread,
> don't cut it
> don't waste it
> God's own bread
> bread stained with the sweat of your father's brow
> true bread of true bread

The counterpoint between the formula *ma mère voulant d'un fils* (my mother wishing her son to be) with which Damas begins each section of his poem and the repeated refrain that follows

> Désastre
> parlez-moi du désastre
> parlez-m'en

Disaster
talk to me about disaster
tell me about it

with which each section ends heightens the principal, middle
section in which his humor erupts:

Un os se mange avec mesure et discrétion
un estomac doit être sociable
et tout estomac sociable
se passe de rots
une fourchette n'est pas un cure-dents
. . . .
un nez bien élevé
ne balaye pas l'assiette

Bones should be eaten with measure and discretion
a stomach should be sociable.
and all sociable stomachs
refrain from belching
a fork is not a toothpick
. . . .
a well brought-up nose
keeps well out of one's plate

The poet's mother wishes him to have a fine colonial upbringing, the main object of which is the winning of a memo-
randum, certifying a proper French education. He explodes in
laughter at the punishments imposed for his lapses in learning
and then on the word *français*, sweeps to a high point of mockery:

Si votre leçon d'histoire n'est pas sue
vous n'irez pas à la messe
. . . .
Taisez-vous
Vous ai-je ou non dit qu'il vous fallait parler français
le français de France
le français du français
le français français

If you haven't learned your history lesson
you can't go to mass

. . . .

Be quiet
Have I told you or not that you have to speak French
the French of France
the French of Frenchmen
French French

His mother's constant show of religiosity and the use of
ceremony by which she measures good breeding, simply bore
the poet:

Et puis et puis
et puis au nom du Père
                du Fils
                du Saint-Esprit
à la fin de chaque repas

And then and then
and then in the name of the Father
                and of the Son
                and of the Holy Ghost
after every single meal

In his mother's view, all good little boys have been baptized:

et que je vous y reprenne dans la rue

. . . .

à jouer
à vous ébattre avec Untel
avec Untel qui n'a pas reçu le baptême

and let me catch you in the street again

. . . .

playing
and romping with So-and-So
who isn't even baptized

All good little boys must also acquire the genteel art of tinkling
with music:

Ma Mère voulant d'un fils très do

très ré
très mi
très fa
très sol
très la
très si
très do
ré-mi-fa
sol-la-si
   do

Il m'est revenue que vous n'étiez encore pas à vôtre leçon de vi-
  o-lon

My Mother wanted her son to be very do
    very re
    very mi
    very fa
    very so
    very la
    very ti
    very do
    re-mi-fa
    so-la-ti
      do
It came to me that you still hadn't gotten to your vi-o-lin lesson

In the shocked indignation of his mother's voice Damas exposes the snobbery inherent in a society where good breeding is
measured by lightness of pigment, class by color:

Un banjo
vous dîtes un banjo
comment dîtes-vous
un banjo
vous dîtes bien
un banjo
Non monsieur
  vous saurez qu'on ne souffre chez nous
ni ban
ni jo
ni gui
ni tare

les *mulâtres* ne font pas ça
laissez donc ça aux *nègres*

A banjo
did you say a banjo
what do you mean
a banjo
did you really say
a banjo
No, sir
      you must know we won't stand for any
ban
jos
or gui
tars
mulattos don't do that
leave that for the *Negroes*

"Hoquet" is a poem in which the poet is laughing. In "Solde," however, his tone is harsh, and his irony biting against those same fatuous gestures and the absurd gentility with which his childhood had been stifled; later exiled in Paris, the poet of Negritude rails against unnaturalness of any kind, rejecting theories and logic which distort the truth. The poem becomes a series of attacks, moving from a rejection of restrictions on dress (*leur smoking, leur faux-col, leur monocle*), an indictment of polite empty gestures (*leurs courbettes, leur multiple besoin de singeries, un peu d'eau chaude/ et des gateaux enrhumés*), to a diatribe against the falsification of truth by means of theory and logic. Finally, as in many of his poems, Damas climaxes "Solde" with a harsh eruption:

J'ai l'impression d'être ridicule
parmi eux complice
parmi eux souteneur
parmi eux égorgeur
les mains effroyablement rouges
du sang de leur ci-vi-li-sa-tion[35]

I feel ridiculous
among them an accomplice
among them a pimp
among them a murderer

my hands frightfully red
with the blood of their ci-vi-li-za-tion

In *pigments* Damas reacts in different ways to all the many
forms of physical and mental exploitation and to his complicity
with them. One reaction is that of threatened violence, of violence which could erupt at any moment, as implied in the ominous repetition that trails off at the end of "Ils Ont":

Il ne faudrait pourtant pas grand'chose
pourtant pas grand'chose
pas grand'chose
pas grand'chose[36]

But it wouldn't take much
no, not much
not much
not much

or again in the dark unanswered question that brings the poem
"Sur une Carte Postale" to a halt:

mais quelle bonne dynamite
fera sauter la nuit
les monuments comme champignons
qui poussent aussi
chez moi[37]

but what fine dynamite
will blow up the night
and the monuments like mushrooms
which also grow
at home

Another reaction to the cumulative oppressions is to wish
wearily for a moment of pause, a respite. In the repetition of
trève de, the poet evokes a fatigue that assails, and he pleads at
the end for

Trève un instant
d'une vie de bon enfant
et de désirs
et de besoins

et d'égoismes
particuliers[38]

A moment's peace
from the life of a well-behaved child
and from any special wants
or needs
or thoughts of self

Again in "Regard," Damas ends by seeking a moment of forgetfulness in a glass of Bordeaux.

But to seek respite or to yearn for a moment of forgetfulness
are but temporary reactions. In general, the poet is overcome
by a sense of shame at not having resisted the highly structured
degradation. Then he seeks not a glass of wine but a shoulder
in which to hide his shame. This overwhelming sense of shame
finds its best expression in the short powerful poem "Réalité":

De n'avoir jusqu'ici rien fait
détruit
bâti
osé
à la manière
du Juif
du Jaune
pour l'évasion organisée en masse
de l'infériorité

C'est en vain que je cherche
le creux d'une épaule
où cacher mon visage
ma honte
de
   la
     Ré
       a
        li
         té.[39]

Because I have as yet done nothing
destroyed nothing
built nothing
dared nothing

like a Jew
or a Chinaman
for the organized mass escape
from inferiority

I vainly seek
a shoulder
in which to bury my face
my shame
at
      Re
        al
           i
              ty.

Of all the emotional reactions, of all the resultant sensations, it is anguish that overwhelms Damas, mounting up, stifling and choking him. Night after night the poet experiences a deep feeling of disgust, revulsion, and horror. In a series of vertical images and of images of flooding he captures the stark anguish by which he is continually oppressed, the bitterness that obsesses him.

Un goût de sang me vient
un goût de sang me monte
m'irrite le nez
la gorge
les yeux

Un goût de sang me vient
un goût de sang m'emplit
. . . .
un goût de sang me vient
âcrement vertical[40]

A taste of blood comes over me
a taste of blood rises in me
irritating my nose
my throat
my eyes

A taste of blood comes over me
a taste of blood fills me
. . . .

a taste of blood comes over me
acridly vertical

The mood is insistent, compelling, and unchanging. Days and nights are without contour or differentiation. Unlike Senghor's nights, which are soft and lulling, which evoke memories of gentleness and peace, the nights of which Damas speaks, whether in infancy or adulthood, call forth bitterness and stifling oppression. They are nights of *asphyxie* and *étouffement*, nights in which Damas, the poet of anguish, is continually tormented by bitter blood that swells and mounts, asphyxiating him in a vertical, stifling movement.

Des nuits sans nom
des nuits sans lune
la peine qui m'habite
m'oppresse
la peine qui m'habite
m'étouffe[41]

Nameless nights
moonless nights
the pain which dwells in me
oppresses me
the pain which dwells in me
is stifling me

This sense of *étouffement*, of being surrounded and engulfed by paralyzing impotence and frustration, is a common theme in *pigments* and calls forth a violent, seething rage:

je me sens prêt à écumer toujours de rage
contre ce qui m'entoure
contre ce qui m'empêche
à jamais d'être
un homme[42]

I always feel ready to froth with rage
at the things which surround me
at the things which prevent me
from ever being
a man

So deep is the feeling of pain and anguish that the poet seems driven even to the point of ending it all with a dagger:

nuits sans lune
sans nom sans nom
où le dégoût s'ancre en moi
aussi profondément qu'un beau poignard malais[43]

nights without moon
without name without name
where disgust takes root in me
as deep as a fine Malay dagger

Damas' long, fuguelike poem, *Black-Label*,[44] with its alternation of surrealistic images and lived reality consolidates and intensifies the different feelings of exploitation and degradation and their resultant moods. The main refrain of the poem

BLACK-LABEL À BOIRE
pour ne pas changer
Black-Label à boire
à quoi bon changer

LET'S DRINK BLACK LABEL
to keep from changing
let's have Black Label
what good is it to change

by its very repetition invokes lassitude and intensifies the escape wish. In the first movement of *Black-Label* Damas repeats the unending monotony of days and nights without contour:

TEL J'AI VU LE CIEL
partout Un le même
ni moins bleu
moins beau
ni moins gris
moins triste
avec ou sans nuages

THE WAY I SAW THE SKY
it was One and the same all over
no less blue
no less beautiful

> no less gray
> no less sorrowful
> with or without clouds

One evening is like another, stretching backward in unbroken monotony:

> ce soir comme hier
> comme tant et tant
> d'autres soirs passés
>
> tonight like last night
> like so many, many
> other nights gone by

The poet reiterates the three faces of exile that continually haunt him: exile from natural youth and infancy, exile brought on by the exploitation and killing of his people, and the physical exile of life in Paris:

> Paris—l'Exil
> mon coeur maintient en vie
> le regret double
> du tout premier éveil à la beauté du monde
> et du premier Nègre mort à la ligne
>
> Paris—Exile
> my heart keeps alive
> the double regret
> for the very first awakening to the beauty of the world
> and the first Negro to die on the line

The note of exile from infancy is struck time and time again in the opening movement of the poem—the infant who will never know the warmth of a mother's milk:

> l'enfant à la tétine comprimée d'air
> que nul sein maternel jamais n'allaitera
>
> the infant at the collapsed air nipple
> whom no maternal breast will ever nurse

the child who is exiled from self even before he becomes aware of his own existence:

je n'étais pas né
que déjà les fauves de tout poil donnant la chasse à l'homme
emplissaient de leurs cris
le néant de mes nuits au néon à naître

I hadn't even been born
before man-hunting beasts of every description
were filling with their cries
the void of my nights of nascent neon

This note of distorted childhood swells out into a full-bodied expression in the third movement of the poem where each variation is introduced by *désirs comprimés*. The tone in this section is nostalgic, droll, and at times bitingly witty, as when Damas recounts having been beaten for picking his nose:

la toute derniere fessée reçue pour t'être
sous le regard acerbe de ta mère offusquée
et à la gêne polie de tous
farfouille le nez
d'un doigt preste et chanceux

the most recent spanking you got for being
caught by your offended mother's sharp eye
to everyone's polite discomfort
for picking your nose
with a quick and daring finger

The results of all these "repressed desires" are nights of bitterness whose acrid taste nothing can sweeten:

Désirs comprimés
dont s'emplissaient tes nuits . . .

Et n'enlevaient ce fort goût d'amertume
que laisse à la bouche au réveil une nuit d'insommie
ni la tiédeur du soleil matutinal qui ranimait déjà toutes choses

Bottled-up desires
with which your nights were filled . . .

And did not take away either the bitter aftertaste
a sleepless night leaves in the mouth at waking

> or the warmth of the morning sun, already bringing all things
>> back to life

Exile in Paris is populated by surrealistic dreams, hallucinations produced by a heart marinated in alcohol. The distortions in these surrealistic evocations alternate with the vivid accumulative presentation of exile and degradation introduced in the first movement. There in baroque accumulation these variations are insisted on by the introductory refrain "Ceux qui . . . Ceux qui . . ."

> ceux parlons-en
> qui vagissent de rage et de honte
> de naître aux Antilles
>
> . . . .
>
> de naître partout ailleurs qu'en bordure
> de la Seine ou du Rhône
>
> . . . .
>
> Ceux qui se refusent une âme
> ceux qui se méprisent
>
> . . . .
>
> Ceux qui croient pouvoir s'amincir les lèvres
> à se les mordre
> jusqu'au sang
>
> . . . .
>
> Ceux dont l'attitude immuable d'esclaves
> insulte à la sagesse antique et belle
> de leurs propres Anciens
>
> let's talk about those people
> wailing with rage and shame
> at being born in the Antilles
>
> . . . .
>
> at being born anywhere except beside
> the Seine or Rhône
>
> . . . .
>
> Those people who refuse to have a soul
> those people who despise themselves
>
> . . . .
>
> Those people who think they can make their lips thinner
> by biting them
> until they bleed
>
> . . . .

> Those people whose unchanging slavish attitude
> insults the beauteous age-old wisdom
> of their own Elders

In *Black-Label* Damas strikes out against all the varied forms of exile and oppression, against physical, mental, and moral exploitation. As in the accumulation of degradation introduced by *ceux qui,* the poet of Negritude introduces a countermovement in which he posits his own reactions by a stark listing of the evils he is determined to end.

> Il s'agit moins de recommencer
> que de continuer à être
> contre
>
> . . . .
> la caserne
> la chapelle
> la doctrine
>
> . . . .
> le pourboire
> la médaille
>
> . . . .
> la résignation
> la pudeur fausse
> la pitié
> la charité
>
> . . . .
> la morale occidentale
>
> It's less a matter of starting over
> as of continuing to be
> against
>
> . . . .
> barracks
> chapel
> doctrine
>
> . . . .
> tips
> medals
>
> . . . .
> resignation
> false modesty
> pity

charity

. . . .

Western morality

Black-Label, through its skillful interweaving of refrains, through its stylistic process of accumulation, through its alternating moods of harsh bitterness and ironic laughter, its juxtaposition of a vivid lived reality with surrealistic dream sequences, becomes a beautiful expression of Damas' dramatic current, a deep poetic vision of exile.

David Diop's *Coups de Pilon* strikes many of the notes already played by Damas in *pigments* and *Black-Label.* But unlike Damas, within the body of each single poem Diop counterpoints notes of exile with recurrent chords of hope and return. Although within each poem harsh and gentle statements, negatives and positives, may alternate, Diop closes, almost without exception, on a note of optimism opening out to a future of reconstruction and hope. This structural device is evident in the lines addressed to his mother:

> Écoute écoute ta voix
> Elle est ce cri traversé de violence
> Elle est ce chant guidé seul par l'amour.

> Listen, listen to your voice
> It is that cry shot through with violence
> It is that song guided only by love.

In this poem "À Ma Mère"[45] Diop compares his exile to an empty drugged state, an abyss into which he strays:

> Souvenirs d'escales anxieuses au bord du gouffre
> De mers glacées où se noient les moissons
> Quand revivent en moi les jours à la dérive
> Les jours en lambeaux à goût de narcotique

> Memories of anxious stopovers on the edge of the abyss
> Frozen seas in which the harvests drown
> When once more I relive the days spent drifting
> Shreds of days that taste of narcotics

Diop does not pick up this motif of drugged days in any of his other poems. Rather, he builds up a sense of exile through the use of words and images denoting harshness, brutishness, destruction. Through the use of connotative words charged with sound effects the poet constructs a picture of harsh material exploitation and its agonizing results:

> Les rires agonisaient dans l'enfer métallique des routes
> Et le rythme monotone des Pater-Noster
> Couvrait les hurlements des plantations à profit
> O le souvenir acide des baisers arrachés
> Les promesses mutilées au choc des mitrailleuses[46]

> The laughter writhed in the throes of death in the metal hell
>   of the roads
> And the Pater Nosters' monotonous rhythm
> Covered the howling from profitable plantations
> Oh, acid memory of kisses torn asunder
> Promises maimed by the shock of machine guns

In "Afrique" Diop extends his presentation of physical exploitation to the whole of Africa, painting the picture of an enslaved continent with images of movement, of diffusion and loss, of humiliation, bowing and scraping:

> Afrique mon Afrique
> . . . .
> Ton beau sang noir à travers les champs répandu
> Le sang de ta sueur
> La sueur de ton travail
> Le travail de l'esclavage
> L'esclavage de tes enfants
> Afrique dis-moi Afrique
> Est-ce donc toi ce dos qui se courbe
> Et se couche sous le poids de l'humilité
> Ce dos tremblant à zébrures rouges
> Qui dit oui au fouet sur les routes de midi[47]

> Africa my Africa
> . . . .
> Your beautiful black blood spilled through the fields
> The blood of your sweat
> The sweat of your labor
> The labor of your slavery

The slavery of your children
Oh tell me, Africa
Is this really you, the back bent
And laid low by the weight of your meekness
This trembling, red-striped back
Which says yes to the whip on the noonday roads

Diop builds up his poems with a series of words and images that are almost synonymous in meaning. Thus, in his admonitions against the falseness of European protestations of friendship, he uses images of facial contortions, of veiled movements which he juxtaposes with words denoting purity and beauty:

Ne cherchez pas la vérité dans la grimace de leurs phrases
Dans leurs claques paternelles et les trahisons d'alcôve
Ne cherchez pas la beauté dans ce masque qui s'agite
Et sature de parfums la hideur de leurs plaies
Non plus l'amour dans ces cuisses dévoilées
Monnayant l'aventure dans les bars à prétexte[48]

Don't look for the truth in their simpering phrases
In their fatherly slaps and their bedroom betrayals
Don't look for beauty in that animated mask
Which steeps the horror of their wounds in scent
Nor for love in those undraped thighs
Coining adventures in undercover bars

The predominant note of the falsification of truth by Europeans in "La Route Véritable" finds further expression in "Aux Mystificateurs."[49] Here David Diop opens the poem with a series of images linked to animals, to caging and chaining, with words denoting bestiality, which induce fear:

Monstres cyniques en cigare
Véhiculés d'orgies en vols
Et baladant l'égalité dans une cage de fer
Vous prêchiez la tristesse enchaînée à la peur

Cynical monsters with cigars
Carted out in orgiastic flights
Parading equality in an iron cage
You preached a sorrow chained to fear

The *mystificateurs* spend their nights pouring out alcohol and poring over meaningless words and religious ideas:

> ∴ vos nuits d'alcool à propagande
> . . . vos nuits écrasées de saluts automatiques
> . . . vos nuits de pieux silence et de sermons sans fin
>
> . . . your nights of propaganda-flavored alcohol
> . . . your nights crushed by automatic salvations
> . . . your nights of pious silence and sermons without end

The poem "Nègre Clochard"[50] brings together many of the motifs and images that Diop employs throughout *Coups de Pilon*. Images of breakage, of extinction and exhaustion, of submersion and caging, all combine in a powerful portrait of the exploited *clochard*:

> Toi qui marchais comme un vieux rêve brisé
> Un rêve foudroyé sous les lames du mistral
> . . . .
> Te voici nu dans ta prison fangeuse
> Volcan éteint offert aux rires des autres
> A la richesse des autres
> A la faim hideuse des autres
>
> You who walked like an old, shattered dream
> A dream ripped to shreds by the blades of the mistral
> . . . .
> Here you are naked in your filthy prison
> An extinct volcano offered up to other people's laughter
> Other people's wealth
> Other people's hideous hunger

The poet cannot comprehend why he failed to aid the naked tramp in his distress, and like Damas he is conscious of the complicity in his action. He too feels a sense of shame:

> Mais moi moi qu'ai-je fait dans ton matin de vent et de larmes
> Dans ce matin noyé d'écume
> Où pourrissaient les couronnes sacrées
>
> But I, what did I do in your windy, tearful morning
> That spume-drenched morning
> Where sacred crowns lay rotting

Like Damas he ridicules and yet pities the Negro who has allowed himself to become whitewashed and who can now go through the same empty grimaces so condemned by the poet of Negritude.

> Mon frère aux dents qui brillent sous le compliment hypo-
>   crite
> Mon frère aux lunettes d'or
> Sur tes yeux rendus bleus par la parole du Maître
> Mon pauvre frère au smoking à revers de soie
> Piaillant et sussurant et plastronnant dans les salons de la con-
>   descendance
> Tu nous fais pitié
>
> My brother, with teeth gleaming at hypocritical compliments
> My brother with golden spectacles
> Worn on eyes rendered blue by the Master's word
> My poor brother in your tux with silk lapels
> Squealing and hissing and strutting around in the parlors of
>   condescension
> We pity you

This renegade would feel quite lost and alone on his return to the red soil of Africa:

> Tu fouleras la terre amère et rouge d'Afrique
> Ces mots angoissés rythmeront alors ta marche inquiète
> Je me sens seul si seul ici![51]
>
> Your feet will tread Africa's bitter red earth
> And these anguished words will keep time to your uneasy step
> I feel alone here, so alone!

His absence from this red soil of Africa lies at the root of Léopold Sédar Senghor's nostalgic exile. His exile is gentler and phrased in softer language than that of Damas or Diop. The poet evokes a sense of nostalgia and regret, a feeling of the loss of something warm and treasured, a mood of rhythmical weariness and fatigue. By contrasting the cold harshness, the strident noisiness of the cities with the warmth and soft sounds of his homeland, Senghor underscores his feeling of absence. The commotion of the city makes the poet ill at ease, dazing him with its many passions. Thus, his sixteen years of wandering through the cities of Europe rest heavily on him.

> Sur ma faim, la poussière de seize années d'errance, et l'inqui-
> étude de toutes les routes d'Europe
> Et la rumeur des villes vastes; et les cités battues de vagues de
> mille passions dans ma tête.[52]

> On top of my hunger lies the dust of sixteen years' wandering,
> and the anxiety of all the roads in Europe
> And the rumble of vast cities; and the cities built from the waves
> of the thousand passions in my head.

In the middle of the city's uproar, the poet feels solitude; Manhattan is a city of horns blowing but a city of emptiness:

> Nuits d'insomnie ô nuits de Manhattan! si agitées de feux
> follets, tandis que les klaxons hurlent des heures vides[53]

> Sleepless nights, oh nights of Manhattan! so stirred up by
> flashing lights, while auto horns blare out the empty hours

This emptiness from exile and wandering abroad oppresses the poet, shriveling his poetic potential:

> Le poème se fane au soleil de Midi[54]

> The poem wilts in the sun of the Midi

For in the cities, especially in Paris, the poet feels excluded, fearing the hardness present in the crowds around him. Thus in the poem "In Memoriam"[55] Senghor creates a feeling of the steely quality of the city by the use of the adjective "blue," of his distance from the city through the image of a glass tower from which the poet peers out on the cold world around him. The scene is misty and indistinct.

> De ma tour de verre qu'habitent les migraines, . . .
> Je contemple toits et collines dans la brume

> From my migraine-haunted tower of glass, . . .
> I contemplate fog-bound rooftops and hills

By repeated mention of the area where he perches ("from this observatory, from my dangerously secure tower") the poet emphasizes the fact that he is outside looking in.

Then by equating parts of the bodies of the crowd with hard metals, the poet shows why he is afraid, why he is outside:

> J'ai peur de la foule de mes semblables au visage de pierre.
>
> . . . .
>
> Aux mains dures
>
> I fear the crowd of my stone-faced fellow men.
>
> . . . .
>
> With their hard hands

The biting cold of the Paris snow increases the poet's feeling of exile from warmth. Even like the parts of the body the snow too is hard—crystal salt, inimical to the poet. Using a stylistic device that appears throughout his poetry, Senghor picks up the feeling of coldness, the lack of warmth, by a series of negative introductory phrases, which further emphasize his sense of exile.

> Une goutte d'eau n'est tombée depuis six mois, pas un mot tendre et pas un bourgeon à sourire.
> Rien que l'aigreur de l'Harmattan . . .
>
> . . . .
>
> Rien que le Vent d'Est dans nos gorges . . .[56]
>
> Quinze jours sans un puits ni pâturage . . .
>
> . . . .
>
> Pas un rire d'enfant en fleur . . .
> Pas un sein maternel . . .
> Pas un mot tendre en l'absence de lèvres . . .[57]
>
> . . . sans main chaude dans la main.[58]
>
> For six months not a drop of water, not a single tender word or flicker of a smile.
> Nothing but the harshness of the harmattan . . .
>
> . . . .
>
> Nothing but the East Wind in our throats
>
> Fifteen days without a well or pasture . . .
>
> . . . .
>
> No laugh from any blossoming child

No mother's breast . . .
No tender word when lips are absent . . .

. . . no warm hand in my own.

The poet of Negritude desires the warmth of emotions, the tenderness of people, the sympathetic touch of the elements. Their absence almost becomes a suspension of living.

> La poitrine succombe à de graves énigmes, et je meurs de ne pas mourir et je meurs de vivre le coeur absent

> My chest succumbs to grave enigmas, and I die of not dying and die of living with absent heart

Over and over Senghor laments his absence with *saudade*, that is, not bitterly but with a feeling of gentle nostalgia.

> Dites! qu'elle est longue à mon coeur l'absence de l'Absente[59]

> Ah! how long to my heart is the absent one's absence

Thus while living abroad, even when sheltered from the harshness of the cold, the poet of Negritude longs for warmth and affection:

> Je dormirai sous le toit d'autres chevelures à l'abri des orages.
> Mais chaque année, quand le rhum du Printemps fait flamber la mémoire
> Je regretterai le pays natal et la pluie de tes yeux sur la soif des savanes.

> I will sleep sheltered from the storm under the roof of other tresses.
> But every year, when memory flames with the rum of Spring-time
> I will miss my homeland and the rain of your eyes upon thirsty savannahs.

And so the poet in exile asks the question:

> Quand reverrai-je mon pays, l'horizon pur de ton visage?
> Quand m'assiérai-je de nouveau à la table de ton sein sombre?[60]

When will I see my land again, the pure horizon of your face?
When will I sit down again at the table of your dark breast?

Unlike the other poets of Negritude, Senghor seldom lists the
accumulated degradations and exploitations suffered by his
people. Even on the few occasions when he does enumerate
them, he does not do it with harshness, bitterness, or irony. His
long poem *Chaka* is one of the few examples in which Senghor
touches on this theme of exploitation, and even here Chaka's
speech is a response to the accusations of the *voix blanche*,
almost an apology for his actions:

> Le tamtam ni la voix ne rythment plus les gestes des saisons.
> Peuples du Sud dans les chantiers, les ports les mines les manu-
> factures
> Et le soir ségrégés dans les kraals de la misère.
> Et les peuples entassent des montagnes d'or noir d'or rouge—
> et ils crèvent de faim.
> Et je vis un matin, sortant de la brume de l'aube, la forêt des
> têtes laineuses
> Les bras fanés le ventre cave, des yeux et des lèvres immenses
> appelant un dieu impossible.[61]

> Neither tom-tom nor voice still keeps time to the seasonal
> gestures.
> Peoples of the South in the work-sites the ports the mines the
> mills
> And segregated at night into misery's kraals.
> And the people pile up mountains of black gold and red gold—
> and they die of hunger
> And one morning I see the forest of woolly heads coming out of
> the misty dawn,
> Their arms limp, their bellies empty, their immense lips and
> eyes calling upon an impossible god.

Yet in spite of his poetic noninvolvement in the treatment of
exploitation, the poet is aware of the intensity and duration of
the struggle which his people have undergone:

> La lutte est longue trop! dans l'ombre, longue des trois époques
> de nuit millésime.[62]

> The struggle has gone on too long! on and on in the shadows
> for three ages of vintage night.

The seeming hopelessness of this long struggle which has
pulled the poet of Negritude away from the center of things,
from the beat of life:

> . . . vous avez arraché de ce coeur trop aimant les liens qui
> l'unissaient au pouls du monde[63]

> . . . from this far too loving heart you have ripped the cords
> which bound it to the heartbeat of the world

and leads to weariness and deepening anguish.

> Lasses lasses mes jambes lasses par les rues de thé à cinq heures.
> Et mon coeur de ma mère lasse, qui oscille toujours entre
> Espoir et Angoisse.[64]

> Weary, weary, my legs are weary in streets of five o'clock tea.
> And weary the heart my mother gave me, always wavering be-
> tween Hope and Anguish.

In *Black-Label*, Damas, through a series of surrealistic
images, dramatized his exile. In *Brush Fire*, U'Tamsi uses a
parallel poetic technique to evoke the destruction that had befallen his country: dislocated images and broken rhythms paint
a hallucinatory picture of a wasteland. Not only U'Tamsi, but
the total landscape suffered exile and loss. For Damas it was
not enough to say *merde*, he had to lash out against a series of
injuries; so also U'Tamsi:

> . . . it is not enough to cry rape
> this is how the first star exploded
>
> . . . .
>
> coffee bananas cotton tapioca
> die die if you want to
> it is not enough to recreate the rape[65]

Yet the poet does precisely this in the connected collection of
poems that form *Brush Fire*. Harshly and brutally, and thus
quite differently from Senghor and more acidly than Diop,
U'Tamsi tells of the rape of himself, his race, and his land. To

be sure return takes place through purification and cleansing.
Yet the poet emphatically states in the title poem:

> my race remembers
> the taste of bronze drunk hot.[66]

Poignantly, but bitterly, the poet tells in the poem "Madness"
of the contamination that has poisoned his laughter, of the
blood clotted in his veins:

> my sheep my fingers my hair
> in which wholesome laughter hangs
> oh my rivers I render you the dirty water
> of my pores
> . . . .
> I want nothing but the moon
> but what slaughter in my poor blood[67]

The poet has undergone not only slaughter, but has suffered
from exclusion and nonparticipation, which he laments:

> day passes zenith
> . . . .
> but I still have no task[68]
> . . . .
> here I am in the limbo of all suffering
> hunchbacked
> what boldness has opened my arms[69]

and with the bitter irony so typical of Damas, cries out in
"Erect" his loss in agony:

> you are lost
> you are not so much
> you are too dirty
> to be a model negro
> jazz blues
> you do not stretch your guts
> as membranes of drums
> your head is not good ebonite
>
> mimed

what agony[70]

In the poets of Negritude solitude is a constant motif, solitude suffered in exile from self, from country, from one's people. U'Tamsi's poem "The Slave" is a harsh pessimistic song telling of solitude, disintegration, and loss. As in Césaire the landscape of misery opens out, extending itself into the vastness of land and sea.

> I have carried my dog days
> along the oceans
> my eyes bent on my misery alone
> I have moaned without revolt
>
> my brothers did not recognise me
> and my integrity
> my youthful days pass.[71]

In "Flight of Vampires," the landscape of desolation is created through distortions of the natural, the repetition of images of freak children.

> and here a mother is delivered
> of a child with two heads
> . . . another mother
> to put into the world
> a child with three heads
> and perhaps no legs[72]

And the river, which symbolizes the poet's land and his life, now flows with "broken thighs," rolling his "scandals down to the dolphins."

Throughout *Brush Fire* the reiteration of images of rot and decay create a sense of death and destruction, a landscape of pollution. In "Long Live the Bride," the poet says:

> the river flows
> and it smells of vomited dew
> a rancid resin that will no longer hunt
> the night moths
> flows from the gaping wound[73]

Through the juxtaposition of dead forms with his gutted
being, the poet, in "Still Life," identifies his suffering with the
land's.

> I have often seen
> carcasses in the air
> where my blood burns[74]

And in "Against Destiny" the recurring images of dungheap
and fire introduced in the very opening of *Brush Fire* are once
again taken up:

> there are no more setting suns
> there is ravenous grass
> there is more ravenous fire
>
> . . . what agony[75]

U'Tamsi, through a play of contrasts, of sea images, of death
and life, of promised and broken dreams, in "Across Time and
River" emphasizes the loss of his path:

> and I have cried
> above the jungles
> the integrity of forgotten paths[76]

Using vertical images and images of entry, so characteristic of
the poets of Negritude, U'Tamsi explores in a personalistic tone
the solitude and loss which inform *Brush Fire*. The poet confesses in "Presence":

> I played with my body
> the ardent poems of death
> . . . .
> I opened myself to the world
> of sea weeds
> where solitudes crawl[77]

Counterpoint creates a tension in "Erect" that heightens the
poignancy and adds to and sharpens the anguish in U'Tamsi's
appeal:

I have the life that kills
give me my death

. . . .

I understand that my congo
wants to live free[78]

The correlation of life, death, and freedom suggest the poet's
desire for mystical sacrifice to save his Congo. Yet, the poet
chafes at the oppression and the need to sacrifice and yearns for
a vital life ("Madness").

I am no longer satisfied
with my sea gull fate
give me the savannah
and its colours of living grass[79]

The play of opposites continues in the broken dream, light
and solitude, in birth experienced by "mother" and death signi-
fied by "rope at neck" (the poem "Dance of the Amulets").

the rainbow coloured dream the rope at the neck

. . . .

solitude
my mother promised me the light.[80]

A sense of having been murdered is reiterated in the lines from
"My Head Is Perfumed":

my country inhabits me no more . . .
my soul is a nail on a dead plank[81]

containing overtones of Christian martyrdom. But the poet
harshly rejects Christianity; it had deceived him with the
preaching of patience and restrained action, with the precepts
of logic that had made him acquiesce to his fate. Ironically, the
poet realizes:

the gibbons . . .
. . . fooled me with patience to explain to me
the problems of life[82]

The result (from "Long Live the Bride") is that:

> . . . I am dead murdered in the altar of christ[83]

The creative genius, western science, had indeed produced a monster. With heightened irony the poet U'Tamsi, in "The Lines of My Head," shows that he need not learn the secrets of the electric chair since he already possesses the power of self-immolation:

> I recreate my head with all the new sciences
> the electric chair
> . . . .
> hence I have lulled to sleep
> my own filth
> my filth of negro-jew
> my race of jew-negro wandering
> in the desert of my country's heart
> but I am well sheltered under my skin
> I am already my own funeral oven[84]

But the poet and his people did not always suffer loss of hope and dreams. The poet did not always live in a solitude of absence and a limbo of time. U'Tamsi, the poet of Negritude, is reinforced by the elements; thus he can assert:

> time need not come to grief
> . . . .
> we are the storm
> in the heart of summer
> thunder leaps
> on the slope of our hearts[85]

The poet in "Across Time and River" affirms his belief and his people's abiding faith:

> we have seen the sand
> we have seen the reef
> who can ignore it

> we have seen rivers and trees
> who will pronounce it
>
> we have believed
> we have believed
> who will deny it[86]

Now his task and mission are to preserve the gentle arch of his laughter, his stream—the safest of streams, his living flesh (from "A Mat to Weave"):

> his stream was the safest of cups
> because it was of bronze
> because it was his living flesh[87]

Before he could not guide his stream; he could not change the flow of his river; only the rainbow could (from "Abortive Joy"):

> I threw stones just to see
> but I could not bestride it
> only the rainbow could[88]

But now, injected with the germ of life, poetic transformation takes place. Transformation brings with it the will to act, makes the poet the executor of his people's destiny. Self-sacrifice is efficacious; death ensures life. He says in "Against Destiny":

> to hoist the harness
> high in the wind
> to safeguard everything
> the white laughter
> and the red and native sun
>
> . . . .
>
> I must arm my people
> against their destiny tonight
> in order to name it later
> in golden figures
> he earned his death
> long live love[89]

Poetic transformation is coupled with a transformation of the landscape. The pattern of destruction is halted, "the rhythms are broken saved," unnatural disfiguration and deformities drawn through dissecting surrealistic images are now metamorphosed. In the poem "March":[90]

> the red blood pounded black
> the red blood pounded one eyed
> the red blood pounded blind
> shall have a beak of the finest steel
> blind but just
> and shall smash the fire thank god

Through the marriage of the vertical with the curved expressed in

> a hundred hysterical women pounded
> with curved loins
> they pounded down to the roots of the day

shapes are altered and balance is restored, things become natural again:

> the child has no more eyelashes
> a hundred women pound the path
> . . . .
> the child finds its eyelashes but one is missing
> . . . .
> the missing eyelash is the river
> he names it
> congo
> what splendour

Splendor is revived, and "now the child will sleep," the rainbow dream is accomplished (in "Abortive Joy"):

> I have dreamt this dream
>   with the rainbow
> curving against the sleeping stream[91]

Purification takes place and the votive lamp is rekindled ("My Head Is Perfumed"):

> come tonight my head is perfumed
> my sweat is good resin
> come tonight and light your lamps

the night will come
my soul is ready.[92]

The barren and burnt landscape of destruction, the destroyed
and mutilated wasteland are restored; the river remains, and
the rainbow. Now in the poem "Presence" U'Tamsi consum-
mates his return, defines his Negritude, which in essence rejects
surfaces and moves deep into the center of all things:

my hands moist to all seeds
carry my feet deep into space
and I resemble slow death with its rich suns[93]

Césaire, too, had lived in a barren and sterile land where
people impotently accepted their wounds, resignedly carried
their anguish. This is the land which Césaire had first rejected
and from which he fled; it is to this country that Césaire symbolically returns, transformed by the poetic word.

Cahier d'un Retour au Pays Natal[94] by Aimé Césaire
bridges the exile, its span reaching out to the return. It dramatically presents the close relationship between the movement away and the return. The movement away takes place in
the first part of the poem; its countermovement in the second.
The structural movement of the former is horizontal; the return
ends in a vertical ascension. Césaire opens his poem with a
refrain, *Au bout du petit matin*, which runs throughout the first
part. This nonspecific time of day is vague enough to set the
poem in no historical time yet by its repetition makes the time
ever-present. The exile is captured in a series of accumulative
statements that lead the poem from the larger geographical
area, the Antilles, to the microcosm, the individual. The poem
moves from the islands themselves to town, to a crowd within
that town, and finally to an individual human being. The Antilles, in which hunger walks supported by alcohol, islands that
are historical failures, form the starting point for Césaire's
geography of exile.

Au bout du petit matin bourgeonnant d'anses frêles les Antilles
qui ont faim, les Antilles grêlées de petite vérole, les Antilles
dynamitées d'alcool, échouées dans la boue de cette baie, dans
la poussière de cette ville sinistrement échouées.

At the end of the early hours budding with fragile handles, the hungry Antilles, pitted by smallpox, dynamited by alcohol, stranded in the mud of this bay, ominously stranded in the dust of this town.

The concatenating process has begun. Next Césaire, in a horizontal movement, picks up the town stretching out into a distance, a town which is inactive and unending, which is buried under the weight of its own problems.

Au bout du petit matin, cette ville plate—étalée, trébuchée de son bon sens, inerte, essouflée sous son fardeau géométrique de croix éternellement recommençante, indocile à son sort, muette, contrariée de toutes façons, incapable de croître selon le suc de cette terre . . .

At the end of the early hours, this flat town, spread out, staggered by its good sense, inert gasping beneath its geometric burden of a cross eternally renewed, chafing at its fate, mute, thwarted in every way, unable to grow according to the juices of this earth . . .

The note of inertia that pervades the first part of the poem is carried forward into the description of the crowd that inhabits this town, a crowd which is paradoxically chatty and mute and which despite its size remains inactive and spineless, devoid of its essential nature.

Dans cette ville inerte, cette étrange foule qui
ne s'entasse pas, ne se mêle pas. . . . Cette foule qui
ne sait pas faire foule, cette foule, on s'en rend
compte, si parfaitement seule sous ce soleil

In this inert town, this strange crowd which
doesn't huddle, doesn't mix . . . this crowd which
doesn't know how to make a crowd, this crowd which is, one sees,
so perfectly alone beneath that sun

Through an extended comparative image Césaire stresses the animality of this crowd in the figure of a woman:

> d'une paysanne, urinant debout, les jambes
> écartées, roides.

> of a peasant woman standing there urinating,
> her spread legs stiff.

Ending the movement with the final word *roides*, the poem moves to the single individual, *le morne*, a figure of anguish, a nameless, tired, beaten figure who leads a life of emptiness and futility.

> le morne oublié . . . le morne au sabot inquiet et docile . . .
> le morne accroupi . . . lentement vomissant ses fatigues
> d'hommes, le morne seul et son sang répandu, le morne et
> ses pansements d'ombre, le morne et ses rigoles de peur,
> le morne et ses grandes mains de vent . . . ce morne bâtard

> the forgotten, brooding man . . . restless, docile in his clogs . . .
> squatting down, brooding . . . slowly vomiting his human weari-
> ness, alone and brooding with his blood spilled, brooding with
> his bandages of shadows, brooding and furrowed by fear, brood-
> ing with his great hands of wind . . . this melancholy bastard

The climax of these scenes of empty anguish and inertia, of futility and boredom, is the act of suicide, which further accentuates the abortive nothingness of the life of the crowd, of life in the city, in the islands.

> le suicidé s'est étouffé avec complicité de son
> hypoglosse en retournant sa langue pour l'avaler

> the suicide choked himself, bending back his tongue to sever
> the connection of the tongue to the bottom of the mouth

Here the young are fed with commandments instead of food. Césaire harshly rejects the teacher and the priest who scorn the inability of the little Negro boy to learn these empty commandments and who are heedless of the gnawing hunger which paralyzes him:

> sa voix s'oublie dans les marais de la faim . . .
> une faim lourde et veule

His voice is forgotten in the swamps of hunger . . .
a hunger heavy and drab

The refrain *Au bout du petit matin* now sweeps us away from
these individualized statements to a more general conception of
rot and decay, both physical and moral. Here the physical
degeneration is inextricably linked to the moral, and both are
laid bare in a long passage infused with a festering unhealthi-
ness. The poet evokes vivid pictures of disease and immorality,
illustrating them through exploding images of fermentation:

> les sodomies monstrueuses de l'hostie . . . les prostitutions, les
> hypocrisies . . . les mensonges . . . les perversions, les
> arlequinades de la misère . . . Ici la parade des risibles et
> scrofuleux bubons . . . les fermentations imprévisibles d'espèces
> putrescibles . . . les hamacs tièdes de la dégénérescence

> the monstrous sodomies of the sacred host. . . . the prostitu-
> tions, hypocrisies . . . the lies . . . perversions, misery's horse-
> play . . . Here, the parade of ludicrous, lymphatic infections
> . . . unforseeable fermentations of putrescent species . . . ham-
> mocks warm with degeneracy

Even the landscape is static and connives in this all pervasive
dégénérescence:

> la grande nuit immobile, les étoiles plus mortes qu'un balafong
> crevé

> the great, motionless night, the stars deader than a broken
> balaphon

This landscape of destitution and poverty is continued in Césaire's description of the road, which leads precariously through
the hills, coming to a dead halt at the skeleton of his house:

> une route bossuée qui pique une tête dans un creux où elle
> éparpille quelques cases . . . une route follement montante,
> témérairement descendante, et la carcasse de bois comiquement
> juchée sur de minuscules pattes de ciment que j'appelle "notre
> maison."

> a bumpy road that dives into a hollow where it scatters a few
> huts . . . a road going crazily up and recklessly down, and

perched comically on tiny cement feet, the wooden carcass which I call "our house."

The interior of this house is gray and dim, its gloom pierced only by unwholesome glitter accentuating its spectral quality:

> le plancher grossier où luisent des têtes de clous . . . la lumière grise de la lampe, celle vernissée et rapide des cancrelats qui bourdonne à faire mal . . .

> the rough floor with its shining nail-heads . . . the lamp's gray light and the glossy flashes of the cockroaches whose buzzing makes you ache . . .

Césaire interrupts the large thematic movement of his poem with a brief but dramatically effective Christmas interlude. By compressing the activities of most of the year into a few lines, he gives poetic expression to the importance of this holiday in the lives of his people, the eager anticipation with which they await it. Christmas comes on with a rush: "c'était Noël qui commençait."

> Il s'était announcé d'abord Noël par un picotement
> de désirs, une soif de tendresses neuves.

> The first sign of Christmas had been a prickling of desires, a thirst for new caresses.

The phrases *picotement de désirs* and *tendresses neuves* are weighted with irony, for the poet has already foreshadowed the gluttonous "hysteria" of the Christmas scene in an image of the sea sucking up the land, the sea's great, hysterical licking. Christmas is not like other festivals where there are fireworks and dancing in the public squares. Christmas preparations are elaborately undertaken, not with a view to pleasure and enjoyment so much as out of a desire to impress others.

> de-peur-que-ça-ne-suffise-pas,
> de-peur-que-ça-ne-manque
> de-peur-qu'on-ne-s'embête

lest-it-be-too-little
lest-it-be-lacking
lest-we-get-bored

With corrosive irony Césaire speaks of "the church . . . which let itself kindly fill with laughter" and states that "it's nice inside." The *banquet de chants* contrasts with a gluttonous scene in which "you eat good food and drink the cup that cheers"—foods are piled up in a vast accumulation with the connective *et*, ending with

> et toutes sortes de bonnes choses qui vous imposent
> autoritairement les muqueuses

> and all sorts of good things which your tastebuds
> thrust upon you with authority

Then with an ironic expression of Negritude in which there is total participation of all parts of the body, Césaire begins a rhythmical climactic movement:

> Et ce ne sont pas seulement les bouches qui chantent,
> mais les mains, mais les pieds, mais les fesses, mais
> les sexes, et la créature tout entière qui se liquéfie
> en sons, voix et rythme.

> And not only do the mouths sing,
> but the hands, feet, buttocks,
> genitals, and the entire creature liquifying
> into sounds, voice and rhythm.

The word *liquéfie* reflects not only the sodden state of the merrymakers but picks up an image of water, which swells, climaxing the Christmas festivities with a burst.

> Arrivée au sommet de son ascension, la joie
> crève comme un nuage.

> Having reached its high point, joy
> burst like a cloud.

From the height of joy a sudden vertical movement plunges the merrymakers back into "the valleys of fear, the tunnels of anguish and the fires of hell." A drugged life of anguished follows in which "l'on somnole . . . comme dans un rêve" to the accompaniment of steady rains; the cloud of joy dissolves in the monotony of rain:

> et la pluie,
> les cloches . . . la pluie . . .
> qui tintent, tintent, tintent . . .
>
> and the rain,
> the bells . . . the rain . . .
> going plink, plink, plink . . .

The longer movement of the poem resumes with the ever-present refrain, *Au bout du petit matin*. The town is afraid; there is no desire to rebel or to take action against the oppressive monotony of life. Even the houses seem afraid:

> Les dos des maisons ont peur du ciel truffé de feu . . . elles ont opté de se poser superficielles entre les surprises et les perfidies.
>
> The ridges of the houses are afraid against the fire-studded sky . . . they have chosen to remain simply poised between surprise and perfidy.

Césaire relentlessly pushes the town forward, picking up the horizontal flatness of its life with the *pourtant*, which retraces the author's incredulity at the power of survival of this town. Reiterating the word *petit*, Césaire captures the bourgeois inanities that govern the emotions of the town's inhabitants, for whom little scandals, little hatreds swell out to fill the vacuum of their lives, aborted lives of boredom and stagnation. From the general life of the town we move to the interior of one house, Césaire's, and to the life of those who dwell there.

Unlike Senghor, who recaptures the softness of his childhood, Césaire evokes the meanness and drabness of his own. A series of adjectives denoting smallness introduces his house, where a father does nothing but waste away, seemingly bewitched by impotence; where a mother tires the night, sewing for the survival of the children. The mood of unending desperation is captured in the repetition of the word "pedaling" and the phrase "and night and day." "And my mother whose legs kept pedaling, pedaling day and night for the sake of our unre-mitting hunger; I was even awakened at night by those tireless legs pedaling in the night and the sharp bite which a Singer takes from the night's soft flesh as my mother pedals, pedals day and night for the sake of our hunger."

The sound of his mother's continuous pedaling alternates with the whistling and creaking of his house, where a whole race is spawned on a bed perched on swollen kerosene tins and covered with rags: "nostalgia for the mattress on my grand-mother's bed." There is no talk of lofty lineage, as in Senghor, nor even of the boredom of the middle-class propriety of Damas' family; here, Césaire is at his most skillful, as he unfolds for us the doomed life of three generations of his line. The heroic exaggeration of the phrase *tout entière ma race* is not once interrupted, but further swollen by the cancerous implication of the word *éléphantiasis*—"that bed made of planks with kerosene tins for feet, as if the bed had elephantiasis." The word *nostal-gie* underscores the futility of their dreams, and *MERCI* the total irony of unrewarding faith—"A meager little flame dances like a fat roach in a pot full of oil underneath the bed . . . golden letters spell out THANK YOU on the pot."

On the rue Paille where the house stands the sea vomits its dead cats and dogs, adding to the filth and sordidness of the street. The sea, violent and threatening, ravenously eats away at houses, streets, and the dark filthy beach. "This beach, too, is distressing, with its rotting heaps of garbage, its furtive back-sides answering nature's call, and the sand is black, funereal; you never saw such black sand." Perhaps the sea will wash away the total, barren, dismal landscape that Césaire, with compressed energy, has hammered out. It is from this land that the poet sets out for another exile in Europe. Here the poem opens out, and the poet cuts across all the regions of the world, wherever people are exploited, wherever his race is oppressed.

Until now the poem has been one vast accumulation of de-spair, a piling up of anguish and horrors, dramatizing the sense of the poet's total alienation from his land. Now begins the slow return to that land. The poet will become the sorcerer and prophet who is to bring deliverance. To rediscover his land is to discover the power of words. "I would rediscover the secret of great communications and great combustions. I would say storm. I'd say river. I'd say tornado. I would say leaf. I'd say tree." As the poet harnesses all the combustive energy of the elements, poetic strength comes through utterance. To give concrete form to disembodied fragments he throws out the challenge: "And you ghosts . . . I'll have words vast enough to hold you."

Nourished by the milk of the earth, the earth of his land, the poet continues his transformation, gathering strength for his task, for his return to his native country. ". . . I'd only need one gulp of your jiculi milk to keep discovering in you . . . the land of liberty and brotherhood, my land." His role will be that of a spokesman: "My mouth will speak for ills that have no mouth, my voice will be freedom for voices dwindling in the dungeon of despair." He sets his own task; moving from passive observer, from describer, the poet becomes an active part of his country, an activist, not a portrayer or even sympathizer: ". . . be careful not to fold your arms in the sterile posture of the spectator, for life is not a stage show, a sea of sorrows is no proscenium, a shouting man is not a dancing bear. . . ." He returns to this life, this living death, "limping along . . . without meaning or piety . . . and all those deaths just futile absurdities beneath the splashing of my open consciousness." Suddenly, the poet stops the process of his transformation with an ironic chuckle and statement. How can he, a mere man, change the hierarchy ordained by Providence? Has he "the right to reckon life by my murky span . . . and thus to turn creation upside down"?

It is not only through a series of poetic transformations that Césaire begins his return to his native country, but it is by his embracing and identifying with "those few thousand carriers of death going round and round in the calabash of an island." But his island is only one of the many that form the Caribbean archipelago so the poet extends his identification, quickly working through the Caribbean Sea, across Guadeloupe to Haiti, the first black republic "where Negritude first stood up tall," to Florida, the tail of America, "where the black is finished by strangulation" and then across on the Gulf Stream to Africa.

Quickly, the poet enumerates the many towns and areas of the world which bear the imprint of his race, which contain the sweat of his race. With his bones and his blood the skyscrapers were built, his filth and his dirt fertilized "Virginia, Tennessee,

Georgia, Alabama." For the poet, the past has been bloody
with futile revolt.

But all revolt has not been useless. Toussaint Louverture, the
liberator of Haiti, with whom the poet identifies, had defied "les
cris blancs de la mort blanche." Now the poem becomes a
panegyric to Toussaint, recounting his imprisonment in the
Jura where the biting whiteness of the snow is part of the death
grip of the white world. In a passage that builds up with
rhythmical cadenced progression, Césaire choreographs a styl-
ized duet in which Toussaint Louverture routs white death.
Death expires in white silence, and the splendor of Toussaint's
vital red blood bursts forth. Here, all is counterpoint of sound;
all is color contrast. The contrast is carried into a dialectical
opposition between the liberating embrace of *la folie* and the
confining rigidity of *la raison*, reason which the poet scorns and
which he equates with the whiplash of servitude.

La folie becomes a transforming force for the poet of Negritude, "madness which remembers . . . howling . . . seeing . . .
going wild." Liberated by this carefree abandon the poet can
freely penetrate nature, absorbing and being absorbed by it.
La raison comprehends only surfaces, *la folie* makes for deeper
involvement, begins the poet's entry into the center of things,
and leads him back to the waters of the Congo:

> A force de regarder les arbres je suis
> devenu un arbre et mes longs pieds
> d'arbre ont creusé dans le sol de larges
> sacs à venin de hautes villes d'ossements
> à force de penser au Congo
> je suis devenu un Congo bruissant de
> forêts et de fleuves
> où le fouet claque comme un grand
> étendard
> l'étendard du prophète
> où l'eau fait
> likouala-likouala
>
> From looking at trees I have
> become a tree and my long tree feet
> have hollowed out large
> sacs of poison from the ground

tall cities made of bones
from thinking about the Congo
I have become a Congo rustling
with forests and rivers
where the whip cracks like a great
banner
the standard of the prophet
where the water goes
likooala-likooala

Now the poet is at the border of his country, when he ironically
declares to the guardian angel customs man his baggage of
sins: "je déclare mes crimes . . . Danses. Idoles. Relaps." In
mocking defiance the poet accepts these sins:

Moi aussi

J'ai assassiné Dieu de ma paresse de
mes paroles de mes gestes de mes chansons obscènes
. . . .
J'ai lassé la patience des missionnaires
insulté les bienfaiteurs de l'humanité.
. . . .
L'étendue de ma perversité me confond!

I too

Have assassinated God with my laziness
with my words with my actions with my obscenc songs
. . . .
I have tired the missionaries' patience
insulted the benefactors of mankind.
. . . .
The extent of my perversity confounds me!

Accepting the sins of ugliness that had been used against
him, the poet-sorcerer begins his work of conjuring the explosiveness of words for the taming of the elements. Through the
force of repetition of the explosive *voum rooh oh* the poet casts
his spell which resurrects a time of his childhood: "—myself
as a child going down a road, chewing on a sugar cane root," recalling a vision of a man garreted by a rope, finally evoking the
twitchings of the garreted man through the repetition of "oh's."
The poet moves away into the "fierce exaltation of forests and

of uprooted mountains," and through the conjuring power of
voum rooh oh almost arrives at "the Promised Time." Then
there is a sudden halt: "But what shapes my voice? . . . It is
you, dirty old world. Dirty old morning. You, dirty hate." The
cumulative weight of the hundred years of slavery momentarily stops him, choking his voice, but he begins again, not simply
mouthing words but threatening destructive violence with them,
"words which are . . . both brushfires, and flaming flesh, and
blazing towns . . ."

Here Césaire's mood becomes fiercer, more defiant; there is a
sudden bursting movement in verbs and nouns: "I burst the
vitelline membrane separating me from myself, I burst the great
cauls which girdle me with blood." Self-stigmatization and
despair had been foisted on him through the blatant egoism
of Europe, which he now answers with his egoism, willing it
beautiful: "je veux cet égoïsme beau."

Strengthened by this egoism the poet can reveal the physical
and psychological brutalization that his race has suffered across
the centuries, and laments its bloody history. "How much blood
within my memory! My memory contains lagoons."

Rapidly and with a tone reminiscent of Damas, he reviews
the many stereotypes that Europe imputes to him, that of the
singing, dancing Negro and such "old saws: Beating a nigger
is feeding him." The *Cahier* sweeps along spiraling upward,
and through a series of harmonic counterpoints, by alternating invocation with magical transformations compelled by
the sorcerer's word, this poem of Negritude becomes a ceremony of purification. The poet will accept all, the total filth and
degradation suffered by his race, the rejected and abandoned of
his kind, the diseased and mutilated of his people, their sores
and their wounds. By accepting he will be revitalized by them
and in turn vivify them. All will undergo change from nonbeing
to being, from absence to presence, and with a series of vertical
images the poet delves deep into the true heart of things, into
their essences. Ironically, Césaire disclaims his heritage:

> Non, nous n'avons jamais été amazones du roi du Dahomey,
> ni princes de Ghana avec huit cents chameaux, ni docteurs à
> Tombouctou Askia le Grand étant roi, ni architectes de Djénné,
> ni Madhis, ni guerriers. Nous ne nous sentons pas sous l'ais-
> selle la démangeaison de ceux qui tinrent jadis la lance. Et

puisque j'ai juré de ne rien celer de notre histoire, (moi qui
n'admire rien tant que le mouton broutant son ombre d'après-
midi), je veux avouer que nous fûmes de tout temps d'assez
piètres laveurs de vaisselle, des cireurs de chaussures sans enver-
gure, mettons les choses au mieux, d'assez consciencieux
sorciers et le seul indiscutable record que nous ayons battu est
celui d'endurance à la chicote . . .

No, we never were horsemen for the King of Dahomey nor
princes of Ghana with eight hundred camels nor doctors in
Timbuktu when Askia the Great was king nor the architects of
Djenné nor Mahdis nor warriors. The pits of our arms do not
itch like those of men who used to wield the lance. And since
I have sworn not to conceal anything of our history (I who
admire nothing so much as a sheep grazing at its afternoon
shadow), I want to confess that from time immemorial we have
been lousy dishwashers, shoeshine boys of limited scope, fairly
conscientious sorcerers (looking on the bright side) and the
only record we've ever beaten indisputably is that of endurance
to the whip . . .

and by so doing reclaims it.

His conniving laughter at the sight of the comic ugliness of a
black man huddling and cowering in a Paris Métro reveals to
the poet the depth of his psychological degeneration, the extent
of his brainwashing:

Et l'ensemble faisait parfaitement un nègre
hideux, un nègre grognon, un nègre mélancholique, un nègre
affalé . . . comique et laid. . . .

And the whole thing added up perfectly to a hideous
Negro, a grumbling, melancholy Negro, a sprawling
Negro, comical and ugly. . . .

Sharply, the poet takes stock of himself, his exile is over, his
return commences:

Par une inattendue et bienfaisante révolution
intérieure, j'honore maintenant mes laideurs repoussantes.

An unexpected and beneficial inner revolution
now makes me honor my repulsive uglinesses.

Now the prophet-poet will sanctify the ugliness of his people and make it holy. The poet who had formerly rejected the call of his destiny, hiding behind his pedantry and debilitating vanity, now accepts his fate.

> je tremble maintenant du common tremblement
> que notre sang docile chante dans le madrépore.

> I tremble with the common trembling now
> which our docile blood sings in the madrepore.

A succession of emphatic negatives introduced by the repeated phrase *ceux qui* reveals the poet's rejection of the art of conquering and taming anything, his acceptance of the positive value of suffering. His people never conquered steam or electricity, but "they know every nook and cranny of the land of suffering."

The pace of the poet's transformation quickens, and once more, after listing the voyages of each of his people, a sudden mystic change comes over him, and the poet wonders, "But what strange pride illuminates me suddenly?"

The poet invokes the sea, repeatedly calling it to his service in the repetition of the word *vienne*. His call is compelling in its insistence, bringing with it a sense of an ever-enlarging horizon of peace and rebirth:

> vienne le bris de l'horizon
> . . . .
> vienne le lotus porteur du monde
> . . . .
> viennent les ovaires de l'eau où le futur agite ses
> petites têtes

> come, horizon's breaking
> . . . .
> come, lotus bearer of the world
> . . . .
> come, ovaries of water where the future moves its tiny heads

Light begins to bathe everything, to flow over everything, to illuminate the poet. He appeals for the poetic impulse from the stars and sensing the contour of light, implores it: "ô lumière amicale/ ô fraîche source de la lumière."

Again, using the structural device of a sequence of negative statements followed and heightened by a set of positive statements, Césaire leaps to his definition of Negritude, deepening it, driving it far into the center of the elements:

> ma négritude n'est pas une pierre, sa surdité ruée
> contre la clameur du jour
> ma négritude n'est pas une taie d'eau morte sur
> l'oeil mort de la terre
>
> my Negritude is not a stone, flinging its deafness
> against the day's clamor
> my Negritude is not a speck of stagnant water on
> the dead eye of the earth

These lines, followed by "it plunges into the red flesh of the soil" without any connective link, completely affirm the positiveness of Negritude.

Using adjectives and adverbs suggesting bottomlessness and infinity, Césaire evokes and praises his people. His is an old race which dances with the winds, which flows from the source of waters, which moves from the total rhythms of the earth. In a sweeping climactic affirmation the poet claims that they are:

> véritablement les fils aînés du monde
> poreux à tous les souffles du monde
> aire fraternelle de tous les souffles du monde
> lit sans drain de toutes les eaux du monde
> étincelle du feu sacré du monde
> chair de la chair du monde palpitant du mouvement même du
> monde!
>
> truly the firstborn sons of the world
> porous to the world's every breath
> fraternal eyrie of the world's every breath
> drainless bed of all the waters of the world
> spark of the world's sacred fire
> flesh of the world's flesh, palpitating with the very movement of
> the world!

Thus, Negritude is man's affinity to the elements, a merging of man's hands with the earth.

A play of negative-positive contrast continues; the poet leads those who have invented and explored nothing to a circle of perfection and "close concordance" whereas those who have conquered and explored arouse his pity. "Pity for our conquerors, omniscient and naive!"

Now indeed, Césaire becomes the suppliant poet, begging for the strength to mold things:

> donnez-moi la foi sauvage du sorcier
> donnez à mes mains puissance de modeler
> donnez à mon âme la trempe de l'épée
> je ne me dérobe point. Faites de ma tête une tête de proue

> give me the sorcerer's rude faith
> give my hands the power to mold
> temper my soul like the sword
> I stand fast. Give my face the shape of valiance

Then with the style of accumulation that characterizes the whole poem, giving it a density and multilayered force, Césaire asks that he be made the executor of his race, the sower as well as the reaper. The poet, altering a structural technique that he has often used throughout the poem, introduces a positive and follows it by a negative, in order to heighten that negative, and he pleads for a humanity that would save him from becoming as hateful as those who have hated him:

> Mais les faisant, mon coeur, préservez-moi de toute haine
> ne faites point de moi cet homme de haine pour qui je n'ai
> que haine

> But in doing so, my heart, preserve me from all hate
> do not turn me into that man of hate for whom I have nothing
> but hatred

He asks that he be deserving of his position as executor of his race, that he be given a strength equal to the *pirogue* which fights its way across turbulent waters. With verbs depicting twisting and turning movements (*danser, galoper, forcer l'eau, se cabre, devie*), Césaire captures the tenacity of the boat as it fights the water; and he uses water images in the same fashion as he recounted Toussaint Louverture's fight and survival in the

Jura Mountains: "he is a man alone in the barren sea of white sand."

Now, through mystical cleansing Césaire loses his anger, and in a tone of religious reconciliation so characteristic of Senghor, humbly accepts—"J'accepte . . . J'accepte . . . entièrement sans réserve"—the total geography of his island, the total biology of his being—"my race which no ablution of mingled hyssop and lily could purify." He creates a mood almost of penitence; the repetition of *J'accepte* has a note of religious self-immolation, of expiation. But then brusquely the tone changes and again the poet becomes self-mocking. "Wait, am I sufficiently humble?"

The poet passes through quickly alternating moods from self-immolation to self-mockery and then fiercely recapitulates the indignities through which his people, covered with mud, have slithered and crawled. "Muddy soil. Muddy horizon. Muddy sky." Once more the poet seems to return to that mood of violent self-assertion, slipping backward from the tone of abnegation he had been slowly summoning.

With rapid strokes the poet summarizes the plight of his islands which he had elaborated in the first part; then, with cosmic force, he offers his poetic strength to their salvation, ritualistically cleansing them.

> Iles annelées . . .
> Et je te caresse de mes mains d'océan. Et je te vire
> de mes paroles alizées. Et je te lèche de mes langues d'algues.

> Ringed islands . . .
> And I caress you with my ocean hands. And I swing you round
> with my trade-wind words. And I lick you with my seaweed
> tongues.

The poet has returned; he no longer rejects the wounds and the destructive forces present in his island but totally accepts them—"hurricanes . . . old wounds, rotten bones, . . . chained volcanoes, poorly rooted deaths, bitter crying. I accept."

The island which had been prostrate, which the poet had blocked out in horizontal images, now stands up. Not only the poet has been transformed, but his people have been transformed as well. Supporting strength flows through their hands; now it is they who hold the poet— "my hand now little inside their enormous fist."

Once again the mood changes, the poet becomes the poet of irony, ridiculing *La vieille négritude* with all its hang-ups and complexes as mordantly as Damas—"those who say to Europe . . . I'm no different from you . . . it's just the sun which turned me into the "good nigger" who has an honest belief in his own unworthiness, and never any perverse curiosity about checking the prophetic hieroglyphs." But this *vieille négritude* also breaks up, and triumphantly the poet proclaims its death. "Hurrah, I say! the old Negritude is becoming more and more a corpse," and the ship in which the larger journey of exile had been made also begins to break up, and with an ecstatic triumphal movement the larger symbolic return begins.

Suddenly, a light pierces through and the horizon expands. As the light rips through, the verbs convey a sense of an agonizing break-up of things—*déchirer, craquer, convulser, ronger*—as the slave ship is destroyed from within. The characteristic movement from negative to positive recurs—after this destruction "the nigger trash is on its feet."

Before, the *pirogue* had to fight its way through the growling water; now the waters recede, the slave ship is purified; "the lustral ship moves undaunted over the toppled waters." With this purification the *flocs d'ignominie* are destroyed. The destroyed ship is the last negative symbol; with the reiteration of *à moi, à moi*, the poet totally affirms his link with his people and their culture. "The master of laughter . . . of silence . . . of dancing . . . the dance called it-is-fair-and-fine-and-legitimate-to-be-a-Negro . . . mine."

Through the use of imperatives and invocations, the poem sweeps up and spirals to its end. The poet implores the wind to engulf him, freeing him from all contamination, for the poet and the cleansing wind can mingle only when the poet has been purified. "My purity is bound only to your purity." The interplay between poet and wind becomes fiercer. From the single embrace of poet and wind the embrace opens out to include all others. "Embrasse-moi . . . embrasse-nous." The embrace as expressed in the verbs used—*embrasser, lie, étranglant, monter*—becomes tighter and tighter in a narrowing upward spiral.

et lie, lie-moi sans remords
lie-moi, de tes vastes bras à l'argile lumineuse
lie ma noire vibration au nombril même du monde

and bind, bind me without remorse
bind me with your vast arms of luminous clay
bind my black vibration to the very naval of the world

The poet of Negritude is reunited with the world.

In the poetry of Léon Damas, the exponent of exile, the Negritude poet of alienation, few motifs of return, few instances of reentry appear, but when they do it is the geography of his native country that informs them. In *Black-Label*,[95] Damas recreates his landscape, lyricising its geography, awakening the throb of his land through a build-up of picturesque geographical names:

—JE SUIS NÉ
disais-tu
tout au bout du Monde
LA-BAS
entre la Montagne-des-Tigres
et le Fort-Céperou qui regarde la Mer dîner de soleil
. . . .
Des Chutes de Rorota dont l'eau est belle et bonne à boire.

—I WAS BORN
you were saying
way at the end of the Earth
DOWN THERE
between Tiger Mountain
and Fort Céperou which watches the Sea dining on sunshine
. . . .
Of the Rorota Falls whose water is fair and good to drink.

and we follow the poet's drama down to the Orinoco River:

des Amandiers
qui n'en peuvent mais de faire
le joli coeur au Ciel
. . . .
le souffle même de l'Orénoque
ton Orénoque

of the Almond Trees
which can't help
flouncing around for Heaven

. . . .
the very breath of the Orinoco
your Orinoco

This land evokes a melodic refrain that runs through *Black-Label*:

dont l'image est à jamais en UNE
FEMME entrevue en l'Ile aux mille et une fleurs
assise au pied des mornes verts
et filaos échevelés
et flûte de bambou du Pâtre éveillé modulant la rengaine en
     sourdine

whose image will ever be that of A
WOMAN glimpsed on the Isle of a thousand and one flowers
Sitting at the foot of green bluffs
and dishevelled filaos
and the wakened Herdsman's bamboo flute modulating the
     muted refrain

There the natural instincts of youth had been squelched and
through the repetition of the phrase *desirs comprimés* Damas
reveals the things he was deprived of, the tasty tropical fruits
and delicious morsels he yearned for:

de bonnes choses en réserve
gelée de goyave
liqueur de monbin
mangues Julie jolies jaunies à point
fruits fruits confits
gâteaux secs et lait
lait condensé chipé toujours meilleur au goût

stores of good things
guava jelly
plum liqueur
pretty Julie mangos, just the perfect yellow
fruits, comfits
cookies and milk
filched condensed milk, always much tastier

The carefree abandon, the unbridled gaiety of childhood, for which he longed, is wistfully and charmingly recalled:

> Les vacances toujours proches à Rémire
> où les Cousins parlaient si librement patois
> crachaient si aisément par terre
> sifflaient si joliment un air
> lâchaient si franchement un rot
> et autres choses encore

> Vacations always near Rémire
> where the Cousins spoke patois so freely
> spat on the ground so casually
> whistled tunes so prettily
> let a belch escape so frankly
> and still other things

And so the poet appeals for a return to that childhood, to a childhood natural and free:

> Rendez-les moi mes poupées noires
> que je joue avec elles
> les jeux naïfs de mon instinct
> resté à l'ombre de ses lois

> recouvrés mon courage
> mon audace
> redevenu moi-même
> nouveau moi-même
> de ce que Hier j'étais
> hier
>   sans complexité
>   hier[96]

> Give my black dolls back to me that I may play
> my instinct's naive games with them
> my instinct kept protected by its laws
> my courage recovered
> and my audacity
> I am myself again
> a new self
> from what I was Yesterday
> yesterday
>   uncomplicated
>   yesterday

David Diop's poems are constructed on two levels: exile and symbolic return. Through antithesis and contrast, he emphasizes various elements of the return. Return comes about through combat and resistance, through singing the praises of African landscape and woman. The poet's memory flows backward through time to select the softness of a mother who becomes the symbol of African mothers. This symbol is one of hope, which pierces the darkness of past exile and illuminates the future. Thus, in Diop images of light and brilliance are reiterated to forecast a hope for the future. Through the play of memory and the pull of blood, the poet symbolically returns to receive regenerative strength from the earth of Africa and so the poet claims:

> Auprès de toi j'ai retrouvé la mémoire de mon sang
>
> Beside you I recovered my blood's memory

and nearness also gives the poet back his name.

> Auprès de toi j'ai retrouvé mon nom
> Mon nom longtemps caché sous le sel des distances[97]
>
> Beside you I found my name again
> My name long hidden from me by time and distance

The poet had not lost his name through distance but instead, far removed from Africa, had never known it. Yet his body, he says in his poem "Afrique,"[98] has received power from Africa.

> Afrique que chante ma grand'Mère
> Au bord de son fleuve lointain
> Je ne t'ai jamais connue
> Mais mon regard est plein de ton sang
> Ton beau sang noir à travers les champs répandu
>
> Africa which my Grandmother sings
> On the bank of her faraway river
> I have never known you
> But my gaze is full of your blood
> Your beautiful black blood spilled along the fields

Diop asserts Africa's obstinate endurance and passionately sings of its power to survive. Thus, in his poems there is always a movement away from the negative effects of oppression to the positive possibility of regeneration in the poetic discovery of truth. Survival comes not only through poetic faith but also from violent combat and action. Hope springs from combat and combat opens out to a happy future.

> Et les mains qui fécondent le ventre de la terre
> Les racines de nos mains profonde comme la révolte
>
> And the hands which fertilize the earth's womb
> The roots of our hands that go down as deep as revolt

They build and create.

> L'espoir vivait en nous comme une citadelle
> Et des mines du Souaziland à la sueur lourde des usines d'Europe
> Le printemps prendra chair sous nos pas de clarté[99]
>
> Hope lived in us like a citadel
> And from Swaziland's mines to the leaden sweat of the mines of Europe
> Springtime will fatten beneath our steps of light

Through images of light ripping through darkness and cutting through mists, Diop finds Africa again:

> Et ton rire comme la flamme trouant l'ombre
> M'a redonné l'Afrique au delà des neiges d'hier
> Dix ans mon amour[100]
>
> And your smile vital as fire piercing the darkness
> Has given Africa back to me beyond yesterday's snows
> Ten years my love

Like Césaire, Diop identifies himself with those who suffered and died; and like all poets of Negritude, he too proclaims the beauty of things African singing the praises of the black woman in what is perhaps his best poem, "À Une Danseuse Noire."

Diop celebrates black woman, through whose movement falsification and stultifying myths are exploded and destroyed,

for she is pure movement and dance, warmth and passionate
life.

> Négresse ma chaude rumeur d'Afrique
> Ma terre d'énigme et mon fruit de raison
> Tu es danse par la joie nue de ton sourire
> Par l'offrande de tes seins et tes secrets pouvoirs
> Tu es danse par les légendes . . . et les rythmes seculaires
> Tu es danse par le vertige
> . . . .
> Par la magie des reins recommençant le monde[101]

> Black girl my warm sound of Africa
> My land of enigma and fruit of my reason
> You are dance in the naked joy of your smile
> By your proffered breasts and secret powers
> You are dance by the legends . . . and time-honored rhythms
> You are dance in dizziness
> . . . .
> By the magic of loins that start up the world again

Now indeed the return is complete. The carnival of exile is
ended, the poet can attempt the reconstruction of African kingdoms and reenter the house where the pestle resounds in the
mortar, preparing the evening meal.

> Pour toi nous referons Ghana et Tombouctou
> Et les guitars peuplées de galops frénétiques
> A grands coups de pilons sonores
> De pilons
> Eclatant
> De case en case
> Dans l'azur pressenti[102]

> For you we will remake Ghana and Timbuktu
> And guitars will gallop wildly
> With great shuddering chords.
> Like the resounding thuds of pestles
> Pounding mortars
> Bursting forth
> From hut to hut
> In the presaged azure

Léon Damas is the Negritude poet of exile; Aimé Césaire the poet who sings of symbolic return to a country. Léopold Sédar Senghor is the Dyâli of the African presence which he invokes and through which he derives a sense of continuity and permanence. Like all the other poets, Senghor assigns himself a task: he invokes infancy recalled through memory and ritualistically summons to his aid the dead, the ancestors who nourish the sources of life. African night, African woman, the earth of Africa, will tenderly offer the poet vivifying sap and nourishment for his task, that of singing his Negritude, of extolling the African presence. A sense of interplay between the cosmic and man infuses all his poetry, often making it heroic and grandiose. The poet's qualities are inordinately vast, perhaps to match the vastness of his poetic task.

In "Le Kaya-Magan" the poet becomes the great provider for his race, provider of reason, nourishment, protection of breath and life, of warmth:

> . . . je . . . suis source de joie . . .
> Roi de la lune, j'unis la nuit et le jour
> . . . Prince du Soleil-levant
> . . . mon empire est celui . . . des grands
> bannis de la raison ou de l'instinct.
> . . . je suis le mouvement du tam-tam, force de l'Afrique
> future.[103]

> . . . I . . . am the wellspring of joy . . .
> King of the moon, I make night one with day
> . . . Prince of the Rising Sun
> . . . my empire is that of . . . the great
> exiles from reason or from instinct
> . . . I am the movement of the tom-tom, strength of the future
> Africa.

In all his work this poet will fit his poetry to the rhythm of all things, the rhythm of all of day and night, sun and moon to sing his Negritude. Poem and poet are charged with substance:

> Mais le poème est lourd de lait et le coeur de Poète brule
> un feu sans poussière.[104]

> But the poem is heavy with milk and the Poet's heart is burning
> with dustless fire.

The milk is the milk of Africa, which will nourish the poet as he seeks the essence of the word, for it is only through the word that the poet can reanimate the dead, of whom he forms a part, and lay the groundwork for the future:

> Chaque mort fut ma mort. Il fallait préparer les moissons à venir
> Et la meule à broyer la farine si blanche des tendresses noires . . .[105]

> Each death was my own. Preparations had to be made for future harvests
> And the mill made ready to grind the flour, so white with black caresses . . .

Not only from milk will the poet be nourished, but also from the greenness of the spring and summer he invokes:

> Eté spendide Eté, qui nourris le Poète du lait de ta lumière
> Moi qui poussais comme blé de Printemps, qui m'enivrais de la verdure de l'eau, du ruissellement vert dans l'or du Temps . . .[106]

> Summer splendid Summer, nourishing the Poet with the milk of your light
> I who sprouted like Spring wheat, drunk with the greenness of the waters, the green streaming in the gold of Time . . .

With images of color, which appear again and again in his poetry, Senghor envisions a night of infancy, recalls its blue glitter:

> Nuit d'enfance, Nuit bleue Nuit blonde ô Lune!
> Combien de fois t'ai-je invoquée ô Nuit![107]

> Night of childhood, blue Night blonde Night oh Moon!
> How many times have I called on you oh Night!

Senghor the poet can invoke the night since from his childhood it was during the night that he heard tales and stories which opened to him a world of poetry. The folk tale, which tells the continuity of the clan and celebrates its warriors, is a natural and ancient source of the creative word. Now the poet can rejoice in his poetic heritage:

> Et nous voilà debout aux portes de la Nuit, buvant des contes
> très anciens et machant des noix blanches . . .[108]

> And there we are standing at the gates of Night, drinking in
> very ancient tales and chewing on white nuts . . .

But a source of inspiration comes also to the poet from the
sculptured lines and structure of the mask. Through it he receives the force and compulsion to sing of Africa:

> Que je bondirai comme L'Annonciateur, que je manifesterai
> l'Afrique comme le sculpteur des masques au regard in-
> tense . . .[109]

> That I will leap like the Bearer of Tidings, that I will reveal
> Africa as the sculptor of masks intensely gazing . . .

The milk of Africa and the African night infused the poet with
strength; the old folk tale and the mask were his artistic heritage. From the masters of Dyong he learned:

> . . . l'art de tisser des paroles plaisantes
> Paroles de pourpre à te parer, Princesse noire d'Elissa.[110]

> . . . the art of weaving pleasing words
> Purple words for your adornment, black Princess of Elissa.

From his Uncle Tokô'Waly he learned to read the hidden signs
in the elements, learned to feel the throb of the African night,
and touched at the source of ancient wisdom, source of his
poetic inspiration:

> Toi Tokô'Waly, tu écoutes l'inaudible
> Et tu m'expliques les signes que disent les Ancêtres dans la
> sérénité marine des constellations
> Le Taureau le Scorpion le Léopard, l'Éléphant les Poissons
> familiers
> Et la pompe lactée des Esprits par le tann céleste qui ne finit
> point.[111]

> You, Tokô'Waly, you listen to what cannot be heard
> And show me the meaning of signs told by the Ancestors in the
> watery serenity of constellations
> The familiar Bull, Scorpion, Leopard, Elephant, Fish

And the milky pomp of Spirits on the celestial tanbark without
end.

Senghor ascribed to Aimé Césaire the same noble poetic
tradition which he has inherited, and in his "Lettre à un Poète,"
written to his "Frère aimé," he wonders:

> Aurais-tu oublié ta noblesse, qui est de chanter
> Les Ancêtres les Princes et les Dieux . . .[112]

> Can you have forgotten your nobility, which is to sing
> The Ancestors, Princes, and Gods . . .

Like Césaire, and like all the other poets of Negritude,
Senghor too seeks purification from the elemental forces, strives
to be cleansed for his poetic task, and searches for the essential
word. In the poem "L'Ouragan," through a series of images
of uprooting and of fire, indicative of the clearing of the ground
before the sowing of seed, the poet prays to the hurricane to
cleanse him for his task:

> . . . arrache en moi feuilles et paroles futiles.
>
> . . . brûle toute fleur toute pensée vaine
>
> La flamme qui illumine ma nuit, comme une colonne et
> comme une palme.
> Embrase mes lèvres de sang, Esprit, souffle sur les cordes de
> ma kôra
> Que s'élève mon chant, aussi pur que l'or de Galam.[113]

> . . . strip leaves and futile words from me
>
> . . . burn every flower each vain thought
>
> The flame which lights my night, like a column and like a palm.
> Kindle my lips with blood, oh Spirit, blow on the strings of my
> kôra
> That my song may rise, as pure as Galam's gold.

The poet begs for help not only from the hurricane but also
from the river Congo, which becomes for him lover, woman,
mother, goddess:

> O toi l'Impaludée de ton lignage, délivre-moi de la surrection
> de mon sang.
>
> . . . .
>
> délivre-moi de la nuit sans joie . . .[114]

> Oh you the Malarial One of your line, deliver me from my
> blood's upheaval.
>
> . . . .
>
> deliver me from the joyless night . . .

These motifs fuse to give direction to Senghor's poetic vision
and to create his poetic impulse. For the poet requires that only
the crucial word be used, that only rhythm should resound in
his poetry. By a process of bracketing, and through poetic reduction, the poet will arrive at a future point of hope:

> Ah! mourir à l'enfance, que meure le poème se désintègre la
> syntaxe, que s'abîment tous les mots qui ne sont pas
> essentiels.
> Le poids du rythme suffit, pas besoin de mots-ciment pour
> bâtir sur le roc la Cité de demain.[115]

> Ah, to die in childhood, that the poem may die, the syntax fall
> apart, all inessential words be swallowed up.
> The weight of the rhythm suffices, no need for words of mortar
> to build the City of tomorrow on rock.

The relationship between purification and poetic reduction is
constantly reiterated, becoming a very important structural
motif in Senghor's poetry. Here the importance is illustrated
through juxtaposition:

> Pour toute nourriture le lait clair, et pour toute parole la
> rumination du mot essentiel.[116]

> Clear milk the only food, and for all speech only the necessary
> word.

And the poet, who becomes "le créateur des paroles de la vie,"
expresses through antithesis the basic humanism that ordains
his poetic creation. Like Césaire, who asks that he be freed
from all hatred in his poetic reconstruction, Senghor too accepts that strength comes from charitableness:

Ma force s'érige dans l'abandon, mon honneur dans la soumission . . .[117]

My strength is founded on abandonment, my honor on submission . . .

Love becomes the essential ingredient transforming the poet as he searches for essences and truth:

Mais je n'ai pas goût de magie. L'Amour est ma merveille.[118]

But I have no taste for magic. Love is my wonder.

Through assumption of his poetic role, through acceptance of his poetic heritage, the poet gives presence to absence, brings equilibrium to disequilibrium:

Ce fut un grand déchirement des apparences, et les hommes restitués à leur noblesse, les choses à leur vérité.[119]

There was a great tearing away of appearances, and men resorted to their nobility, things to their truth.

Thus, Negritude attempts to restore a natural order to the cosmos, to restate the basic rhythmical relationships between man and forces, to reassert the harmony of emotions. At the center of Senghor's poetry of Negritude lies the nostalgic recreation of infancy:

Et comme il est splendide! C'est l'heure de la re-naissance.
Le poème est mûr au jardin d'enfance, c'est l'heure de l'amour.[120]

And how splendid it is! This is the hour of rebirth.
In the garden of childhood the poem is ripe, this is the hour of love.

The *jardin d'enfance* becomes as soft and serene as that of the Dark Child. While in exile in Paris, Camara Laye nostalgically yearned for that serenity and peace of early childhood, wished for romantic return to mother and motherland: "Oh how I wish I could be with you once again to be a little child beside you."[121] Senghor, the poet of Negritude, romantically recreates this childhood, and charging his infancy with emotion, sings of a Paradise which in fact he has lost, which the African has lost, perhaps which all men have lost. Senghor expresses man's basic yearning for childhood peace after struggle:

> Je sais le Paradis perdu—je n'ai pas perdu souvenir du jardin d'enfance où fleurissent les oiseaux
> Que viendra la moisson après l'hivernage pénible . . .[122]

> I know that Paradise is lost—I have not lost sight of the childhood garden where birds are in flower
> That the harvest will follow the hard winter season . . .

The power that Senghor ascribes to childhood provides a poetic climax to his long, dramatic poem, *Chaka*. After his long struggle, after his heroic fight, reentry into childhood and return to earth bring peace and give an end to Chaka's passion:

> Me voilà rendu à la terre. Qu'il est radieux le Royaume d'enfance!
> Et c'est la fin de ma passion.[123]

> Here I am restored to earth. How radiant the Kingdom of childhood!
> And this is the end of my passion.

The poet, too, after yearning for it, can realize the symbolic return to childhood where mother, Earth Mother, soothes her Prodigal Son:

> Ah! de nouveau dormir dans le lit frais de mon enfance
> Ah! bordent de nouveau mon sommeil les si chères mains noires
> Et de nouveau le blanc sourire de ma mère.[124]

> Ah, back sleeping again in the cool bed of my childhood
> Ah, again my sleep bounded by black hands so dear
> And once again my mother's white smile.

Perhaps Senghor's poem, "Nuit de Sine,"[125] best recaptures the softness and repose of childhood, and soothing presence of mother and night's rhythmic silences. "Nuit de Sine," through the use of alliteration and soft vowel sounds, evokes a beautiful

lullaby scene at close of day. The poem opens with a gentle
plea to woman, which is almost a request for a blessing:

> Femme, pose sur mon front tes mains balsamiques, tes
> mains douces plus que fourrure.

> Woman, place your balsamic hands on my forehead, your soft
> hands softer than fur.

These opening lines immediately set the gentleness of the scene,
of this delicately painted word picture. The woman's hands, like
so many of the hands portrayed in Senghor's poems, are cleansing (*balsamique*), and the inner vowel rhyme between *douces*
and *fourrures* captures their softness. A series of words with
sibilants, *bruissents*, *brise*, *nourrice*, picks up the gentle swaying
of the palm trees in the night wind. The poem has moved from
woman to nature to rhythm, which pulses through a series of
initial b's. It is a silent night, but full of murmurs and sounds
which tell of the throb of life in misty villages:

> Écoutons son chant, écoutons battre notre sang sombre, écou-
>   tons
> Battre le pouls profond de l'Afrique dans la brume des villages
>   perdus.

> Let us listen to its song, listen to our dark blood beating, listen
> To Africa's deep pulse beating in the mist of lost villages.

The play of rhythm and silence, of night and man continues.
With a skillful use of onomatopoeia the poet paints the falling
asleep of both nature and man. The liquid l's in the line:

> Voici que décline la lune lasse vers son lit de mer étale

> Now the weary moon moves downward to her bed of wide-
>   spread sea.

bring out the gradual slipping off to rest of moon and man. The
breaking up of short syllables with d's and t's beats a staccato
rhythm accompanying the slow jerks of his head as the man
falls asleep:

> Dodelinent de la tête comme l'enfant sur le dos de sa mère.

Nodding their heads like a child on its mother's back.

Slowly, both storytellers and dancers grow heavy with sleep, the starry night dresses for sleep, the glittering rooftops and the stars merge in confidence:

> C'est l'heure des étoiles et de la Nuit qui songe
> S'accoude à cette colline de nuages, drapée dans son long pagne de lait.
> Les toits des cases luisent tendrement. Que disent-ils, si confidentiels, aux étoiles?

> This is the hour of stars and of the dreaming Night
> Leaning on this hill of clouds, draped in her long milky robe.
> The cabin roofs shine tenderly. What secrets do they tell the stars?

The poem moves from the world outside to the intimacy of inside, and its entry is marked by a harder rhythm in the line:

> Dedans, le foyer s'éteint dans l'intimité d'odeurs âcres et douces.

> Inside, the hearth grows dim in the intimacy of bitter and sweet odors.

The lighting of a votive lamp conjures up the dead, the ancestors, and those who, like the poet, had wandered afar. A sense of continuity between the living and the dead is felt in the ritualistic lamplight and smoking fire wherein dance the shadows of kindred spirits. In a series of appeals the poet prays for rest, *que je*, that [I] may

> . . . respire l'odeur de nos Morts, que je recueille et redise leur voix vivante, que j'apprenne à
> Vivre avant de descendre, au-delà du plongeur, dans les hautes profondeurs du sommeil.

> . . . breathe the odor of our Dead, that I may gather up and reveal their living voice, that I may learn to
> Live before descending further than the diver into the lofty depths of sleep.

Throughout the poem the link between several realms of phenomena is clearly established. In the final stanza, by the use of
a series of vertical images by which Negritude is described as
entering into the essence of things, the poet clearly demonstrates the continuity of the living and the dead, between earth
and center of earth. In "Nuit de Sine" appear many of the
motifs that inform Senghor's Negritude: African night, African
woman, childhood, ritual, the dance, and the dead ancestors,
which, when fused together, bespeak the continuity and
permanence of the African presence. Through poetic transposition and through the qualitative merging of space, African night
becomes African earth and is then transmuted into African
woman. One of Senghor's concepts of Negritude is clearly evident in the following description of African night. Negritude
does not know the clash of angles and the discontinuity inherent
in joints; rather it knows the flow of curves and the melody of
roundness. Senghor's Negritude in his *Songs of Shadow* and his
Nocturnes celebrates the softness of shadow, the beauty of
blackness, and so the poet sings the praise of African night:

> Nuit d'Afrique ma nuit noire, mystique et claire noire et bril-
> lante
> Tu reposes accordée à la terre, tu es la Terre et les collines
> harmonieuses.
> O Beauté classique qui n'es point angle, mais ligne élastique
> élégante élancée!

> African night my black night, mystical and clear black and
> shining
> You rest attuned to earth, you are the Earth and the harmoni-
> ous hills.
> Oh classic Beauty in no way angle but elastic elegant willowy
> line!

The poet, through use of mystic geography, shows the rhythmical harmony and similarity between contours of landscape and
those of woman. Earth and woman fuse and together are ex-
tolled:

> O visage classique! depuis le front bombé sous la forêt de
> senteurs et les yeux larges obliques jusqu'à la baie graci-
> euse du menton et

> L'élan fougueux des collines jumelles! O courbes de douceur
> visage mélodique!
> O ma Lionne ma Beauté noire, ma Nuit noire ma Noire ma
> Nue!

> Oh classic face! from the domed forehead beneath the forest of
> fragrances and the large slanting eyes down to the graceful
> bay of the chin and
> The passionate surge of the twin hills! Oh curves of sweetness
> melodious face!
> Oh my Lioness my black Beauty, my black Night my Black One
> my Naked One!

The beauty which Senghor ascribes to African night and the
purity which he attributes to hands of the African woman together brought solace to the poet in his exile, and saved him
from the dehumanizing results of such an exile. The African
night

> . . . qui fonds toutes mes contradictions, toutes contradictions
> dans l'unité première de ta négritude
> Reçois l'enfant toujours enfant . . .[126]

> . . . which dissolves all my contradictions, all contradictions in
> the primary oneness of your Negritude
> Receive the ever childlike child . . .

African woman is symbolized in the figure of Nolivé, who
brought solace to Chaka and by extension to the poet:

> O ma Nuit! ô ma Noire! ma Nolivé!
> Cette grande faiblesse est morte sous tes mains d'huile
> . . . .
> . . . ma Noire au secret de diamant
> Chair noire de lumière, corps transparent comme au matin du
> jour premier.
> Mais elle est morte cette angoisse de la gorge, iorsqu'on est
> nu l'un devant l'autre . . .[127]

> Oh my night! Oh my Black One! my Nolivé!
> This great weakness has died beneath the balm of your hands
> . . . .
> . . . my Black One with the diamond's secret

Black flesh of light, body transparent as the morning of the first
day.
But dead is this anguish in the breast when both are naked
before each other.

Senghor, throughout his poetry, reiterates the soothing quality
of the hands of the African woman. In the touch of these hands
there is repose and sleep, dispelling anquish:

Croire qu'il y a des mains plus calmes que des palmes, plus
douces que berceuse nyominka
Mains douces à bercer mon coeur, ô palmes sur ma peine et
mon sommeil.[128]

To think that there are hands calmer than palms, softer than a
Nyominka lullaby
Soft hands to rock my heart, oh palms over my trouble and my
sleep.

Not only do hands soothe, they also explore the mystery of
things;

—*Ma Soeur, ces mains de nuit* sur mes paupières!
—Devine la musique de l'Enigme.[129]

—*My Sister, these hands of night* upon my eyelids!
—Guess the music of the Enigma.

African night, African woman, African landscape, all unite to
cleanse the poet of his impurities. He appeals to the hurricane:

O désert sans ombre désert, terre austère terre de pureté, de
toutes mes petitesses
Lave-moi, de toutes mes contagions de civilisé.
Que me lave la face ta lumière . . .[130]

Oh desert shadeless desert, land austere and pure, wash from me
All my pettiness, all my civilized contagions.
Let your light cleanse my face . . .

It is not surprising, therefore, that the poet can claim to have
retained a measure of purity in his exile:

> Mon coeur est resté pur comme Vent d'Est au mois de
> Mars.[131]

> My heart has remained pure like the East Wind in the month
> of March.

At the heart of the poetry of Negritude is return from exile,
rejection of Europe, reclamation of the oppressed peoples of
the world, and the acceptance of and identification with those
who still live close to the earth:

> Me voici cherchant l'oubli de l'Europe au coeur pastoral du
> Sine.[132]

> Here I am trying to forget Europe in the pastoral heart of Sine.

Like Aimé Césaire, the poet's vision transforms the peasant
stock, leading them from enslavement to liberating dignity:

> Cette colonne solennelle, ce ne sont plus quatre mille esclaves
>   portant chacun cinq mithkals d'or
> Ce sont sept mille nègres nouveaux, sept mille soldats sept
>   mille paysans humbles et fiers
> Qui portent les richesses de ma race sur leurs épaules musi-
>   cales.[133]

> This solemn column, no longer four thousand slaves each bear-
>   ing five mithkals of gold
> But seven thousand new Negroes, seven thousand soldiers seven
>   thousand peasants, humble and proud
> Who bear the riches of my race upon their musical shoulders.

Thus, Negritude opens out, redeeming not only those who live
close to the soil of Africa, but all people who work the land:

> J'ai choisi mon peuple noir peinant, mon peuple paysan, toute
>   la race paysanne par le monde.[134]

> I have chosen my toiling black people, my peasant people, the
>   entire peasant race throughout the world.

Senghor not only sings of the people who live close to the
land but attempts to capture in his poetry the very rhythms of
the earth, the total musical interplay of all things. Rhythm lies

at the center of his poetry of Negritude; it informs many of his verses. There is rhythm in the movement of the elements, the changes of season; there is rhythm in the vibrations of all landscape and the cadences of African woman. Here, through alliteration, the poet captures the rhythm of the dance:

> Rythmez clochettes rythmez langues rythmez rames la danse
> du Maître des rames.[135]

> Keep time little bells keep time tongues keep time oars to the
> dance of the Master of oars.

The harmonious interplay of all of nature which the poet postulates is echoed in the rhythmical balance and movement of his poetry. Thus rhythm not only provides poetic basis and structure but becomes a constantly repeated motif; with music it is invoked in many ways, in many tones:

> J'ai choisi le verset des fleuves, des vents et des forêts
> L'assonance des plaines et des rivières, choisi le rythme de sang
> de mon corps dépouillé
> Choisi la trémulsion des balafongs et l'accord des cordes et
> des cuivres qui semble faux, choisi le
> Swing le swing oui le swing![136]

> I have chosen the Verse from the rivers, winds and forests
> The assonance of plains and streams, chosen the blood rhythm
> of my stripped body
> Chosen the tremolo of balafongs and the harmony of strings
> and brass which seems discordant, chosen
> Swing, swing, yes swing!

Rhythm provides the poet with metaphor, and African woman becomes

> Tamtam sculpté, tamtam tendu qui grondes sous les doigts du
> vainqueur . . .[137]

> Carved tom-tom, tautened tom-tom booming beneath the victor's fingers . . .

The tam-tam has its own power, its music its own force. Its

echoes recall pilgrimage and exile, its throb and resonance hint
at rebirth after death:

> Et que je meure soudain pour renaître dans la révélation de la
> Beauté!
> Silence silence sur l'ombre . . . Sourd tamtam . . . tamtam lent
> . . . lourd tamtam . . . tamtam noir . . .[138]

> And may I suddenly die to be born again in the revelation of
> Beauty!
> Silence silence on the shadows . . . Muffled tom-tom . . . slow
> tom-tom . . . heavy tom-tom . . . black tom-tom . . .

The rhythms of the tam-tam not only drum out sounds to the
initiates telling of a second birth but symbolically protect the
poet from death:

> Le rythme chasse cette angoisse qui nous tient à la gorge. La
> Vie tient la mort à distance.[139]

> Rhythm chases away this anguish which has us by the throat.
> Life holds death at a distance.

The rhythmical play of d's and t's creates an onomatopoeic
effect of drumming, the throbbing of the poet's blood:

> Écoute ton sang qui bat son tamtam dans tes tempes rythmi-
> ques lancinantes . . .[140]

> Listen to your blood beating its tom-tom in your temples that
> throb rhythmically . . .

The poet accepts the rhythm of his blood; its pull and throbbing
with the rhythm of the tam-tam spells out Negritude. In its
essence it becomes the entry into the center of all things, the
marriage of the vertical with the curve, the vertical continuity
of line that unites man to earth and raises him to the sky:

> Et moi je suis celui-qui-accompagne, je suis le genou au flanc
> du tamtam, je suis la baguette sculptée
> La pirogue qui fend le fleuve, la main qui sème dans le ciel, le
> pied dans le ventre de la terre
> Le pilon qui épouse la courbe mélodieuse.[141]

And I, I am the-one-who-accompanies, I am the knee at the
　　tom-tom's side, I am the carved drumstick
The canoe cleaving the river, the hand sowing in the sky, the
　　foot in the earth's belly
The pestle wedding the melodious curve.

Now the poet, through the use of negative statements, begins to
affirm his Negritude:

　　. . . Ma gloire n'est pas sur la stèle
　　Ni ma voix ne sera sur pierre pétrifiée, mais voix rythmée d'une
　　　　voix juste.[142]

　　. . . My glory is upon no stele
　　Nor shall my voice be petrified in stone, but shall carry the
　　　　rhythm of a voice that rings true.

These lines echo Césaire's affirmation that Negritude is not
superficial:

　　ma négritude n'est pas une pierre, sa surdité ruée
　　contre la clameur du jour . . .[143]

　　my Negritude is not a stone, its deafness flung
　　against the day's clamor . . .

Senghor's Negritude has the power to transform, to change and
make what was futile and impotent into an assertive and productive vital force. Like the Negritude which Césaire, Damas,
U'Tamsi, and Diop exalt, Senghor's Negritude has power.

　　. . . la farine futile pour nourrir tout un peuple . . .[144]

　　. . . flour futile to nourish an entire people . . .

It germinates, ripens, to the point where the poet claims:

　　Donc je nommerai les choses futiles qui fleuriront de ma
　　nomination—[145]

　　Thus I will name the futile things which flourish at my nam-
　　　　ing—

And in the style of invocation so characteristic of all poets of
Negritude Senghor heralds a victorious return—a rhythmical
rebirth:

> Mais vous ô jeunes feuilles, chantez la victoire du Lion dans
> l'humide soleil de Juin
> Je dis chantez le diamant qui naît des cendres de la Mort
> O chantez la Présente qui nourrit le Poète du lait noir de
> l'amour.[146]

> But you, oh young leaves, sing the Lion's victory in the humid
> sun of June
> Sing the diamond I say born from the ashes of Death
> Oh sing the Present that nourishes the Poet with the black milk
> of love.

Negritude seems to postulate that man is not sufficient unto
himself, that he receives regenerative force from without. Thus,
do the poets of Negritude appeal to forces outside of themselves for strength, inspiration. The following lines pick up
Damas' *Rendez-moi*, and Césaire's oft repeated *Faites-moi* and
Faites de moi:

> Donne-moi la science fervente des grands docteurs de Tom-
> bouctou
> Donne-moi la volonté de Soni Ali, le fils de la bave du
> Lion . . .
> Souffle sur moi la sagesse des Keïta.
> Donne-moi le courage du Guelwar . . .
> Donne-moi de mourir pour la querelle de mon peuple . . .
> Conserve et enracine dans mon coeur libéré l'amour premier
> de ce même peuple.
> Fais de moi ton Maître de Langue; mais non, nomme-moi
> son ambassadeur.[147]

> Give me the fervent science of Timbuktu's great doctors
> Give me the will of Soni Ali, son of the Lion's foam . . .
> Breathe on me the wisdom of the Keitas over me.
> Give me the Guelwar's courage . . .
> Grant that I may die for my people's cause . . .
> May the love of these same people take root and stay fast within
> my liberated heart.
> Make me your Master of Speech; rather, appoint me its am-
> bassador.

Through this poetic progression the poet assumes will and strength and wisdom and becomes the executor of his peoples' trust. Now he is imbued with the power to call forth the sounds, the smells, the movements of the earth and by renewing them, to garner the potential of earth. Through repetition, a stylistic device which is so often used by all the poets of Negritude, Senghor intones a song of praise:

> Mais lors je ressuscite la rumeur des troupeaux . . .
> Je ressuscite la théorie des servantes . . .
> Je ressuscite la caravane des ânes et dromadaires dans l'odeur
>   du mil et du riz
> Dans la scintillation des glaces, dans le tintement des visages et
>   des cloches d'argent.
> Je ressuscite mes vertus terriennes![148]

> But then I revive the murmur of the flocks . . .
> Revive the serving maids' theories . . .
> Revive the caravan of donkeys and dromedaries in the smell of
>   millet and rice
> In the mirrors' sparkle, the tinkling of faces and silver bells.
> I revive my earthly virtues!

Again, through accumulation and repetition of the phrase *je me rappelle*, Senghor's Negritude tells of rituals and ceremonies and of lost splendors. The poet sensuously recalls his birthplace, Joal:

> Je me rappelle les signares . . .
> Je me rappelle les fastes du Couchant . . .
> Je me rappelle les festins funèbres fumant du sang des trou-
>   peaux égorgés
> Du bruit des querelles, des rhapsodies des griots.
> Je me rappelle les voix païennes . . .
> Et les processions et les palmes et les arcs de triomphe.
> Je me rappelle la danse des filles nubiles . . .[149]

> I remember the signs
> I remember the feasts of the Setting Sun . . .
> I remember the mourning banquets steaming with blood from
>   the slit throats of flocks
> The sound of arguments, the griots' rhapsodies
> I remember the pagan voices . . .

And the processions and palms and triumphal arches.
I remember how the nubile maidens dance . . .

In the sounds of shadow in *Chants d'Ombre* Senghor's style is a lyrical, votive offering wherein the poet celebrates the sensory qualities of the earth of Africa, its rituals linking infancy to ancestry and the dead. With it he welcomes Aimé Césaire and chants of the relationship that binds all poets of Negritude. News of Césaire's symbolic return comes:

> Mêlées aux épices, aux bruits odorants des Rivières du Sud et des Iles.[150]

> Mingled with spices and the fragrant sounds of the Rivers of the South and of the Islands.

With a vertical image so characteristic of Negritude poets, Senghor delves into his memory and recalls the shared enthusiasm, the mood of exhilaration which accompanied their creative endeavors:

> Me charme par-delà les années . . .
> . . . ta musique vers quoi nous tendions nos mains et nos coeurs d'hier.
> Au fond du puits de ma mémoire, je touche
> Ton visage où je puise l'eau qui rafraîchit mon long regret.[151]

> Charms me beyond the years . . .
> . . . your music towards which we stretched our hands and hearts of yesterday.
> At the bottom of the well of memory, I touch
> Your face whence I draw the water to cool my long regret.

Through the symbolic power of poetry Césaire's return is assured:

> Mon ami mon ami—ô! tu reviendras tu reviendras! . . .
> Tu reviendras au festin des prémices.[152]

> My friend my friend—oh! you will return you will return! . . .
> You will return to the banquet of the first fruits.

The lyrical, votive style of *Chants d'Ombre* becomes in *Ethiopiques* one of declamatory exaltation, one of eulogies which sing the strength of the forces of nature in "The Congo" and exalt the glories of warriors in "Chaka." In *Ethiopiques* Senghor's poetry is heroic, decorative and ornate. Here things swell out, burst out, in sensual imagery:

> . . . Mais cette rumeur dans nos jambes, ce surgissement de la sève
> Qui gonfle les bourgeons à l'aine des jeunes hommes . . .
> Écoutez jeunes filles le chant de la sève qui monte à vos gorges debout.
> Vert et vert le Printemps au clair mitan de Mai, d'un vert si tendre ho! que c'est ravissement.[153]

> . . . But that clamoring in our legs, that sap erupting
> To swell the buds in the young men's groins . . .
> Listen, maidens, to the song of the sap rising in your poised breasts.
> Green, green the Springtime in bright mid-May, ho! a green so tender as to be enrapturing.

The tone of ritual worship in *Chants d'Ombre* gives way to one of pomp and splendor in *Ethiopiques*. Images of precious metals, gold and jewels recur, and this Ethiopian becomes:

> . . . fauve comme l'or mûr incorruptible comme l'or
> Douce d'olive, bleu souriante de son visage fin souriante dans sa prestance
> Vetue de vert et de nuage . . .[154]

> . . . tawny as ripe gold incorruptible as gold
> Olive softness, smiling blue of her fine face smiling in her noble bearing
> Clothed with green and cloud . . .

In *Nocturnes* the style changes again. Now there is a feeling of things declining, of reclining and setting down:

> De la colline, j'ai vu le soleil se coucher dans les baies de tes yeux . . .[155]

> From the hill I saw the sun set in the bays of your eyes . . .

The style is elegiac, images of *ombres* and *ténèbres* pervade, and the poet warns that time is pressing on him:

> *Ne t'étonne pas mon amie si ma mélodie se fait sombre*
> *Si je délaisse le roseau suave pour le khalam et le tama*
> *Et l'odeur verte des rizières pour le galop grondant des*
> tabalas.[156]

> *Do not be surprised my love* if my melody grows somber
> If I abandon the sweet-voiced reed for the khalam and the tama
> And the green smell of ricefields for the thundering gallop of
> wardrums.

The rhythms in *Nocturnes* are *éloges cadencés* through which the poet sings not of the bursting out and blossoming of nature, but rather captures the pure vibrations of space as he searches through it for the renaissance of his spirit:

> . . . feu de la Mort qui prépare la re-naissance
> Re-naissance du Sens et de l'Esprit . . .
> . . . dans la vibration pure et l'espace fervent.[157]

> . . . fire of Death that prepares the rebirth
> Rebirth of the Senses and the Spirit . . .
> . . . in pure vibration and fervent space.

And so Senghor, the poet of Negritude, using his many styles, seeks essences and truths and gives them poetic definition:

> L'éternel un ciel sans nuage, une forêt bleue sans un cri, la voix
> toute seule mais juste.[158]

> Eternity a cloudless sky, a blue forest without a cry the voice all
> alone but true.

The rebirth takes place, the symbolic return is achieved as the *pirogue*

> . . . renaîtra par les nénuphars de l'écume
> Surnagera la douceur des bambous au matin transparent du
> monde.[159]

. . . will be reborn through the waterlilies of foam
Will float above the bamboos' sweetness in the transparent
morning of the world.

So finally, through the singing of the chorus in *Chaka*, Negritude can celebrate the life of black peoples, the life of all peoples.

LE CORYPHEE　　Rosée ô Rosée qui reveilles les racines soudaines de mon peuple.

LE CHOEUR　　*Bayêté Baba! Bayêté ô Bayêté!*

LE CORYPHEE　　Là-bas le Soleil au zénith sur tous les peuples de la terre.[160]

CORYPHEE:　　Dew oh Dew which wakens the sudden roots of my people.

CHORUS:　　Bayêté Baba! Bayêté oh Bayêté!

CORYPHEE:　　Yonder the Sun at its zenith over all the peoples of the earth.

Notes

1. Aimé Césaire, *Cahier d'un Retour au Pays Natal* (Paris: Présence Africaine, 1956), p. 75.
2. Léopold Sédar Senghor, *Poèmes* (Paris: Editions du Seuil, 1964), p. 189.
3. Felix Tchikaya U'Tamsi, *Brush Fire*, tr. from the French *Feu de Brousse* (Ibadan, Nigeria: Mbari Publications, 1964), p. 4.
4. Senghor, *op. cit.*, p. 23.
5–12. *Ibid*: 5. p. 18; 6. pp. 16–17; 7. p. 42; 8. pp. 148–149; 9. p. 41; 10. p. 15; 11. p. 31; 12. p. 101.
13. U'Tamsi, *op. cit.*, pp. 8–53.
14. Senghor, *op. cit.*, p. 207.
15–17. *Ibid*: 15. p. 41; 16. p. 24; 17. p. 143.
18. Césaire, *op. cit.*, pp. 71–82.
19. Léon G. Damas, *Black-Label* (Paris: Gallimard, 1956), p. 52.
20. U'Tamsi, *op. cit.*, p. 4.
21. Léon G. Damas, *pigments* (Paris: Présence Africaine, 1937), p. 11.
22. U'Tamsi, *op. cit.*, p. 5.
23. David Diop, *Coups de Pilon* (Paris: Présence Africaine, 1956), p. 20.

24. Senghor, *op. cit.*, p. 13.
25. Césaire, *op. cit.*, p. 41.
26. Damas, *pigments*, p. 45.
27–43. *Ibid:* 27. p. 71; 28. p. 37; 29. p. 29; 30. p. 45; 31. pp. 49–50; 32. pp. 42–43; 33. p. 58; 34. pp. 33–36; 35. p. 40; 36. p. 71; 37. p. 75; 38. p. 21; 39. p. 69; 40. p. 17; 41. p. 23; 42. p. 47; 43. p. 24.
44. Damas, *Black-Label*, pp. 10–65.
45. Diop, *op. cit.*, p. 7.
46–51. *Ibid:* 46. p. 8; 47. p. 21; 48. p. 9; 49. pp. 15–16; 50. pp. 26–27; 51. p. 17.
52. Senghor, *op. cit.*, p. 47.
53–64. *Ibid:* 53. p. 116; 54. p. 202; 55. pp. 9–10; 56. pp. 111–112; 57. pp. 115–116; 58. p. 38; 59. p. 111; 60. p. 172; 61. p. 124; 62. p. 100; 63. p. 50; 64. 184.
65. U'Tamsi, *op. cit.*, p. 4.
66–93. *Ibid:* 66. p. 8; 67. p. 10; 68. p. 19; 69. p. 21; 70. p. 44; 71. p. 40; 72. pp. 15–16; 73. p. 28; 74. p. 17; 75. p. 20; 76. p. 3; 77. p. 18; 78. pp. 45–46; 79. p. 10; 80. p. 29; 81. p. 30; 82. p. 31; 83. p. 28; 84. p. 34; 85. p. 33; 86. p. 1; 87. p. 5; 88. p. 37; 89. pp. 20–22; 90. pp. 49–52; 91. p. 38; 92. p. 32; 93. p. 18.
94. Césaire, *op. cit.*, pp. 26–91.
95. Damas, *Black-Label*, pp. 38–64.
96. Damas, *pigments*, p. 42.
97. Diop, *op. cit.*, p. 20.
98–102. *Ibid:* 98. p. 21; 99. p. 8; 100. p. 20; 101. p. 12; 102. p. 27.
103. Senghor, *op. cit.*, pp. 104–105.
104–120. *Ibid:* 104. p. 115; 105. p. 126; 106. p. 198; 107. p. 200; 108. p. 131; 109. p. 26; 110. p. 182; 111. pp. 36–37; 112. p. 12; 113. p. 11; 114. p. 102; 115. p. 201; 116. p. 109; 117. p. 102; 118. p. 206; 119. p. 109; 120. p. 127.
121. Camara Laye, *The Dark Child*, tr. from French by James Kirkup (London: Collins Press, 1955), dedication.
122. Senghor, *op. cit.*, p. 43.
123–142. *Ibid:* 123. p. 118; 124. p. 52; 125. p. 14–15; 126. p. 37; 127. p. 131; 128. p. 180; 129. p. 176; 130. p. 35; 131. p. 47; 132. p. 13; 133. p. 35; 134. p. 30; 135. p. 103; 136. p. 30; 137. p. 17; 138. p. 195; 139. p. 201; 140. p. 151; 141. p. 132; 142. p. 113.
143. Césaire, *op. cit.*, p. 71.
144. Senghor, *op. cit.*, p. 113.
145–160. *Ibid:* 145. p. 114; 146. p. 114; 147. p. 51; 148. pp. 50–51; 149. pp. 15–16; 150. p. 11; 151. p. 12; 152. p. 13; 153. p. 112; 154. p. 113; 155. p. 172; 156. p. 174; 157. p. 194; 158. p. 132; 159. p. 103; 160. p. 133.

SIX

BELIEF AND MAN'S FAITH

> TIME for worship:
>
> softly sing the bells of exile
> softly sings the angelus
>   unto my ears,
> softly sings
>   my guardian angel.
>
> Mask over my face—
>
>   my own mask
> not ancestral—
>   I sign:

Thus Christopher Okigbo in his long poem *Heavensgate*[1] elegiacally opens the fifth part, "Newcomer."

The bells of exile now softly ring, distant and muted as the poet symbolically assumes a mask, his own being. Here the mask is not, as in some poets of Negritude, an ancestral one; rather it will be his own single self, arching upward to the time of worship. "Newcomer" is the sequel to the passage "Initiation," and "Watermaid" comes about only after the cleansing "Lustra," in which the poet ascends to the hills.

So would I to the hills again
so would I
to where springs the fountain
there to draw from

and to hill top clamber
body and soul
whitewashed in the moondew
there to see from

So would I from my eye the mist
so would I
thro moonmist to hilltop
there for the cleansing

But the cleansing does not always take place, for a single man
who is still linked to the sources of the fountain and tied to his
guardian angel cannot extricate himself, even when the bells of
exile sing softly and the time for worship has begun. The works
under discussion in this chapter treat of man as an ontological
being set in a qualitatively historic and mythic time, controlled
by worship and belief, family and ancestry, sacrifice and mediation. Man is linked to all the forces of the earth, affecting and
being affected by them, seeking for his own mask and his own
destiny, often his own tragic fulfillment.

In Wole Soyinka's *A Dance of the Forests*,[2] Demoke the
carver, the bondsman of the god Ogun, has carved the totem
for the gathering of various tribes, a "work of ten generations," with "hands that are very old . . . and with fingers of the
dead." Yet he is tied to the frailty of his body, a frailty which
also extends far back in time and from which he cannot free
himself. And so he laments the brittleness of his being: "Where
my hands are burning to work, where my hands are trembling
to mould, my body will not take me. Is that not a lack of
fulfilment? If I can pull my body up, further than it will go, I
would willingly fall to my death after." Even though Demoke's hands circle backward for thousands of years, thereby
reiterating the philosophical affirmation of duration and continuity advanced in Negritude, this affirmation, even while giving power to man through his link with the past, ties him to a
future from which he seems powerless to extricate himself. The
postulate of continuity and endurance advanced in Negritude

writings is not used to demonstrate that the black man is indeed one of the oldest members of the human race, but rather it is in this and in other works cited as an operative, structural ingredient.

The question that will be reiterated in some of the works under discussion is whether at one and the same time man can be linked to the Earth Mother and not be controlled by her. In John Pepper Clark's play *The Raft*, Kengide says:

> People learn to shed
> Their umbilical cords in the dust
> Under baobab trees although it was
> What tied them centre to centre to their mothers
> For nine blind moons.[3]

Yet, in Soyinka's *The Strong Breed* and Clark's *Song of a Goat* and *The Masquerade*, the chief protagonists are pulled by and contend with the curse in their line, finally succumbing to their tragic historical destiny. For man is linked to his nature, to his past, to his family, to the dead, to all phenomena. All phenomena, all visions of the world are contiguous and inextricably mingled.

In these works, time and space are not quantitative durations but qualitative crisscrossings of moment and regions.

A *Dance of the Forests* is built upon a cyclical history in which the past and the present, the dead and the living cohere; their axes and revolutions are coincidental. Thus, it is only at the high point of return that past generations meet present ones. Forest Head, Godhead of all creatures, persons and things, at the bidding of the living can summon up the unburied dead from the underbelly of the world.

> Only such may regain
> Voice auditorial as are summoned when their link
> With the living has fully repeated its nature, has
> Re-impressed fully on the tapestry of Igbehinadun
> In approximate duplicate of actions, be they
> Of good, or of evil, of violence or carelessness;
> In approximate duplicate of motives, be they
> Illusory, tangible, commendable or damnable.
> Take note, this selection, is by the living.
> We hold these rites, at human insistence.

By proclamation, let the mists of generations
Be now dispersed, Forest Father, unveil, unveil
The phantasmagoria of protagonists from the dead.

Two awaiting summons are a dead woman and a warrior.
Through these two figures, as well as through the Half-Child,
its mother, and many other characters in the play, the cyclical
nature of history is reiterated and augmented through imagery
and through recurrent poetic motif. In the intonement of the
Half-Child, who is seeking an end to his wanderings, and in the
answers of his mother, Soyinka skillfully incorporates Yoruba
ritual and belief into this cyclical view. For this Half-Child is
the "Abiku" of Yoruba mythology, one who repeatedly dies
and revisits a mother's womb, to be born again only to die
again. This cycle of belief can only be broken through ritualistic purification. At the climactic ritualistic end of the play the
Half-Child and its mother are seeking purification:

HALF-CHILD:　　Still I fear the fated bearing
　　　　　　　　Still I circle yawning wombs.
DEAD WOMAN:　. . . . .
　　　　　　　　Shall my breast again be severed
　　　　　　　　Again and yet again be severed
　　　　　　　　From its right of sanctity?
　　　　　　　　Child, your hand is pure as sorrow
　　　　　　　　Free me of the endless burden.
　　　　　　　　Let this gourd, let this gourd
　　　　　　　　 Break beyond my hearth . . .

The dead warrior also laments the unending cycle of his destiny:

Three lives I led since first I went away
But still my first possesses me
The pattern is unchanged.

For he is still wandering in the world of the dead seeking
surcease from his unending bodily corruption.

Three hundred rings have formed
Three hundred rings within that bole

Since Mulieru went away, was sold away
And the tribe was scattered
Three hundred moultings of
The womb-snake of the world
And does the son return now
Empty-handed?

Indeed in *A Dance of the Forests*, Soyinka seems to be constantly preoccupied with time as it relates to history and how together both past and present open out to a vision of the future.

One of the most vivid scenes in the play is the historical flash back to the Kingdom of Mata Kharibu; one of the most beautifully dramatized scenes of ritual is the danced "chorusing of the future" at the end of the play, where the earthlings assume the voices of various spirits in the welcoming of the Dead. In the latter scene, Spirit of the Palm, Spirit of Darkness, Spirit of Precious Stone, Spirit of Pachyderms, Spirit of the Rivers, Spirit of the Sun, and Spirit of Volcanoes are summoned to chorus the future of man and all things. Through images of red and black and through the use of shifting body dance patterns, Soyinka evokes the historical relationships—in most instances inimical—the eternal links through time and space between the forces of nature. Man and the Spirits of all phenomena perform under the direction of Forest Head on the huge panoramic stage of the Dance of the Forest. At the beginning of the scene Forest Head gives his directive:

Let the one whose incompletion denies him rest be patient till the Forest has chorused the Future through lips of earth-beings.

But creatures too dance the future, often giving a vertical movement to the cyclical movement of history which Soyinka propounds. All things, even the ant kingdom, are interdependent in the continuity of the world.

Down the axis of the world, from
The whirlwind to the frozen drifts,
We are the ever legion of the world,
Smitten, for—'the good to come.'

All things open out toward a possible future, the Second Triplet says:

> I am the Greater Cause, standing ever ready,
> excusing the crimes of today for tomorrow's mirage.
> Hungry I come, hearing there was a feast for the dead . . .
> Am I expected?

The whole scene conveys the endless cycle of deception, suffering, and corruption.

Soyinka's vision of historical continuity is a cynical one, but we are never certain of the true depth of this cynicism or whether future history ever brings with it its own regeneration. The dead woman cries out that "a hundred generations has made no difference." When Forest Head is questioned by Eshuoro, a wayward cult spirit, as to his purposes in bringing up the dead, Aroni, the lame one, who seems to be the interpreter for Forest Head answers: "It is enough that they discover their own regeneration. . . . Let the future judge them by reversal of its path or by stubborn continuation." Eshuoro counters that Forest Head is bluffing and that the future will not be chorused since all the Forest Spirits have gone to the gathering of the tribes. But Aroni argues: "Forest Head has provided for the default of your brothers. The living ones will themselves speak for the future." And so the mists of generations are rolled back, and "the phantasmagoria of protagonists from the dead is 'unveiled.'" All, except the dead woman and the warrior, have living counterparts, and Soyinka dramatizes the lived reality of both the live counterparts and that of the dead. The play becomes a shifting kaleidoscopic dance presented through the use of recapitulations of past events, a double-tiered manifestation of concomitant lives.

Rola is now, as in previous life, a whore; and inevitably she has regained the name by which they knew her centuries ago: Madame Tortoise. Demoke the Carver was court poet to Mata Kharibu. Adenebi in previous life was the court historian to Mata Kharibu. Adenebi, who expounds great causes and acts as protector of great myths of history, now proclaims, "Mali, Chaka, Songhai, Glory Empires." Now at the gathering of the clans it is not the illustrious of the Kingdom of Mata Kharibu or of Mali, Chaka, Songhai, Glory Empires who are summoned, but rather a dead woman who lies "with the living in her grave" and who is seeking rest, and a dead warrior seeking rest from his wanderings in the understreams:

> When I died
> And still they would not let my body rest;
> When I lived, and they would not let me be
> The man I felt, cutting my manhood, first
> With a knife, next with words and the dark
> Spit of contempt, the voice at my shoulder said,
> Go seek out Forest Head. If I am home, then
> I have come to sleep.

A *Dance of the Forests* becomes a ritualistic atonement for the two dead ones and a trial for those accused of corruption and violence—Adenebi, Rola, and Demoke. It is before the whole hierarchy of the forest that the dance ritual unfolds; all things, all phenomena interplay with history, reality, and man:

> To all such as dwell in these Forests; Rock devils,
> Earth imps, Tree demons, ghommids, dewilds, genie
> Incubi, succubi, windhorls, bits and halves and such
> Sons and subjects of Forest Father, and all
> That dwell in his domain, take note, this night
> Is the welcome of the dead.

Soyinka is clearly concerned with those events and tendencies that repeat themselves in history, yet his attempts to link this concern with his ideas on man's destiny and fate in a larger sense are not always self-evident. The relationship between choice, accident, and history—where choice ends and accident begins, how choice or accident generate or interrupt an historical process—is not clearly established in A *Dance of the Forests*. In the introduction, Aroni states: "Their choice was no accident. In previous life they were linked in violence and blood with four of the living generation." When the living rejected these mementos from their past, Aroni declares: "I took them under my wing. They became my guests and the Forests consented to dance for them. Forest Head, the one who we call OBANEJI, invited Demoke, Adenebi, and Rola to be present at the dance. They followed him, unwillingly, but they had no choice."

We must assume here that Forest Head is omnipotent, for it is not clear what force propels these cycles of history and makes the choice of the dead man and woman no accident, giving Demoke, Adenebi, and Rola no recourse but to follow Forest Head. Yet, it is only through Demoke's initial assertive and violent action that the dance can begin: "Demoke reached a hand and plucked him down . . . the final link was complete—the Dance could proceed."

Again, paradoxically and inexplicably, it is Demoke who seems to have prior awareness of events when, early in the play, he says: "Perhaps we will meet," and when later he affirms: "I know we are bound to meet somewhere." Furthermore, Demoke suddenly recognizes Rola as Madame Tortoise:

> Why? Why? Why? The man said nothing. Only a feeble effort to be cruel. Why do you take it to heart? . . . Madame Tortoise! Blind. Blind. (*Hitting himself on the forehead.*) Madame Tortoise, that is who you are! (*Rola stands stock-still, her face drained of expression.*)

Does Demoke derive his foresight and hindsight from his profession of creative carver, bondsman to the God Ogun, and from his aesthetic thought process? He says to Rola at their first meeting:

> I carved something to you. Of course, I didn't know you then, I mean, I had never met you. But from what I heard, you were so. . . .
> Madame Tortoise is the totem—most of it anyway. In fact, you might almost say she dominated my thoughts . . .

Here Soyinka creates another link between different times, between the past and present, through the power of man's thought process. Yet, it is not clear whether the creative artist Demoke has the power of divination, whether his recognition of Rola's link with Madame Tortoise is sheer accident, or whether it is generated through creative thought. The relationship between choice, accident, and historical process and thought is further elaborated in the historical flash-back to the Court of Mata Kharibu where the dead man, the warrior, sets a precedent, not only through asserting his right to choose his own destiny but also by being the first to think about that right. In Mata Kharibu's court, the warrior, attempting to exercise a power of choice, refuses to continue in the service of Mata Kharibu and says: "Perhaps I have started a new disease that catches quickly." Soyinka is questioning whether a simple man's action has any relevance, whether a man has a choice as to how he must die:

PHYSICIAN: You think your own life is yours to dispose of?
WARRIOR: I have the right to choose how I mean to die.
PHYSICIAN: Your own life. Are you sure that no one else may waste your life except you?

The soldier's attempt to make a free choice causes Mata Kharibu to fear, and he asks: "Will there be more like him, born with this thought cancer in their heart?" But it is not only Mata Kharibu who sees independent thought and dissension as having a corrupting influence; even the soldier finds it so: "What have they thought that it fills the air so suddenly with stench?"

The cycle of self-being is seen to be little affected by the outspoken integrity of one man—the warrior. Soyinka expresses this through the soothsayer, who compares the warrior's action to a soiling smudge:

Mata Kharibu, have you ever seen a smudge on the face of the moon? . . . Once in every million years, one of the sheep that trail the moon in its wanderings does dare to wipe its smutty nose on the moon. Once in a million years. But the moon is there still. And who remembers the envy-ridden sheep?

This pessimism concerning the efficacy of thought and the exercise of free will is further echoed through the words of Adenebi, in his ideas on individual freedom. That the historian Adenebi, a charlatan and a most pompous character, is made to express the following thought either underscores Soyinka's pessimistic view of history and choice, or further obscures the dramatist's own ideas about these concepts:

Nations live by strength; nothing else has meaning. . . . War is the only consistency that past ages afford us. It is the legacy which new nations seek to perpetuate. Patriots are grateful for wars. Soldiers have never questioned bloodshed. The cause is always the accident your Majesty, and war is the Destiny.

Throughout *A Dance of the Forests*, Soyinka is not only concerned with choice, accident, and destiny, but he is constantly preoccupied with the motifs of freedom and the free act; thus many scenes, indeed the climactic unraveling of the play, revolve around the free act. The ant leader, when asked the question by Forest Head, "Are you free?" answers:

> Freedom we have
> Like the hunter on a precipice
> And the horns of a rhinoceros
> Nuzzling his buttocks.

Perhaps it might be argued that Demoke's carving of the totem for the gathering of the tribes was, as Abaneji, Forest Head, claims—"the kind of action that redeems mankind . . ." Yet, Demoke's work was not his own; it had been inspired by the hands of Ogun in jealous rivalry with Eshuoro, whose slave carving above the head of his master Demoke had boasted:

> No one reduces Oro's height, while I serve
> The wind. Watch Oremole ride on Aja's head,
> And when I shift the dust, master, gather it
> Below.

To be sure, Demoke does act to liberate his own creative potential, but this potential is not solely his own; it is, in part, inheritance from his father and in part infusion from his Orisha Ogun. Yet the speech with which Demoke rejoices in his liberating act, soars with jubilation and sings of freedom:

> Down, down I plucked him, screaming on Oro.
> Before he made hard obeisance to his earth,
> My axe was executioner at Oro's neck. Alone,
> Alone I cut the strands that mocked me, till head
> And boastful slave lay side by side, and I
> Demoke, sat on the shoulders of the tree,
> My spirit set free and singing, my hands,

> My father's hands possessed by demons of blood
> And I carved three days and nights till tools
> Were blunted, and these hands, my father's hands
> Swelled big as the tree-trunk. Down I came
> But Ogun touched me at the forge, and I slept
> Weary at his feet.

Here it is evident that freedom and choice are not the prerogatives of the individual, who seems to be controlled by forces outside of himself and dominated by the cosmic crisscrossing of elements and realms.

In *A Dance of the Forests* there is no clear role assigned to any of the members of the various hierarchies; we do not know who finally controls, dictates, or even guides action. We are certain, however, that there is an interaction of all forces, and that Soyinka's cosmological concepts derive from an interplay between these inimical forces; there is constant enmity between gods and realms. Human emotions find correspondences in those of Gods; rivalries between Gods trigger off a human emotional reaction in the Godhead, Forest Head:

> Soon, I will not tell you from the humans, so closely have their habits grown on you. Did I summon this welcoming for your prowess or for ends of my own? Take care how you tempt my vanity. Eshuoro, you came here to bathe in blood, Ogun, you to defend the foibles of your ward. Let this night alone, when I lay out the rites of the dead or my anger will surpass your spleen. Aroni, you know my will. Proceed.

The Spirit of the Rivers exalts in its control over the deserts:

> From Limpopo to the Nile coils but one snake
> On mudbanks, and sandy bed
> I who mock the deserts, shed a tear
> Of pity to form palm-ringed oases
> Stain my bowels red!

Again, Forest Head asks the Spirit of Volcanoes:

> Who are you?
> Why do you blanket earth and swarm
> Like molten rocks?

Along with the competition within the realms, there is also that between the various realms. Answering Eshuoro's complaints Murete says: "We have claimed our own victims," and "it seems to me that, limb for limb, the forest has always proved victor." Yet, in this hierarchy of forces, although Forest Head seems himself unable to bring about change in the nature of phenomena and man, he has the power to summon up a dance wherein all forces confront one another, and in which a single action may break the pessimistic cycle of history.

Trouble me no further. The fooleries of beings whom I have fashioned closer to me weary and distress me. Yet I must persist, knowing that nothing is ever altered. My secret is my eternal burden—to pierce the encrustations of soul-deadening habit, and bare the mirror of original nakedness—knowing full well, it is all futility. Yet I must do this alone, and no more, since to intervene is to be guilty of contradiction, and yet to remain altogether unfelt is to make my long-rumoured ineffectuality complete; hoping that when I have tortured awareness from their souls, that perhaps, only perhaps, in new beginnings. . . . Aroni, does Demoke know the meaning of his act?

But in the end, A Dance of the Forests is not a chronicle of overwhelming pessimism and cynical hopelessness, for Soyinka makes Demoke, through his own individual action, break the cycle of the Half-Child's wonderings, redeeming the Abiku through an unpremeditated act which could lead to his immolation and sacrifice. Demoke is warned through Aroni by Forest Head: "Demoke, you hold a doomed thing in your hand. It is no light matter to reverse the deed that was begun many lives ago. The Forest will not let you pass."

Through the play of shadow and through the dramatic incorporation of stage directions into which movement is injected, the Dance of the Unwilling Sacrifice rushes A Dance of the Forests to its climactic moment. For the consequence of Demoke's action is certain doom, the risk, the worst possible death for him, that of being burned as sacrifice at the top of the tallest tree:

(The Woman appeals mutely to Demoke. All eyes are intent upon Demoke until he makes up his mind; gives the child to *the Dead Woman. Immediately, Aroni leads out the Dead Woman with the Half-Child, Forest Head takes a final look at the gathering, goes off. Eshuoro gives a loud yell of triumph, rushes off-stage . . . The Triplets follow gleefully. A silhouette of Demoke's totem is seen. . . . Eshuoro's Jester leaps on stage, bearing the sacrificial basket which he clamps on to Demoke's head . . . Dance of the Unwilling Sacrifice, in which Eshuoro and his Jester head Demoke relentlessly towards the totem and the silent dancing figures.*)

However, Ogun is able to save Demoke from his doom, unaccountably forestalling his rival Eshuoro's plans, and defeating his deadly purpose. That Ogun redeems Demoke from death clearly attests to Soyinka's final optimistic vision of the possibility of action and its efficacy; through it the light pierces the darkness of the wilderness. Now all the human characters receive strength from the cosmic forces and, in a series of images of entry, reminiscent of the poetry of Negritude, plunge their hands into the center of the elements:

DEMOKE: Darkness enveloped me, but piercing
Through I came . . .
Child of the Moon's household am I.

AGBOREKO: . . . The crocodile scratching taught me then
My veins run with the oil of palms.

OLD MAN: . . . Ruler of the Forest depths am I.

ROLA: . . . Palm of the storm's hand am I.

ADENEBI: My saddle is the torrent of the flood.
Serpent of the ocean depths am I.

DEMOKE: I lodge below, with the secrets of Earth.

And so *The Dance of the Forests* plays itself out, structurally united through ritualistic sequences, through a mask play linking the dead to the living who ordered the dance and who, with spirits of creatures, pronounce the future. Nothing is left as background; all phenomena, a multilayered piling up, are externalized, linked together through concomitant images of space and time to produce a stratified, if at times unclear, vision of history and man's destiny. Time and space are historically defined, thoughts and feelings are given an historical dimension. Characters, although they are immersed in actions of the present, nonetheless seem to be aware of their past, for Soyinka builds through the consonance of images a multitiered and many-sided dance.

In Soyinka, Tutuola, and Clark the realm of nature and that of man are hardly distinguishable; there is no fixed point of demarcation as both realms constantly interact and interplay. In these writers, phenomena are conceived in terms of human events, natural events are reflected in and reflect human reactions or emotions. A reciprocity is established between the world of man and the world of nature. Thus, in Soyinka's *The Road*[4] the nature of the road, which is the central symbol along which the play is constructed, is consonant with his pessimistic expression of the trajectory of man's life:

> Be even like the road itself. Flatten your bellies with the hunger of an unpropitious day, power your hands with the knowledge of death. In the heat of the afternoon when the sheen raises false forests and a watered haven, let the event first unravel before your eyes. Or in the dust when ghost lorries pass you by and your shouts your tears fall on deaf panels and the dust swallows them. Dip in the same basin as the man that makes his last journey. . . . Breathe like the road. Be the road. Coil yourself in dreams, lay flat in treachery and deceit and at the moment of a trusting step, rear your head and strike the traveller in his confidence, swallow him whole or break him on the earth. Spread a broad sheet for death with the length and the time of the sun between you until the one face multiplies and the one shadow is cast by all the doomed. Breathe like the road, be even like the road itself . . .

In the preceding passage, Soyinka with a skillful interplay between parts of the human body and time of day, or time of journey, brings about an assimilation of man and phenomena, a concurrence of emotions or destinies. Here, Soyinka's imagery is not based on allegory. The imagery of *The Road* becomes a vehicle for Soyinka's abstract thoughts about man's journey through life. Imagery and thought are fused to produce a conscious philosophical statement. In the first sentence of the passage the movement is from the animate—physical flattened "bellies" and "hands" extending—to the overall pessimistic view stated in "an unpropitious day" and "death." In *The Road*

Soyinka's preoccupation is with various kinds of death that occur along its way; the chief protagonist, the Professor, is ritualistically attempting to comprehend the true meaning of death, to apprehend its reality. In the next two sentences of the passage the movement is reversed. The passage of time, day's decline expressed in the words "heat of the afternoon" and "dust" parallels man's decline, the growing anguish of man as events unravel before his eyes, and "shouts" and "tears fall on deaf panels." Like the road, man's last journey falls and, dipping away into the distance like the road, sighs and disappears, breathes and expires.

In the second part of the passage, another species of phenomenon is added to that of concrete road and animate man by the use of snake imagery; man, the road, and snake all lie in wait for the unsuspecting traveler waiting to ambush him. "Coil yourself in dreams, lay flat in treachery and deceit and at the moment of a trusting step, rear your head and strike the traveller in his confidence." Soyinka's vision has fused together realms and phenomena; whether they be hostile or friendly, destructive or productive, alien or familiar, all have an emotional texture. They are variegated patterns seen under varying aspects and painted in diverse ways.

The principal motifs of *The Road* intersect in the figure of Murano, who lives suspended between life and death. This state of suspension gives a time structure to the play, as the author attempts to explore the various significations of death and the philosophical relevance of chance and accident.

Murano has suffered an accident, and he is picked up by the Professor, who through him is exploring the meaning of death and its relationship to accident. Here, the playwright himself explains in the notes 'For the Producer' the correspondences between time and the suspension of death, the mask dance and death:

The dance is the movement of transition; it is used in the play as a visual suspension of death—in much the same way as Murano, the mute, is a dramatic embodiment of this suspension. He functions as an arrest of time, or death, since it was in his 'agemo' phase that the lorry knocked him down. Agemo, the mere phase, includes the passage of transition from the human to the divine essence (as in the festival of Ogun in this play), as much as the part psychic, part intellectual grope of professor towards the essence of death.

Thus, dance and song become the link between the lived dramatic moment and the Professor's search for essence, for the meaning of death. Every accident, all the varying manifestations of death add another link to the Professor's attempted reconstruction of the meaning of death and its relationship to the word:

> My bed is among the dead, and when the road raises a victory cry to break my sleep I hurry to a disgruntled swarm of souls full of spite for their rejected bodies. . . . There are dangers in the Quest I know, but the Word may be found companion not to life, but Death. . . . They died, all three of them crucified on rigid branches. . . . But you must not think I accept all such manifestations as truth. . . . I know this is not the Word, but every discovery is a sign-post.

The Professor continually needs to be near those who expose themselves to death—drivers and thugs. He sleeps in the cemetery and is continually seeking for the word through the figure of Murano. Although the Professor is unable to fathom the cause of death on the road, he never imputes it to mere accident and chance.

> PROFESSOR: Come then, I have a new wonder to show you . . . a madness where a motor-car throws itself against a tree—Gbram! And showers of crystal flying on broken souls.
>
> SAMSON (*suddenly alarmed*): Wait! What was that about an accident?

And again later on in a cynical speech the Professor expresses the prime reason for his association with the drivers and thugs whom he has collected around him:

> It is true I demand little from you, just your presence at evening communion, and the knowledge you afford me that your deaths will have no meaning. . . . I would live as hopefully if you were ant-heaps destined to be crushed underfoot. But I

suppose you my friend [Kotonu], would dare to call this also, accident?

Kotonu, who has stopped driving because he fears he might kill someone, seems dazed throughout most of the play; he remains affected, however, through his having struck Murano, of whom he says: "It was almost as if he was determined to die. Like those wilful dogs getting in the way of the wheels." Since he has stopped driving he has taken over the running of the Professor's store, which collects parts from wrecked lorries and the belongings of those who have been killed, a job to which Samson objects. For Soyinka, all material objects have their own spirit, all professions their own essential nature. The link between the animate and the inanimate, an animistic interpretation of phenomena, is revealed in Samson's relationship with the lorry. He says: "You see Professor, the magic of a motor engine simply refused to reveal itself to me. Kotonu was the clever one. . . . I knew that driving was not for people like me."

Like Demoke, who because of an inherent physical defect could not ascend to great heights, and thus was unable to completely fulfill his desire to be the greatest of carvers, Samson is unable to become a great lorry driver because of insensitive feet: "A driver must have sensitive soles on his feet. . . . and he has to be able to judge the pressure on the pedals exactly right. I have such thick soles you see so I always revved the engine too much or too little." But in *The Road*, it is Say Tokyo Kid who best reflects, in a modern setting, the image of Demoke the Carver. He feels a real affinity to the timber he carries, and in an American motion picture idiom says:

> You think a guy of timber is dead load. What you talking kid? . . . You kidding? There is a hundred spirits in every guy of timber trying to do you down cause you've trapped them in, see? There is a spirit in hell for every guy of timber. . . . Until that guy is sawn up and turned to a bench or table, the spirit guy is still struggling inside it . . .

The revelation that matter is animate, that all elements have their own spirits which extend and correspond with those of other things, forces, and beings, is not merely a manifestation of ontological relationships but indeed controls the play's denouement and brings about its climax, for Say Tokyo Kid, like many of Soyinka's other characters, is concerned not simply with death but rather with the style and manner of dying. Some deaths are ennobling, others degrading. Since Say Tokyo Kid is a son of timber and only drives timber, the noblest death for him would be to die pitting his strength against the strongest spirits of woods and high-class timbers: "Golden walnut. Obeche. Ironwood. Black Afara. Iroko. Ebony. Camwood. And the heartwood's gorra be sound. (*Thumps his chest.*) It's gorra have a solid beat like that. Like mahogany."

As in A *Dance of the Forests,* where Demoke, the carver of wood, breaks the cycle of history and brings repose to the dead who are wandering and to the unborn child lying suspended between life and death, so too in *The Road* Say Tokyo Kid, through an act of strength, pits his force against that of the Spirits of Wood and breaks the Professor's hold over all those whom he has gathered around him; principally he frees Murano, releasing him from his state of suspension. In the climactic dance of the "egungun," the wild dance of possession, Say Tokyo Kid hoarsely says: "I ain't afraid. Even if he's master of the spirits of every timber I ever wrestled with, I can teach him a lesson." Then he locks in combat with the Professor, whom he believes is sacrilegiously trespassing on the spirit world by ordering the dance of possession, kills the Professor, and is killed by the spirit of timber, the masked "egungun." The Professor has finally achieved what he had felt approaching: ". . . a true excitement of the mind and spirit. As if that day has been lowered at last which I have long awaited." Say Tokyo Kid is broken on timber and dies clutching timber, thereby achieving a noble death: "The still mask appears to come to life suddenly, lifts Say Tokyo in a swift movement up above his head . . . smashes him savagely on the bench. Say Tokyo . . . rolls over onto the ground and clutches the train of the mask to him." Murano's agemo phase is ended, the link is complete, and the natural flow of time can now continue.

Whereas in A *Dance of the Forests* the different realms are like overlapping circles, in *The Road* the different realms seem to be marching along in parallel lines, meeting at certain climactic and decisive points, as for instance in the dance of the masked egungun.

In *The Swamp Dwellers,* the realms intersect in the image of the swamp, which like the road demands sacrifice so that man may continue to exist. Thus, sacrifice often becomes the intercessor between the different realms in nature and between different times. In *The Road* the god Ogun demands that dogs be sacrificed to the road, which if not appeased would make sacrificial victims of man. Samson prays: "May we never walk when the road waits, famished." He pleads to Kotonu:

> Kill us a dog Kotonu, kill us a dog. Kill us a dog before the hungry god lies in wait and makes a substitute of me. . . . Ogun likes it that's all that matters. . . . Serve Ogun his tit-bit so the road won't look at us one day and say Ho ho you two boys you look juicy to me. But what's the use? The one who won't give Ogun willingly will yield heavier meat by Ogun's designing.

The swamp too, like the road, might lie in wait for the unsuspecting traveler unless it is offered sacrifice. The climactic moment of *The Swamp Dwellers*[5] comes when the reason for such sacrifice is challenged and the traditional power of the priest of the swamp is questioned by Igwezu:

> Who takes the gifts of the people, in order that the beast may be gorged and made sleepy-eyed with the feast of sacrifice? . . . And so that the Serpent might not vomit at the wrong season and drown the land, so that He might now swallow at the wrong moment and gulp down the unwary traveller, do I not offer my goats to the priest?

The expression of such doubts and questions is the free act that will break the cycle of tradition which has become corrupt.

In *The Swamp Dwellers* where the swamp is the functional background and the immediate foreground of the play, the interrelationship of man, swamp, and serpent creates an historical and spacial perspective, demonstrates the unchanging inimical nature of animistic belief. A blind beggar who has traveled far from the north following the river's path and wishing to find fulfilment in treading where the land is moist and in working the wet clay between his fingers inadvertently is the first to challenge the traditional power of the swamp: "But if a man is willing to take a piece of the ground and redeem it from the swamp—will they let him? If a man is willing to drain the filth away and make the land yield cocoyams and lettuce—will they let him?" Makuri, who outwardly adheres strictly to tradition even while inwardly despising the conductor of such tradition, the Kadiye, the priest of the swamp, hastens to reply:

> The land that we till and live on has been ours from the beginning of time. The bounds are marked by ageless iroko trees that have lived since the birth of the Serpent, since the birth of the world, since the start of time itself. What is ours is ours. But what belongs to the Serpent may never be taken away from him.

It is because of Makuri's and the older generation's belief in the omnipotence of the serpent to whom sacrifice must be continually given, that the priest of the swamp, a charlatan grown fat from the benefits of such sacrifice, can continue to exercise control over the people of the swamp. But the swamp, like the road, can be inimical, swallowing up the unwary, the unquestioning believer. The conflict of the play arises when Makuri's son Igwezu, one of the twins born with "the very colour of the swamp," questions tradition, doubts the omnipotence of the serpent and the validity of sacrifice to it, and unmasks the mediator between man and swamp, the priest of the swamp.

The swamp is multidimensional, presenting a variety of images to the different characters for whom it becomes the most important force. The swamp is many things; it is despair and disaster, an evil malignant force, an all-powerful controlling influence, the hope of fertile land. For Alu and Makuri it is a living thing, but it lives as the serpent does beneath the surface demanding an unquestioning allegiance. To them it is familiar for it was their bridal bed: "Where the rivers meet, the marriage must begin. And the river bed itself is the perfect bridal bed." But the swamp became threatening and the bed of conception fell in over them:

> We did not know that the swamp came up as far as that part of the stream. . . . The ground . . . gave . . . way beneath us!

and Alu was "left kicking in the mire." Yet the memory of the swamp is dear to them. Now they still pay allegiance to it, and bound to it by traditional belief they cannot countenance any blasphemy against it or its priest. "Unsay it my son. Unsay that at once," Makuri cries when Igwezu is shaving both the beard and the hypocrisy from the Kadiye.

The swamp is the Kadiye's power; as long as the swamp is feared, he is respected and revered. Through the perpetuation of the myth of the swamp he perpetuates his own hold over the dwellers of the swamp. When through his actions he destroys Igwezu's belief in the myth, when his powers of mediation between swamp and people seem to be ineffectual, when he does not give to the swamp the sacrificial offerings of the swamp dwellers but rather feeds himself with these offerings, then he is revealed in the folds of his flesh and the lie is seen in the "fat of his eyes." When Igwezu rips the mask of deceit from the Kadiye he becomes, for a moment, "master . . . slayer of serpents." Corrupt tradition has been unmasked and the hold of the serpent over the people of the swamp perhaps broken. Igwezu leaves knowing that "only the children and the old stay . . . only the innocent and the dotards." He flees into the dark night refusing the company of the blind beggar: "No, I want to paddle as I go, like a little child."

Yet this play too ends on a note of optimism. The blind beggar who came from the arid north, following the river, and who will now work the soil of the swamp between his fingers gives optimistic assurance to the departing Igwezu:

> I shall be here to give account. . . . The swallows find their nest again when the cold is over. Even the bats desert dark holes in the trees and flap wet leaves with wings of leather. There were wings everywhere as I wiped my feet against your threshold. I heard the cricket scratch himself beneath the armpit.

In many of the plays of both Soyinka and Clark, tradition in its various forms is the constantly reiterated functional motif. But often tradition and its cultural legacies are scathingly satirized by the dramatist. The inimical nature of the outward manifestations of tradition is presented, even as its pervasive powerful influence on the living is demonstrated through the pull of blood.

In *The Strong Breed*,[6] it was ordained that in Eman's village only those of the line of the strong breed could carry away from their village the total corruption of the dying year enabling the cycle of the new year to occur uncontaminated and cleansed. In the village to which Eman goes as a stranger, attempting to flee the pull of his blood, it is the weak and the wayward on whom this burden is placed. For man in this play is the intermediary between the cycles of time, the year's end and its beginning, the sacrifice of a single man, the atonement for the communal guilt. Like the road and the swamp which demand sacrifice, in *The Strong Breed* both villages offer up a carrier to ensure a propitious year for their inhabitants. Time (the past and the present) and space (the distance between two villages) are linked by the blood of the strong breed, which too demands its own sacrifice, which has its own compulsion.

Eman's mother, Eman's father's mother, and Eman's wife, as ordained, had died giving birth to men of the strong breed: "You killed your mother. She died giving birth to you. Son, it is not the mouth of the boaster that says he belongs to the strong breed. It is the tongue that is red with pain and black with sorrow." The old man, Eman's father, had received regenerative strength from this pain and sorrow, from his unending task of carrying. When Eman attempts to interrupt this recurrent task, which had asked for the sacrifice of his wife, his father again reminds him of the strength of his heritage: "Ours is a strong breed my son. It is only a strong breed that can take this boat to the river year after year and wax stronger on it. I have taken down each year's evils for over twenty years. I hoped you would follow me."

In *The Strong Breed*, man is still connected to his umbilical cord and seems unable to free himself from the pull of his blood, from the call of his inherited profession. Even though Eman's grief at the death of his wife drives him away from his village, his father wills that he return: "It had to be. But you know now what slowly ate away my strength. I awaited your return with love and fear. Forgive me then if I say that your grief is light. It will pass. This grief may drive you now from your home. But you must return."

And his father, in his wisdom, knowing the strong pull of the blood among those of the strong breed, urges patience: "It is only time you need son. Stay longer and you will answer the urge of your blood." So strong is the force of this blood that it not only protects its members from contamination, but conversely, if not used, it turns in on one, gestates, and breeds its own contamination. Thus, in pleading with his son not to interrupt the race of the strong breed Eman's father uses two arguments: only by being a carrier can those of the strong breed achieve fulfillment, and only a carrier can expose himself to the weight of contamination without rotting: "Other men would rot and die doing this task year after year. It is strong medicine which only we can take. Our blood is strong like no other. Anything you do in life must be less than this, son." Yet, Eman flees from his village, attempting to flee the responsibility of his lineage, even though warned by his father that: "Your own blood will betray you son. Because you cannot hold it back. If you make it do less than this, it will rush to your head and burst it open. I say what I know my son."

And indeed Eman's blood does turn back on him, for the village to which he flees does not use men of the strong breed as carriers, but harbors idiots and strangers so that they may assume the burden, willingly or unwillingly, of removing the year's evil. This village reeks with contamination and is so shrouded in evil that Sunma, the daughter of the executor of the carrier custom, confesses to Eman with whom she has fallen in love: "I wonder if I really sprang from here. I know they are evil and I am not. From the oldest to the smallest child, they are nourished in evil and unwholesomeness in which I have no part."

The play opens with Sunma, who feels an overwhelming presentiment of this evil, attempting to convince Eman with whom she has been living that they should leave the village on this last day of the year. For the first time she brutally turns the idiot Ifada, the other stranger in the village, out of their house so that he might be made carrier, but neither her pleas to Eman nor this unusually cruel attitude to Ifada convince him to leave. Eman's demonstration of ignorance in the opening of the play, his naive ignorance of the custom of the carrier, is dramatically necessary for the eventual unraveling of the plot, but there ensues an unconvincing narrative exposition. Not only does Eman demonstrate his ignorance of the custom but further takes into his house the idiot Ifada, who is being pressed into service as carrier, and gives to a strange little girl some of his own clothing for her effigy.

In the first scene this little girl, a miniature of the village, states the custom. She enters dragging an effigy, which she calls her carrier, and in answer to Eman's question about it, she states: "I am unwell you know. My mother says it will take away my sickness with the old year." The words of this shadowy little waiflike girl to Ifada early in the play foretell its denouement: "But just because you are helping me, don't think it is going to cure you. I am the one who will get well by tomorrow, do you understand? It is my carrier and it is for me alone."

Here, Soyinka has united two dramatic elements—exposition and denouement. Structurally, the past and the present are linked by flash backs. The flash back that presents Eman's flight from his initiation camp and his first departure from his own village reveals the corruption and lechery of the tutor in charge of performing the initiation ceremony. Here, too, as in *The Swamp Dwellers*, it is a member of the younger generation who unmasks and challenges the corrupt executor of custom. The hero, Eman, is visited at his initiation camp in violation of a very strong taboo by his girl friend, Omae, who mimics the custom and reveals the perversity of the tutor in charge:

EMAN: . . . What do you think will happen if my tutor turns up now.

OMAE: He won't.

EMAN [*mimicking*.]: He won't. I suppose you are his wife and he tells you where he goes. In fact this is just the time he comes round to our huts. He could be at the next hut this very moment.

The action of the play is presented in the form of a chase, for Eman has become the unwilling carrier and is pursued by the villagers led by two elders who are the executors of the ritual. The chase dramatically illustrates the perversity of the ritual and how quickly ritual observance can become a mania for persecution. In Soyinka's plays the executors of custom are often either corrupt or inhuman, and frequently they are so set on rigidly performing ritual that they pervert the meaning of the custom or even violate taboos themselves. Angered by Sunma's attempt to forestall the execution of the ritual, Jaguna defiles the proper observance of the custom through a brutal act of temper:

JAGUNA: My daughter! Does this one look like my daughter? Let me cripple the harlot for life.
OROGE: That is a wicked thought Jaguna.
JAGUNA: Don't come between me and her.
OROGE: Nothing in anger—do you forget what tonight is?

Further riled by Eman's flight through the night and the village, which almost spreads contamination into the new year, Jaguna orders a drastic cleansing:

It is no longer enough to drive him past every house. There is too much contamination about already. . . . I said there is too much harm done already. The year will demand more from this carrier than we thought.

The flash backs merge well, becoming more and more integrated into the present action of the play until past and present join in Eman's final chase. All during the flight, Eman sees a vision of his father in the act of courageously taking his last journey down to the stream as carrier of his own village. The blood of the strong breed has betrayed Eman; he has become the carrier of a village that does not have the heroic tradition of the strong breed, and by so doing he has lost the fiber and essential courage of those of the strong breed. His father had warned him:

I am very sad. You only go to give to others what rightly belongs to us. You will use your strength among thieves. They are thieves because they take what is ours, they have no claim of blood to it. They will even lack the knowledge to use it wisely. Truth is my companion at this moment my son. I know everything I say will surely bring the sadness of truth.

Now in the final vision the link of the strong breed is complete as father and son meet as carriers; the father who has been carrier for twenty years and is courageously facing his last journey and the son who is carrying out his first and last task as carrier. Symbolically, Eman tells his father at their last meeting: "My throat is burning. I have been looking for the stream all night." And heedless of his father's warnings that he should turn back Eman inevitably follows his father to his death. But as in *A Dance of the Forests*, *The Road*, and *The Swamp Dwellers*, where a single act brings an end to suffering and sacrifice, here Eman's death and Sunma's consequent madness may bring an end to the sacrificial custom of the carrier. Indeed, it can be said that Soyinka's vision, although initially rooted in a deep pessimism, opens out to an optimistic future: "A man must go on his own, go where no one can help him, and test his strength."

The final optimism that we discern in Soyinka is nowhere present in the plays of John Pepper Clark. In Soyinka, through some act of defiance man interrupts the cycle of unending history and brings to an end an inherited and tragic destiny. As we have seen in *The Strong Breed*, it is implied that with Eman's death the tragic destiny of the strong breed would be ended and that the tight pull of his heritage would be weakened, if not totally suspended. Clark holds out no such optimistic hope for an end to the tragic pull of man's inheritance, sees no solution through action to the destructive force of the curse that has befallen a man, a race. Thus, neither Zifa in *Song of a Goat* nor Tufa in *The Masquerade* is able to forestall the tragedy of his line. To be sure, Clark implies in *Song of a Goat* that had man rigorously adhered to the traditional ways of behavior, Zifa's ensuing tragedy could have been averted; but Clark does not advance any ideas as to how the curse suffered by Zifa—contamination through contact with his dead father—could be broken. Even as Soyinka accepts the possibility of accident and ensuing death, Clark predicates in his play *The Raft* accident and chance (for we do not know how the raft was set adrift), and that man is indeed adrift and his actions to escape the drift are futile. Therefore, Clark's vision of history is based on the uninterrupted continuity of man's tragic destiny. This treatment of phenomena, too, differs in one basic way from that of Soyinka. In Clark, not only is man's tragic destiny presaged by phenomena but also it is totally reflected in phenomena's various manifestations. The anxiety of the men on the raft is marked by the ebb and flow of the tide and by the movement of the whirlpool and the winds. In many instances, Soyinka's phenomena, as in *The Road*, are, a priori, inimical. Yet, in *The Swamp Dwellers* the gluttonous and destructive swamp may be contained through the creative act of a believer such as the blind beggar. Whereas in Soyinka the sacrifice of an individual, the end result of an action, is efficacious, in Clark sacrifice and mediation are ineffectual. Time and transitions in the plays of Clark are marked by changes in the natural order of things, which, mirroring the various aspects of a curse, also reflect changes in the characters' fortunes. Unlike Soyinka, Clark does not question the validity of tradition and belief; he implicitly accepts them and from this acceptance constructs his plays. A series of events are not mere associations; rather they are causally connected. Every connection in space or time creates a link between subject and object making it possible to see in the one the reason for changes in the other. An initial incident occurs, needs no other explanation except that it sets off a process, generates a series of happenings which unite it to the final action. The irrational, predominant situation, concretized and expressed in parallel movements in space and time, gives a multidimensional character to Clark's images. Metaphor is often conceived through juxtaposed relationships and not through direct comparative links.

Soyinka is basically concerned with historicity, Clark with causality. Clark's view of history is implicitly revealed or expressed through the continuity and permanence of a curse that affects a total household, a complete clan. Clark traces the curse suffered by Zifa in *Song of a Goat*, shows its effect on the other members of the family, and then extends it to the offspring of the cursed line. Thus, the play becomes the unraveling of a man's fate, unwinding inevitably to a tragic end. In the three plays, Clark cuts his characters adrift and watches them move, powerless to steer their own course.

The verse in *Song of a Goat*[7] sings and wails the lament of a man, Zifa, who is caught in the toils of his curse and is unable to free himself from them. The story is of Zifa's cursed family, of the pride and fall of its race, of man, of man's frustration at his loss of fertility and creativity. The loss is as great to Zifa as it is to his wife, Ebiere. When they challenge their fate, destruction ensues and corruption sets in:

> But you are
> As yet not cleansed, and for that matter all
> The concession is reeking with rot and
> Corruption.

The tale is told through a fisherman's family; the rhythm is that of the continuous beat of a pulse, the pulse of man's being and the pulse of the sea, which brings life and death. The ebb and flow of the tide reflect the changing fortunes of the family:

> See how like waters whipped by the wind you
> Have run amok.

A series of earth images depicts the play of sterility and fertility. The floods come in, as fate exists, and the tide, as the Masseur knows, will turn back upon one.

The opening dialogue of the play immediately introduces the contrapuntal motifs of loss of fertility and creativity. The loss is enlarged upon by the poet's imagery, which always links the tragedy of his characters to the larger universe. For Clark, there is an inherent irony in the cosmic interplay of forces and phenomena; nature is whimsical and capricious: miraculously and suddenly creative, it is just as suddenly and ultimately destructive. What is natural may become unnatural; what seems rational in the order of things may become irrational and destroy that order. The Masseur, the doctor and priest, warns Ebiere, who has sought his advice because she cannot conceive:

> An empty house, my daughter, is a thing
> Of danger. If men will not live in it
> Bats or grass will, and that is enough
> Signal for worse things to come in.

Images are linked with the natural universe; the Masseur suggests that since the seed of her husband, which had previously given them a son, Dode, had now lost its power to "bring forth green leaves and fruit," she should allow another to bring life into her house. Since in nature there is a natural solution to everything, since "for every ailment in man there is a leaf in the forest," the Masseur advocates what he considers the natural and traditional solution, that:

> . . . a good proposition
> Would be for your husband to make you over
> To another in his family.

He tries to quiet Ebiere's shame at Zifa's sterility, indicating that all things in nature, even the very strongest, can undergo change: "Worst things/ Have been seen before. Why, even leopards go lame." The Masseur's harsh realism is now juxtaposed with Ebiere's youthful exuberance and optimism in a lyrical image:

> After all, you are just stepping out
> On the morning dew of life with mist all prostrate
> On the ground before you.

The wistful, ephemeral quality of these lines is harshly broken by the next line; the Masseur continues, "But when the sun is up/ You'll see better." We are reminded that this reality of loss and destruction is to Ebiere death itself. But to attempt to recreate life through what seems a violation of the natural order is "what the dead forbid you to speak of." To Ebiere, the wisdom of the doctor has caught her in its "crooked hands."

Another image, similarly expressive of the beauty and sadness of Ebiere, is caught in Zifa's words and further reflects his inability to capture this beauty:

> I heard her skirt flutter
> In the wind as I came in but even as I called
> Her footsteps died out on the grass.

The Masseur accuses Zifa of wasting the land that should bear fruit:

> You have allowed the piece of fertile
> Ground made over to you to run fallow
> With elephant grass.

The images "elephant grass" and "harmattan" emphasize sterility and wastage, accentuating the ineffectiveness of Zifa's love, which the Masseur calls "a cloak of dew." For the Masseur, and implicitly for Clark also, "the soil is sacred," its tilling and sowing man's duty. Here, once again, is reiterated one of the basic concerns of Clark, Soyinka, and Tutuola—man's relationship to the earth, the inherent potential of earth, which in *The Swamp Dwellers* the blind beggar reverently brings out with his hands. Here, too, is the relationship between earth and woman. The power of earth, its relationship to man, which was reiterated in Negritude, becomes the functional structural motif as it does for many of the works discussed in this chapter. Earth as well as woman should be productive, for earth is mother; its productivity not only ensures the continuity of the clan but should be assured by that clan. So when Zifa comes to the Masseur seeking a way out:

> What I want is
> A way out, a way to lead me
> Out of this burnt patch of earth.

The Masseur suggests:

> Have you ever considered another should
> Take over the tilling of the fertile
> Soil, and had wet mud flung back at you?

Zifa's mind is already closed to the Masseur's suggestion:

> I am not such a child as to set fire
> To my land for fowls of the air to scratch
> And pick up the grubs.

The mixture of images and the shock of mixing opposites to express one idea reveals the tension and conflict in that idea:

>   People
> Will only be too pleased to pick at me
> As birds at worms squirming in the mud. What,
> Shall I show myself a pond drained dry
> Of water so their laughter will crack up the floor
> Of my being?

The idea that through overripeness creative power may be destroyed or cause its own destruction, if it is not used, is expressed, too, through fertile images—"the rains," "the moistness of the earth," and the warning of the Masseur:

> Don't you see the entire grass is gone
> Overlush, and with the harmattan may
> Catch fire though you spread over it
> Your cloak of dew?

The images are direct; the comparison and the meaning are
stated. Sterility is contrasted with fertility and blossoming
things; the metaphor heightens the unnaturalness of Zifa's impotence while all the world is bursting forth. Zifa's anxiety to
regain the power to create is expressed in the metaphor of the
floods' rise and fall; his hopes are elevated on its crest, his
being raised up "only to be left aground," helpless to use the
rains that symbolize his wife's fertility, and he cries out in the
agony of this hopeless waiting: "I will not give up my piece of
land." By saying: "One learns to do without the masks he can/
No longer wear," the Masseur reminds us once again of harsh
reality. This ends a dialogue of images that brought us into
conversation with the forces of nature, with the earth, floods,
fire, wind, a new dawn, the push and thrust of life. Agitated,
Zifa retorts, "I cannot follow the drift of your talk." The use of
the word "drift" is a denial by Zifa of the harsh reality and
persuasive force of the Masseur's proposition. The image of
man's being adrift, an image that forms the basis of Clark's
play *The Raft*, is now picked up by the Masseur, who warns
Zifa that while he awaits the return of his potency, all the world
and especially his wife Ebiere are heady with sap and lie waiting for fertilization. In such a situation the propitious floods
and rains, which have prepared the lands for sowing, can become ominous; a bounteous tide may bring destruction:

> In a situation
> Like yours one may be content to drift as do
> The weeds of the stream. But that carries very
> Little, because the tide always turns
> Back on one.

Zifa alienated his people by bringing his father's corpse home
for burial, even though, apparently, it still carried the danger of
his disease.

> And for that they have picked my flesh
> To the bones like fish a floating corpse.

> Others grumble it was in time
> Of flood. They will all be too ready now
> To smirk if they hear I am become
> Drained of my manhood.

In Clark's plays, fish often are destructive, preying and feeding on corruption. Images of corruption pervade Clark's vision of reality. Corruption in one sphere leads to that in another; a curse leads to corruption which leads to a death, and the dead thing will be assailed by beasts of prey, mocked by the unsympathetic:

>   . . . there
> Goes the cock with the flaming red crest
> But touch the thing and you'll find it
> Colder than a dog's nose.

When the Masseur suggests the same thing to Zifa as he had to Ebiere, Zifa's fierce pride and loyalty breaks out in a furor. The lines that follow are contrived:

> You lame thing, you crawling piece
> Of withered flesh with the soul of a serpent.

Also, the witch images are equally unnatural:

> The Witch of Nine Plumes has your stomach
> For her cauldron.

Clark often uses artificial statements and metaphors such as these, destroying the correspondence of images that he has been carefully building up. At the end of this scene there is a skillful incorporation of proverb in the dialogue. Zifa challenges the doctor: "They say the crooked/ Wood tells the expert carver," but the Masseur replies: "Not when the tree/ Is blasted, my son." The end of the first movement, and the foreshadowing of the final movement, is well stated in the river image, which will become the dominant metaphor of Clark's play *The Masquerade*: ". . . there goes a man deep and furious as/ A river underground."

The second movement reaches the climax: the sacrifice of

the goat, the symbol of fertility, and the destruction of Zifa and
his family, whose fate is sealed. Zifa's father's sister, Orukorere, acts out the role of the mad woman who has "double
vision" or insight into the passion of the sacrifice that is about
to take place. Orukorere is a seer whose comments link together the relationships between man and the forces around
him; it is she who sees the goat being destroyed by the leopard.
From the chorus, which becomes the narrator of events, the
impassive commentators of the action, we learn that Orukorere
had been a beautiful woman on whom, because of her arrogant
rejection of many suitors, a spell had been cast by the people of
the sea, of whom she was the handmaiden:

> But although she has this double vision
> Nobody believes a word she says, even
> Outside the gourd.

But not only does the chorus tell of Orukorere's curse, it also
tells of the curse besetting the whole family: "That's a queer
family/ A curse lies heavy on it" and the chorus further elaborates on the effects of the curse: "Bring up a chicken among
hawks/ And if she is not eaten she will eat." The voice of the
chorus telling the sequence of tragic incidents merges with
Orukorere's voice, which is heard wailing but is not listened to;
it is a voice that foretells tragic events but cannot forestall
them. All forces, man, nature, and the extraterrestial, interact
and Orukorere, the prophetess, seems to be their explicator. In
his suffering, Zifa appeals to Orukorere for help:

> The very trees in my
> Grove are being
> Felled level with the ground, you yourself say
> You hear them crashing one upon another,
> And yet you do nothing to stop them.

Orukorere had heard the bleating of the goat, had tried to warn
her family of the impending tragedy:

> I must find him, the he-goat;
> His cry is everywhere, don't you hear it?
> It is all over the house: I say, can't

You hear the poor billy bleating.
It's bleeding to death.

But in fulfillment of the curse Orukorere's foreshadowing had gone unheeded. The Masseur had also attempted unsuccessfully to forestall the tragedy:

I sought
To bring them water but all
I had was a basket. Now, see
How burnt to charcoal the land
Lies, even to the shrubs on the hedge.

He, too, suffers the pain of foreseeing tragedy without being able to prevent it, and he states Clark's idea that man's coming into the world is a coming into anguish: "You know now that each day we live/ Hints at why we cried out at birth."

The leopard destroys the goat, and with the destruction of fertility, Zifa, Ebiere, and Tonye are destroyed. Again, it is Orukorere who had stated the impending doom:

The leopard, I have missed the leopard
That will despoil the prime goat of our yard
But I do not hear the victor's cry.

The absence of the victor's cry reveals that the person who performs the sacrifice on the goat does not benefit from the sacrifice. The leopard is then symbolically merged with the snake:

I knew it was no proper leopard.
There, I see it sports the long slide
Of the earth one.

The snake image is picked up in the beginning of the third movement by Ebiere, who hisses like a snake, thus assuming its destructive role. Tonye asks:

Why, what do you make that sound for? . . .
From a snake such a sound is only to be
Expected; it is the signal of spite and
Sinister motives.

Ebiere challenges Tonye to prove the fertility of his family or she will laugh to scorn his proud race.

In the final movement, Zifa returns from sea to find he has been betrayed. The sacrifice is performed; the head of the goat is forced into the pot, which breaks, proving without doubt that the race is truly cursed. The act of sacrifice of the goat climaxes the play as the blood spurts erect.

One of the neighbors recounts Zifa's death, stating that the thunder noise was "But the lowing of a ship coming in." Orukorere laments: "Oh, I see. So they have come and taken/ Him to the other shore before me?" The ancestors of the cursed family have reclaimed them. The neighbors tell of Zifa's last words, appropriately spoken to the dead and to the sea; they tell of the final destruction of their house:

> The owls . . . that should
> Hoot at night have this afternoon blown down
> His house as they have the ancestral hall
> Open in the market place. And the stalls there
> That should crowd with voices are filled now
> Not even with the buzz of houseflies.

And so the curse has been fulfilled. But even as he has submitted to the fate of their curse, Zifa refuses to be reclaimed by his ancestors: "you may blow and hoot . . . from here to the other shore/ But I will not come to you tonight," and he walks on into the sea, claiming his right to create, even if it is his own destruction.

Orukorere is full of anguish for her son Tonye, who "hangs dangling like a fruit full/ Before its time and for her boy Zifa, "who walked of his own will into the dusk." The gods and the ancestors have failed. The end is ominous and dismal as she is led away.

> You see, black birds whose immortal
> Knot both my sons have tied and slung
> Have gathered the loot, all the loot,
> And left behind not one seed of my fruit.

Out of a very simple plot Clark skillfully builds a play through the elaboration of images and their continuous correspondences. Wordy explanations of the denouement by the

Masseur in *Song of a Goat*, or by the Priests in *The Masquerade*, are contrivances that falsify the dramatic action and give to the final scenes a static immobility.

This explanatory process destroys the visual intensity of the end of *The Masquerade*, where the narrative exposition of the Priests takes the place of dramatic action. It also destroys the dramatic moment at the beginning of *The Raft*, where four men, suddenly finding themselves adrift, do not take any immediate steps to steer a course but inactively launch into a long dialogue. *The Masquerade* is a dramatic variation and an extension of *Song of a Goat*. The curse that had befallen Zifa's race contaminates and destroys Diribi's line through the association of Tufa, the son born of the incestuous act between Ebiere and Tonye, with Titi, Diribi's beautiful daughter. Through a chain of images of water, tree, river, fish, dog, and many others, the play elaborates the process of contamination, unswervingly unfolds the playing out of the curse, demonstrating its historical continuity. No one seems to be able to interrupt the enactment of the curse, and the chief protagonists, Tufa, Titi, and Diribi, are driven irrevocably to their destruction.

From very opening of *The Masquerade*,[8] disturbances in the natural order foretell the tragedy that is to come. A multiplicity of omens in all spheres of nature—in the moon and in the river, in the animal world and in the world of man—foreshadow the doom that awaits the race of Tufa and of Diribi. A chorus of neighbors, unlike the chorus in *Song of a Goat*, are not merely commentators; active participants, they see the impending tragedy mirrored in natural phenomena:

> The moon's fresh bowl
> Is quite upturned. It is clearly
> Spilling over towards my left.
>
> . . . .
>
> It is never so but there is disaster
> General down the whole delta.

And even though one takes precautions to escape from the rising tide, such precautions avail little:

> Twice already within this one tide
> I've been forced to move boat

And post farther ashore
For safe tethering but each time
The river refusing confinement like
Goats to a hearthstead, has moved up
Its shore line.

Umuko, Diribi's wife, also had been given a sign of the burden
that would oppress her husband:

> Why,
> Only this morning I opened my fishbasket
> To have stock for our pepper soup; but
> What was it I told you I found in there?
> A python, coil after coil, had engirdled
> It close, and poor old man, he was fast
> Asleep. Now I know his burden.

These many omens that presage the disaster also reveal the
ontological correspondences around which Clark's plays are
structured. Nature reflects all things—evil and good, disaster
and love. A beautiful metaphor tells of Titi's love and of her
eventual mating with Tufa:

> Oh, what magic moonlight! Look at the sands,
> They are like a silver spawn
> In their first outing with the tide.
> And see how they glide to meet the moon!

Clark captures Titi's tragic hope in an image similar to that
which painted Ebiere's youthful exuberance:

> But what could this gazelle of a girl, so
> Abruptly invested with the weed of death,
> Just when she was gathering her skirt of cam
> To mount her bridal bed?

Both Ebiere and Titi full of youthful desire, achieve momentary
fulfillment but as a consequence suffer death. At first, Diribi
had sanctioned Titi's marriage to Tufa; the ancestors of the
race and the spirits of the earth, too, had been propitious:

> Before the dead
> And living of the land, you asked us to kneel
> At your paternal feet, and there in words
> I have come to carry close
> To heart as a newborn child
> You called all the clan to witness
> A union you said the soil herself must welcome
> To sweet fruition.

But as had been hinted in the early part of the play, a halt is put to this happy prospect. Now, indeed, Titi's coy words: "I see a simple watermaid, and a wicked/ Wicked traveller between her and home," take on symbolic overtones, her coquettish banter, a tragic turn, for she had challenged Tufa:

> Well, come catch the dragon-fly
> First, will you? After, you may tie to her wings
> The stoutest string at hand.
> . . . .
> And what if some wild wind sweep the prize
> Out of reach, or the loops tangle among
> The woods?

Rumors of Tufa's history are at first insinuated by the chorus to Diribi, and as the rumors gain credence the plot unwinds, the loops tangle. Tufa's story, which is presented in a well-cadenced monologue, is a tragic one:

> Others for no reason but that they prefer
> To travel double, or too impatient, fail
> To collect their kits complete.
> Get instant snuffing out or
> Are tossed among reeds to rot away
> Far from contamination of the stream.
> But I whose coming, right from conception
> To this apparent deception, has
> Been the draining of all that was pure and
> Lovely, how is it they left me loose
> To litter such destruction?

He had become a successful trader, but even this could not interrupt his predetermined destiny. Diribi, too, had been emi-

nently successful, a great hunter and the head of a prosperous
household, constant in his worship to the gods who protect his
family and his house:

> No
>
> Festival has passed but I have been
> On both my knees at their feet. What man
> Has offered fatter sacrifice? Yam tubers
> As high as thigh, fish enough to beat
> A wrestler's span? All this and more
> I render to them below and above without
> Stint or stop. Now they let this bilge
> Come into my blood. No, no, they have done
> Hard by me.

Such a man should, the chorus of women confidently assures
him, not succumb to any trivial disaster:

> Master, you are lashed by forces fit
> To confound forests. But you are no simple
> Reed, and therefore should ride this tide.

But Clark makes all of his characters accept their fate as something inevitable, their destiny as irrevocable:

> Who I have hugged to myself as
> A river laps an island, now seeks
> To dam my path, even as I answer
> The unavoidable call to sea.

As in Soyinka's work, man seems powerless to break the
unending cycle of his curse; he can only try to extirpate corruption and in so doing sink deeper into it. In a harsh image
symbolizing corruption, Diribi refers to the mating of Titi and
Tufa:

> The bitch was not in her bed, do you
> Get that? She is even now not asleep
> In the bridal bed I myself built for her before
> That mongrel ran in, tongues down, to foul us all.

For this he kills his daughter who has damned his house and for
whom there seems to be no protection, even from nature, which
Clark presents as less than benign:

> She tried tears, tried prayers and like some bird
> Already struck, but still struggling
> For sunlight, skipped from one twig
> To another, but leaves and boughs shrunk in her path
> And none could offer her closet.

Now Diribi lies broken:

> What chains? For a cripple?
> Why, look at him who was so tall and strong
> Before. Nobody knew him shave his head
> As tributary to the flood. Now at one stroke
> See him splintered to the ground.

and Tufa attempts to destroy his contaminated line:

> Mud oozes out of me, see it flowing hot and thick down
>   my side; I must go
> Before I smear more with it.

and both lines are broken. The playing out of a curse or the
enactment of an indeterminate accident as in *The Raft* becomes
the principal action of Clark's plays. A number of images are
repeated throughout the three plays, linking them together. For
instance, the tragedy which befalls Titi is the same which had
befallen Ebiere. In both, endemic disaster stems from their
lushness:

> Like sparks of fire
> On grass at harmattan, it bounced off
> One lip to another and knew no break
> Till it had burnt itself out with feeding on its source
> The girl in glory.

In *The Masquerade* as well as in *The Raft*, images of containment or of things slipping the bounds of their containment
hint at the ineffectualness of man's action and his consequent
drifting. Tufa says:

Because the tide
Has all of a sudden turned on us while
Others stayed out of sea, the nets we cast
With pride over shaols sure as shallows
Have had the floors cut from under them, and
The prime shark we set out to catch has got
Clean away, filtered right through and left
Us dangling adrift . . .

Whereas in *The Masquerade* the river is a powerful metaphor whose tide turns, whose waters flood and destroy men's
hopes, in *The Raft*[9] the river is the stage, the forefront on which
four men—Olotu, Kengide, Ogro, and Ibobo—drift to their
destruction. In this play, too, Clark introduces omens which
foreshadow doom: "The pilot fish now smell rot among/ The
logs: they don't jump on board any more."
The course of the raft's drift is blocked out in a set of chance
happenings, accidents of fate that pull the raft under. From the
very beginning the raft is accursed and has been cut adrift by
"Some ghost or evil god," and even before realizing how helpless they are, Kengide cries out impotently. "Truly we are a
castaway people," whose only hope lies in the turning of the
tide, "With the swift ebb tide coming/ And some better lot, we
ought to get out/ Before the sun goes down." Man's impotence
has been established, the river in its force and strength has
already asserted itself, clutching man in its grasp:

And we are water-logged here
In Osikoboro—the confluence of all
The creeks!
. . . .
The drain pit of all the earth

Caught in this drainage pit of the earth, man's actions merely
anticipate doom:

Bundling up mats [which were later hoisted as masts in an
    effort to escape from the drain pool] like this always puts
Me in mind of a corpse ready for the castoff.

And the image of containment, which in *The Masquerade* illustrated the ineffectualness of man's action, is again reiterated:

Worse, the net he cast out
Attracted many, but could not retain
A single fish. It had too many loopholes.

And Ogro is hit by a bat in the daytime:

A bat? On the river and at daytime? Now,
What evil errand does it run?

Of the four men adrift, Kengide is the one who is worldly
wise, knows the ways of the river and of the town, can dis-
course on William Tell and homosexuals; he is a cynic and says
of the people of the city:

You should see crabs out of their holes
In the peat and swamp, making splendid
Salutations with hairy forearms under those
Same lamps. And the scorpions never stop
Stalking below the windows aglow with light.

Yet none of his worldly knowledge generates any action, and
during the course of the drifting offers no practical solutions.
Kengide seems continually at odds with Olotu, a townsman
who does not know the ways of the river and is the first to drift
away to his destruction as a "calabash on water."

Ibobo seems to be the catalyst who often comments sympathetically on the actions of other characters, interpreting their
destinies. Of his own fate he says:

I try to shut my eyes, gateways to my head
Which is one great cage where misfortune
Like an alligator trussed within, batters
At my temples, forehead and back.

In *The Raft*, also, sacrifice, or offers of sacrifice, are ineffectual and can neither offset the seeming inevitability of their
drifting nor put an end to it. Again and again, Ibobo makes
promises of sacrifice to his ancestors:

I promised you a goat
At the next festival, my great-grandmother, Now
How have you led us into this?

Later he cries out:

> My grandfather and your gods on land
> And sea, just see us safely make port
> And I'll slaughter that goat long since assigned
> For your sacrifice.

But mediation is of no avail, and the men continue to drift. Once "the drift" has been initiated by chance, no extrahuman force seems able to intervene to control its course and forestall man's doom.

Ogro, the man from the river people, sings sad songs which foretell the doom that is to overtake them all, a doom which seems preordained:

> Death that has nothing to do
> With God is what has struck;
> Death that has nothing to do
> With God is what has struck;
> It's Ozidi, the all-strong,
> Who's come to strike down man.

Faith in sacrifice is of little avail, action of little use.

Ogro often acts positively; for instance, he tries to bait fish with excrements. His two attempts to reach safe harbor fail. When the mast is hoisted by Ogro, the strength of the wind cracks the raft, and Olotu goes adrift. Ogro, a good swimmer, leaps overboard to swim to a passing ship; but he is stoned with coals and his hands are beaten with bars of iron. He does not drown but is "caught in the mortal arms/ Of that stern-wheeling engine."

Kengide and Ibobo drift on past towns that become mirages, lost eventually in the fog which:

> . . . has stuffed its soot and
> Smoke in our eyes, has shut up the world
> Like a bat its wings.

and both men, fearing aloneness, shout together into the night:

> Shout, shout, Ibobo, let's shout
> To the world—we woodsmen lost in the bush

But none of Tutuola's heroes get lost in the bush, for his vision of the universe and ontological relationships between man and phenomena differs from that of Soyinka and Clark.

In the kaleidoscopic world of Amos Tutuola's novels all realms flow together, various manifestations of reality merge and coalesce. Yoruba myth, customs, and manners are synchronized with western artifacts; the concepts are made concrete, the imagery taut. All details are in the foreground, all illuminated by the author's total experience. There is no inherent clash of cultures, for all cultures are his domain and he derives his material from all of them. This material is transmuted through the author's imagination, and the fusion gives to reality a sense of otherness, to myth a veracity. Heroes are carriers of divinity through juju, yet they are fallible and subject to torture, beating, and punishments. Such events bend and shape them into myriad forms. They often are saved from degradation and humiliation by chance or juju, but, as in folklore, they also triumph through the greed of their captors or the use of their wits.

Much in Tutuola is legendary, but much springs from ordinary, everyday lived reality. Time (qualitative and quantitative) and space (charged with emotion) become actualized by the journeying of Tutuola's myth heroes. Only after being fortified by juju, prepared by sacrifice, do these heroes cross over into an imaginary realm contunguous to their own real world to pursue their searches and continue their wanderings. But the imaginary world has all the qualities of the real world: its codes of behavior, social structure, and institutions. The heroes are not, as Clark's, adrift in the world. Rather, they take on the characteristics of the realms in which they wander; they become socialized: the palm-wine drinkard learns the habits of the Dead, gets married, and has children during his search for the palmwine tapster; the hero of *My Life in the Bush of Ghosts* grows to manhood there, marries and procreates, and indeed almost assumes the qualities of the ghosts; Simbi in *Simbi and the Satyr of the Dark Jungle* also marries and brings forth children; Adebisi in *The Brave African Huntress* learns the lore of the jungle, the manners of the pygmy world.

At the center of Tutuola's vision of the world is man, mastering his environment through the acquiring of knowledge of it or through the simple acceptance of the propitiousness of chance and the belief in the benign intervention of a never clearly defined deity. Therefore, Tutuola's vision of the world is much more optimistic than Soyinka's predominantly pessimistic, even though ultimately optimistic, belief in the power of a single man's actions. Indeed, Tutuola's novels are the ultimate expression of a return to the acceptance of tradition in all its varying manifestations. For even though his own native traditions and customs have come into contact with and been influenced by foreign mores, Tutuola accepts the dynamics of his evolving traditions. Further, though exposed to trials and dangers during his symbolic journeys through hostile regions, man always returns strengthened by such wanderings.

Tutuola begins all his novels with a biographical sketch of his heroes, outlining the reasons for their journeys. The palm-wine drinkard is the oldest of eight sons and thus the heir to his wealthy father's estate. Like Tutuola's other heroes, Adebisi and Simbi, the palm-wine drinkard lives a privileged life:

> My father got eight children and I was the eldest among them, all of the rest were hard workers, but I myself was an expert palm-wine drinkard. I was drinking palm-wine from morning till night and from night till morning. By that time I could not drink ordinary water at all except palm-wine.[10]

The privileged life is shattered by the death of his father, the death by falling of their irreplaceable palm-wine tapster, and the consequent loss of all his "uncountable friends." Thus, quickly Tutuola not only sets up the necessity of his character's search for the palm-wine tapster, but also introduces a moral lesson. He introduces reasons for the palm-wine drinkard's journey, sets the locale of the journey, and notes preparations.

> When I saw that there was no palm-wine for me again, and nobody could tap it for me, then I thought within myself that old people were saying that the whole people who had died in this world, did not go to heaven directly, but they were living in one place somewhere in this world. So that I said that I would find out where my palm-wine tapster who had died was.
> One fine morning, I took all my native juju and also my

father's juju with me and I left my father's hometown to find out whereabouts was my tapster who had died.[11]

The hero in *My Life in the Bush of Ghosts* does not undertake his journey willingly; rather, he falteringly chances on it through the jealousies of wives in a polygamous household. It was a time of African wars, "general wars, tribal wars, burglary wars and the slave wars which were very common in every town and village and particularly in famous markets and on main roads of big towns at any time in the day or night."[12] The seven-year-old hero, whose mother, a petty trader, leaves him alone one day with his eleven-year-old brother, is not warned by his father's other wives of an impending slave war. His brother attempts to carry him to the safety of their grandmother's house but reluctantly abandons him at the foot of a tree, from which his journey begins. As in *The Palm-Wine Drinkard*, two motifs have been introduced: one a moral lesson; the other a journey.

My Life in the Bush of Ghosts opens with the line, "I was seven years old before I understood the meaning of 'bad' and 'good,'"[13] but the author does not develop the boy's apprehension of these moral states.

In *Simbi and the Satyr of the Dark Jungle*, the principal motive for the heroine's journey is her desire to learn the meanings of poverty and punishment. Simbi, like the palm-wine drinkard, has had a very privileged life. Although his only work was to drink palm-wine, hers was "not working at all, except to eat and after that to bathe and then to wear several kinds of the costliest garments. Although she was a wonderful singer whose beautiful voice could wake deads and she was only the most beautiful girl in the village."[14]

But desirous of knowing the meanings of poverty and punishment she first approaches her mother and then an old man. Rebuked by them she "remembered to go to the soothsayer who could solve the words to her."[15] Before she can undertake this allegorical journey she is told by the soothsayer to make two sacrifices:

Firstly, you will sacrifice one cock to your head. The cock must be of three years of age. And to sacrifice the cock to your head means to safe your life throughout your journey and to help you to return to your mother. Because you will travel for many years and it is in your travel you will know and experience of what you ask now from the Ifa, the god of oracle.[16]

Thus, Simbi will certainly undergo severe punishments and experience many misfortunes, but she is assured of a safe return. Thus Tutuola, unlike Clark, accepts the value of sacrifice in mediating between her reality and the reality of the realm through which she will search for the meaning of poverty and punishment.

In *The Brave African Huntress*, Adebisi's interest in venturing out to the bush is not merely a whimsical wish to experience certain moral states; she undertakes her journey to retrieve not only her brothers but many of her townsmen who had been lost in the Jungle of the Pygmies. Like Simbi, her curiosity is awakened and her desire for the journey prompted by an overheard conversation. The biographical story line in *The Brave African Huntress* is much more elaborate than in the three preceding novels. First, Adebisi's father is described as an ancient brave hunter who hunted in very dangerous jungles, killed thousands of wild and wonderful animals, and conquered gnomes, genie, and countless curious creatures. "He had plenty of supernatural powers" and innumerable gods to whom he sacrificed before his hunting trips. Second, the terrain and its economic geography are mapped out. One hundred miles from town was the jungle of the pygmies where strange and wild creatures, wonderful birds and boa made their home among many kinds of fruit trees and precious metals.

Adebisi trains for her journey to this jungle, becoming a skilled hunter, and is finally inducted into the hunting profession. After inheriting her father's profession and possessions, she is transformed: "All were telling me not to attempt to go and hunt in this jungle, because they thought that I would not be able to return. But I did not listen to them, because I had become wild at the same moment that I had put on the hunting dress and jujus." With her new powers, she undertakes her journey: "So, I thank you all for the warm affection you have on me. I pray to God to let us meet again. Good-bye to you all! good-bye!"[17]

None of Tutuola's four heroes simply enters the region where he will have his adventure, where he will experience his trial.

Rather, each is faced from the beginning with the choice between his lived reality and the realm in which he will wander.

The palm-wine drinkard uses his wits to ascertain the road that will lead him to "Death":

> I lied down on the middle of the roads, I put my head to one of the roads, my left hand to one, right hand to another one, and my both feet to the rest, after that I pretended as I had slept there. But when all the market goers were returning from the market, they saw me lied down there and shouted thus: —Who was the mother of this fine boy, he slept on the roads and put his head towards Death's road.[18]

Even before he has to make this choice the palm-wine drinkard has wandered for several months through the bush; already a dislocation of time has occurred:

> I was travelling from bushes to bushes and from forests to forests . . . and again I could spend two or three months before reaching a town or a village. Whenever I reached a town or a village, I would spend almost four months there. . . . After the seventh month that I had left my home town, I reached a town.[19]

Dislocation of time and space, or rather "mythic" time, transports the hero in *My Life in the Bush of Ghosts* into the bush. Symbolically he finds himself under a fruit tree, which verges on the bush of ghosts, and instantly the location of the tree is given a temporal definition:

> ". . . so I entered into the bush under this fruit tree. This fruit tree was a 'SIGN' for me and it was on that day I called it— THE 'FUTURE SIGN.' "[20]

Unlike the other heroes, he does not possess juju, but he symbolically eats the fruit of this tree. Immediately he enters the bush of ghosts, and like the palm-wine drinkard, he must choose between three routes:

> But as I stood at the junction of these passages with confusion three kinds of sweet smells were rushing out to me from each of these three rooms, but as I was hungry and also starving

before I entered into this hole, so I began to sniff the best smell so that I might enter the right room at once from which the best sweet smell was rushing out.[21]

Since most of the hero's adventures and escapes revolve around feasting and banqueting, we see that one of the principal motifs has been introduced. Similarly, many of Simbi's escapes in *Simbi and the Satyr of the Dark Jungle* are the result of luck and supernatural occurrences. Her adventures begin with sacrifices at the junction of the three roads from which she is carried off by Dogo, the villain: "And from there she carried the sacrifice without looking at her back, to the junction of three paths, and she put it down there."[22]

Adebisi, who has been the most calculating in preparing for the journey, consciously attempts to select the correct road to take her to the Jungle of the Pygmies. In this novel, Tutuola makes structural use of calendar time, synchronizing Adebisi's actions with the symbolic character of each day:

This was the junction of roads that which used to confuse the stranger, because I did not know which of these roads to travel to the jungle. . . . At last when I did not know which was the right one that led to the jungle, I slept there till following morning which was "The Day of Three Resolutions" Saturday.[23]

In the very first adventure in *The Palm-Wine Drinkard*, Tutuola introduces many elements that will recur throughout the novel. The palm-wine drinkard's access to divine powers is not explained; it is merely stated: "I replied that my name was 'Father of gods' who could do everything in this world. . . ."[24] This fact will be repeated from time to time throughout the novel to help the palm-wine drinkard resolve seemingly insolvable dilemmas.

In his first errand to retrieve an unknown thing, the palm-wine drinkard uses juju, as he does throughout the novel, to change into a bird and overhear what the thing was. In the second episode, in which God challenges the palm-wine drinkard to capture Death, Tutuola employs all the structural devices of a folk tale grounded in everyday reality. The palm-wine drinkard comes upon Death planting yams in his garden;

Death is given the customary welcome, the offer of food and lodging. Although the concept of death is personified, Death is no ordinary farmer: ". . . he was using skeleton bones of human-beings as fuel woods and skull heads of human-beings as his basins, plates and tumblers, etc."[25]

The trickster element common to many folk tales appears here: "but as this bed was terrible to look at or to sleep on it, I slept under it instead, because I knew his trick already."[26]

As in subsequent adventures, the hero effectively uses his wits and ensnares Death in a net. To repay God for his attempted guile, the drinkard releases Death upon the world. Thus, the moral of the folk tale is enforced.

In the second adventure, most of the motifs that appear in other Tutuola novels are skillfully woven together through the author's narrative technique. In this adventure, the hero uses juju and relies on chance to rescue a young woman who refused the suitors chosen by her father and willfully followed a most beautiful and "complete gentleman." She is punished not only for her disobedience to her father, but also for not heeding the advice of the complete gentleman:

> I had told you not to follow me before we branched into the endless forest which belongs to only terrible and curious creatures, but when I became a half-bodied incomplete gentleman you wanted to go back, now that cannot be done, you have failed. Even you have never seen anything yet, just follow me.[27]

A moral condemnation has been established, and now the hero can rescue the lady from her purgatory. At this juncture Tutuola reiterates how frail human is judgment, how subject to change are human emotions, for even the hero is jealous of the complete gentleman's beauty: "After I looked at him for so many hours, then I ran to a corner of the market and I cried for a few minutes because I thought within myself why was I not created with beauty as this gentleman."[28] The hero, like the lady, follows the complete gentleman from the marketplace into the endless forest.

In the description of the complete gentleman, who is really only a skull, Tutuola uses all his syncretic power, fusing a symbol of death with an image of human vitality and beauty:

> . . . if this gentleman went to the battle field, surely, enemy
> would not kill him or capture him and if bombers saw him in a
> town which was to be bombed, they would not throw bombs
> on his presence, and if they did throw it, the bomb itself would
> not explode until this gentleman would leave that town, be-
> cause of his beauty.[29]

Strengthening the power of his juju by sacrifice, the hero is
able to transform himself into a lizard and also into air. Later
he changes the lady into a kitten, and even more marvelously
puts the kitten into his pocket and then makes himself a spar-
row. Like all good mythic heroes he is rewarded with the lady
he rescues. They beget a son who springs to the height of three
feet from the left thumb of his mother. Like so many children
in Tutuola's novels, he is so malignant and hostile that his
parents attempt to get rid of him. He is rescued by Drum, Song,
and Dance, personifications who recur throughout Tutuola's
novels as structural devices.

The drinkard and his wife suffer many tortures and punishments, but they symbolically find rest at Faithful-Mother's
house, a luminous hotel-like structure. In this episode, Faithful-
Mother retains images of those travelers who suffered trials in
order to afford them a place of rest and a point of respite. "So
we asked from Faithful-Mother what she was doing with all of
the images. She replied that, they were for remembrance and to
know those she was helping from their difficulties and punishments."[30]

No one is allowed to overstay in the house of the Faithful-
Mother. Refreshed and equipped, everyone must continue his
journey to face new trials and dangers. Transmuted by Tutuola's imagination, fantasy and reality merge, yet lie separate.
The Faithful-Mother cannot come out: "Then we went to her
and told her we were ready to leave and we wanted her to lead
us to our destination because of fearful creatures in the bush.
But she told us that she could not do such request, because she
must not go beyond their boundary." Nothing lies between the
world of fantasy within and reality without: "but what made us
very surprised was that we saw the tree opened as a large door,
and we simply found ourselves inside the bush unexpectedly,
and the door closed at once and the tree seemed as an ordinary
tree which could not open like that."[31]

The palm-wine drinkard's journey is now affected in two ways. Since he sold his death before entry into the tree, he no longer is concerned with dying. Yet, since he only "loaned his fear" and had to retrieve it on his departure, his fear is a constant motif throughout his search, which ends in his arrival at the Deads' town where he meets his tapster.

Like Tutuola's other realms, the Deads' town has its own customs and institutions to which one must adhere. To default is to trespass. Throughout his novel, Tutuola constantly delineates the boundaries in which a creature can exercise his potential to the fullest. Therefore, for Tutuola potential is entirely relative to the area in which it is exercised. Each single region has its own characteristics, which imbue the creatures with extensive powers within its confines and define the limits of their activity. Thus, the myth heroes, able to cross boundaries, can move from reality to fantasy, can escape from creatures who are powerless to move out of their domains: "But although we did not know it these long white creatures were bound not to trespass on another's bush, and they did not enter into that field at all . . . , and the creatures of that field must not enter into their bush either."[32]

Although the Bush of Ghosts is contiguous to and in many ways similar to the region inhabited by earthly persons, it has its own specific physical characteristics, its own clearly defined ethics. Thus, earthly persons are unwelcome: "[She] warned me seriously that I must not attempt to enter into the Bush of Ghosts forever, because 90% of ghosts hate any of the earthly persons to enter this bush . . ."[33]

Nor do human creatures willingly enter the Bush of Ghosts: "This 'Bush of Ghosts' was so dreadful so that no superior earthly person ever entered it." Yet, once a human has entered this region it is against the ghosts' ethics to show him the way back to earth: "Yes, I know the right way to your town, but to tell you such a thing is against our rule in this Bush of Ghosts."[34]

Like earthly persons, ghosts attend many functions and ceremonies. Wryly, Tutuola states that "ghosts like to be in conference at all times." Ghosts seem quite hedonistic and given to wining and dining, dancing, birthday parties, and marriage ceremonies. Thus, the hero often becomes an unwilling entertainer, such as when he was trapped with a snake inside a log: ". . . first of all they would eat and drink to their most entire satisfaction, after that he would knock the wood as a sign . . . and when hearing my cry then the whole of the ghosts of that town would be dancing till a late hour."[35]

Like the earthly region, the Bush of Ghosts has government, courts of law, hospitals, educationl institutions, and churches. Indeed, one of the regions of the Bush of Ghosts even undergoes colonization, curiously by the evangelizing dead cousin of the hero:

> I went direct to H. M. the King of the Bush of Ghosts and informed him that I want to establish the Christianity works in this 10th town, so he agreed after several meetings to consider this request with himself and his councillors . . . there are many supervisors, directors of education and education officers who are carrying on their tasks according to the rules and regulations given them to my satisfaction.[36]

Within this Bush of Ghosts, with its own ghostlore, the hero is gradually socialized, learns the ways of ghosts, assumes many of their qualities, and almost becomes a full ghost. He makes many friends with ghosts, learns their language, falls in love with ghostesses, and is so thoroughly at home in the Bush of Ghosts that he begins to forget his original home: ". . . then I remembered to continue to be looking for the way to my home town as I had forgotten that for a while, because of love."[37]

Not only does he acquire the habits of ghosts, but at times he excells in these habits. Thus, he can go farther into the bush than any other ghost: ". . . so whenever I was following the short ghosts to the bush in which we were killing the animals, I would go farther than them."[38] Indeed, his journeys into Bush of Ghosts and his escapes, many of which take place at the height of festivals, become an initiation through trial into the society of the ghosts. Unlike the palm-wine drinkard, the hero of *My Life in the Bush of Ghosts* grows to manhood in the Bush of Ghosts and will even wish to revisit the place in which he grew. However Simbi, the heroine of *Simbi and the Satyr of the Dark Jungle,* after her wanderings and trials in search of poverty and punishment, has absolutely no desire to return to the jungle.

Simbi's journey is not so much an initiation as a physical experiencing of moral states. Thus, every physical torment experienced is given a moral and emotional texture. Throughout

his novels Tutuola differentiates between appearance and reality, between externalized sensory reactions and more sincere,
internalized feelings, between what the heart truly feels and the
mouth utters. Thus, many of the decisions of the Bush of Ghosts
are decisions of the heart.

Indeed, despite the outward transformations undergone by
characters, each retains his basic nature, his essential being.
Thus, even after having been transformed into a cow, the hero
of the Bush of Ghosts is still essentially human:

> As I was unable to explain to these cow-men that I am not
> really a cow, so I was showing them in my attitude several
> times that I am a person . . . and whenever they were discuss-
> ing some important matter with arguments within themselves I
> would be giving signs with my head which was showing them
> the right and wrong points on which they were arguing.[39]

Tutuola's insistence on emotional states and reactions even
makes the heart the giver of reason. The heart of Simbi is the
counselor of faith in whom she places her trust:

> Can I free from these punishment? Simbi asked from her
> heart seriously. Certainly, you will free from it, her heart re-
> plied quietly. How long that will be? she asked sorrowfully.
> In the near future.
> I don't believe so, she asked.
> You must believe, her heart assured her.[40]

For Simbi, who comes seeking poverty and punishment, is
made to suffer such severe want and hunger, such deep pain
and torture that she continually regrets having ventured from
her home. Thus, in *Simbi and the Satyr of the Dark Jungle*
Tutuola gives material shape to fear, emotional dimension to
want, concretizing these moral and physical states. From the
very beginning Simbi is warned that she would know: ". . . the
'Poverty' and the 'Punishment,' even you shall see them personally. And you shall experience their difficulties even farther
than as you are expecting them to be. Because the difficulties of
the 'Poverty' etc. are almost without the end."[41]

The novel becomes a vivid recitation of various states of
suffering, of unending beatings and tortures, which culminate in

Simbi's methaphorical entry into the very terrain of poverty and punishment:

> This land of poverty was too wonderful because all the clothes of her body turned into ashes immediately she started to travel on it. She was then in nakedness.
>
> Having travelled for many hours she was ambitious to eat. Then she went to a tree to pluck some fruits and eat them. But to her great horror, immediately she touched the fruits just to pluck them, they turned into small stones. She was unable to eat them. Then she left there. A few minutes later, she travelled to a pond of water. As she was hungry badly for food she thought to drink some water perhaps she would be more powerful. But when she bent down just to start to drink that water it dried at once.[42]

A rapid physical transformation ensues and Simbi is suddenly startled by her reflection in a pond of water:

> She stopped there and drank some water, though there was no food at all. But as she needed the looking glass and there was none, she sat down closely to this stream. She bent her head downward onto the water. And her shadow proved that she had leaned, the hairs of her head had become almost dust for want of care and she was greatly ashamed to see herself in nakedness.[43]

All things combine to ensure her punishment. After marrying within the jungle and conceiving and bearing in gladness, not only are her two children demanded as sacrifice for the good of the area in which she is a stranger, but in one instance she is forced to perform the sacrifice. Simbi herself almost becomes an element of sacrifice, in preparation for which she is made to undergo extreme physical torment.

Unerringly, Tutuola propels his heroine from one difficulty to another, from one form of punishment-chastisement to another: All realms merge, combine to produce Simbi's total immersion in the experience of the poverty and punishment. Driven by hunger, Simbi plucks and eats two pawpaws from a tree, thereby unwittingly unleashing the fury of elements:

After a while, she travelled to some pawpaw trees. She plucked two pawpaws. Hardly ate all when she noticed that all the living creatures were running helter-skelter. And within that moment a heavy wind started. The wind was so blowing with its full power that the top-mosts of small and big trees were touching the ground and then getting up at once. All the refuses as leaves, dried sticks and dusts were full up in the sky, everything was in disorder. . . .

It was from that spot she started to experience the punishment and poverty of the Dark Jungle, because immediately she started to find the shelter a heavy rain came. She was so drenched by the rain that all her clothes were stuck to her body and a few minutes after, they tore into rags, but she was still going on with them because she could not remain in this heavy rain or in the powerful wind.[44]

The corollary to such punishments is regret, the stating of which becomes a constant refrain throughout the novel. Over and over, Simbi laments her initial desire for experience; her every utterance is a whine; at every mishap, at every misadventure she chides herself: "When it was twelve o'clock of the third night, the pains were so much that she started to blame herself. 'Hah! if I had obeyed my mother's warnings not to try to know the poverty and the punishment, all these should have not happened to me.'"[45]

Unlike many of her village friends who had been kidnaped by Dogo, Simbi manages to survive. In her duels with Dogo the kidnaper, the ferocious eagle, many evil creatures, and the phoenix, and in her running battle with the Satyr of the Dark Jungle, she is aided by chance, by a benign God, by deities to whom she offered allegiance, by a gnome whom she had rescued, by a woodcutter she marries. She gives credit to her gods: "But with the help of my three gods, I killed the phoenix and several of the rest evil creatures were wounded."[46]

When imprisoned in the bottle by the Satyr and by his many evil creatures, Simbi appeals to her gods and is immediately saved from the death with which the Satyr threatened her: "'Please the god of thunder, help me to come out from this bottle.' She hardly said like that when the god of thunder sent the lightning onto that rock suddenly. It broke the rock and the bottle into several pieces and the Satyr with his invitees ran far away with fear."[47]

Again later, overwhelmed with the poverty and punishment when joined to a rock by her arms and legs that have been petrified by the Satyr, she cries a lament that brings the gnome to her aid: "After the gnome explained to Simbi like that, he rubbed her body with his left palm and at the same time Simbi changed to her usual form, and all the pains of the beats went away. She was then in sound health and was so powerful that if she dashed to a tree it would fall down at once."[48] Here again she is saved from the final punishment. It is clear that Tutuola accepts the power of mediation and implicitly believes that a benign force comes to the aid of those in dire circumstances, saving them from the tragic end. This implicit belief is at complete variance with the tragic inevitability of man's fate postulated by John Pepper Clark; it differs, too, from the courageous action that breaks the cycle of suffering in Soyinka's plays. In Tutuola, all things are possible, nothing is inevitable. Thus, although Simbi follows the Path of Death, where "no a person . . . could travel . . . for two days without being killed by the noxious creatures"[49] toward the Dark Jungle, which is guarded by the Satyr, she eventually kills the Satyr, perhaps thereby triumphing over the poverty and punishment.

Unlike Simbi, Adebisi, the brave African huntress, never whines, never complains. To be sure, she is afraid when confronting her adversaries, but so steadfast are her aims:

> To see that I kill the whole of the wild animals. To see that I kill the whole of the pigmies who were detaining many hunters or to drive them away from this jungle and the third work was to see that I bring my four brothers back to my town, because I had promised my people and the people of my town to do these three works before I left them for this jungle.[50]

that they cushion this fear and give her renewed strength and courage:

> But when I was about to throw away my gun, hunting bag, etc., and then to start to run away for my life, it came to my mind suddenly this moment that all my four brothers were still held up in the custody of the pigmies and that it was in respect of them I was going to hunt in the Jungle of the Pigmies perhaps I would see them and bring them back to the town.

When it came to my mind like that, my bravery returned to my body at the same time.[51]

Thus, unlike Simbi, whose confrontations are happenings from which she flees, Adebisi, better equipped, better prepared, and better motivated, journeys to adventure and seeks confrontations.

The stress in *The Brave African Huntress* is not on the punishment and tortures suffered by the heroine, but rather on her daring exploits and cinematographic fights from which she emerges victorious. Hers is not a pilgrimage as is Simbi's, nor is her journey the search for continued gratification as is the palm-wine drinkard's, nor, as in *My Life in the Bush of Ghosts*, does Adebisi gain maturity in the course of her wanderings. Her journey is that of a generous spirit.

Professionally mature, altruistically purposeful, aided by ancestral inheritance, Adebisi perseveres for the good of the present and future generations. Here the generational link is complete, continuity is not in doubt. The possible inimical strength of generational ties will only be problematic insofar as one does not persevere:

> The son of thief inherits "thieving"
> The son of poor man inherits "poverty"
> The son of lazy man inherits "laziness"
> The son of rich man inherits "wealth"
> The son of philosopher inherits "philosophy"
> The son of hunter inherits "gun, etc."
> so the "poverty," "misery," "wretchedness," and
> "sorrow" shall never finish in the generation
> that there is no "perseverance."[52]

Adebisi accepts unquestioningly the productive strength of her juju; its intercessory power repeatedly saves her from physical harm. Not only is her juju a deterrent, counteracting the venom from snake bites, but also it is a lethal weapon:

> When they climbed the tree to where I hid they were biting at my legs and ankles so that I might give them chance to hide in there and I was very lucky that the poisons of their teeth did not harm me but they were falling back to the ground and they

were dying at once instead because my ankles had already been injected with a kind of medicine before I left my town.[53]

In her fight with Odara whose coming is heralded by and disturbs all of nature:

> This wind was so strong that the whole jungle was in disorder at the same moment. This wind was blowing to the trees so heavily that their tops or branches were touching the ground and all the dried leaves and refuses were blown to the great height in the sky . . . all the hills and trees were shaking, his voice was hearing all over the jungle.[54]

Adebisi is again saved from death by her juju: "Immediately he [Odara] saw me there he threw one of his poisonous cudgels to me but I snatched that one easily because it did not hit me, and he threw another one at the same time which hit my breast so heavily that I should had died at once if I had had no juju in my body."[55]

Adebisi survives and triumphs over all her adversaries not only through the intercessory power of her juju, but through her own cunning, her professional skill as a huntress, and at times through luck. She diligently cares for her weapons, and although her Shakabula gun is of no avail against many of the evil creatures, she calls it her sister. With keen foresight she acquires from those whom she defeats artifacts and weapons which will aid her in her later encounters.

Like all of Tutuola's heroes, Adebisi at times is aided by luck and by a benign godhead, but more than any of the others she uses wit and cunning and her own daring to escape from her perils:

> But God was so good, as I was just thinking in mind to come out from the pot with which I covered myself or protected myself all the while and then to run away perhaps I would be saved, luckily it came to my mind this moment to throw one of the two poisonous cudgels to him perhaps the poison which was in this cudgel would kill him.[56]

In the preceding, she not only acknowledges the goodness of God, the efficacy of luck, but also the power of her thoughts.

Thus, throughout the novel Adebisi carefully plans her strategy. Aided by her juju, her own weapons, and those which she acquires from her defeated enemies, and assured in her knowledge of hunting, Adebisi liquidates all the dangerous creatures and the hostile pygmies from the jungle. Many of the fight scenes, in which Adebisi seems continuously to hang precariously from trees and dangle from beards, are bloody and melodramatic, yet they are visually graphic and precisely detailed:

> When he was hearing what I was saying repeatedly he became more angry and he ran to me and held my right leg unexpectedly. But as he was trying to tear it away from my body, it hooked his long beard and then I began to dangle here and there as he was trying to take it away from his beard as quickly as possible, because his lower jaw was then paining him very badly. When the pain was too much for him and my leg did not come out from his beard in time. He left it there but he was then running along to where he had made a big fire just to put me inside this fire so that I might be burnt to death at once . . .[57]

The plots of *Simbi and the Satyr of the Dark Jungle* and *The Brave African Huntress* are more cohesive than those of *The Palm-Wine Drinkard* and *My Life in the Bush of Ghosts*. Indeed, in the former novels Tutuola gives more attention to themes, more centrality to action, more definition to his main characters. Yet, none of the four novels has the totality of suspense, the dramatic intensity that forces an action along, catapulting it to a climactic moment. Situations and adventures begin and end, a fluid sequence that terminates in the hero's return to his point of departure. Tutuola insists on precisely merging the end of one adventure with the beginning of another; this folkloric device, that of rounding off the telling of the folk tale with a coda, when employed through a long narrative that combines several intrinsically complete episodes, becomes boring and tiresome:

> It was like that I left my town and my people and started to go to this jungle.

> It was like that I left this town and continued my journey unexpectedly to the Jungle of the Pigmies.

It was like that I won this powerful gate-keeper, of course it was not easy for me before I saw the end of him.

It was like that this old man, who took great care of me as if he was my father, and I departed from one another without our wish.[58]

But the multiplicity and variety of adventures, each containing its own dramatic dimension, the diversity and descriptive power of his grotesque creations, each possessing its own vital shadings, the broad satirical comic inventions, all contort and give dynamic shaping to repetitiousness, sudden contours to a levelness of tone.

The novels are not static or immobile, but flow along. They are a richly textured, broad kenti cloth, whose fabric is woven from strands plucked from everywhere. Tutuola's realms are many, moving inward from the land of the Deads through the Bush of Ghosts, across the jungle with its Satyr into the area inhabited by pygmies; the play of imagination on the various realms lessens as the realms move closer to the reality lived by human beings. In Tutuola, all things join together, all realms intersect at the common point of experience. Thus, the works abound with adaptations, transformations, syncretic formulations.

In the creation of the juju compass three realms crisscross in the wind: the realm of animistic belief, that of nature, and that of science:

This juju was just like the tail of a big cow, it was very bushy and it was a very sure "juju-compass" which had never deceived my father once throughout the time that he hunted.
And when I stretched this inherited "juju-compass" up the breeze blew it to my left and then I started to travel to that direction at once.[59]

For Tutuola accepts the graftings from a culture that momentarily seemed to dominate his, then prunes and shapes these graftings to his own culture. Thus, there is essentially no cleavage of time, no movement away. There is a total absorption of foreign influences into an ever-flowing, ever-evolving culture—his culture. Not only is there a television-handed ghostess, but the television is actually a manual portable set affected

by juju and dating two hundred years back in time. The grafting
has taken place, and time has been fragmented in the palm of
the television-handed ghostess who was "born over two hundred years ago with sores on my head and all over my body."[60]
The hero of *My Life in the Bush of Ghosts* not only sees his
mother and the people of his town, but luckily sees on television the way in which his mother cured many sores similar to
the ones that afflict the television-handed ghostess. Through
this medical television lesson he is able to cure the "sores with
uncountable maggots which were dashing here and there on her
body."[61]

The television-handed ghostess does not have the medical,
herbalist skill of the hero's earthly mother, but her palms possess a power to cut through mythic space and time. The hero,
who has been lost in the Bush of Ghosts, and has been searching for the way to his home town, in recompense for having
cured the television-handed ghostess is suddenly transported
back to the fruit tree where he made his entry into the Bush of
Ghosts: "Then she opened her palm as usual, she told me to
look at it, but to my surprise, I simply found myself under the
fruit tree [the Future-Sign] which is near my home town."[62]

Many of Tutuola's supercreatures blend the macabre and the
animalistic with the scientific appurtenances, especially elec-
trical appliances. For instance, in *The Brave African Huntress*
one of the animals which Adebisi fights:

> . . . had two curious eyes which were as accurate as full moon
> of the dry season. Both were on the right part of his head as
> the other animals did, but each was bigger and could see ev-
> erywhere without moving head. The powerful light that these
> eyes were bringing out could not go far or straight but they
> were bringing out the clear and round light. The ray of this
> light was always round him and it could be seen clearly from a
> long distance.[63]

Light and its power to penetrate darkness is a recurrent descriptive motif, indeed perhaps *the* most recurrent descriptive
motif.

In Tutuola's descriptions of creatures he slips easily from the
realm of the real to the superreal. In some of his ironic satirical
creations he distorts the ordinary, blurring the accepted aspects

and proportions of things. In the description of the multicol-
ored town that discriminates against the monocoloreds, the
question of color is implicitly derided:

> "Not at all! we shall not allow you (refugees) to stay in our
> town, since you are the mono-coloured persons and we are the
> multi-coloured people." And the king himself said sharply "We
> don't hate yourselves but your mono-colour."[64]

His laughter riotously explodes time and time again.

Through the juxtaposition of antithetical propositions, by
giving a positive value to what is usually negative, Tutuola
elaborates the grotesque. Thus, there are smelly ghosts who
have an exhibition of smells:

> It was in this town I saw that they had an "Exhibition of
> Smells." All the ghosts of this town and environs were assem-
> bling yearly and having a special "Exhibition of Smells" and
> the highest prizes were given to one who had the worst smells
> and would be recognized as a king since that day as all of them
> were appreciating dirt more than clean things.[65]

Tutuola not only deforms reality to effect his grotesque creations, but distorts concepts to produce his whimsical caricatures:

> . . . but before Rev. Devil could finish the baptism I re-
> gretted it. Then I told him to let me go away from their
> church and I do not want to marry again, because I could not
> bear to be baptized with fire and hot water any longer, but
> when all of them heard so, they shouted, "Since you have
> entered this church you are to be baptized with fire and hot
> water . . ." But when I heard so from them again, I exclaimed
> with a terrible voice that—"I will die in their church." So all
> of them exclaimed again that—"you may die if you like, no-
> body knows you here."[66]

At times, Tutuola moves away from the purely satirical to
the comic, hurling his humor into the realm of pure buffoonery:

> This young ghostess was so ugly that if she hid under a bush
> and if she looked at her ugly body she would burst suddenly

into a great laugh which would last more than one hour and this was detecting her out of the hidden place she might hide herself. She could not live with any ghost or any other kind of creature because of her ugly appearance . . . I determined to see or to look at the ugliness of this ghostess to my satisfaction and said—"It is better for me to die than to leave this ugly ghostess and run away without seeing her ugliness clearly to my entire satisfaction."[67]

In Tutuola these stylistic devices play and slide together to create an ever-shifting kaleidoscope. Tutuola, sensitizing all matter, transmutes it. All substances, human, animal, plant, and mineral, metamorphose, slice into one another, as through graphic exaggeration he pushes the bounds of belief and creates his real, superreal world. All phenomena too are at play, made real through activity, concretized by the author's vision of reality. All realms merge and run together, space is shattered, and time is pushed back into the beginnings of all folklore.

. . . when "Drum" started to beat himself, all the people who had been dead for hundreds of years, rose up and came to witness "Drum" when beating; and when "Song" began to sing all domestic animals of that new town, bush animals with snakes, etc., came out to see "Song" personally, but when "Dance" (that lady) started to dance the whole bush creatures, spirits, mountain creatures and also all the river creatures came to the town to see who was dancing. When these three fellows started at the same time, the whole people of the new town, the whole people that rose up from the grave, animals, snakes, spirits and other nameless creatures, were dancing together with these three fellows. . . . But at last "Drum" was beating himself till he reached heaven before he knew that he was out of the world and since that day he could not come to the world again. Then "Song" sang until he entered into a large river unexpectedly and we could not see him any more and "Dance" was dancing till she became a mountain and did not appear to anybody since that day."[68]

For Tutuola time is not static but a relative quotient regulated by experience and qualified by the knowledge of the area to be traversed, the deed to be accomplished.

Then we continued our journey as usual to the Deads' Town and when we had travelled for 10 days we were looking at the Deads' Town about 40 miles away and we were not delayed by anything on the way again. But as we were looking at the town from a long distance, we thought that we could reach there the same day, but not at all, we travelled for 6 more days, because as we nearly reached there, it would still seem to be very far away to us or as if it was running away from us. We did not know that anybody who had not died could not enter into that town by day time, but when my wife knew the secret, then she told me that we should stop and rest till night. When it was night, then she told me to get up and start our journey again. But soon after we started to go, we found that we need not travel more than one hour before we reached there. Of course we did not enter into it until the dawn, because it was an unknown town to us.[69]

A man is forever journeying, or impelled to journey, to experience his moment in history. His departures as well as his returns are made through qualitative time, relative to the depth and intensity of the experience undergone when moving away, when journeying and when returning. Tutuola's heroes all return, all having suffered, all having grown. As the *Brave African Huntress* returns:

They first shouted greatly with great joy just to show that they were leaving this jungle safely. And as they were singing this song they began to paddle the canoes along homeward as hastily as they could, because hastily, hastily the sun is going back to its place of yesterday.[70]

.   .   .

I have listened in cornfields
    among the windplayers
I have listened to the wind leaning
    over its loveliest fragment.[71]

The reality of Christopher Okigbo's *Heavensgate* is not within the realm of nature, but moves through and modifies many Christian ordinances, soaring into the realm of belief and of spirit. The prodigal poet stands a naked supplicant, seeking to elucidate the mystery of the genesis, of his initiation, of his purification. Time is not only a linear chronological progression from innocence to spiritual awareness, but also a structurally lyrical moment in which the poem arcs from the dark waters of the beginning across the waters of noon to the fountain of lustration, to its final descent as the moon goes under the sea, bringing the song's ending. Yet, before the end, the eyes of the prodigal open:

> Eyes open on the sea,
> eyes open, of the prodigal;
> upward to heaven shoot
> where stars will fall from.[72]

His spirit is in the ascent and with the returning cycle of nature's rebirth, a newcomer is born:

> In the chill breath
> of the day's waking
>
> comes the newcomer
>
> when the draper of May
> has sold out fine green
> garments, and the hillsides
> have made up their faces[73]

The invocation at the beginning of *Heavensgate* immediately introduces the linear imagery on which the poem is based, the finely etched spatial indications introducing less clearly defined metaphysical concepts:

> Before you, mother Idoto,
> 　　naked I stand,
> before your watery presence,
> 　　a prodigal,
>
> leaning on an oilbean;
> lost in your legend . . .
>
> Under your power wait I on barefoot,
> Watchman for the watchword at
> 　　HEAVENSGATE;
>
> out of the depths my cry
> give ear and hearken.[74]

From the beginning, innocence is confounded by the divergent promises of the elements, fire and water:

> Dark waters . . . foreshadow the fire that is dreamed of.
> . . . a rainbow . . . foreshadows the rain that is dreamed of.[75]

The image of innocence is mirrored in the picture of "the young bird at the passage."[76] The image is carried forward and is now presented on two levels—the bird has learned the power of flight and the boys the joys of innocence:

> And when we were great boys . . .
> we sang words after the bird—
>
> And we would respond,
> great boys of child—innocence

Soon the song of the bird, which stood indecisively at the passage, moves under a lamp, becomes a stale song:

> still sings the sunbird
>   under the lamp,
> stale song the dumb bell
>   loud to me.[77]

Within "the hot garden where all roads meet,"[78] the song becomes a canticle of pipe organ music, introducing a festival of mourning. Forgiveness to the newly naked at pentecost does not lead to resurrection but merely opens to a "vision of the hot bath of heaven/ Among reedy spaces."[79]

In the second section, initiation is the crisscrossing of lines in the synthesis of religion and belief. The initiation ritual reaffirms innocence through the purity of line:

> Scar of the crucifix
> over the breast
> by red blade inflicted
>
> .   .   .   .
>
> witnesseth
> mystery which I initiate
> received newly naked
> upon water of the genesis
>
> .   .   .   .

> Elemental, united in vision
> of present and future,
> the pure line, whose innocence
> denies inhibitions.[80]

Intuition and sensation blend and save man from the unnatural, from sham. Through his initiation moral man is led to free living, away from sophistry, and saved from "the errors of the rendering"[81] that distorted logic or religion produce.

In "Bridge" all movement is momentarily suspended as the poet, treading water at noontide, waits in listening anticipation:

> I am standing above you and tide
>   above the noontide,
> Listening to the laughter of waters
>   that do not know why:
> Listening to innocence . . .
> I am standing above the noontide
>   with my head above it[82]

In "Watermaid" the waiting soon is replaced by an effervescent, momentary encounter with a presence. Images of containment, of vertical movement, the play of reflected light and shadow splice together the poet's swiftly fleeting, but experientially necessary, sensations:

> and the waves escort her,
> my lioness,
> crowned with moonlight.
>
> So brief her presence—
> match-flare in wind's breath—
> so brief with mirrors around me.[83]

Yet after this brief encounter, the poet is once more left alone, aspiring to fulfill his monody:

> The stars have departed,
> and I—where am I?
>
> Stretch, stretch, O antennae,
> to clutch at this hour,

fulfilling each moment in a
broken monody.[84]

Lustration now takes place, and the poet accepts the ritual of
a newly laid egg performed with "thundering drums and can-
nons in palm grove,"[85] and the spirit is in the ascent to the hills,
"to where springs the fountain," and "body and soul whitewashed in the moondew"[86] clamber to the hilltop. The newcomer arrives, even though in the chill May morning the welcome is synthetic. Yet the fledgling that had stood at the passage
on one leg, now a heron, attempts a perilous flight toward the
infinite:

in flight into the infinite—
    a blinded heron
thrown against the infinite—
    where solitude
weaves her interminable mystery[87]

Man's journey is at an end; his spirit freed, he goes searching
for essences.

Notes

1. Christopher Okigbo, *Heavensgate* (Ibadan, Nigeria: Mbari
   Publications, 1962), pp. 35, 30.
2. Wole Soyinka, *A Dance of the Forests* (London: Oxford
   University Press, 1963).
3. John Pepper Clark, "The Raft," *Three Plays* (London:
   Oxford University Press, 1964), p. 92.
4. Wole Soyinka, *The Road* (London: Oxford University
   Press, 1965).
5. Wole Soyinka, "The Swamp Dwellers," *Three Plays*
   (Ibadan, Nigeria: Mbari Publications, 1963).
6. Wole Soyinka, "The Strong Breed," *Three Plays* (Ibadan,
   Nigeria: Mbari Publications, 1963).
7. John Pepper Clark, "Song of a Goat," *Three Plays* (London: Oxford University Press, 1964).
8. John Pepper Clark, "The Masquerade," *Three Plays*
   (London: Oxford University Press, 1964).
9. John Pepper Clark, "The Raft," *Three Plays* (London:
   Oxford University Press, 1964).

10. Amos Tutuola, *The Palm-Wine Drinkard* (London: Faber and Faber, Ltd., 1962), p. 7.

11. *Ibid.*, p. 9.

12. Amos Tutuola, *My Life in the Bush of Ghosts* (London: Faber and Faber, 1954), pp. 17–18.

13. *Ibid.*, p. 17.

14. Amos Tutuola, *Simbi and the Satyr of the Dark Jungle* (London: Faber and Faber, Ltd., 1955), p. 7.

15–16. *Ibid*: 15. p. 11; 16. p. 12.

17. Amos Tutuola, *The Brave African Huntress* (London: Faber and Faber, 1958), p. 20.

18. Tutuola, *The Palm-Wine Drinkard*, pp. 11–12.

19. *Ibid.*, pp. 9–10.

20. Tutuola, *My Life in the Bush of Ghosts*, p. 21.

21. *Ibid.*, p. 23.

22. Tutuola, *Simbi and the Satyr of the Dark Jungle*, p. 14.

23. Tutuola, *The Brave African Huntress*, pp. 22–23.

24. Tutuola, *The Palm-Wine Drinkard*, p. 10.

25–32. *Ibid*: 25. p. 13; 26. p. 14; 27. p. 20; 28. p. 25; 29. p. 25; 30. p. 68; 31. p. 71; 32. p. 43.

33. Tutuola, *My Life in the Bush of Ghosts*, p. 165.

34–39. *Ibid*: 34. p. 139; 35. p. 51; 36. pp. 146, 148; 37. p. 135; 38. p. 111; 39. p. 44.

40. Tutuola, *Simbi and the Satyr of the Dark Jungle*, pp. 116–117.

41–49. *Ibid*: 41. p. 19; 42. p. 97; 43. p. 98; 44. pp. 109–110; 45. p. 61; 46. p. 118; 47. p. 103; 48. p. 120; 49. p. 52.

50. Tutuola, *The Brave African Huntress*, p. 60.

51–59. *Ibid*: 51. p. 51; 52. p. 18; 53. pp. 28–29; 54. p. 27; 55. p. 30; 56. p. 39; 57. p. 53; 58. pp. 21, 46, 54, 132; 59. p. 48.

60. Tutuola, *My Life in the Bush of Ghosts*, p. 162.

61–62. *Ibid*: 61. p. 161; 62. p. 166.

63. Tutuola, *The Brave African Huntress*, p. 66.

64. Tutuola, *Simbi and the Satyr of the Dark Jungle*, p. 53.

65. Tutuola, *My Life in the Bush of Ghosts*, p. 35.

66–67. *Ibid*: 66. p. 60; 67. pp. 86–87.

68. Tutuola, *The Palm-Wine Drinkard*, pp. 84–85.

69. *Ibid.*, p. 95.

70. Tutuola, *The Brave African Huntress*, p. 149.

71. Okigbo, *op. cit.*, p. 10.

72–87. *Ibid*: 72. p. 24; 73. p. 37; 74. p. 5; 75. p. 8; 76. p. 8; 77. p. 9; 78. p. 10; 79. p. 11; 80. p. 14; 81. p. 15; 82. p. 21; 83. p. 25; 84. p. 27; 85. p. 31; 86. p. 30; 87. p. 39.

CODA

REBIRTH

FLUTE-PLAYERS, by Jean-Joseph Rabéarivelo

Your flute,
Cut from the thighbone of a mighty bull,
Polished on the bleak hillsides
Scourged by the sun.
Her flute,
Cut from the reed that quivers in the wind
Pierced on the banks of running water
Drunken with moonlight dreams.

In the deeps of evening, play them together
. . . .
Your flute
And hers—
Longing for their past
In the songs of your grief.[1]

And so the notes of a strong dramatic flute merge with the
dreamy lyric and the search for a past in songs of grief. The
grief may be a song of death in the wind before fulfilment and
Rabéarivelo, the poet of death and rebirth, laments the pre-
mature death of the black cow at nightfall:

The hide of the black cow is stretched,
stretched but not set to dry,
stretched in the sevenfold shadow.
But who has killed the black cow,
dead without having lowed, dead without having roared,
dead without having once been chased
over that prairie flowered with stars?[2]

The puzzlement that seeks to solve the question of the black
cow's death—"But who has killed the black cow"—gives way
to a deep curiosity which wonders at the reason for the seeming
leprous sickness of the "Cactus":[3]

Fathom the cave from which they came
if you seek the origin of the sickness which ravages them—
origin more shrouded than the evening
and further than the dawn—

A song of pity and grief should arise in the evening for the
unending ceaseless journeys of "that slave all clothed in pearls
of glass," for the suffering of the black glassmaker "whose
countless eyeballs none has ever seen," but one seems oblivious
to his agony, unmindful of his toil:

And you are witness of his daily suffering
and of his endless task;
you watch his thunder-riddled agony
until the battlements of the East re-echo
the conches of the sea—
but you pity him no more
and do not even remember that his sufferings begin again
each time the sun capsizes.

But for Rabéarivelo the death of the black cow, the sickness
of the cactus, or the burden of the black glassmaker are but
momentary; metamorphosis takes place and the ensuing birth is
hailed with songs of gladness. The cactus, "That multitude of
moulded hands/ holding out flowers to the azure sky," the
moulded fingerless hands of the cactus crown the sky and come
from an inner source which

refreshes thousands of cattle
and numberless tribes, wandering tribes
in the frontiers of the South.

All the strength in the elements flows through the cactus, transforming it, beautifying it:

The blood of the earth, the sweat of the stone,
and the sperm of the wind,
which flow together in these palms
have melted their fingers
and replaced them with golden flowers.

Through images that shimmer with light and pulse with vibrations, the shadowed darkness is infused with life; rebirth is echoed in the reverberations of the drum, its incantations transforming the death sleep of the black cow. The incantatory dreams of the drum interweave with the moonlight dreams of the flute, and the black cow is born again:

And the drum is ready
when the new-born calf,
her horns crowned with spear grass
leaps
and grazes the grass of the hills.

It reverberates there
and its incantations will become dreams
until the moment when the black cow lives again,
white and pink
before a river of light.[4]

Now the agony of the black glassmaker opens the way for the continuous rhythm of night and day and reveals that all things flow together, that movement away leads to movement back, return follows exile, a new day follows the agony of night:

Have you ever seen dawn marauding
in the orchards of night?
Behold her returning now
on the footpaths of the East

overgrown with flowering speargrass:
she is entirely stained with milk
like her children, raised of old by heifers;
her hands that carry a torch
are black and blue like the lips of a girl
chewing ripe berries.

The birds she caught in her net escape,
They fly before her.[5]

. . . .

The moon has now gone under the sea.
The song has now gone under the shade.[6]

Notes

1. *A Book of African Verse*, eds. J. Reed and C. Wake
   (London: Heinemann Educational Books, Ltd., 1964),
   pp. 54–55.
2. *Modern Poetry from Africa*, eds. Gerald Moore and Ulli
   Beier (Baltimore: Penguin, 1963), pp. 33–34.
3. Reed and Wake, eds., *op. cit.*, pp. 55–56.
4. Moore and Beier, eds., *op. cit.*, p. 34.
5. Jean-Joseph Rabéarivelo, "Birth of Day," *Twenty-Four
   Poems* (Ibadan, Nigeria: Mbari Publications).
6. Christopher Okigbo, *Heavensgate* (Ibadan, Nigeria:
   Mbari Publications, 1962), p. 39.

INDEX

WILFRED CARTEY was born in Port of Spain, Trinidad, in 1931, was graduated from University College of the West Indies in Jamaica, and holds a Master's Degree and a Ph.D. from Columbia University, where he is Associate in African Literature. He is also Professor of English and Comparative Literature and Director of Black and Puerto Rican Studies at City College in New York. Previously, from 1957 to 1962, Professor Cartey had been an Instructor in Spanish at Columbia College. Among the numerous prizes and grants he has been awarded is a Fulbright Travel Grant, from 1955 to 1959, to study Afro-Antillian and Latin American Literature. In 1967 Dr. Cartey was Visiting Scholar at the University of Legon, Ghana.

Since 1962 Professor Cartey has been a regular lecturer to Peace Corps groups on African and Caribbean literature and culture. Dr. Cartey appears frequently on television, lectures across the country, writes widely on African and Black literature, and contributes to numerous journals and magazines here and abroad. In addition, he is Literary Editor of *African Forum*, and the author of a book on the Caribbean called *Islands in the Sun*. Dr. Cartey is also the editor of an anthology of African literature, and the author of *Black Images*, both to be published in the near future.

At present Professor Cartey is at work on an authoritative two-volume reader on African history, culture, and politics in collaboration with Dr. Martin Kilson of the Department of Government at Harvard University.